The Air Pilot's **Manual**

Volume 1

Flying Training

Trevor

Revised & edited by
Peter D. Godwin

Airlife England

Nothing in this manual supersedes any legislation, rules, regulations or procedures contained in any operational document issued by The Stationery Office, the Civil Aviation Authority, the manufacturers of aircraft, engines and systems, or by the operators of aircraft throughout the world.

ISBN 1 84037 267 2

First edition published 1987
by Airlife Publishing Ltd

Second revised edition 1987
Reprinted with revisions 1989
Reprinted with revisions 1990
Third revised edition 1991
Reprinted 1992
Reprinted with revisions 1993
Reprinted 1994
Reprinted 1995
Fourth revised edition 1997
Reprinted 1997
Reprinted 1998
Reprinted with revisions 1999
Fifth revised edition 2000

Origination by Bookworks Ltd, Ireland.

Printed in England by Livesey Ltd, Shrewsbury, England.

A Technical Aviation Publications Ltd title
under licence by

Airlife Publishing Ltd
101 Longden Road, Shrewsbury SY3 9EB, Shropshire, England
Website: www.airlifebooks.com E-mail: airlife@airlifebooks.com

The Air Pilot's **Manual**

Volume 1

Contents

Under the European Licence (JAR), some changes to exercise numbering occur. The content of the exercises remains the same.
- *The order of Exercises 16 and 17 is reversed, i.e. Forced Landings becomes Ex.16 and vice versa.*
- *Low-level flying is in Exercise 18b.*

Under JAR-FCL, radio navigation has been added to the PPL syllabus (Ex. 18c). Radio navigation is covered in depth in Vol. 3 of The Air Pilot's Manual.

The Air Pilot's **Manual**

Flying Training

Airwork Diagrams

Editorial Team

Trevor Thom

A former Boeing 757 and 767 Captain with a European airline, Trevor has also flown the Airbus A320, Boeing 727, McDonnell Douglas DC-9 and Fokker F-27. He has been active in the International Federation of Airline Pilots' Associations (IFALPA), based in London, and was a member of the IFALPA Aeroplane Design and Operations Group. He also served as IFALPA representative to the Society of Automotive Engineers (SAE) S7 Flight-Deck Design Committee, a body which makes recommendations to the aviation industry, especially the manufacturers. Prior to his airline career Trevor was a Lecturer in Mathematics and Physics, and an Aviation Ground Instructor and Flying Instructor. He is a double degree graduate from the University of Melbourne and also holds a Diploma of Education.

Peter Godwin

Head of Training at Bonus Aviation, Cranfield (formerly Leavesden Flight Centre), Peter has amassed over 14,000 instructional flying hours as a fixed-wing and helicopter instructor. He has edited this series since 1995 and recently updated it to cover the JAR-FCL. As a member of the CAA Panel of Examiners, he is a CAA Authorised Examiner (AE), Instrument Rating and Class Rating Examiner, Fellow of the Royal Institute of Navigation (FRIN), and is currently training flying instructors and applicants for the Commercial Pilot's Licence and Instrument Rating. Previously he was Chief Pilot for an air charter company and Chief Instructor for the Cabair group of companies based at Denham and Elstree. Peter has been Vice Chairman and subsequently Chairman of the Flight Training Committee on behalf of the General Aviation Manufacturers' and Traders' Association (GAMTA) since 1992.

Graeme Carne

Graeme is a BAe 146 Captain with a dynamic and growing UK regional airline. He has been a Training Captain on the Shorts 360 and flew a King Air 200 for a private company. He learned to fly in Australia and has an extensive background as a flying instructor in the UK. He has also been involved in the introduction of JAR OPS procedures to his airline.

John Fenton

A Flying Instructor for over 20 years, John was joint proprietor and assistant CFI of Yorkshire Flying Services at Leeds/Bradford, a PPL examiner, and has received the Bronze Medal from the Royal Aero Club for his achievements and contributions to air rallying. John has made considerable contributions to the field of flying instruction in this country and pioneered the use of audio tapes for training.

Edward Pape

Director of MSF Aviation, Manchester and Portugal, and a former Chief Flying Instructor of the Lancashire Aero Club, Ed has amassed over 5,000 instructional flying hours and is dedicated to private pilot training.

Ronald Smith

A senior aviation ground instructor, Ron's 25 years in aviation include considerable time as a Flying Instructor, specialised flying in remote areas, fish-spotting, and a period operating his own Air Taxi Service. He is an active member of *International Wheelchair Aviators* and holds a Commercial Pilot's Licence.

Robert Johnson

Bob produced the first three editions of this manual. His aviation experience includes flying a Cessna Citation II-SP executive jet, a DC-3 (Dakota) and light aircraft as Chief Pilot for an international university based in Switzerland, and seven years on Fokker F27, Lockheed Electra and McDonnell Douglas DC-9 airliners. Prior to this he was an Air Taxi Pilot and also gained technical experience as a Draughtsman on airborne mineral survey work in Australia.

Warren Yeates

Warren has been involved with editing, indexing, desktop publishing and printing Trevor Thom manuals since 1988 for UK, US and Australian markets. He currently runs a publishing services company in Ireland.

Acknowledgements

The Civil Aviation Authority; Allied Signal, Bendix, Cessna, Piper, and Gulfstream American and Slingsby for technical material; Airtour International Ltd; Captain R. W. K. Snell (CAA Flight Examiner [ret.]), Captain Horace Galop (British Aerospace Flying College, Prestwick), Bill Bennet, Bill Constable, Peter Grant, Robyn Hind, Rick James, Mark Miller, John Monroe, Bill Ryall and Ian Suren (ex-ICAO, Montreal); and the many other instructors and students whose comments have helped to improve this manual.

Introduction

Becoming a Pilot

Every pilot begins as a student pilot, whether the aim is to fly for a hobby or to fly for a career.

■ ***Becoming a pilot***

Learning to fly does not take long – within the first 20 hours of flying training you will have learned the basic skills. Since the training period is so short, good habits must be developed right from the start. Patterns formed in the first few hours will stay with you throughout your flying life, and so, to gain the maximum benefit from each hour in the air and to develop good habits, you should be well prepared. This manual will help you to do this.

An advanced formal education is not a requirement to become a pilot, although use of the English language is required for radio calls and a knowledge of basic mathematics is useful. Beyond that, no special academic skills are required.

The basic training aeroplane is simple in design and straightforward to operate. It has a control column (or control wheel) to raise or lower the nose and to bank the aeroplane, a rudder to keep it in balance and a throttle to supply engine power. The largest and fastest airliners have basically the same controls.

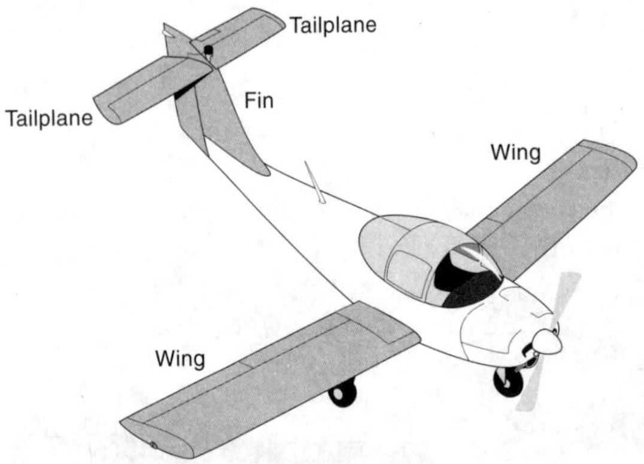

■ ***The main aerodynamic surfaces of the aeroplane***

How an Aeroplane Flies

When not in flight, an aeroplane is supported by the ground, but when airborne it must generate its own support. It does this by modifying the flow of the air over the wings, generating a force known as **lift**.

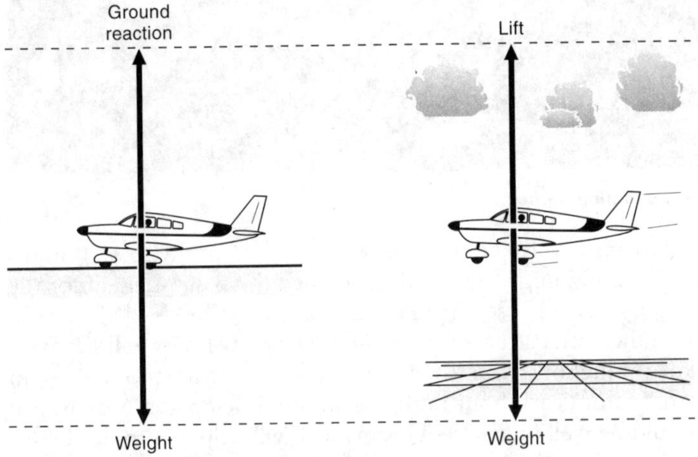

■ ***In flight, the aeroplane is supported by lift***

The air is made up of many molecules, all of which are moving at high speed and in random directions, even though the parcel of air itself might be stationary. The molecules act like small tennis balls, bouncing off any surface that they come in contact with and thus exerting a force on it.

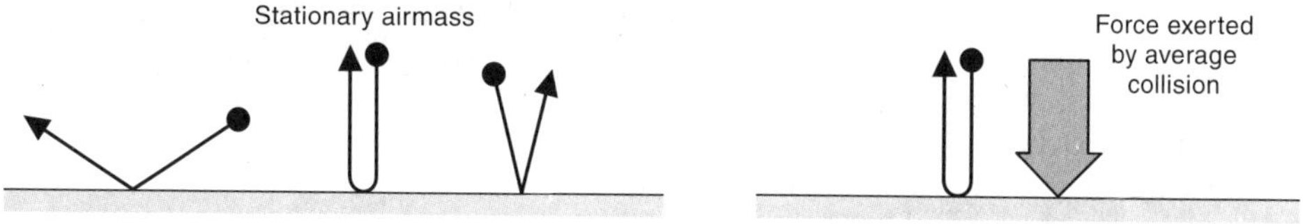

■ ***Static pressure exerted by a stationary parcel of air***

The size of the force is greatest when the collision is 'head-on', and becomes less with glancing blows. All of these small forces, when added up over an area, exert a pressure on the surface. This is known as **static pressure.**

If the parcel of air is moving relative to the surface, the collisions are more likely to be glancing blows than 'head-on', and so the pressure exerted on the surface will be less. **The faster the air flows** past the surface, **the lower the static pressure** that it exerts.

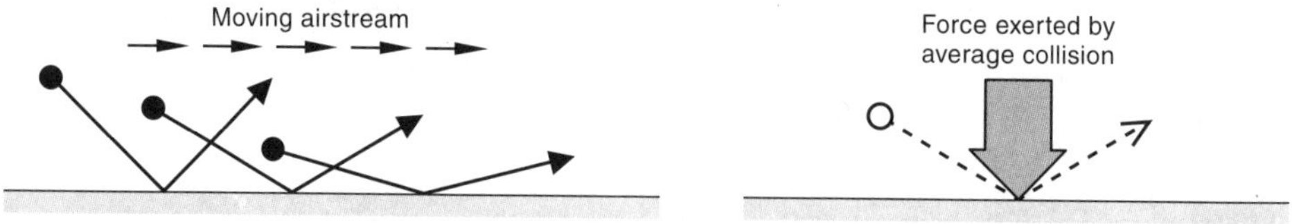

■ ***Static pressure decreases with the speed of airflow***

A wing is shaped so that the airflow speeds up over its upper surface. This results in a lower static pressure above the wing than below it and so a lifting force is created.

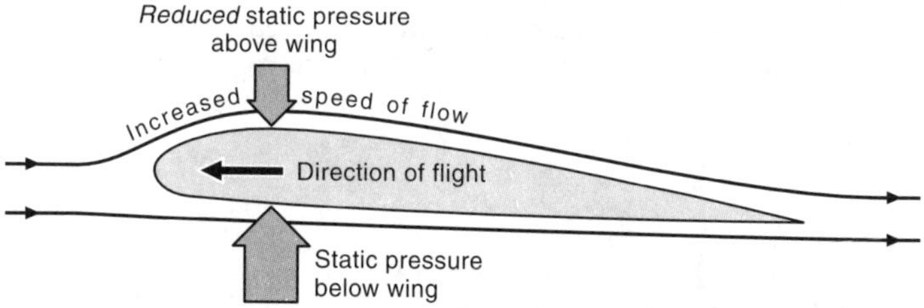

■ ***The airflow is faster over a wing than under it, causing a lower static pressure to be generated***

NOTE The decrease in static pressure with an increased speed of airflow is known in physics as **Bernoulli's principle.** It is usually stated as: *static pressure + dynamic pressure = a constant total pressure* (related to speed).

The effect is the same when air flows past the wing as when the wing moves through the air – it is the **relative motion** of one to the other that is important.

The actual lift generated by a wing depends on its shape and also on the angle at which the wing is presented to the airflow. This angle is known as the **angle of attack.** The greater it is in the flight range, the faster the air will travel over the upper surface of the wing and the lower the static pressure will be – thus, the greater the angle of attack, the greater the lifting ability of the wing. The practical result is that sufficient lift to support the weight of the aeroplane can be generated at a lower airspeed.

Increasing the angle of attack of a wing increases its lifting ability.

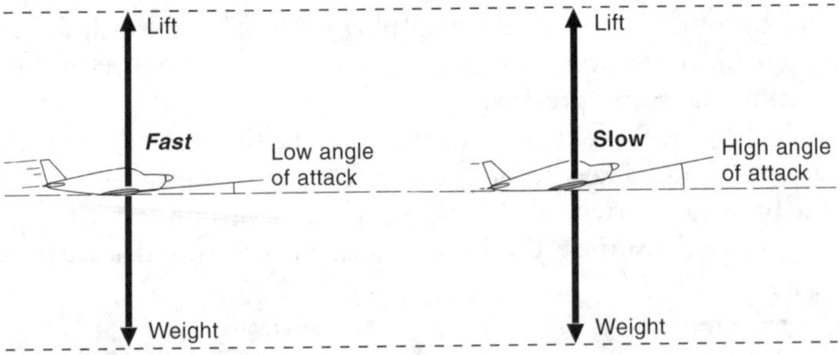

■ ***In level flight the aeroplane can fly slower at high angles of attack***

A limit occurs when the aeroplane slows to an airspeed at which the angle of attack reaches a critical value. Beyond this angle of attack the **smooth airflow** over the wing breaks down and becomes **turbulent,** causing a marked decrease in lift. The wing is then said to be **stalled.** Exercise 10a of this manual discusses stalling and stall recovery in detail.

The force that opposes the motion of the aeroplane through the air is called **drag.** In straight and level flight, drag is balanced by thrust from the propeller.

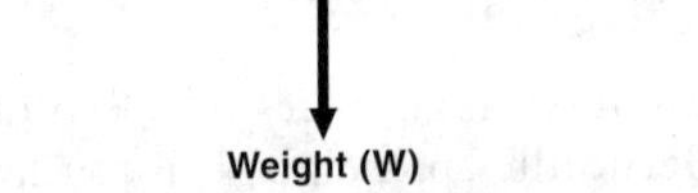

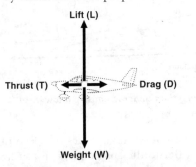

■ ***The four main forces that act on an aeroplane in flight***

To control the aeroplane, control surfaces, operated from the cockpit by the pilot, are used to alter the airflow around the wings and the tail-section. This causes different aerodynamic forces to be generated, and thus allows the pilot to manoeuvre the aeroplane as desired.

That summarises briefly the basic principles of flight. Volume 4 of *The Air Pilot's Manual* covers this topic in depth and prepares you for the *Aircraft (General)* technical examination.

Be Prepared for your Flying Lessons

For each stage of your training, this manual sets out:

- a clear aim:
- the principles and considerations involved:
- how to fly the manoeuvre;
- the *Airwork* exercise, summarised graphically;
- any further points relevant to the exercise.

It will prepare you well and help to minimise your training hours (and your expense). As your training progresses, it can be used for revision. Earlier manoeuvres can be revised by scanning the sub-headings and margin notes within the relevant exercise and referring to the Airwork pages, which act as a summary.

Your flight training will consist of various phases:

PHASE 1. Upper airwork, learning the four fundamental manoeuvres (climbing, straight and level, turning and descending), with an introduction to stalling and slow flight. Throughout this phase you will also be practising starting and stopping the engine, and taxiing on the ground.

PHASE 2. Take-offs, circuits and landings, leading to first solo.

PHASE 3. Advanced manoeuvres and procedures, including steep turns, low-level flying and practice forced landings.

PHASE 4. Cross-country navigation and VFR radio navigation, and basic instrument flying.

You will feel a great sense of achievement as you progress through these phases towards your Private Pilot Licence.

NOTE The order and breakdown of flying training exercises in this book follows our preferred sequence of instruction, and has been agreed with the CAA. You may find that this differs slightly from some other syllabuses.

Pre-flight Briefings

Each new flight exercise should be preceded by a pre-flight briefing by your instructor. This briefing will outline the principles of the exercise to be flown. A typical briefing appears on page 90.

Flight Tests for the PPL(A).

The culmination of your training is to demonstrate that you have achieved (or even surpassed) the required standard for the PPL (Aeroplanes). There is one Flight Test to be completed at the end of your training, which may be split into two parts – General

Handling and Navigation. Details of this test are included in Appendix 1 of this manual.

The Air Pilot's Manual and JAR-FCL1

This book is the first in a series of seven volumes, designed to prepare you for the UK Private Pilot's Licence or the JAR European Licence and associated ratings (and equivalent qualifications in many other countries).

Note that while these books now cover the new European JAR-FCL (Joint Aviation Regulations Flight Crew Licence), they still cover the existing UK PPL training syllabus. Students who began their training before 30 June 1999 under the UK syllabus have until 30 June 2002 to complete it under that syllabus. Students beginning their training after 30 June 1999 must follow the new JAR-FCL syllabus.

THE AIR PILOT'S MANUAL SERIES	
Volume 1	***Flying Training***
Volume 2	***Aviation Law, Flight Rules and Procedures; Meteorology***
Volume 3	***Air Navigation*** *includes Operational Procedures*
Volume 4	***The Aeroplane – Technical*** *covers Aircraft (General) and Aircraft (Type) – principles of flight; airframe, engines and systems; airworthiness and performance.*
Volume 5	***Instrument Flying, Radio Navigation, IMC Ratings, Night Rating***
Volume 6	***Human Factors and Pilot Performance; First Aid and Survival***
Volume 7	***Radiotelephony***

NOTE In the JAR-FCL syllabus some flying training exercises are numbered differently to their counterparts in the existing UK syllabus. The difference is in name and number only; the content of the exercises is the same. Differences of note are:

JAR-FCL1 SYLLABUS	EXERCISE IN THIS MANUAL
5E *Emergencies*	*covered in* **Ex. 5** *and* **Ex. 1**
12/13E *Emergencies*	*covered in* **Ex.12**
16 *Forced Landing without Power*	**17a** *Forced Landing without Power*
17 *Precautionary Landing*	**16** *Low-level Flying & Precautionary Landing* **and** **17b** *Precautionary Search & Landing*
18b *Navigation Problems at Lower Levels and at Reduced Visibility*	**16** *Navigation at Minimum Level and in Reduced Visibility*
18c *Radio Navigation**	*Radio navigation not required*

*Radio navigation is covered in depth in the navigation volume of *The Air Pilot's Manual* series, Vol. 3.

Exercise 1
Aircraft Familiarisation

The basic training aeroplane consists of a **fuselage** to which the **wings,** the **tail,** the **wheels** and an **engine** are attached. A **propeller,** driven by the engine, generates thrust to pull the aeroplane through the air. This enables the airflow over the wings to generate an aerodynamic force, known as **lift,** that is capable of supporting the aeroplane in flight. The aeroplane can fly without thrust if it is placed in a gliding descent.

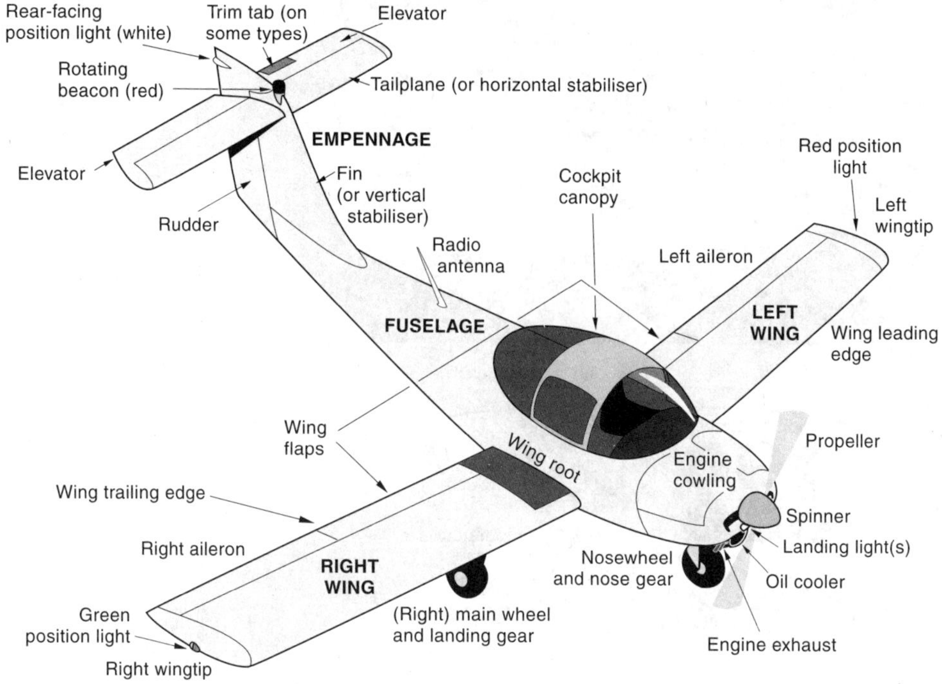

■ *Figure 1-1* ***The aeroplane***

The tail section of the aeroplane is situated some distance to the rear of the main load-carrying sections of the fuselage, and provides a balancing or stabilising force much like the tail feathers on an arrow or a dart. The tail section consists of a **vertical stabiliser** (or fin) and a **horizontal stabiliser,** both of which are shaped to produce suitable aerodynamic forces.

The pilot and other occupants of the aeroplane are accommodated in the **cockpit,** usually in two-abreast seating – the pilot-in-command sitting on the left-hand side. Various controls and instruments are available in the cockpit to enable safe and efficient operation of the aeroplane and its systems.

The main controls used to fly the aeroplane are the **flight controls** and the **throttle.** The throttle, which is operated by the pilot's right hand, controls the power supplied by the engine–propeller combination. 'Opening' the throttle by pushing it forward increases the fuel/air supply to the engine, resulting in increased revolutions and greater power being developed. Pulling the throttle back, or 'closing' it, reduces the power.

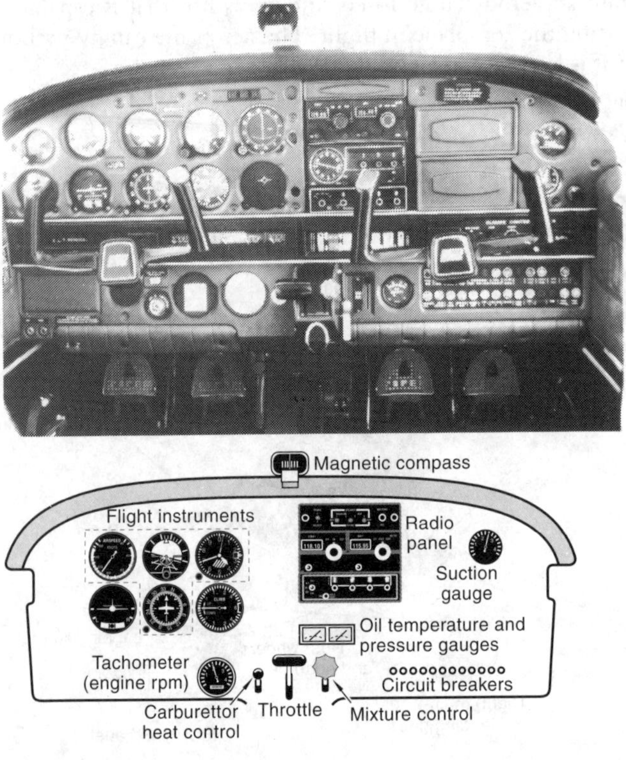

■ *Figure 1-2* ***The cockpit***

The **attitude** (or position in flight) of the aeroplane is controlled using the main flight controls. These are surfaces which, when deflected, alter the pattern of the airflow around the wings and tail, causing changes in the aerodynamic forces that they generate.

THE ELEVATOR (hinged to the trailing edge of the horizontal stabiliser) controls pitching of the nose up or down and is operated from the cockpit with fore and aft movements of the control column.

THE AILERONS (hinged to the outer trailing edge of each wing) control rolling of the aeroplane and are operated by sideways movement of the control column.

THE RUDDER (hinged to the trailing edge of the vertical stabiliser) controls the yawing of the nose left or right and is operated by the rudder pedals.

Other flight controls include:

- **the wing flaps** (situated on the inner trailing edge of each wing); and
- **the elevator trim tab** (on the trailing edge of the elevator).

There will be other controls in the cockpit to operate the **cabin heating** and **ventilation systems.**

Variations in Design

There are variations in design between different types, but the same basic principles apply to all aeroplanes.

Instead of a **control column** in the form of a 'stick', many aeroplanes are fitted with a **control wheel,** which serves exactly the same function. Moving the control wheel in or out operates the elevator, rotating it operates the ailerons. In this manual the term *control column* refers to both types.

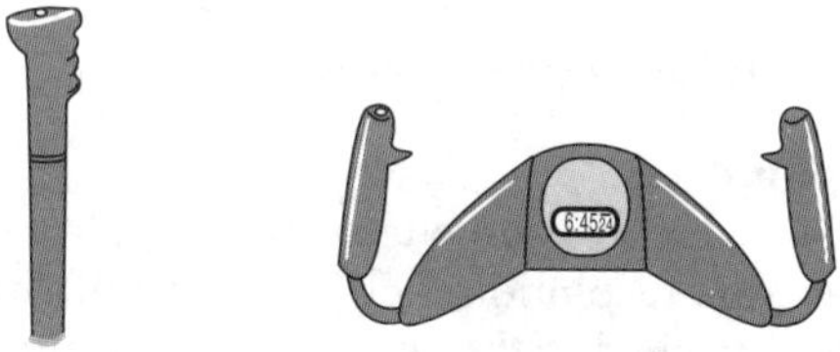

■ *Figure 1-3* ***The control column and the control wheel***

Even though the aerodynamic sections of various aeroplane types serve the same basic functions, their actual location on the structure and their design can vary. For example, the wings may be attached to the fuselage in a high, low or mid-wing position; the horizontal stabiliser is sometimes positioned high on the fin (known as a T-tail), and the combined horizontal stabiliser and elevator is sometimes replaced by an all-flying tailplane (or stabilator).

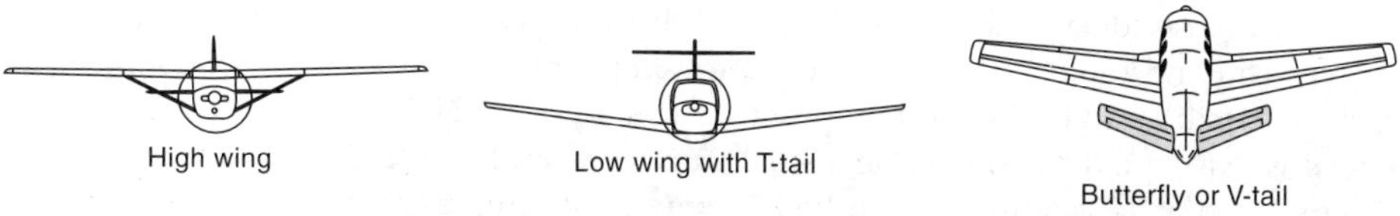

■ *Figure 1-4* ***Different aircraft designs***

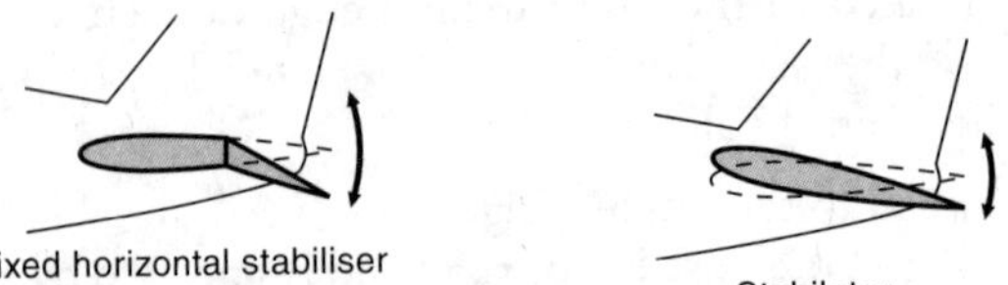

■ *Figure 1-5* ***Different tailplane designs***

Most modern training aeroplanes have a tricycle **undercarriage** or **landing gear** that consists of two main wheels and a nosewheel to provide support on the ground. Other aircraft have a tailwheel instead of a nosewheel. The nosewheel on most types is connected to the rudder pedals so that movement of the pedals will turn it, assisting in directional control on the ground.

Most aircraft have **brakes** on the main wheels which are operated by pressing the top of the rudder pedals or by using a brake handle.

■ *Figure 1-6* ***The tricycle undercarriage and the tailwheel type***

The Engine and Propeller

The typical training aeroplane has a **piston engine** that uses **Avgas** (aviation gasoline). The engine revolutions per minute (rpm) are controlled by the **throttle.** Attached to the engine is a fixed-pitch **propeller** (its blade angle cannot be altered) that converts the power from the engine into thrust. A measure of the power developed is the engine **rpm** (revolutions per minute) which is indicated in the cockpit on the **tachometer** (or 'rev counter').

The fuel is usually stored in **wing tanks;** low-wing aeroplanes require a fuel pump to deliver it to the engine, high-wing aeroplanes usually rely on gravity. There are **fuel gauges** in the cockpit to indicate quantity, but it is good airmanship (common sense) to check the contents of the tanks visually prior to flight.

It is also wise to confirm both that the fuel is of the correct grade (which is identified by its colour) and that it is not contaminated – the most likely contaminant being water, which is denser than Avgas and gathers at the low points in the fuel system. The check is performed by inspecting a small sample taken from **fuel drains** fitted at low points in the fuel system, for example from beneath each fuel tank.

Fuel management is a high priority item.

The **fuel tank selector** in the cockpit allows fuel to be supplied from each tank as desired or possibly from all tanks. It is vital that a tank containing fuel be selected.

Oil for **lubricating** and **cooling** the engine is stored in a sump in the engine compartment. Its quantity should be checked with a dip-stick prior to flight. There are two cockpit gauges in the oil system to register **oil pressure** and **oil temperature** when the engine is running. These gauges are often colour-coded, with the normal operating range shown as a green arc.

The fuel is mixed with air in a **carburettor** attached to the engine and passes through the induction system into the cylinders, where combustion occurs. The **mixture control,** situated near the throttle, is used to ensure that a suitable fuel/air mixture is provided to the engine by the carburettor. The **carburettor heat control,** also located near the throttle, is used to supply hot air to protect the carburettor from ice.

The engine has **dual ignition systems** which provide sparks to initiate the combustion process in the cylinders. The electrical current for the sparks is generated by **two magnetos** geared to the engine. The dual ignition systems provide more efficient combustion and greater safety in the event of one system failing.

An **ignition switch** in the cockpit is normally used to select BOTH, although it can select the LEFT or RIGHT systems individually, as well as having an OFF position. Most ignition switches have a further position, START, which connects the battery to an electric starter to turn the engine over. Once the engine starts, the ignition switch is returned to BOTH and the red starter warning light (if fitted) should go out to verify that the starter motor has indeed disengaged.

■ *Figure 1-7* ***The ignition switch***

The Electrical System

The **battery** is a source of electrical power to start the engine and provides an emergency electrical back-up supply if the engine-driven alternator (or generator) fails.

The electrical system will have an **alternator** or a **generator** to supply various aircraft services, such as some flight instruments, the radios, cabin lights, landing lights, navigation lights, the wing-flap motor, pitot heater and stall warning system. It is important that aeroplanes fitted with an alternator have a serviceable battery so that the alternator can come on-line.

The electrical system has an **ammeter** and/or **warning light** incorporated to verify that electrical current is flowing.

Note that the two magneto systems providing the ignition sparks to the engine are totally separate from the electrical system (alternator/generator, battery, circuit breakers and fuses). Each electrical circuit is protected from excessive current by a **fuse** or a **circuit breaker.**

One very useful electrical service is the **radio,** which is used for air/ground communications. It has an ON/OFF and volume control (usually combined in the one knob), a squelch control to eliminate unwanted background noise, a microphone for transmitting and speakers or headphones for receiving messages.

■ *Figure 1-8* ***Control panel of a typical VHF-COM radio***

The Instruments

The panel in front of the pilot contains various instruments which can provide important information – the main groups being the **flight instruments** (which are directly in front of the pilot) and the **engine instruments** (which are generally situated near the throttle).

The flight instruments include an airspeed indicator, an attitude indicator to depict the aeroplane's attitude relative to the horizon, an altimeter to indicate height, a vertical speed indicator to show climb or descent, a heading indicator and a turn coordinator with an associated balance ball.

The instruments related to airspeed and height are operated by air pressure obtained from the **pitot-static pressure system,** while those related to attitude, direction and turning are operated by internal spinning **gyroscopes** (with the exception of the magnetic compass). The gyroscope rotors may be spun electrically or by a stream of air induced by 'suction' from the vacuum system. The **magnetic compass** is usually located well away from the magnetic influences of the instrument panel and radio.

The engine instruments include the **tachometer** (to read engine rpm), and the **oil pressure** and oil **temperature gauges.** Some aircraft also have a cylinder head temperature gauge.

Other instruments may include an **ammeter** to monitor the electrical system and a suction gauge for the vacuum system.

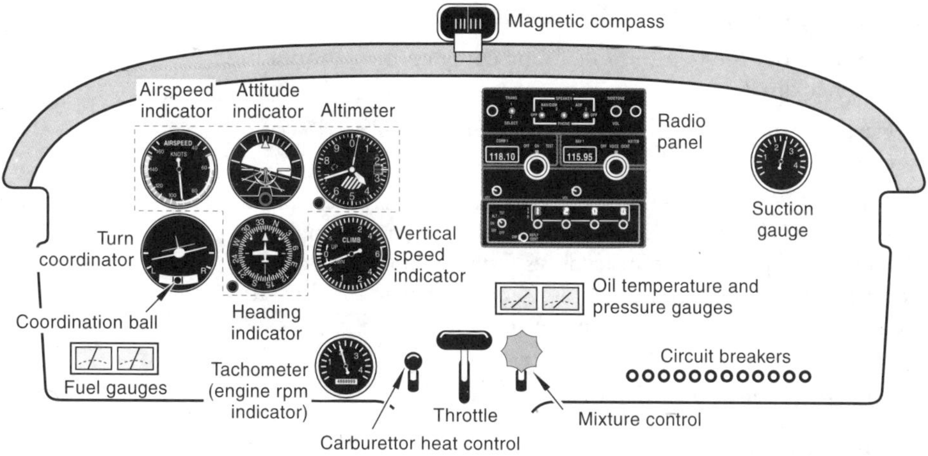

■ *Figure 1-9* ***A typical instrument panel***

Other Items

There may be a **fire extinguisher** provided in the cockpit, which should be checked for serviceability and security in its fitting. Light aircraft fire extinguishers are normally of the dry-chemical (powder) type, which are non-toxic. You should learn how to use the extinguisher in your aircraft.

Control locks may be carried. These fit both internally to lock the control column and/or externally on the actual flight controls. Their purposes is to prevent control-surface movement and damage from the wind when the aeroplane is parked. It is vital of course that they be removed prior to flight.

A **pitot cover** may be carried to protect the pitot head from blockage by insects and water while the aeroplane is parked. It must be removed prior to flight if the airspeed indicator is to read correctly.

Wheel chocks may be carried, to place ahead of and behind the wheels when the aeroplane is parked as a precaution against movement. There may also be a tie-down kit of ropes, pegs and mallet to secure the aeroplane to the ground and prevent strong winds lifting the wings or tail.

A **first-aid kit** may be carried.

Checklists

Written checklists are used in some aeroplanes to confirm that appropriate drills have been carried out: for example, the 'pre-take-off drill' or the 'engine fire drill'. The method of using checklists may be one of:

1. Carrying out the items as the checklist is read.
2. Carrying out the items in full, followed by confirmation using the checklist.
3. Carrying out the items without reference at all to a written checklist.

Vital drills are best committed to memory so that they may be actioned quickly and efficiently, followed by confirmation using a checklist if required. The procedures for your training organisation will be made quite clear by your flying instructor. If checklists are used, they must be carried in the cockpit.

1E. Emergency Drills

The **Pilot's Operating Handbook** for the aircraft will specify the drills to be followed in coping with certain emergencies, for example:

- **engine fire** on start-up or taxiing;
- **engine fire** in flight;
- **engine failure** in flight followed by a forced landing;
- **electrical fire;**
- **cabin fire;**
- **flat main tyre;** and
- **brake failure.**

If any problem occurs in flight, the most essential task for the pilot is to maintain flying speed and control the flightpath of the aeroplane. The emergency must be handled in conjunction with this primary task.

The more serious emergencies are considered in detail in the appropriate exercises of this manual. However, since you are about to commence flying training, and become part of the flight crew, you should have a basic awareness of emergency procedures even at this early stage.

Fire

Fire is a hazard to aviation and is to be avoided at all costs. For a fire to occur, three things are required:

- **fuel** (Avgas, oil, papers, fabric, cabin seating, etc.);
- **oxygen** (present in the air); and
- **an ignition source** (cigarettes, matches, electrical sparks, etc.).

The usual method of extinguishing a fire is to eliminate one or more of these items, e.g. blanketing a fire with 'dry chemical' from a fire extinguisher to starve the fire of oxygen.

It is, of course, preferable that fire is prevented by keeping 'fuel' and possible sources of ignition separate. For example, when **refuelling** an aeroplane, ensure that there is no smoking in the vicinity, that the aeroplane and refuelling equipment are adequately grounded to avoid the possibility of static electricity causing a spark, and that no fuel is spilled. As a precaution, however, a fire extinguisher should be readily available. Know how to use it!

Engine Fire during Start-Up

The best procedure in this situation is to keep the engine turning with the starter, but to move the mixture control to IDLE CUT-OFF (or the fuel selector to OFF) to allow the engine to purge itself and the induction system of fuel. The fire will probably go out. If not, then further action should be taken:

- **fuel** – OFF;
- **switches** – OFF;
- **brakes** – ON;
- **evacuate**, taking the extinguisher.

Engine Fire in Flight

If there is an engine fire in flight, shut down the engine and do not restart it. Maintain flying speed.

A fire in flight will probably be caused by a leakage of fuel or oil under pressure, so a typical procedure to stop the leakage is:

- **throttle** – CLOSED;
- **mixture** – IDLE CUT-OFF, or fuel selector – OFF (so that fuel will be eliminated from the induction system and engine);
- **ignition switches** – OFF;
- **cabin heat** – OFF (to avoid fumes from the engine entering the cockpit).

Electrical Fire

A peculiar smell often indicates that the fire is electrical. Switch off any associated electrical circuits. If required, a fire extinguisher can be used, but ensure that cabin ventilation is sufficient and the windows are open to remove smoke and toxic fumes from the cabin once the fire is out. An immediate landing is advisable. Whether or not to shut the engine down in flight is a command decision and will, of course, mean a forced landing without power.

A typical drill for an electrical fire is:

- **master switch** – OFF (to remove power from the electrical services);
- **all other switches** (except ignition) – OFF;
- **cabin heat** – OFF;
- **fire extinguisher** – use as required (and open fresh air vents);
- **on the ground,** shut down the engine and evacuate; **in flight,** decide whether to keep the engine running and make an early landing or shut down the engine and make an immediate forced landing.

Cabin Fire

A cabin fire may be caused by such things as a cigarette igniting a seat or other matter. The source of the fire should be identified and the fire eliminated using the fire extinguisher. In flight, maintain flying speed and a suitable flightpath while the emergency is resolved; on the ground, consider an immediate evacuation after securing the aeroplane (shut down the engine, switches and fuel – OFF, brakes – ON).

Brake Failure

If the brakes fail while taxiing, then:

- **throttle** – CLOSED;
- **steer away** from other aircraft and obstacles; and, if a collision is imminent
- **stop the engine** (mixture control to IDLE CUT-OFF);
- **fuel** – OFF;
- **ignition** – OFF;
- **master switch** – OFF.

Exercise 2a
Preparation for Flight

Aim

To prepare for flight.

Considerations

The success of a flight depends very much on thorough preparation. In the course of your training a pattern of regular pre-flight actions should be developed to ensure that this is the case. They must be based on the checks in the Pilot's Operating Handbook for your aeroplane.

Preparation for a flight commences well before you actually enter the aeroplane, and consists of:

- **personal preparation;**
- **satisfying the pre-flight documentation requirements;**
- **'booking out'** the flight with an Air Traffic Service Unit;
- **the pre-flight inspection** of the aeroplane;
- **start-up and taxi checks;**
- **the pre-take-off check.**

Personal Preparation for Flight

The pilot is the key person on any flight and must be properly prepared. If you are planning on a flight some days hence, then calm, unhurried and thorough long-term preparation a day or two ahead of time might be useful, be it preparing the maps for a cross-country flight or reading up on 'turning' for an imminent lesson on that exercise.

Short-term preparation involves such things as being properly equipped, arriving early enough at the aerodrome for any briefing or flight preparation to proceed in an unhurried manner, and carrying out the required pre-flight checks of the aeroplane calmly and thoroughly.

A typical list of items to check before even leaving home should include:

- **Am I fit to fly?**
  - Have I consumed alcohol in the last eight hours?
  - Am I using pills, tablets, drugs, etc. that could impair my abilities?
  - Do I have a cold, blocked nose, blocked ears or any other upper respiratory complaint?

- **Do I have the required equipment** for this particular flight?
- **Am I suitably clothed?** (Natural fibres and materials are generally best, such as a cotton shirt, woollen slacks and leather shoes; these allow the body to 'breathe' as well as being somewhat fire-resistant.)

Pre-Flight Documentation

A high level of flight safety is maintained partly because of the thorough documentation required. Items that are recorded include the history of the aeroplane in terms of hours flown and maintenance carried out, and the details of each particular flight and the experience of the pilot.

The Flight Authorisation Sheet

Each flight must be authorised by your flying training organisation and will be recorded on a Flight Authorisation Sheet with appropriate details. There may also be a book containing local rules and regulations appropriate to your flying training, which you should check prior to flight.

The Flight Plan and the Weather

It is not usual to compile a flight plan prior to a local training flight, but it is a consideration during more advanced training when cross-country flights will be undertaken. Weather is a consideration for every flight and, if a 'weather man' is available, you should consult him, and also read through the appropriate weather forecasts or discuss the weather with your flying instructor.

Weight and Balance

*The aeroplane must **always** be within weight and balance limitations.*

It is essential to the safety of every flight that no weight limit is exceeded and that the load is arranged to keep the centre of gravity within approved limits. The ability of the aeroplane to fly and be controllable depends on this.

Most training aeroplanes, however, will be satisfactorily loaded with one or two persons on board and so there may be no need to actually compile a load sheet or check the weight and balance prior to every training flight. All the same, you should develop the habit of considering weight and balance before each and every flight.

Airworthiness Documents

It is the pilot's responsibility to check certain documents prior to flight to ensure that the aeroplane is **airworthy.** These documents include the:

- **Certificate of Airworthiness;**
- **maintenance documents;**
- **aircraft weight and balance schedule;**
- **aircraft technical log.**

Do not accept responsibility for the aeroplane if it has defects which may make it unacceptable for flight. If in any doubt, discuss the matter with your flying instructor or with a licensed engineer.

Booking Out

Booking out with Air Traffic Services (ATS) makes them aware of your flight and allows them to document its progress and safe completion. You can book out with the ATS unit in person before going to the aeroplane or by radio prior to taxiing.

Preparing the Aeroplane for Flight

The Pilot's Operating Handbook for your aeroplane will contain a list of items that must be checked during:

- **the external inspection** of the aeroplane;
- **the internal inspection;**
- **the pre-start, starting and after-starting checks;**
- **the engine power check;** and
- **the pre-take-off check.**

At first, these checks may seem long and complicated but, as you repeat them thoroughly prior to each flight, a pattern will soon form. It is vital that these checks are carried out thoroughly, strictly in accordance with your Pilot's Operating Handbook. The comments that follow are only general comments that will apply to most aeroplanes, however they may or may not apply to yours.

The External Inspection

***Always** perform a thorough external inspection.*

The external inspection can commence as you walk to the aeroplane, and should include:

- **the position of the aeroplane** as being suitable for start-up and taxi (also, note the wind direction and the likely path to the take-off point);
- **the availability of fire extinguishers** and emergency equipment in case of fire on start-up (a very rare event, but it does happen).

A list of typical 'walk-around' items follows. Each item must be inspected individually, but do not neglect a general overview of the aeroplane. Be vigilant for things such as buckling of the fuselage skin or 'popped' rivets, as these could indicate internal structural damage from a previous flight. Leaking oil, fuel forming puddles on the ground, or hydraulic fluid leaks from around the brake lines also deserve further investigation. With experience, you will develop a 'feel' for what looks right and what doesn't.

The **walk-around inspection** starts at the cockpit door:

- Check or take action to ensure that:
  - the magneto switches are OFF;
  - the fuel contents are indicated on the gauges;
  - the control locks are removed;
  - the flaps are lowered (in anticipation of an external inspection);
  - the brakes are set to PARK.
- Check the door to ensure that it is securely attached and can be latched correctly.
- Check the fuel contents by visually inspecting the tanks, replacing the fuel caps securely.
- Carry out a fuel drain (following refuelling or on the first flight of the day) from the drain valves into a glass bottle, visually checking for water (which will sink to the bottom), for any sediment, and for correct coloration of the fuel.

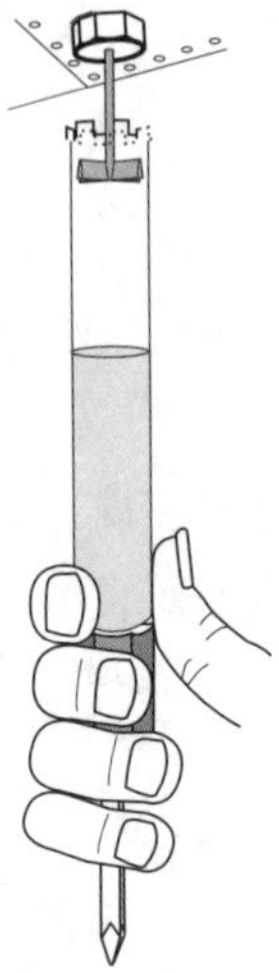

■ *Figure 2a-1* ***Take fuel samples from the fuel system***

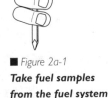

> *If the fuel is contaminated by water, all of the water should be drained away. If the fuel is contaminated by dirt or other solid contaminants, the whole fuel system may have to be drained.*
> ***Do not fly with contaminated fuel!***

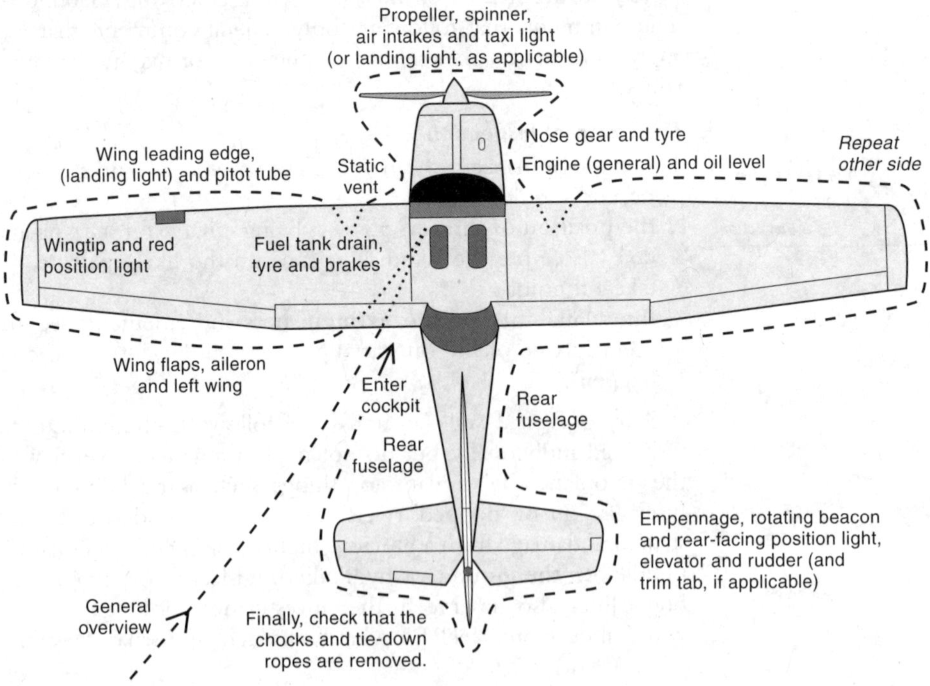

■ *Figure 2a-2* ***Typical walk-around pattern for the external check***

- Check the hydraulic lines to the wheel brakes for cracks and leaks and check that the brake disc is secure.
- Check the undercarriage leg and its attachment to the fuselage. Popped rivets, buckling of the skin or other damage should be brought to the attention of an engineer.
- Check the tyre for correct inflation, cuts and creep, and check that the wheel is secure.
- Check the undersurface of the fuselage for any buckling of the skin or other damage.
- Check the flap surfaces and flap actuating mechanism; check the trailing edge of the wing and aileron for free and correct movement (one up – one down).
- Check the wingtip and navigation light for damage and security.
- Check the leading edge of the wing for smoothness – contamination from ice, frost or insects can greatly diminish the lifting ability of the wing.
- Check that the cover is removed from the pitot tube (otherwise the airspeed indicator will not operate correctly in flight).
- Check that the fuel vent is clear (to allow pressures inside and outside the tanks to equalise as fuel is used and/or altitude is changed).
- Ensure that all inspection panels on the wing are secure.
- Check that the wing strut (if one exists) is secure at both ends.
- Check that the static vent is open and clean (for correct operation of the airspeed indicator, altimeter and vertical speed indicator).
- Check the nose section of the fuselage – loose screws, popped rivets and any buckling of the skin could indicate structural damage from a previous flight.
- Check the propeller for damage (especially nicks along its leading edge), cracks and security.
- Check the propeller spinner for damage, cracks and security.
- Check that the engine air intake and filter is clean, secure and not blocked by things such as a bird's nest, rags, etc.
- Check the nosewheel and tyre.
- Check the nose oleo strut for correct extension (usually 2–3 inches), and the shimmy damper and other mechanisms for security.
- Open the engine inspection panel and check the oil contents (replacing the oil cap securely), inspect for any obvious loose cables or wires, cracked manifolds, etc., and then lock the inspection panel.
- Ensure that the windscreen is clean.
- Continue the check around the other side of the aeroplane.
- Check that luggage lockers are securely closed.

- Check radio aerials for security and no loose wires.
- Check all visible cables, lights, etc.
- Check the tailplane, rudder, elevator (for free movement) and trim tab.
- Remove and stow tie-down ropes and chocks (provided the parking brake is on).
- Stand back and check the general appearance of the aeroplane.

It cannot be emphasised enough just how important this pre-flight inspection by the pilot is. Even if you have no experience of mechanical things, you must train yourself to look at the aeroplane and notice things that do not seem right. Bring any items that you are unsure of to the attention of your flying instructor or an engineer.

At this stage, you are now ready to seat yourself in the aeroplane and begin the internal inspection.

The Internal Inspection

The internal inspection should include:

- Confirm the brakes are – ON (parked).
- Fuel – ON.
- Seat position and harness.
- Ignition switch (magnetos) – OFF (i.e. the engine is not 'live').
- Master switch – ON (for electrical services such as fuel gauges).
- Flight controls for full and free movement (elevator, ailerons, rudder and trim wheel or handle – set the trim to the take-off position).
- Engine controls for full and free movement (throttle, mixture control and carburettor heat control).
- Scan the instruments systematically from one side of the panel to the other for serviceability and correct readings.
- No circuit breakers should be popped nor fuses blown (for electrical services to operate).
- The microphone should be plugged in if you are to transmit on the radio.
- Safety equipment (fire extinguisher, first-aid kit) on board.
- Loose articles stowed.
- Checklists available (if required).

__Always__ perform a thorough internal inspection.

Once the pre-flight inspection is completed and you are comfortable in your seat, you should then brief your passengers on the use of their safety belts, and on any relevant emergency procedures. Now the engine starting procedure can begin, and this is covered in the next exercise.

Exercise 2b
Starting and Stopping the Engine

Aim

To start and stop the engine

Considerations

Prior to starting the engine, check that the surrounding area is suitable for start-up. The aeroplane should be on a surface suitable for taxiing and well away from any buildings, fuel storage areas and public areas. The aeroplane should be parked facing in a direction that will not cause loose stones or gravel to be blasted back over other aircraft or into open hangars when the engine is running. Also, there should be no fuel spills in the vicinity as this creates a fire risk.

The engine then needs to be properly prepared for the start-up. The correct procedure for this is found in your Pilot's Operating Handbook.

The Pre-Start and Starting Check

The pre-start and starting check will include such items as:

- Brakes – ON.
- Unnecessary electrical equipment – OFF.
- Fuel – ON.
- Carburettor heat control – COLD.
- Mixture – RICH.
- Throttle – CLOSED (or cracked ¼ inch open).
- Fuel primer – LOCKED (following 1–3 priming strokes, if applicable).
- Rotating beacon – ON (as a warning to other people).
- 'All clear' – the area around the aeroplane, especially near the propeller, should be all clear. The pilot is responsible for people around the aeroplane. Loudly call, "Clear propeller!" to warn anyone who may be approaching the aeroplane.
- Starter – ENGAGE to crank the engine; then, once the engine has started, release the starter and check that it has disengaged (which, in most aeroplanes, is indicated by a red light going out).

After Starting

After engine start, various items to be checked may include:

- Starter warning light – OUT.
- Oil pressure – sufficient pressure within 30 seconds of start-up (slightly longer in very cold weather).
- Set idling rpm with the throttle (usually 1,000 to 1,200 rpm) to ensure adequate cooling.
- Ammeter – indicating recharging of the battery following the drain on it during start-up.
- Vacuum gauge (if fitted) – check for sufficient suction to operate the gyro instruments.
- Magneto check of the LEFT and RIGHT magnetos individually, as well as with the ignition switch in the usual BOTH position (the rpm should decrease slightly on each individual magneto and return to the previous value when the switch is returned to BOTH), but, if the engine stops, then a problem exists.
- Radio – ON, correct frequency selected, volume set and squelch set.

The Pre-Take-Off Check of the Engine

After the aeroplane has been taxied to the holding point or run-up bay prior to entering the runway, it is brought to a halt and the brakes parked while the **pre-take-off vital actions** are performed. One of these actions is a check of the engine. This is detailed in Exercise 12 of this manual.

Shutting Down the Engine

There will be a shut-down procedure specified in the Pilot's Operating Handbook for your aircraft which will include such items as:

- Brakes – PARKED, with the aeroplane (ideally) pointing into any strong wind.
- Ensure the engine is cool (having taxied or set 1,000 to 1,200 rpm for a minute or two should be sufficient).
- Magnetos – CHECK: both magnetos should be checked individually. There should be a slight rpm drop as you go from BOTH to an individual magneto, and a return to the set rpm when the switch is returned to BOTH.

NOTE Sometimes a 'dead-cut' check is made by moving the ignition switch very quickly from BOTH to OFF and back to BOTH, to check that the engine will actually cut. This checks that the OFF position does indeed break the circuit to each magneto by earthing them. If this were not the case, the engine and propeller would be *live* even with the magneto switched to OFF. An innocent movement of the propeller could start the engine unexpectedly – a dangerous situation! Some engine manufacturers advise against this check as it may damage the engine, especially if the switch is held too long in the OFF position. Seek your instructor's advice.

- Electrics – OFF (radio, lights, etc.).
- Mixture control – IDLE CUT-OFF (fully-out), to starve the engine of fuel and stop it running.
- After the engine stops, switch the ignition OFF and remove the key.
- Consideration should be given to switching the fuel cock OFF.

Problems During Start-Up

Most engine starts are uneventful if correct procedures are followed but, occasionally, problems may arise.

A Flooded Engine

It is possible to 'flood' an engine with too much fuel, making a start difficult and placing a strain on the battery which supplies electrical power to the starter motor. If 'flooding' is suspected, adopt the following procedure:

- Ignition switches – OFF.
- Throttle – FULLY OPEN.
- Fuel – ON.
- Mixture control – IDLE CUT-OFF (i.e. no fuel supplied to the engine).
- Crank the engine through several revolutions with the starter (which should clear the intake passages of excess fuel); then
- Repeat the starting procedure without priming the engine.

Engine Fire on Start-Up

Engine fires are a very rare event these days but they can still occur, possibly as a result of over-priming the engine with fuel. In such a case:

- Starter – if still engaged, CONTINUE CRANKING.
- Mixture control – IDLE CUT-OFF.
- Fuel selector – OFF.
- Throttle – OPEN (to allow maximum airflow through to purge the induction system and engine of fuel).

Once the fuel has been eliminated, the fire should stop. Release the starter.

If the fire continues:

- Ignition switch – OFF.
- Master switch – OFF.
- Brakes – ON.
- Evacuate, taking any suitable fire extinguisher with you. Do not attempt to restart the engine.

Exercise 2c
Post-Flight Actions

The post-flight duties required of each pilot are to secure the aeroplane and complete the post-flight documentation.

A flight is not really completed until the engine is shut down and the aeroplane parked and secure. The post-flight documentation must be finalised, since it is a requirement that certain records be kept and that any faults in the aeroplane be made known so that maintenance action will be taken.

An aeroplane has a life of its own in the sense that it passes continually from the command of one pilot to the command of another – the post-flight check of one being followed by the pre-flight check of the next. To a certain extent, each pilot relies on the fact that previous pilots have performed their duties, even though we must all accept individual responsibility.

Securing the Aeroplane

The aeroplane should not be left unattended unless it is adequately secured against movement and possible damage.

- Ensure that the parking brake is ON (if required) and that the wheel chocks are in place, in front of and behind the wheels.
- Carry out a brief external inspection.
- Fit the pitot covers, control locks and tie-down ropes if required.
- Secure the seat belts.
- If yours is the last flight of the day, consider refuelling to minimise overnight condensation of water in the fuel tanks.
- Lock the door and return the key.

Post-Flight Documentation

- 'Book in' the flight if necessary with the Air Traffic Service Unit.
- Complete the **Flight Authorisation Sheet,** recording the time and nature of the flight.
- Report any aeroplane defects to your flying instructor or to an engineer and, when appropriate, note them on the maintenance document to ensure that necessary maintenance will be attended to and that the following pilot will have a serviceable aeroplane.
- Complete your personal **logbook.**

During your training, debriefing by your flying instructor will probably occur following the completion of your post-flight duties.

Exercise 3
Air Experience

Your First Flight

This flight is not part of your formal instruction, but rather an opportunity to get the 'feel' of being airborne. Your flying instructor, an experienced and professional pilot, will use this first flight to let you experience some of the more common sensations of flying an aeroplane.

In the Cockpit

Sit comfortably in your seat and **relax.** Since you will be trained to become the captain of your aeroplane, you may as well start by sitting in the left-hand seat – the captain's seat by tradition and design. It needs to be positioned so that you can reach the appropriate controls comfortably with your hands and feet. The seat belt or harness should be firm.

Even though this may be your very first flight, it is important that your seat is positioned correctly, since the position of the natural horizon in the windscreen is a vital element in assisting the visual pilot to fly accurately.

Fresh air is available through vents, and directing these towards your face and body makes the cockpit more comfortable.

Communication in the cockpit is very important, so ensure that your headset is comfortable and the intercom is working properly.

Leaving the Ground

While **taxiing out,** you can assist in maintaining a good **lookout** for other aircraft and for obstructions.

During the **take-off roll** you should look well ahead. Maintaining a straight path down the runway, and also judging height above it, is best achieved by looking into the 'middle distance'. Develop good habits right from the start! Even though the take-off appears full of action, in reality it is a straightforward manoeuvre and you will soon master it.

As the aeroplane climbs, ground features take on a different perspective, being viewed more in plan than in profile – towns, roads, rivers, mountains and coastlines appearing as they would on a map. The sensation of speed also diminishes and the aeroplane feels as if it is flying in slow motion.

In Flight

You will have the opportunity to 'follow' your instructor on the flight controls by placing:

- your left hand lightly on the control wheel (or control column);
- your right hand on the throttle or on your lap; and
- both feet lightly on the rudder pedals (with your heels on the floor to ensure that the toe brakes are not applied).

■ *Figure 3-1* ***A light touch on the controls***

Control of the Aircraft

During the course of your training, control will be passed from your instructor to you and then back again quite frequently. Your flying instructor will say "You have control". (or words to that effect), when he wishes you to take control. On hearing this instruction, you should place your hands and feet on the controls lightly, but firmly, and, once you feel comfortable to take control, respond by saying "I have control." Each change of control should be preceded by an initial statement followed by a response from the other pilot.

■ *Figure 3-2* ***Be clear at all times as to who has control***

Keep a Good Lookout

'Visual' flying requires that the pilot maintains a **high visual awareness of the environment outside the cockpit,** to relate the attitude (or nose position) of the aeroplane to the natural horizon, to look out for other aircraft, to check passage over the ground and to remain clear of cloud.

■ *Figure 3-3* ***The view from the cockpit***

The most efficient means of scanning for other aircraft takes into account the fact that the eyes see better when they are stationary. Use a series of short, regularly spaced eye movements, moving the eyes about 10° each time, to position them to scan an area for about one second before moving on.

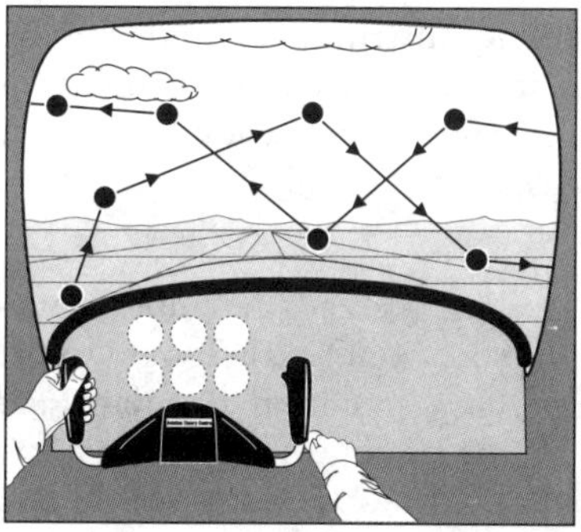

■ *Figure 30-4* ***Scanning for other traffic***

There is a **blind spot** under the nose of the aeroplane that the pilot cannot see, which you should periodically clear by making shallow turns that enable you to see this area out of the side window. Get to know the blind spots of your aeroplane, and periodically take action to clear the areas normally obscured.

The position of other aeroplanes in relation to your own is best described by using the **clock code,** based on a horizontal clock face aligned with the aeroplane's heading.

An aeroplane ahead of you, but higher, would be described as '12 o'clock high', while one slightly behind and below you on the left-hand side would be at '8 o'clock low'.

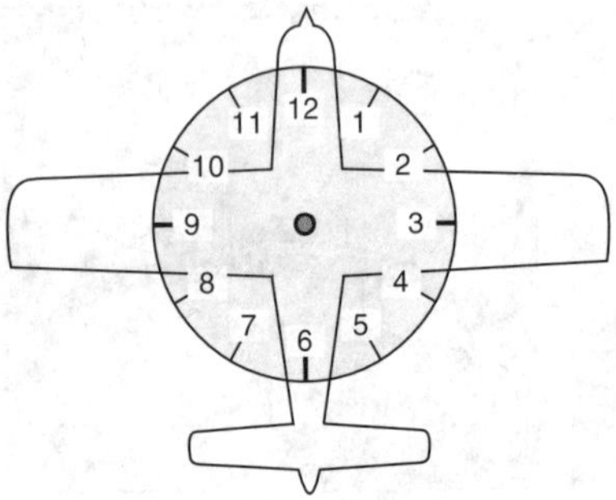

■ *Figure 3-5* ***The clock code***

Note any **landmarks** that can assist in your return to the aerodrome and remain **well clear of cloud** at all times.

The Instruments

The aeroplane has instruments which can provide useful information regarding altitude, direction, airspeed and engine operation. The basic division is into **flight instruments** and **engine instruments.** An occasional glance at a particular instrument for one or two seconds is all that is necessary for visual pilots – your visual awareness of the world outside the cockpit must not suffer.

Landing

As the **descent, approach** and **landing** proceed, the pilot's workload increases. During the landing, you should again look into the 'middle distance', to allow better judgement in the **flare** and **touchdown** when you are making the landing. The approach and landing seems full of action, but it will not be long before you have mastered this manoeuvre!

A flight is not complete until the aeroplane is parked and secured, and the post-flight duties of the pilot completed. Your first flight is now over, but a marvellous hobby or career awaits you. Preparing for the next flying lesson carefully on the ground by reading the appropriate exercise of this manual (as outlined by your instructor) will ensure that you derive the maximum benefit from your next lesson in the air.

Exercise 4a
The Primary Effect of Each Main Flight Control

Aim

To observe the primary effect of moving each main flight control.

Considerations

Aeroplane Movement

An aeroplane moves in three dimensions.

To describe an aeroplane's attitude, or position in flight, three mutually perpendicular reference axes passing through the centre of gravity (CG) are used. Any change in aeroplane attitude can be expressed in terms of motion about these three axes.

Motion about the lateral axis is known as ***pitching****.*
Motion about the longitudinal axis is known as ***rolling****.*
Motion about the normal axis is known as ***yawing****.*

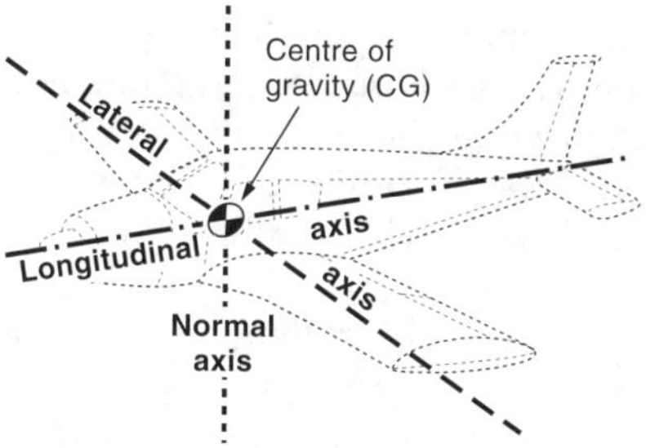

■ *Figure 4a-1* ***Angular motion is described using three reference axes***

NOTE The word *normal* in geometry means perpendicular. We therefore refer to the yaw axis as the *normal axis,* because it is perpendicular to both the longitudinal axis and the lateral axis. It is preferable not to call it the vertical axis, because it is only vertical when the aeroplane is in the cruise attitude. Whenever the aeroplane is banked, or the nose is pitched up or down, the normal axis is not vertical.

Motion about an axis can be described as *motion in a plane.* For instance, the nose pitching up and down can be described as either rotation about the lateral axis, or motion in the pitching plane.

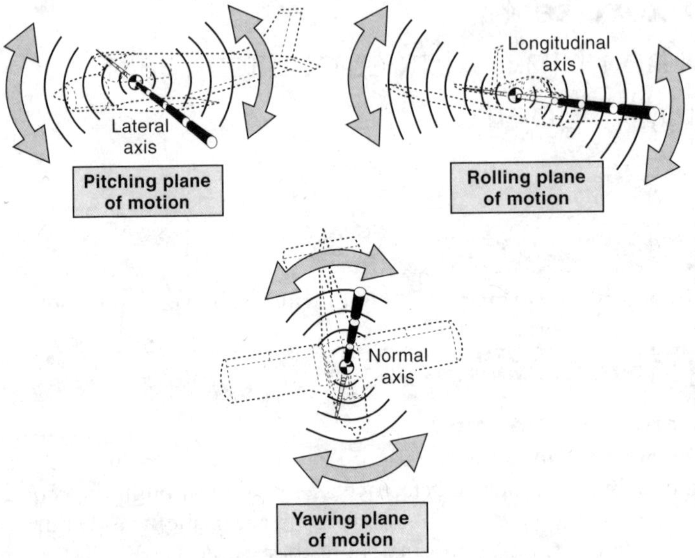

■ *Figure 4a-2* ***Angular motion can occur in three planes***

Aeroplane Stability

Stability is the natural ability of the aeroplane to remain in its original attitude or to return to it following some disturbance (such as a wind gust), without any action being taken by the pilot.

Most training aeroplanes are reasonably stable in the **pitching** plane. If correctly trimmed, they will maintain steady flight with the pilot flying 'hands-off'. In other words, the nose position relative to the horizon will remain reasonably steady without too much attention from the pilot.

The stability of most aeroplanes in the **rolling** and **yawing** planes, however, is usually not as great as in the pitching plane. If the wings are moved from their position (say by a gust), the aeroplane will eventually enter a descending spiral turn unless the pilot actively does something about it – in this case by levelling the wings.

The Main Flight Controls

The pilot controls motion about the three axes (or in the three planes) with the main flight controls:

- the **elevator** controls pitch;
- the **ailerons** control roll; and
- the **rudder** controls yaw.

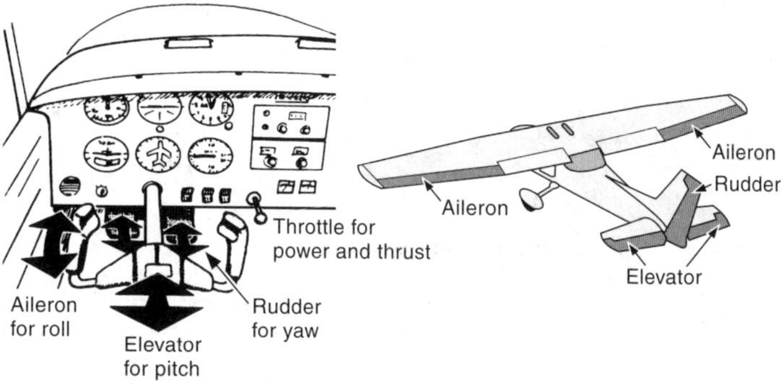

■ *Figure 4a-3* ***The three main flight controls: elevator, ailerons and rudder***

The Elevator

The elevator controls pitching.

The elevator is operated by fore and aft movements of the control column and controls pitching. The **conventional elevator** is a control surface hinged to the rear of the tailplane (also known as the horizontal stabiliser). Some aircraft have an **all-flying tail** (or **stabilator**) which is a single moving surface acting as both the tailplane and the elevator. Either type has the same effect on the aeroplane when the control column is moved.

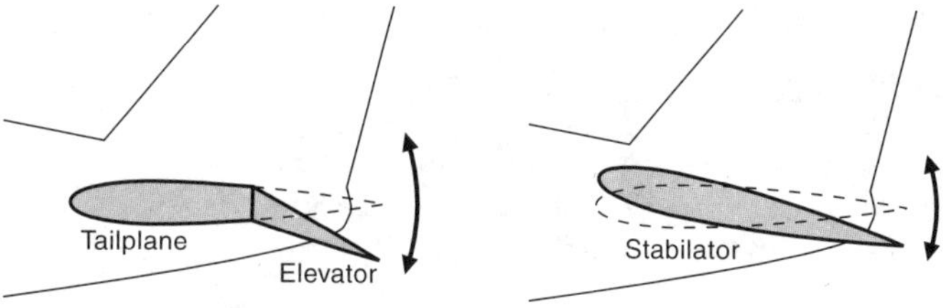

■ *Figure 4a-4* ***Fixed tailplane and moving elevator (left), and the all-flying tail (right)***

Deflecting the elevator with the control column alters the airflow around the tailplane and changes the aerodynamic force generated by it. Moving the control column back deflects the elevator up, causing an increased speed of flow beneath the tailplane and reducing the static pressure in that area. This results in a downward aerodynamic force on the tailplane, causing the aeroplane to rotate about its centre of gravity. The tail moves down and the nose moves up.

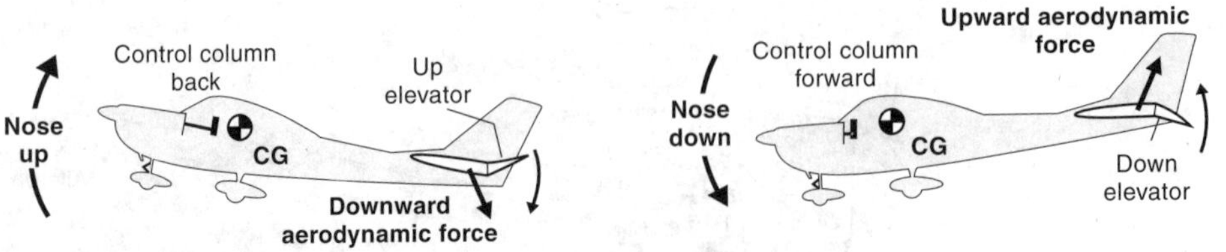

■ *Figure 4a-5* ***The elevator controls pitching***

The rate of pitching of the aeroplane increases with larger elevator deflections. At normal flight speeds, the movement of the control column can be quite small and may feel more like pressure changes than actual movements. Fore and aft movement of the control column is used to place the nose in the desired position relative to the horizon (i.e. to set the **pitch attitude**).

The Ailerons

The ailerons control roll.

The ailerons are hinged control surfaces attached to the outboard trailing edge of each wing. The ailerons in some aeroplanes are controlled by rotation of the control wheel and in other aeroplanes by left/right movements of the control column. The control column or control wheel therefore serves two functions:

1. Fore and aft movement operates the elevator.
2. Rotation or left/right movement operates the ailerons.

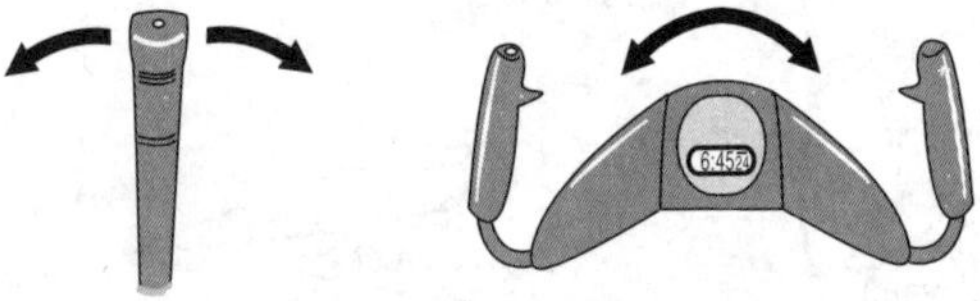

■ *Figure 4a-6* ***A control column and a control wheel perform the same function***

As one aileron goes down and increases the lift generated by that wing, the other aileron goes up and reduces the lift on its wing, causing the aeroplane to roll. For example, moving the control column to the left causes a roll to the left by raising the left aileron and lowering the right aileron.

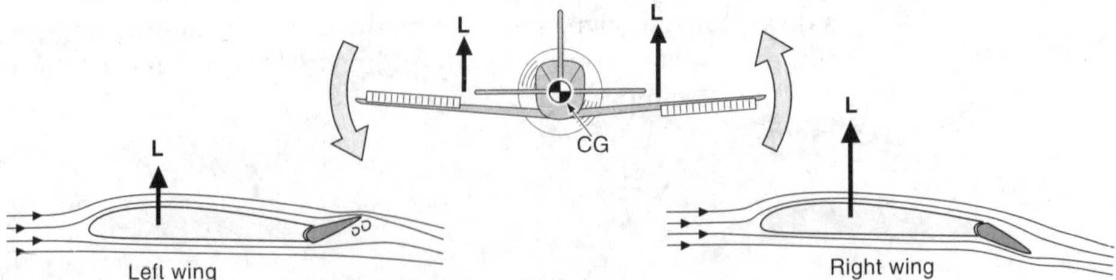

■ *Figure 4a-7* ***A roll to the left***

The aeroplane will continue to roll while the ailerons are deflected, the roll rate being determined by the amount of aileron deflection. Holding the control column central places the ailerons in the neutral position and stops the roll.

The Rudder

The rudder controls yaw.

The third (and final) main flight control is the rudder, which is a hinged control surface at the rear of the fin (vertical stabiliser). The rudder is controlled with both feet on the rudder pedals. These pedals are interconnected so that as one moves forward the other moves back.

Moving the left rudder pedal forward deflects the rudder to the left. This increases the speed of airflow on the right hand side of the fin, reducing the static pressure there and creating an aerodynamic force to the right. The aeroplane rotates about its centre of gravity and so, with left rudder, the nose yaws left. Conversely, moving the right rudder pedal forward yaws the nose of the aeroplane to the right.

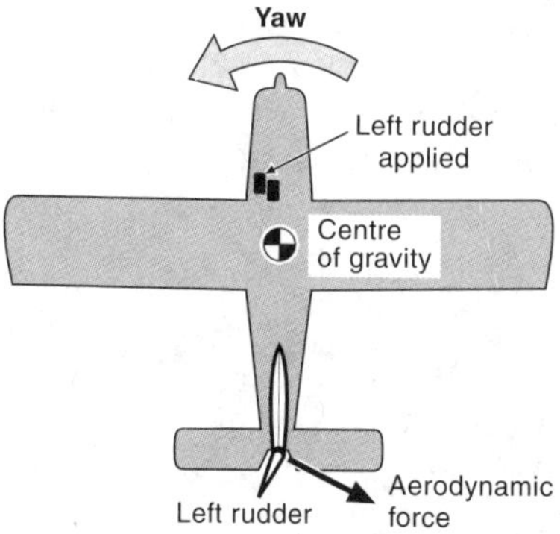

■ *Figure 4a-8* ***The left rudder pressure yaws the nose left***

Yawing the aeroplane can be uncomfortable and is aerodynamically inefficient because it causes drag to increase. It is neither a comfortable nor efficient means of turning an aeroplane in flight; a yawing turn falls into the same category as trying to turn a bicycle without leaning it into the turn.

Although it can yaw the aeroplane, one of the main functions of the rudder is to **prevent unwanted yaw,** a function known as 'maintaining balanced flight'. This is indicated to the pilot by the small balance ball on the instrument panel and also by the 'seat of his pants'. If the aeroplane is out of balance, the ball moves out to one side (and the pilot, reacting in the same way as the ball, will feel pressed to the same side).

Balance can be restored by applying **same-side rudder pressure,** i.e. if the ball is out to the right, apply right rudder pressure (and vice versa).

■ *Figure 4a-9* **Apply 'same-side' rudder pressure to centre the balance ball**

Aeroplane Attitude and Control

Each of the three primary aerodynamic controls operates in the same sense relative to the aeroplane, irrespective of its attitude in pitch or bank. For example, moving the control column forward will move the nose in a direction away from the pilot, even if (taking an extreme case) the aeroplane is inverted.

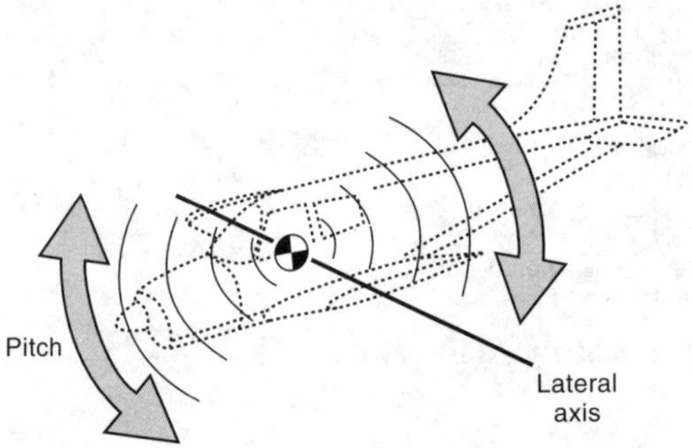

■ *Figure 4a-10* **Motion is referred to the aeroplane axes**

Flying the Manoeuvre

Good flying requires the coordination of all three flight controls; however, in this exercise we will use them individually. It is a necessary step because the individual effects need to be appreciated before smooth coordination of the flight controls in normal flight is possible.

From straight and level flight move each of the controls *individually* and relate the effects to the three axes. Repeat with the aeroplane banked.

Airmanship

You are training to be a visual pilot, so develop good habits early. **Look out** of the cockpit most of the time, both to check the attitude of the aeroplane relative to the horizon and to look for other aircraft. Identify their position using the clock code. Follow the correct "You have control" – "I have control" procedures so that it is quite clear at all times who has control.

Hold the controls lightly and move them smoothly and fluently. Occasionally, large control movements are required to achieve the desired effect but, at normal flying speeds, *firm pressures* rather than large movements will achieve the desired effect.

Airwork 4a
The Primary Effect of Each Main Flight Control

Aim *To observe the primary effect of moving each main flight control during flight.*

1. The Primary Effect of the Elevator is to Pitch the Aeroplane

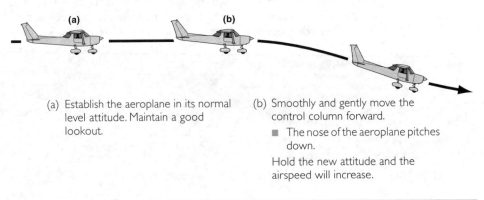

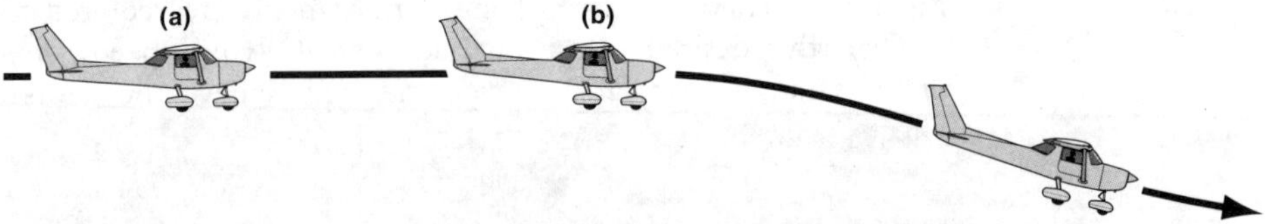

(a) Establish the aeroplane in its normal level attitude. Maintain a good lookout.

(b) Smoothly and gently move the control column forward.
- The nose of the aeroplane pitches down.

Hold the new attitude and the airspeed will increase.

2. The Primary Effect of the Ailerons is to Roll the Aeroplane

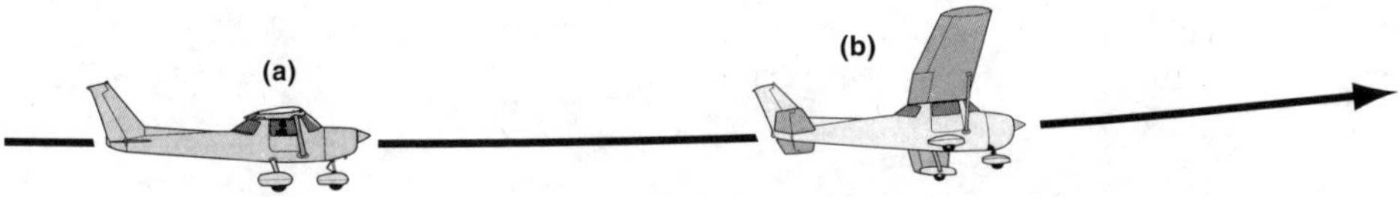

(a) Establish the aeroplane in its normal level attitude. Maintain a good lookout.

(b) Initially hold the wings level. Then smoothly rotate the control column to the left.
- The aeroplane rolls to the left.

Airwork 4a

(c) Smoothly and gently move the control column rearward.

- The nose of the aeroplane pitches up.

Hold the new attitude and the airspeed will decrease.

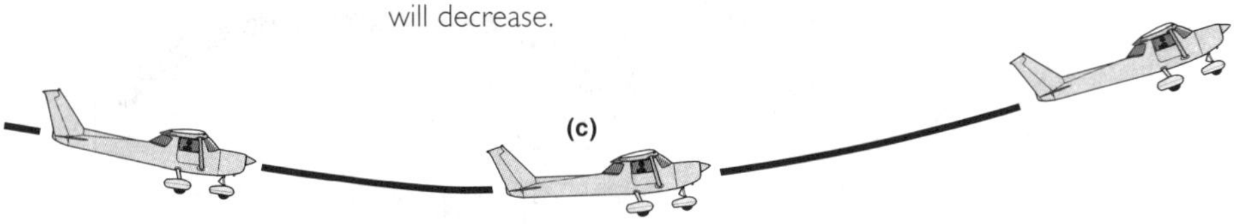

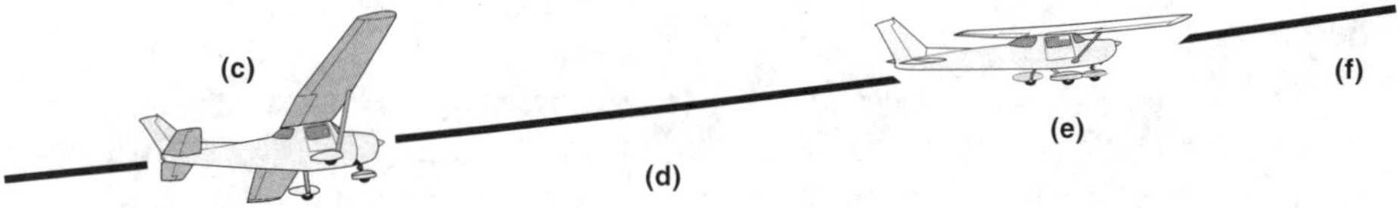

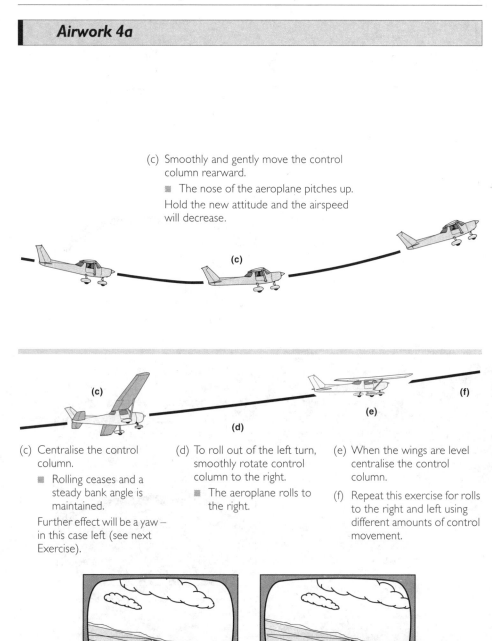

(c) Centralise the control column.

- Rolling ceases and a steady bank angle is maintained.

Further effect will be a yaw – in this case left (see next Exercise).

(d) To roll out of the left turn, smoothly rotate control column to the right.

- The aeroplane rolls to the right.

(e) When the wings are level centralise the control column.

(f) Repeat this exercise for rolls to the right and left using different amounts of control movement.

Airwork 4a

The Primary Effect of Each Main Flight Control

3. The Primary Effect of the Rudder is to Yaw the Aeroplane

(a) Establish the aeroplane in its normal level attitude. Maintain a good lookout.

(b) Select a reference point on the horizon.

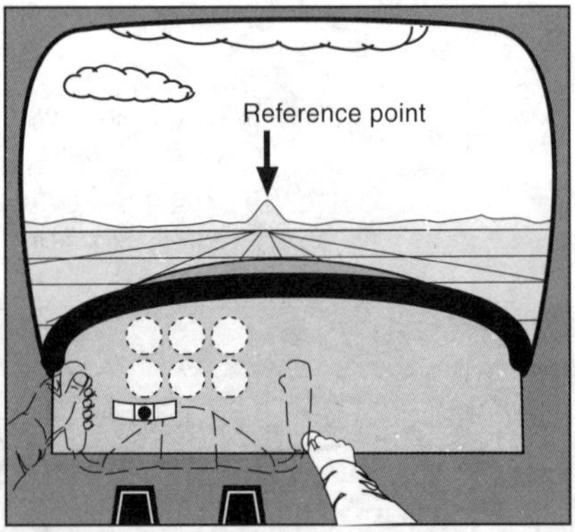

■ ***Steady, straight and level flight***

(c) Smoothly apply left rudder pressure.

- The nose of the aeroplane yaws left (and the balance ball is thrown out to the right).

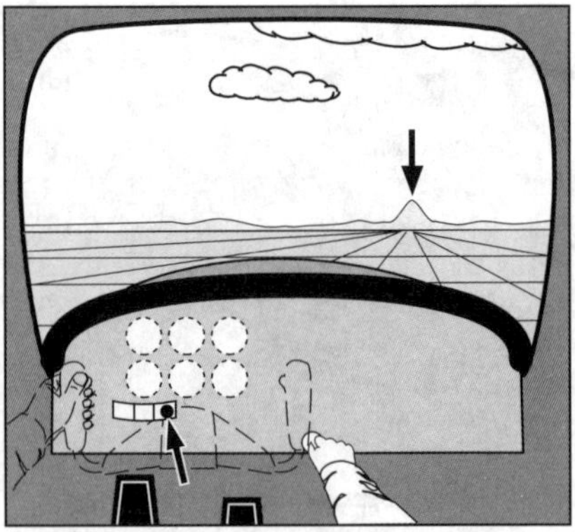

■ ***Left rudder – nose yaws left and balance ball thrown right***

(d) Centralise the rudder pedals (by removing left rudder pressure).

(e) Repeat using right rudder pressure and observe the reverse results.

Airwork 4a

4. The Controls Work the Same when the Aeroplane is not Flying Straight and Level

(a) Establish the aeroplane in its normal level attitude. Look out.

(b) Bank the aeroplane with the aileron control.

- Forward pressure on the control column pitches the nose down and away from the pilot.
- Aft pressure on the control column pitches the nose up and towards the pilot.

■ ***Aeroplane banked to the left – forward control column pressure still pitches the nose down***

(c) Set the aeroplane with a high nose attitude.

- Rotating the control column left causes the aeroplane to roll left.
- Rotating the control column right causes the aeroplane to roll right.

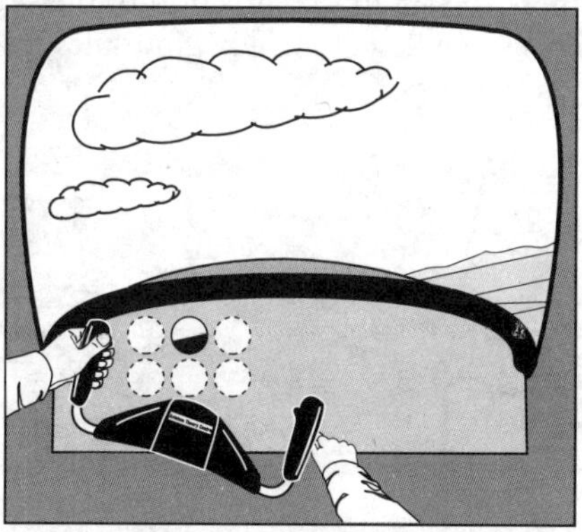

■ ***With a high nose attitude the aeroplane still responds to the aileron control – rolls right (and left)***

(d) Bank the aeroplane with the ailerons.

- Pushing the left rudder pedal causes the nose to yaw left relative to the pilot.
- Pushing the right rudder pedal causes the nose to yaw right relative to the pilot.

Exercise 4b
The Further Effect of Each Main Flight Control

Aim

To observe the further effect of moving each main flight control.

Considerations

Control Effects

Operating a single flight control can have more than one effect. When either the ailerons or rudder are used individually there is both a primary and a secondary (or further) effect.

Roll Causes Yaw

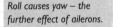

Roll causes yaw – the further effect of ailerons.

Banking the aeroplane tilts the lift force generated by the wings. A sideways component of the lift force now exists, causing the aeroplane to 'slip' towards the lower wing. In this **sideslip,** the large keel surfaces behind the centre of gravity (such as the fin and the fuselage) are struck by the airflow, which causes the aeroplane's nose to yaw in the direction of the sideslip. The nose will drop and a spiral descent will begin (unless prevented by the pilot levelling the wings).

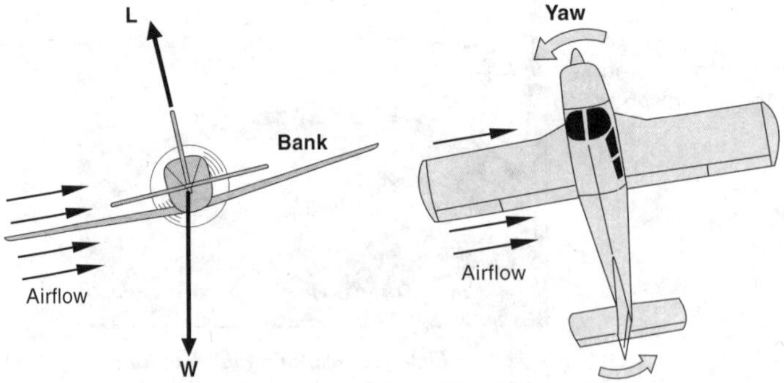

■ *Figure 4b-1* ***Bank causes sideslip followed by yaw***

Moving the ailerons with left/right movements of the control column has two effects – a **roll** followed by a **yaw.** Therefore:

- the **primary effect** of the **ailerons** is to **roll** the aeroplane; and
- the **further effect** is to **yaw** the aeroplane.

Yaw Causes Roll

Yaw causes roll – the further effect of rudder

Applying rudder will yaw the nose of the aeroplane – a yaw to the left if left rudder pressure is applied, a yaw to the right if right rudder is applied. As a result of the yaw, the outer wing will tend to rise because:

- **it is moving faster** than the inner wing and so generates more lift; and
- **the aeroplane** will continue to move in its original direction due to inertia, causing the outer wing, if it has dihedral, to be presented to the airflow at a greater angle of attack, generating increased lift. (*Dihedral* describes a wing that is angled up towards the wingtip.)

The inner wing will be somewhat shielded from the airflow by the fuselage, and therefore produce less lift.

Operating the rudder, therefore, causes yaw followed by roll, and unless the pilot takes corrective action (by preventing unwanted yaw with opposite rudder or by levelling the wings) a spiral descent will result.

When rudder is applied:

- **the primary effect** is to **yaw** the aeroplane; and
- **the further effect** is to **roll** the aeroplane.

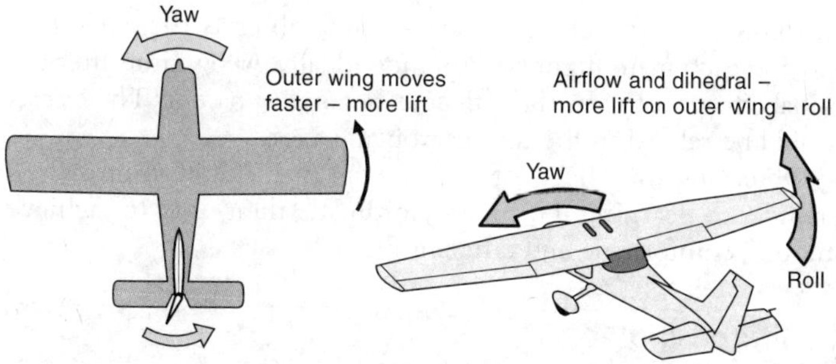

■ *Figure 4b-2* ***Rudder causes yaw followed by roll***

Pitch and Airspeed

The further effect of the elevator is an airspeed change.

The primary effect of elevator is to change the pitch attitude. For example, by moving the control column back the nose is raised.

Following a pitch change, the inertia of the aeroplane (i.e. its resistance to any change) will cause it to follow the original flight-path for a brief period. The airflow will then strike the wings at a greater angle of attack and, as a consequence, they will generate a different aerodynamic force. Drag will increase, causing the aeroplane to slow down. Thus, raising the nose with the elevator will lead to an airspeed decrease.

Conversely, by moving the control column forward, the nose is lowered and the airflow will strike the wings at a lesser angle of attack, less drag will be created and so the airspeed will increase. Thus, lowering the nose with the elevator will lead to an airspeed increase.

When deflected by moving the control column, the elevator has:

- **the primary effect** of pitching the aeroplane; and
- **the further effect** of changing the airspeed.

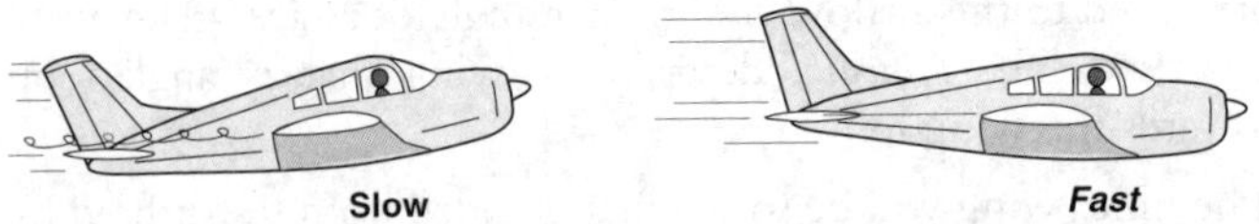

■ *Figure 4b-3* ***The further effect of elevator is to change the airspeed***

NOTE When the elevator changes the pitch attitude of the aeroplane, it will gradually settle at a new airspeed. Whether the aeroplane climbs, descends or stays at the same level depends on the power that is set. The effect of power is discussed shortly.

Flying the Manoeuvre

Established in straight and level flight, observe the effects of moving each main flight control individually. Allow time after the initial effect for the further effect to become apparent. The effects should be related to the three aeroplane axes.

Observing the effects of each of the main flight controls is a prelude to learning how to coordinate their use to achieve smooth, comfortable and efficient flight.

Airmanship

Maintain a good **lookout,** both with respect to the horizon and landmarks and looking for other aircraft. Be very clear at all times about who has control of the aeroplane. When you have control, exert gentle, but firm and positive pressure on the controls as required.

Airwork 4b
The Further Effect of Each Main Flight Control

Aim *To observe the further effect of moving each main flight control.*

1. Roll Causes Yaw – the Further Effect of the Ailerons

(a) Establish straight and level flight, maintaining a good lookout.

(b) Remove your feet from the rudder pedals.

(c) Apply aileron by moving the control column.

- The aeroplane banks and then, because of the resulting sideslip, yaws towards the lower wing, i.e. the nose drops into the turn.

■ **Aileron applied** ■ **Left bank ...** ■ **Causes a yaw to the left**

2. Yaw Causes Roll – the Further Effect of the Rudder

(a) Establish straight and level flight, maintaining a good lookout.

(b) Take your hands off the control column.

(c) Apply rudder pressure.

(d) The aeroplane yaws and then, because of the yaw, rolls in the same direction.

■ **Left rudder applied** ■ **Left yaw ...** ■ **Causes a roll to the left**

NOTE The effects seen in steps 1 and 2 will also be the same when the aeroplane is banked, is climbing, or is descending.

Airwork 4b

3. *Changing the Pitch Attitude Alters the Airspeed – the Further Effect of the Elevator*

(a) Establish straight and level flight, and look out.

(b) Ease the control column forward:

- The nose pitches down and the airspeed increases.

(c) Ease the control column back:

- The nose rises and the airspeed decreases.

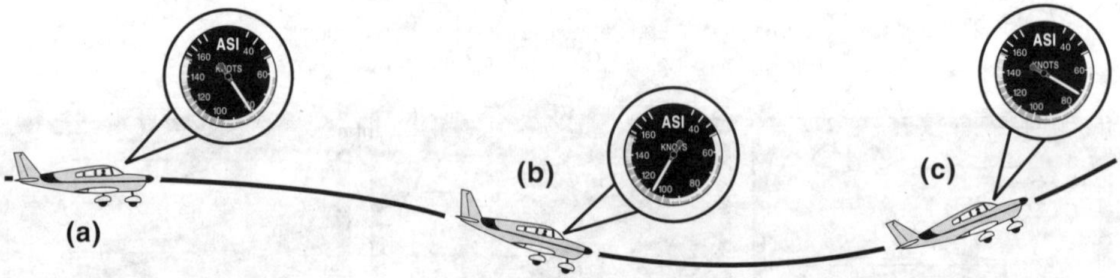

Exercise 4c
The Art of Trimming

Aim

To use the trim to relieve prolonged control pressures.

Considerations

Trimming is Vital to Accurate Flight

The trimming devices can decrease your workload tremendously.

All training aeroplanes have an elevator trim that can relieve the pilot of steady fore and aft pressures on the control column. Some aeroplanes also have a rudder trim to relieve steady pressures on the rudder pedals.

The trim is used to relieve prolonged control pressures in steady conditions of flight, such as straight and level, climbing and descending. The trim should not be altered in transient manoeuvres, such as turning.

Using the trimming devices can ease the workload on the pilot tremendously, so the effect of trim and how to use it correctly should be clearly understood at an early stage.

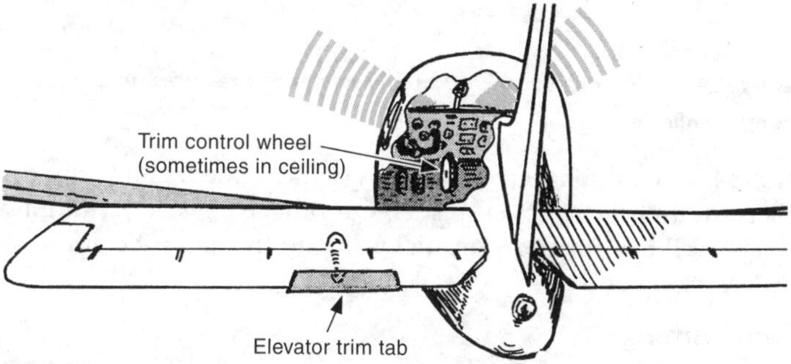

■ *Figure 4c-1* ***The elevator trim tab and trim wheel***

Why is Trim Needed?

*Use trim to relieve **steady** control pressures.*

The elevator is controlled by fore and aft movement of the control wheel and is used by the pilot to hold the desired pitch attitude. If this requires a *steady* pressure, then flying becomes quite tiring, making precision flight almost impossible. Trim can be used to relieve this steady pressure on the control column and, used precisely, can reduce it to zero.

Trim is *not* used to alter the attitude of the aeroplane; it is only used to relieve steady control pressure.

Elevator Trim

Elevator trim can hold the elevator deflected.

Elevator trim in most aeroplanes is achieved using a small **trim tab** located on the trailing edge of the elevator. The trim tab is operated by a trim wheel (or handle) in the cockpit. The purpose of the trim tab is to hold the elevator displaced with an aerodynamic force, rather than a force that the pilot exerts via the control column.

If the trim tab is deflected downwards, the airflow over the upper surface of the elevator speeds up, reducing the static pressure. An aerodynamic force now exists to deflect the elevator upwards.

Trimming Technique

While you are trimming the aeroplane, the pitch attitude should not change.

A steady back pressure exerted by the pilot on the control column to hold the elevator up can be relieved by winding the trim wheel back. This deflects the trim tab down, reducing the static pressure above it. If the static pressure is sufficiently low for the elevator to remain deflected upwards to the same degree, then the pilot need not continue to hold steady back pressure on the control column. Flying now becomes less tiring.

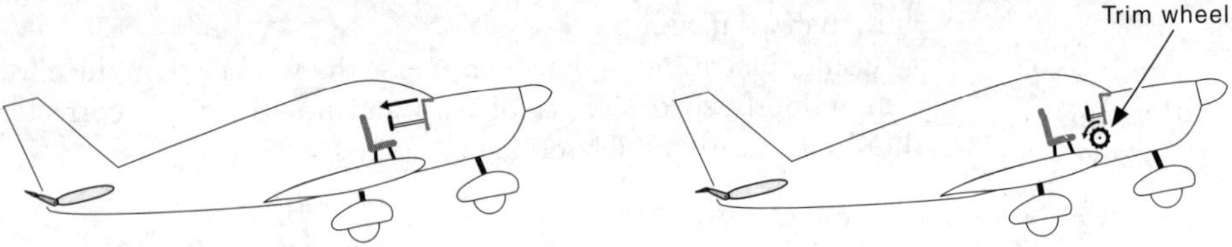

■ *Figure 4c-2* ***Using elevator trim to relieve steady pressures on the control column***

NOTE The description above applies to the 'aerodynamic' trim tab that is found on most aeroplanes. On others, however, trimming is achieved by applying a spring loading to the control column to relieve the pilot.

Retrimming

The demands placed on the elevator change from time to time and so retrimming will be necessary:

- **after a new pitch attitude** is selected;
- **after a power change;**
- **after a configuration change** (e.g. alteration of flap position);
- **after a change in the position of the centre of gravity** (say as fuel burns off, passengers move, baggage is shifted or parachutists depart).

Whenever a steady pressure is required on the control column in steady flight, then trim it off.

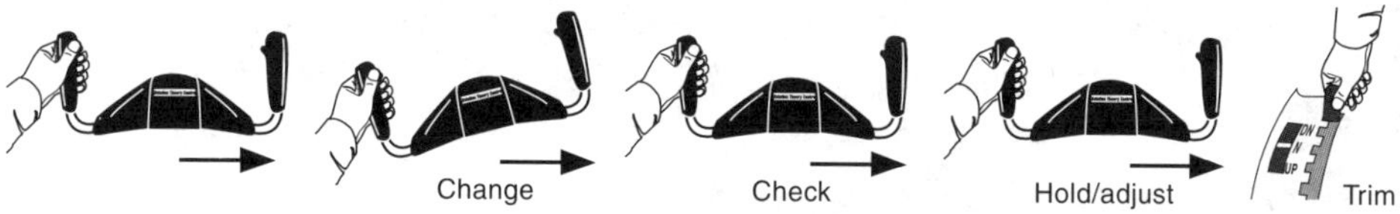

■ *Figure 4c-3* ***Control sequence when trimming***

Flying the Manoeuvre

Correct trimming is achieved by moving the trim wheel in a natural sense. If you are holding back pressure on the control column, then wind the trim wheel back, gradually releasing the pressure so that the pitch attitude does not change.

Conversely, if forward pressure is needed to maintain pitch attitude, then wind the trim wheel forward until there is no steady pressure required on the control column.

While you are trimming the aircraft, the pitch attitude should not change.

NOTE In aircraft fitted with a rudder trim the same procedure is used. With the aeroplane in balance, trim off any steady rudder pressure without allowing the nose to yaw. Throughout this manual, the word *trim* implies use of the elevator trim, and also use of rudder trim, where it is installed.

Airmanship

Maintain a good **lookout.**

Do not be reluctant to use the trim. If you feel a steady pressure then trim it off, but do not use the trim in transient manoeuvres such as turns. Use the trim only to remove steady pressures. Do *not* use the trim to change the attitude of the aeroplane.

Trimming is an art. As you develop the skill of trimming an aeroplane, smooth and precise flying becomes much easier.

Airwork 4c
The Art of Trimming

Aim *To use the trim to relieve steady pressures on the control column.*

1. Trimming the Aeroplane Correctly

This exercise involves use of the pitch trim wheel or control.

To trim the aeroplane correctly in pitch:

- Hold the desired pitch attitude with pressure on the control column; then
- Without looking, place your hand on the trim wheel and trim (in a natural sense) to relieve pressures so that the desired attitude is held without exerting any pressure on the control column. If the load is high, trim quickly. As the load reduces, trim more finely. Gradually, the pressure on the control column can be relaxed.

2. Getting the Feel of Incorrect Trim

(a) To get the feel of incorrect trim, fly straight and level, holding the desired pitch attitude with elevator.

(b) Then, without letting the pitch attitude change, gradually wind the trim wheel fully forward.

- You will need considerable back pressure on the control column to hold the nose up in the level flight attitude.

(c) Gradually wind the trim wheel back until the control column back pressure is again reduced to zero.

(d) Repeat the procedure, winding the trim fully aft this time, noting the considerable forward pressure required on the control column to maintain the level flight attitude.

NOTE This is not a normal procedure. It is done only for you to experience the effect of incorrect trim, which makes flying almost impossible.

3. Common Situations Requiring Retrimming

Practise trim changes by holding a particular pitch attitude and then:

(i) adopt a new pitch attitude;
(ii) change the power setting; or
(iii) change the aircraft configuration (e.g. lower flaps).

After each change, hold the pitch attitude constant for a short period (10 or 20 seconds) and allow the aeroplane to settle into the new flightpath and/or airspeed before retrimming.

- If strong pressure is required on the control column, it is advisable to relieve most of it fairly quickly and then, after the aeroplane has settled down, trim more finely.

NOTE For aeroplanes fitted with rudder trim these exercises can be repeated. The same technique applies – use rudder trim to relieve steady pressure on the rudder pedals which are necessary to balance the aeroplane.

Exercise 4d
The Effect of Airspeed and Slipstream

Aim

To observe the effect of an increased speed of airflow over the control surfaces.

Considerations

Control Effectiveness

Increased airflow increases control effectiveness.

The effectiveness of the three main flight controls and the rate at which the aeroplane moves in all three planes (pitch, roll and yaw) depends on:

- the amount of control deflection;
- the airflow over the control surface, which can be increased by:
  - a higher airspeed; and/or
  - slipstream from the propeller.

Airspeed

All flight controls are more effective at higher airspeeds.

The elevator, ailerons and rudder will all experience an increased airflow when the aeroplane is flying at a higher airspeed. Each control will feel firmer and only small movements will be required to produce an effective response.

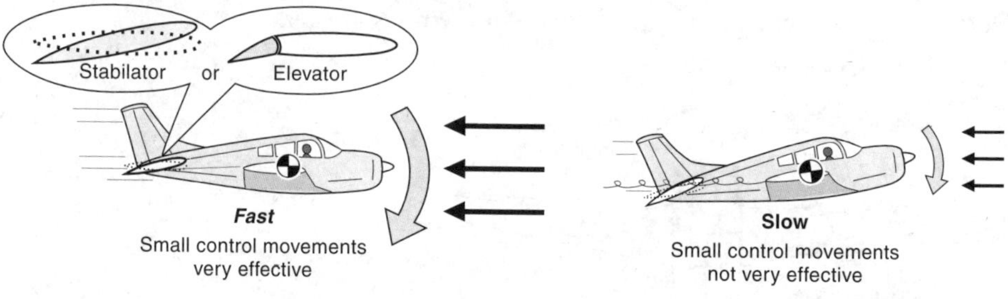

■ Figure 4d-1 ***All of the flight controls are more effective at high airspeeds***

Conversely, at low airspeeds the airflow over each of the flight controls is less and their effectiveness is reduced. The elevator, ailerons and rudder will all feel 'sloppy' and large movements may be required to produce the desired effect.

The Propeller Slipstream

The slipstream from the propeller flows rearwards around the aeroplane in a corkscrew fashion, which increases the airflow over the tail section, making the rudder and elevator more effective.

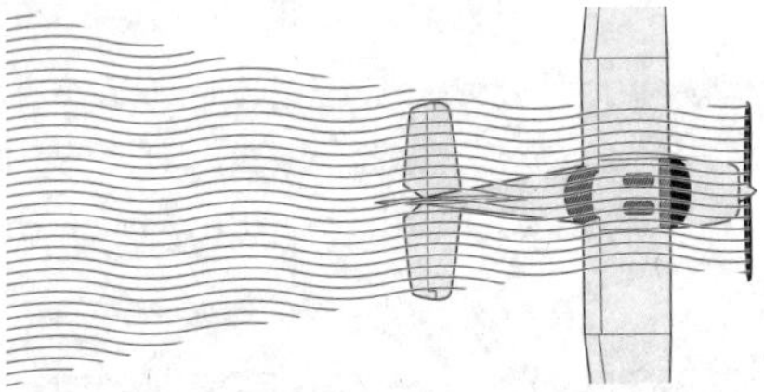

■ *Figure 4d-2* ***The slipstream increases elevator and rudder effectiveness***

The ailerons, being outside the slipstream airflow, are not affected by it and will remain 'sloppy' at low airspeeds irrespective of the power set. The elevator on T-tail aircraft may also be somewhat out of the slipstream and therefore not affected by it to the same extent as the rudder.

The Slipstream Causes a Yaw Tendency

The slipstream from the propeller flows back in a corkscrew fashion over the tailplane, meeting the fin at an angle of attack. This generates a sideways aerodynamic force, which tends to yaw the nose of the aeroplane. The pilot can balance this yawing effect with rudder pressure.

Slipstream effect is most pronounced under conditions of high power and low airspeed (e.g. during a climb), when the 'corkscrew' is tighter and its angle of attack at the fin is greater.

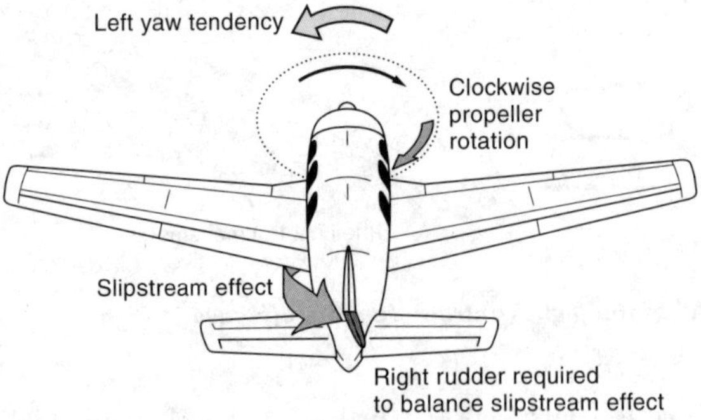

■ *Figure 4d-3* ***Slipstream tends to yaw the aeroplane***

The direction of the yaw resulting from the slipstream effect depends on the direction of propeller rotation. If the propeller rotates clockwise when viewed from the cockpit (as is the case for many modern training aircraft), the slipstream passes under the fuselage and strikes the fin on its left-hand side. This causes a tendency for the nose to yaw left, which can be balanced with right rudder.

If the propeller rotates anti-clockwise as seen from the cockpit (e.g. the *Tiger Moth, Chipmunk,* and *ARV Super 2*), the slipstream passes under the fuselage and strikes the fin on the right-hand side. The nose will tend to yaw right and will require left rudder to balance.

Flying the Manoeuvre

To observe the effect of airspeed on the flight controls, first establish a glide (to eliminate the effect of slipstream) at a high airspeed and operate each of the three main flight controls. Each one will feel firm and be effective.

Then raise the nose to glide at a lower airspeed and operate each of the three main flight controls. Each will feel 'sloppy' and less effective than before.

Next apply climb power, maintaining the same low airspeed by raising the nose. This will introduce a strong slipstream effect, but keep the airspeed effect constant. The elevator and the rudder, being in the slipstream, will feel firm and effective. The ailerons, which are outside the slipstream, will still feel 'sloppy' and less effective.

Airmanship

Maintain a high visual awareness. Keep an eye out for other traffic and remain aware of the position of the aeroplane and the direction to be flown back to the aerodrome. Exert firm, positive, but smooth control over the aeroplane.

Airwork 4d
Effect of Airspeed and Slipstream

Aim *To observe the effect of increased airflow over each of the main flight control surfaces as a result of airspeed and slipstream.*

1. The Effect of Airspeed

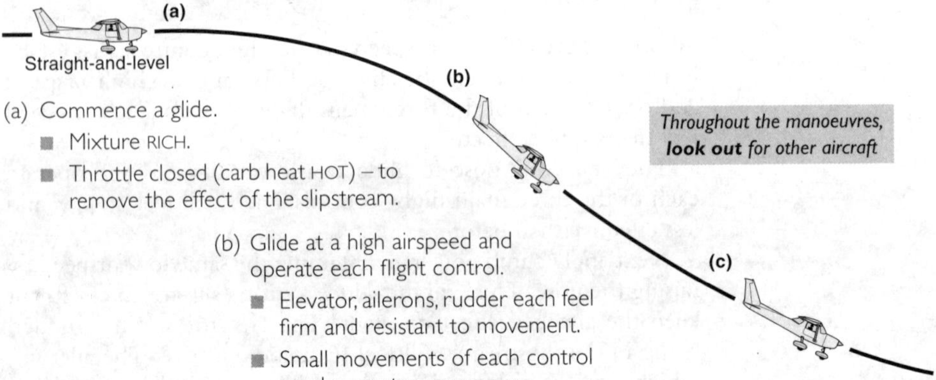

Throughout the manoeuvres, ***look out*** *for other aircraft*

(a) Commence a glide.

- Mixture RICH.
- Throttle closed (carb heat HOT) – to remove the effect of the slipstream.

(b) Glide at a high airspeed and operate each flight control.

- Elevator, ailerons, rudder each feel firm and resistant to movement.
- Small movements of each control produce a strong response.

(c) Glide at a low airspeed.

- Each of the primary controls feels 'sloppy'.
- Large control deflections are easy to make against little resistance.
- The aeroplane is less responsive to movements of the controls and so large movements may be required to elicit a response.

2. The Effect of Slipstream

Continuing directly from the exercise above, with the aeroplane in a glide at low airspeed.

(d) Apply climb power (carb heat COLD) and raise pitch attitude to maintain same low airspeed.

- Ailerons (outside slipstream) still feel 'sloppy'. Large aileron control movements necessary to roll the aeroplane.
- Elevator and rudder are firmer and more effective due to the higher airflow over them from the propeller slipstream.
- Result of a low airspeed and high climb power (and, therefore, strong slipstream) – aeroplane is responsive in pitch and yaw, but not in roll.

Exercise 4e
The Effects of Power Changes

Aim

To observe the effects of applying and removing power, then to counteract any undesirable tendencies resulting from power changes.

Considerations

Throttle movements to increase and decrease power should be smooth and not too fast.

Pushing the throttle in (or 'opening' it) increases power, which is indicated by increased rpm on the tachometer. This causes the propeller to rotate faster and generate increased thrust. Pulling the throttle out (or 'closing it') reduces power.

Reducing Power

Reducing power causes a pitch-down tendency.

Most aeroplanes are designed so that, if power from the engine is lost, the aeroplane will 'automatically' assume the glide attitude without action being taken by the pilot. This is a safety feature designed into the aeroplane to ensure that flying speed is maintained in case of engine failure.

In normal flight, when power is reduced with the throttle, the tendency for the nose to pitch down still occurs but can be counteracted with back pressure on the control column.

Adding Power

Increasing power causes a pitch-up tendency.

When adding power, the reverse effect occurs; the nose will tend to pitch up. This can be counteracted with forward pressure on the control column.

Yawing

Changing power also causes a yawing tendency.

Adding power increases the slipstream effect on the tail of the aeroplane, causing the nose to yaw to the left (for propellers rotating clockwise when viewed from the cockpit). This yawing tendency can be counteracted with right rudder pressure to keep the aeroplane balanced (i.e. balance ball centred).

Conversely, reducing power reduces the slipstream effect on the tail, causing a yawing tendency in the other direction, which can also be counteracted with opposite rudder.

Some aircraft are fitted with rudder trim, which is used to trim off any steady pressure on the rudder pedals, e.g. on the climb.

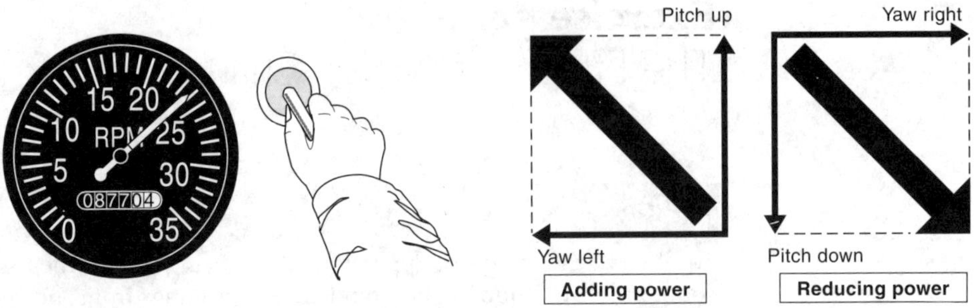

■ *Figure 4e-1* ***The effects of power changes (for a clockwise-rotating propeller)***

The Mixture

Under certain conditions the fuel/air mixture can be 'leaned' using the mixture control in the cockpit (a procedure considered later in this section). Opening the throttle to a high power setting with the mixture lean can cause damage to the engine, so it is usual to have the mixture fully RICH prior to making any significant power changes.

*Set the mixture to **RICH** for significant power changes.*

Carburettor Ice

The air mixing with fuel in the carburettor is cooled and, if moisture is present, there is always the possibility of ice forming, even at temperatures of +25°C and higher. This can block the flow of induction air/fuel to the cylinders, and so, if you intend to close the throttle for a prolonged period, apply full hot carburettor heat.

When closing the throttle, protect against carburettor ice.

Flying the Manoeuvre

The Throttle

The engine has moving parts that should not be subjected to shock treatment, so operate the throttle smoothly. As a guide to how rapidly the throttle should be opened, from idle power to full power should take approximately the same time as to count '1-2-3'. This also applies when closing the throttle.

Operate the throttle smoothly.

Pitch/Yaw

INCREASING POWER (clockwise-rotating propeller) will cause the nose of the aeroplane to **rise** and **yaw left.** These unwanted tendencies can be counteracted with:

- **forward pressure** on the control column to hold the desired attitude; and
- **right rudder pressure** to prevent the unwanted yaw and keep the ball centred.
- **Residual pressures** can then be trimmed off.

Counteract any pitch/yaw tendency with elevator and rudder control.

DECREASING POWER will cause the nose of the aeroplane to **drop** and **yaw right.** These unwanted tendencies can be counteracted with:

- **back pressure** on the control column to maintain the desired attitude; and
- **left rudder pressure** to balance the unwanted yaw.
- **Residual pressures** can then be trimmed off.

Airmanship

Maintain a high visual awareness. **Look out** for other aircraft and note landmarks so that you do not get lost. Make full use of the natural horizon when holding the pitch and bank attitude.

Have the mixture control in full RICH prior to any significant power changes.

When about to reduce power, consider whether you need protection from carburettor ice. If so (and this is usually the case when reducing the power to idle), apply full hot carburettor heat before closing the throttle.

When changing power, consider the engine. It has lots of reciprocating and rotating parts moving at high speeds and any sudden shock to the system is not good for it. Move the throttle smoothly and handle the engine with care. Monitor the engine gauges, especially during the climb when high power is set and there is reduced cooling because of the lower airspeed.

Handle the aeroplane smoothly, but firmly. Anticipate the effect of power changes – be prepared to hold the desired pitch attitude and prevent unwanted yaw.

Airwork 4e
Effect of Making Power Changes

Aims *1. To observe the effect of changing power.*
2. To counteract undesirable tendencies resulting from power changes.

1. The Effect of Changing Power

(a) Trim the aeroplane to cruise straight and level.
- Remove your hands from the control column and your feet from the rudder pedals.

(b) Smoothly open the throttle to full power.
- Nose pitches up; and
- Yaws.*

(c) Smoothly close the throttle:
- Nose pitches down; and
- Yaws.**

■ ***Cruise power, straight and level***

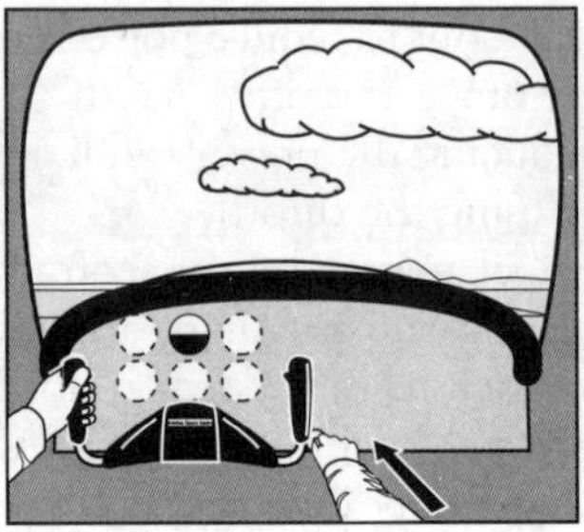

■ ****Yaw to left in most training aircraft***

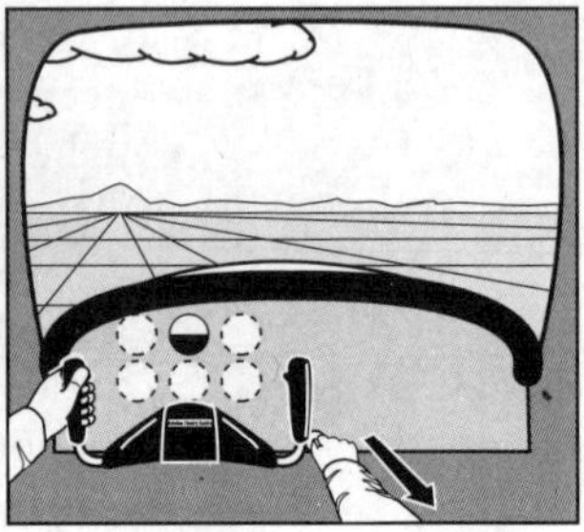

■ *****Yaw to right in most training aircraft***

2. The Correct Pilot Response When Changing Power

(a) When increasing power:
- Hold desired nose attitude with elevator (forward pressure).
- Balance with rudder pressure.
- Trim.

(b) When reducing power:
- Hold desired nose attitude with elevator (back pressure).
- Balance with rudder pressure.
- Trim.

NOTE A good means of practising this is to maintain the straight and level pitch attitude with the nose on a reference point on the horizon.

Smoothly move the throttle from idle to full power and back again, anticipating the changes and holding pitch attitude constant and balancing the unwanted yaw.

Increasing airspeed (by lowering the nose) will cause an increase in engine rpm without any throttle movement.

Exercise 4f
The Effect of Using Flaps

Aim

To observe the effect of altering the flap position and to control the aeroplane smoothly during flap alteration.

Considerations

Flaps move symmetrically.

The flaps are attached to the inboard trailing edge of each wing. They are operated from the cockpit – in some aeroplanes electrically by a switch and, in others, mechanically by a lever. They operate symmetrically on each wing.

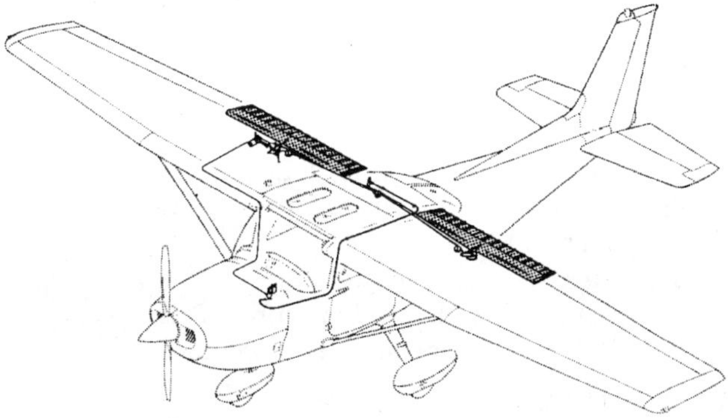

■ *Figure 4f-1* **The wing flaps**

Flaps increase the lifting ability of the wing by changing its shape.

Flaps alter the shape of the wings and the airflow around them. This changes the lifting ability of the wings, altering both the lift and drag generated. In a sense, flaps create new wings. They are used to:

- **generate the required lift at a lower speed** (allowing safe flight at low airspeeds as well as reducing take-off and landing distances);
- **increase drag** and steepen the descent path on approach to land;
- **improve forward vision** as a result of the lower nose attitude.

The flaps may be used to serve various purposes simultaneously: for example, to steepen the descent path while at the same time allowing better forward vision and safe flight at a lower airspeed.

As the flaps are lowered the changes in lift and drag will cause a pitching tendency. This will result in the aeroplane 'ballooning' unless counteracted with pressure on the control column. Conversely, when flap is raised, there will be a pitching tendency in the opposite direction and a tendency to sink.

Once attitude and power changes are complete, and the airspeed has stabilised at the desired value, these pressures can be trimmed off. In general, a **lower pitch attitude** is required to achieve the same airspeed when flaps are lowered compared to when the wings are 'clean'.

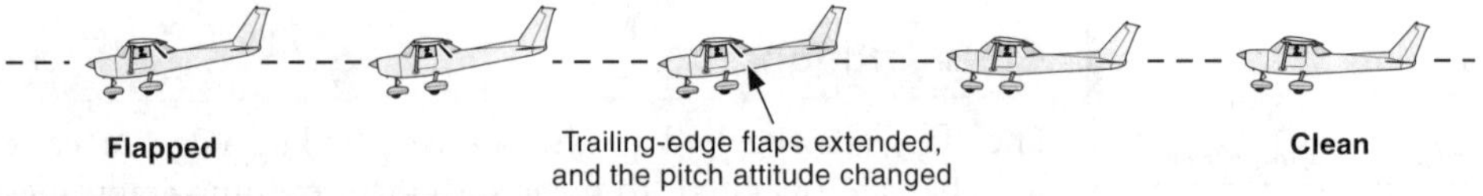

■ *Figure 4f-2* ***Flaps require a lower pitch attitude***

The initial stages of flap are sometimes called *lift flaps,* because the lifting ability of the wing is increased considerably even though there is the cost of a small amount of extra drag. Flaps allow the required lift to be generated at lower speed.

The larger flap settings are sometimes called *drag flaps,* because they cause a marked increase in drag for little improvement in lifting ability. If airspeed is to be maintained, the increased drag must be balanced by either:

- **additional thrust;** or
- a greater component of the **weight force** acting along the flightpath (achieved by steepening the descent).

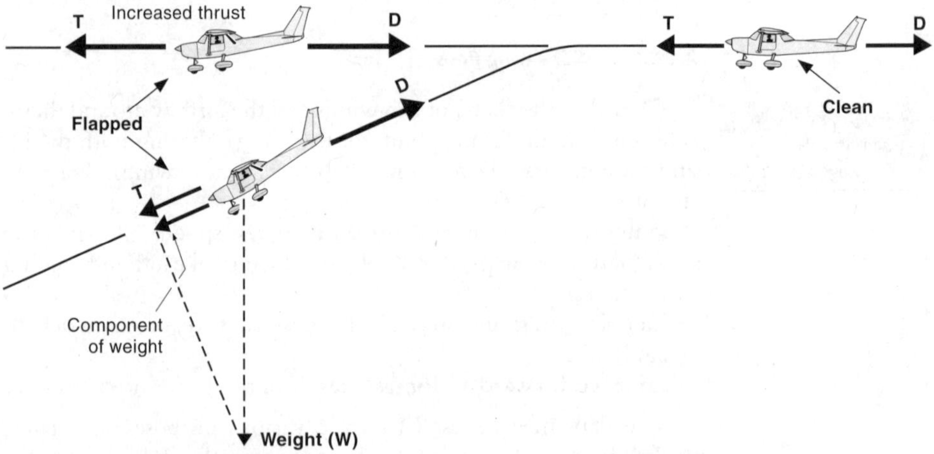

■ *Figure 4f-3* ***Flaps require increased power or a steeper flightpath if airspeed is to be maintained***

The Flap Operating Speed Range

To avoid overstressing the structure, ensure that the airspeed is less than the maximum speed allowed for flap extension (V_{FE}). This figure is stated in the Pilot's Operating Handbook and is shown on the airspeed indicator as the high speed end of the white arc.

Two straight and level stalling speeds (at maximum aircraft weight) are available on the airspeed indicator:

1. With full flap – the low speed end of the white band;
2. With a 'clean' wing – the low speed end of the green band.

They mark the approximate minimum flying speeds straight and level that the aeroplane is capable of in these configurations.

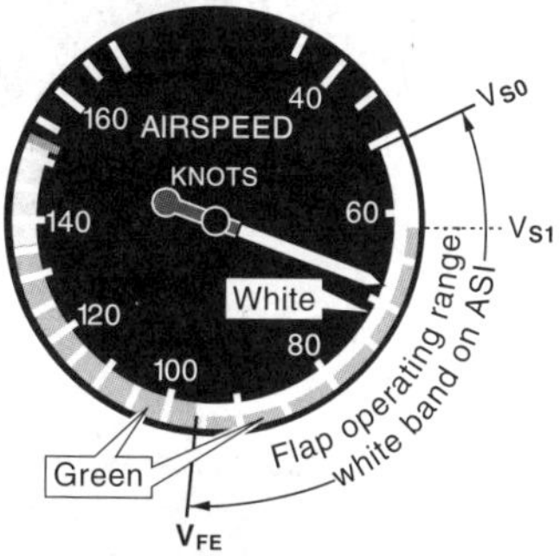

■ *Figure 4f-4* ***The flap operating range on the airspeed indicator***

Flying the Manoeuvre

Move flaps in stages, and retrim.

Raising or lowering large amounts of flap may cause large changes in pitch attitude and in the trim required. For this reason it is usual to operate the flaps in stages, retrimming after each selection.

To operate the flaps:

- **lower** (or raise) one stage at a time;
- **hold the desired pitch attitude** with elevator and make any necessary power changes;
- **trim off the steady pressure** on the control column.

Airmanship

Do not exceed the maximum flap operating speed (V_{FE}) and do not raise them below the 'clean' stalling speed.

Airwork 4f
The Effect of using Flap

Aims *(a) To observe the effect of altering flap position.*
(b) To control the aeroplane smoothly during flap alteration.

1. *Changing Flap Position Causes a Pitching Tendency*

(a) With the wing 'clean' (i.e. flaps up), establish straight and level flight.

(b) Reduce the airspeed to within flap operating range (white arc on ASI) and retrim. (Higher nose attitude required to maintain height as airspeed is reduced.)

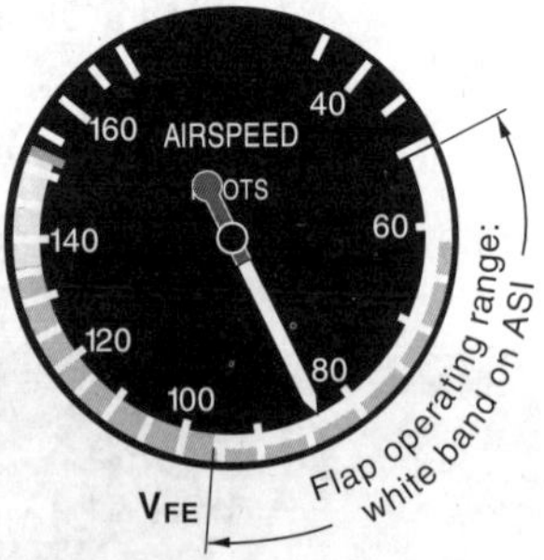

2. *The Flaps Increase Lifting Ability and Drag*

(a) Fly straight and level.
- Wings clean (flaps up).
- Airspeed below V_{FE} (high speed end of white arc).

Leave the power constant throughout the operation.

(b) Lower first stage of flap, holding pitch attitude constant.
- The aeroplane gains some height (due to the wing's increased lifting ability).
- And slows down (due to the increased drag).

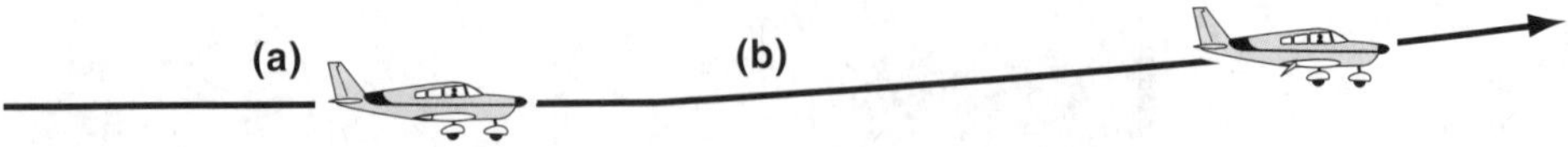

Airwork 4f

(c) To illustrate the pitching tendency when lowering the flaps, remove your hands from the control column (although normally you never do this).

Lower flap in stages (using a firm, steady movement if the flaps are manually operated).

- Note the pitching tendency.

Trim for the desired attitude.

(d) To illustrate the pitching tendency when raising the flaps, once again temporarily remove your hands from the control column.

Raise the flaps fully in one selection (an incorrect procedure not used in normal operations).

- Note the effect. (There will most likely be a strong pitching tendency, accompanied by a height loss.)

Re-establish straight and level flight and retrim.

NOTE In normal flap operations you will control any unwanted pitching tendency when flap is changed with pressure on the control column.

(c) Lower the nose to maintain height and retrim.

- Notice the lower nose position – improved vision – and lower airspeed.

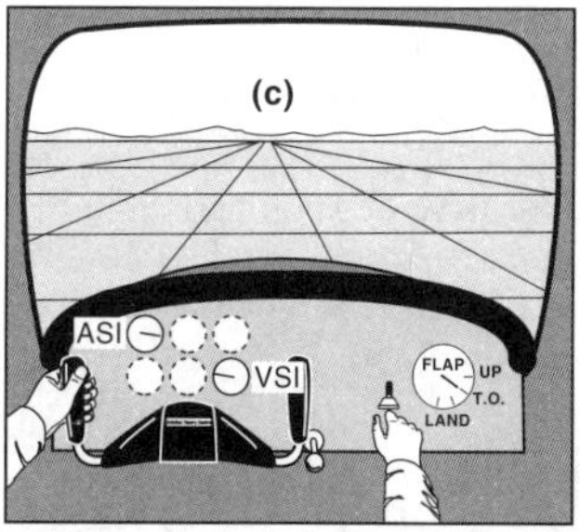

(d) Lower the rest of the flaps in stages and maintain height by lowering the nose; retrim after each flap selection.

- Notice the lower airspeed as the extra drag slows the aeroplane.

(e) Raise the flaps in stages and maintain height by raising the nose; retrim after each selection.

- Note the higher airspeed resulting from the reduced drag.

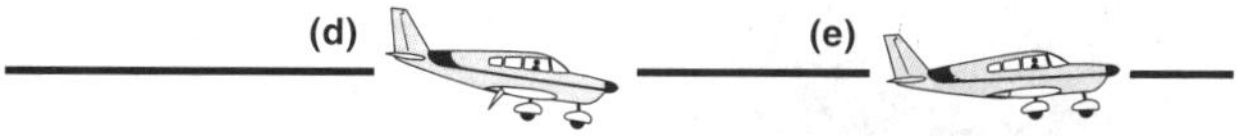

Airwork 4f
The Effect of Using Flap

3. Using Flap to Steepen the Descent Path

(a) Fly straight and level with wings 'clean' at a constant airspeed below V_{FE}. Leave the power constant throughout this exercise.

(b) Lower the first stage of flap. Maintain airspeed by holding a lower pitch attitude.

- The aeroplane descends.

Trim.

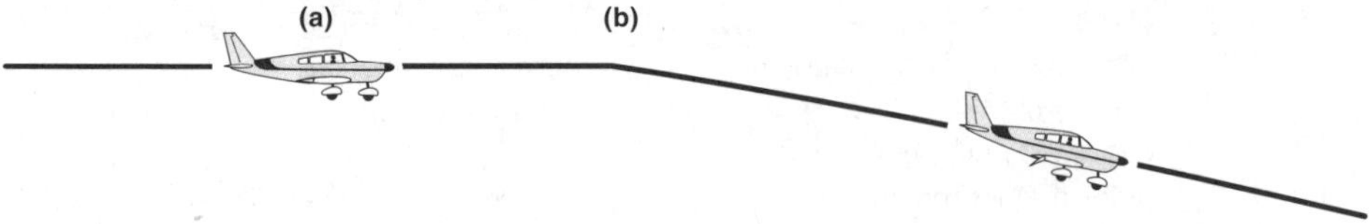

4. Using Flaps to Allow Safe Flight and to Improve Forward Vision

(a) Establish straight and level flight at a speed less than V_{FE}, but within the green arc.

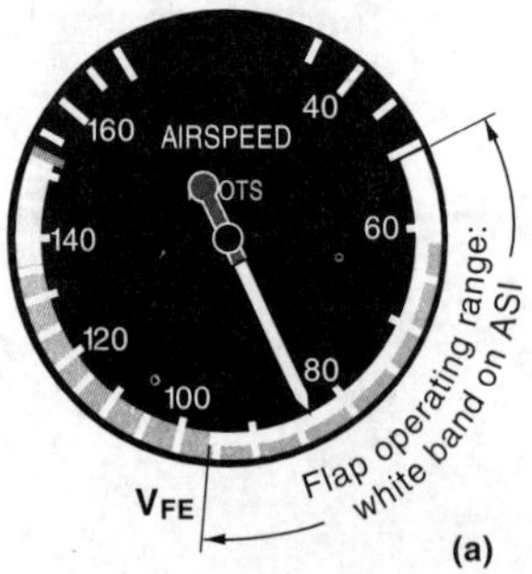

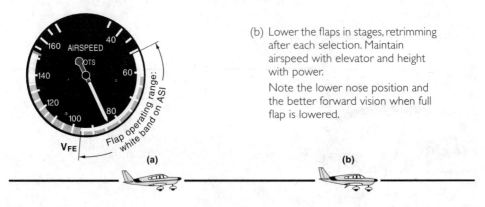

(b) Lower the flaps in stages, retrimming after each selection. Maintain airspeed with elevator and height with power.

Note the lower nose position and the better forward vision when full flap is lowered.

Airwork 4f

(c) Repeat for each stage of flap until full flap is extended. Note:

- A lower nose attitude is required to maintain a constant airspeed.
- Improved forward visibility.
- Increased rate of descent.

This is similar to an approach to land.

(d) Raise the flaps in stages, retrimming after each selection.

Resume straight and level flight.

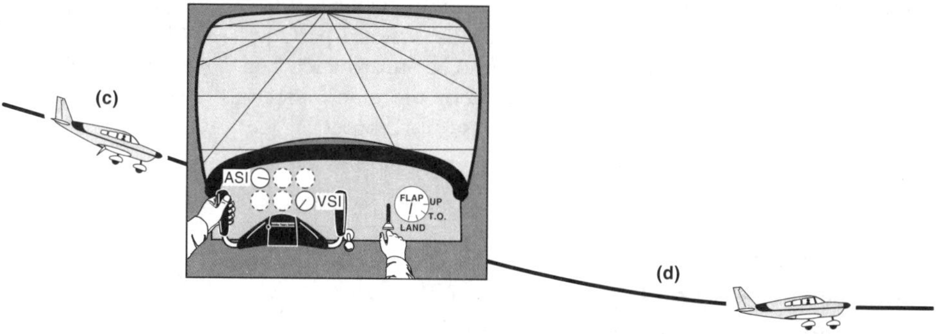

(c) Reduce airspeed to a figure just less than the clean stalling speed (i.e. to below the green arc on the ASI). Maintain height with power.

- The aeroplane can fly quite comfortably at lower airspeeds with flaps extended compared to when the wing is 'clean'.

(d) Increase speed (by applying power) and raise the flaps in stages, retrimming after each selection.

Do not raise the final stage of flap until you are above the 'clean' stalling speed (low speed end of green arc).

Exercise 4g
Carburettor Heat

Aim

To operate the carburettor heat control correctly.

Considerations

Why is Carburettor Heat Necessary?

Vaporisation of the fuel causes cooling in the carburettor, which may reduce the temperature to below freezing. If the air is sufficiently moist, ice may form in the induction system, partially blocking the flow of fuel/air to the cylinders. **Carburettor ice** can occur at outside air temperatures of +25°C or more and affects engine power adversely. Noticeable effects of carburettor ice include:

- **a drop in rpm;**
- **rough running;** and
- **possible engine stoppage.**

Carburettor heat is used to prevent or remove ice that can form in the carburettor under certain conditions.

How Carburettor Heat Works

The **carburettor heat control,** which is usually a knob situated near the throttle, can be used to direct hot air into the carburettor to prevent ice forming or to melt any ice which has already formed. Being less dense that cold air, hot air lowers the mass of each fuel/air change burned in the cylinders, reducing the maximum power available from the engine. Consequently, as carburettor heat is applied, the engine rpm will drop. If ice is present, the rpm will rise following the initial drop as the ice is melted by the warm air.

As a precaution when operating at low rpm it is usual to apply FULL HOT carburettor heat, such as in a prolonged descent. The control is returned to FULL COLD when higher power is required (and if protection from carburettor ice is not required).

TAXIING. In many aeroplanes, the hot air for carburettor heat is supplied from around the engine exhaust and is unfiltered (unlike the cold air which is filtered in the normal engine air intake). For this reason, it is usual to taxi with the carburettor heat control in the full COLD position to avoid introducing dust and grit into the engine, as this would seriously affect engine life.

As carburettor heat air is not filtered, taxi with carburettor heat off.

Airwork 4g
Use of Carburettor Heat

Aim *To learn the correct use of carburettor heat*

1. If Carburettor Icing is Suspected (rough running and/or rpm decay)

- Apply FULL carburettor heat (by pulling the carb heat control knob fully OUT).
- Note drop in rpm (due to the less dense air now entering the engine cylinders).
- If carburettor icing was present and has been melted, a slight rise in rpm will occur following the initial drop.
- Push carb heat knob to FULL COLD. Note rpm rise (denser air is now entering the cylinders).

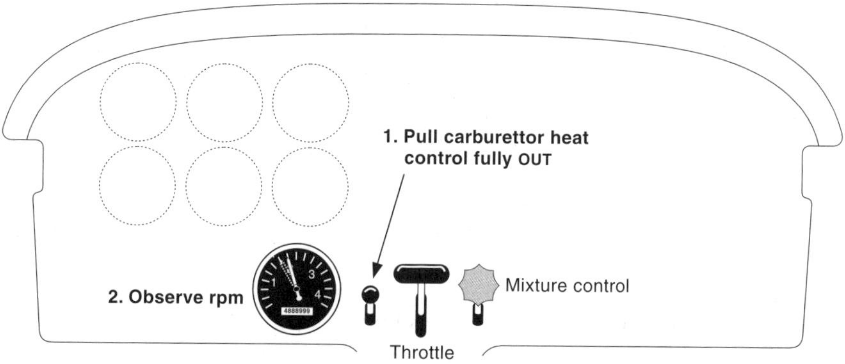

2. Using Carburettor Heat as a Precaution

(Normal procedure on descent and approach to land.)

(a) When reducing power to IDLE:

- Select carb heat to FULL HOT.
- Throttle CLOSED.

(b) When about to increase power:

- Carb heat to FULL COLD (if hot air to carburettor no longer required).
- Apply power with the throttle, as required.

NOTE Your flying training organisation's procedure for using carb heat as a precaution may differ from that given above, in which case you should follow it. (There may be variation in the order of operating the throttle and carb heat when both reducing and increasing power, perhaps due to manufacturer's recommendations.)

If in doubt as to the correct procedure to follow, consult your flying instructor.

Exercise 4h
The Mixture Control

Aim

To operate the mixture control correctly.

Considerations and Operation

The mixture control is usually a red knob situated near the throttle. Its two functions are:

1. To 'lean' the mixture and achieve optimum fuel usage; and
2. To cut off fuel to the carburettor and stop the engine.

Air density decreases with increase in height. This results in a lower weight of air being mixed with the same weight of fuel in the carburettor as an aeroplane climbs. Thus, the fuel/air mixture becomes 'richer' as height is gained and an increasing amount of fuel will remain unburned because of the reduced air available for the combustion process. This fuel is wasted in the exhaust.

The mixture is normally leaned on the cruise to improve fuel economy.

Corrective action to avoid the fuel wastage is usually taken on a high-level cruise (usually above 5,000 ft and when the power is less than 75% maximum continuous power). This action is called **leaning the mixture** and is accomplished by moving the mixture control partially out, which reduces the weight of fuel mixing with the air being taken into the carburettor.

As the 'fuel/air' mixture is leaned and returns to its optimum value, the engine rpm will show a slight increase. Leaning the mixture past the optimum ratio will cause the rpm to fall, at which point the mixture control should be moved back in slightly to the rich side of optimum. It is preferable to operate an engine slightly on the rich side, rather than too lean (when detonation may occur and damage the engine). Note that range figures published by the manufacturer assume cruising with the mixture correctly leaned.

It is prefererable to operate an engine slightly on the rich side.

Moving the mixture control fully out to the IDLE CUT-OFF position cuts off fuel to the carburettor completely. This is a safe way of shutting an engine down, since there will be no fuel left in the cylinders or induction system.

Shut down the engine by moving the mixture control to IDLE CUT-OFF.

Airwork 4h
Use of the Mixture Control

Aim *To operate the mixture control (red knob) correctly.*

1. To Lean the Mixture at Altitude

(for improved range and fuel economy)

- Set desired engine rpm (with the throttle).
- Slowly move red mixture control knob OUT towards lean position.
- Observe the rpm rise. If rpm doesn't rise, return mixture to RICH.
- Continue moving mixture control OUT until a slight drop in rpm occurs.
- Move the knob IN slightly to restore maximum rpm. It might be advisable to move the mixture control slightly further in so that the mixture is slightly on the rich side (too rich is preferable to too lean), where rpm will be slightly lower than peak value.

NOTE Whenever the power setting or cruise level are changed, repeat the above procedure.

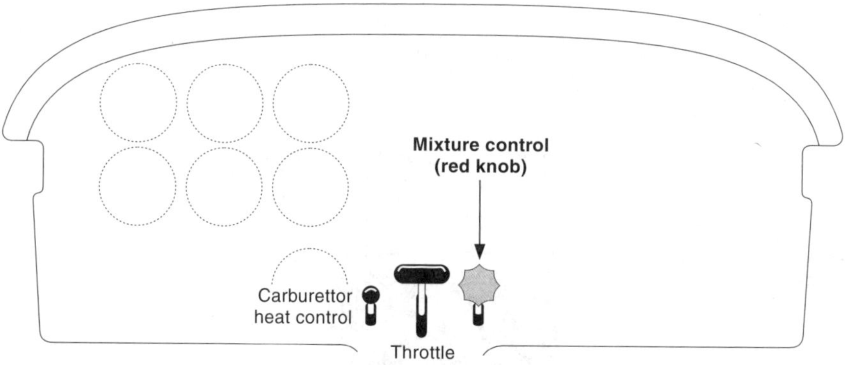

2. On Descent

Prior to commencing descent and reducing power:

- Select mixture to FULL RICH.

3. After Landing

To stop the engine:

- Close the throttle (pull it fully out) to reduce engine rpm.
- Move the mixture control to IDLE CUT-OFF by pulling it fully out – this starves the engine of fuel.
- Complete other actions as per the procedure in your Pilot's Operating Handbook.

Exercise 4i
Using the Radio

Most aeroplanes are equipped with at least one high-quality communications set. It operates in the very high frequency (VHF) radio band. Such a set, known as a VHF-COM, is both a transmitter and a receiver and is quite simple to operate. VHF provides high-quality 'line-of-sight' communications and is the usual form of communication used in aviation.

Many VHF-COM sets are combined in the same unit as a radio navigation receiver – and the whole unit is called a COM/NAV or NAV/COM. It is usual for the COM set to be on the left-hand side.

Connected to the radio are:

- **a microphone** for transmitting and a **speaker** for listening;
- **an optional headset** with a boom microphone;
- **the electrical master switch** (and possibly an avionics power switch) to connect the power supply to the radio;
- **an audio control panel** (in some aircraft) to connect the radio set to the microphone and speaker or headset.

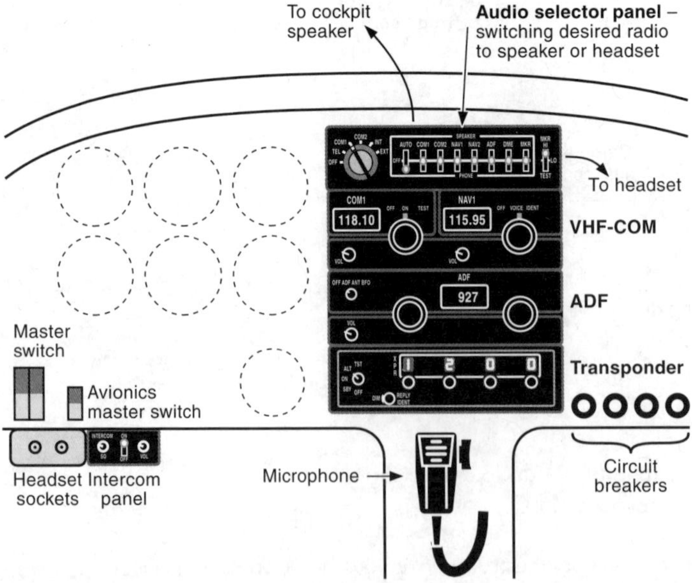

■ *Figure 4i-1* ***Controls for a typical VHF-COM radio set (or 'transceiver')***

Switching On the VHF-COM

1. Check the master switch ON (and avionics power switch if applicable).
2. Switch the radio ON.
3. Select the desired frequency.
4. Select audio to speaker of appropriate radio.
5. Adjust the volume to desired level and adjust 'squelch' control (if fitted) to cut out undesired background noise.
6. Check that the microphone and headset (if used) is plugged in correctly.
7. Select the transmitter to the desired radio, e.g. VHF No. 1.

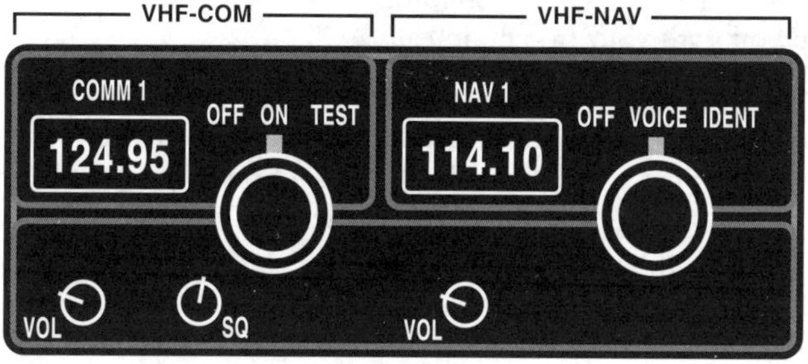

■ *Figure 4i-2* ***A typical VHF-COM/NAV radio set***

Squelch

The function of **squelch** is to eliminate unwanted weak signals that cause background noise (static or hiss). Noise makes it difficult to hear the desired stronger signals. Some squelch controls are automatic and others manual. Your flying instructor will advise you on your particular set.

To Adjust the Squelch Manually

- **Turn the squelch control up high** (i.e. clockwise) until background noise or 'hash' is heard; then:
- **Rotate the squelch knob anti-clockwise** until the noise just disappears (or is at least at an acceptably low level). This causes the unwanted noise from weak signals to be suppressed, allowing only the strong signals to be heard.

NOTE Take care adjusting squelch – turning it right down may cut out the signal that you want to hear as well as the unwanted noise.

What If the Radio Doesn't Work?

Occasionally you may find that the radio is not functioning correctly. If so, then follow a simple fault-finding procedure:

1. Check switching as above under *Switching on the VHF-COM.*
2. Check the circuit breakers or fuses.
3. Check that the squelch is not turned down too far.

Transmitting

Before Transmitting

Before you begin transmitting:

1. Listen out on the frequency to be used and avoid interference with other transmissions.
2. Decide exactly what you are going to say – your instructor will help you with your first radio calls.

The Microphone

There are various microphone types, each having its own operating characteristics. The hand-held microphone incorporates a transmit switch. The boom microphone attached to a headset worn by the pilot usually has its transmit switch situated in a convenient position on the control column.

Training aeroplanes are usually equipped with a hand-held microphone.

■ *Figure 4i-3* ***The hand-held and the boom microphone***

When using a microphone the following rules are generally satisfactory:

- **actuate the transmit switch** before commencing to talk and do not release it until after your message is completed;
- **speak with the microphone** one or two centimetres from your lips;
- **do not significantly vary the distance** between your lips and the microphone;
- **speak directly into the microphone** and do not speak to one side of it.

The microphone is used like a telephone, except that:

- **the transmit button** must be depressed for you to transmit;
- **while transmitting,** most radio sets are unable to receive simultaneously; and
- **only one transmission** from one station within range can occur on the frequency in use without interference. While you are transmitting, no-one else can.

NOTE Your COM set will continue to transmit as long as the transmit switch is depressed, even if you are not speaking. This will block out other stations that may be trying to call on that particular frequency. So at the end of your transmission ensure that the transmit switch (or 'mike button') is released.

The Transponder

A transponder unit is fitted in most light aircraft and when 'squawking' enables an air traffic radar controller to identify a particular aircraft more easily on his screen. There is no voice communication through the transponder. Transponder code selection is accomplished by dialling in the required code with the knobs. When selecting a new code, avoid passing through the emergency codes (**7700 emergency, 7600 radio failure** and **7500 unlawful interference**) when the transponder is switched ON, unless you really want to activate one of them.

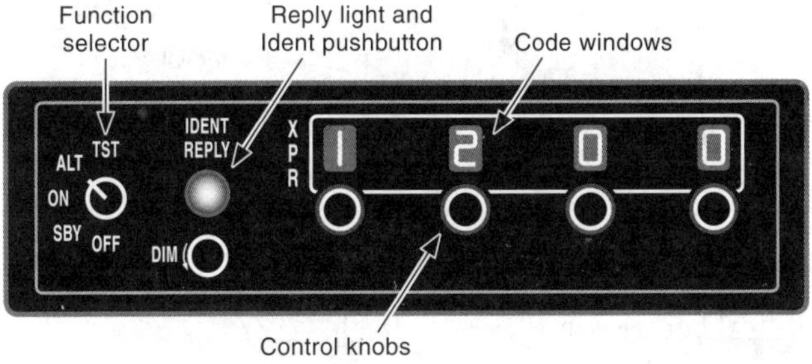

■ *Figure 4i-4* ***Typical transponder control panel***

R/T and transponder phraseology, procedures and equipment are covered in detail in Vol. 7 of *The Air Pilot's Manual – Radiotelephony.* You should also refer to the CAA's *Radiotelephony Manual* (CAP 413), and check for amendments to procedures in Aeronautical Information Circulars (AICs) and the Aeronautical Information Publication (AIP). Your flying instructor will introduce you to these documents.

Exercise 4j
Cabin Heating and Ventilation

Your comfort and well-being is most important to flight safety, so maximise it with correct use of the cabin ventilation and heating systems as explained in the Pilot's Operating Handbook. Ventilation generally improves the cockpit environment significantly.

The hot air for cabin heating is usually taken from around the engine exhaust system. To protect the occupants of the aeroplane from any fumes escaping from a leaking exhaust system, it is good practice to use the fresh air vents in conjunction with cabin heating. Carbon monoxide is colourless, odourless and extremely dangerous. It is present in the exhaust gases and ventilation provides good protection against it!

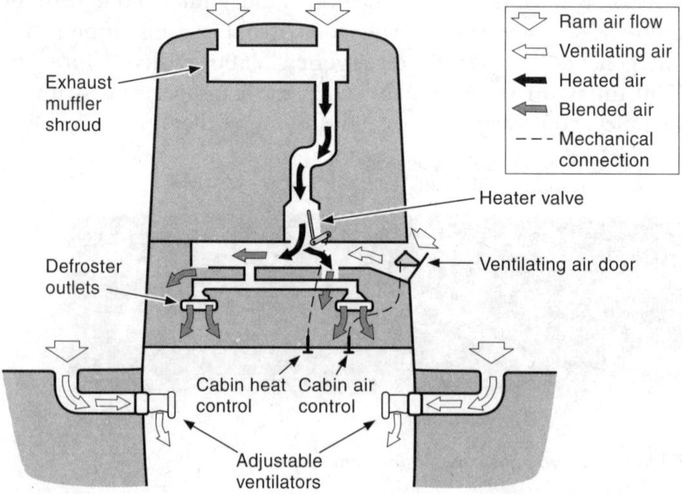

■ *Figure 4j-1* ***Typical cabin heating and ventilation systems***

Exercise 5
Taxiing an Aeroplane

Aim

To manoeuvre the aeroplane safely on the ground.

Considerations

Taxiing Speed

Use power and brakes to control taxiing speed.

Power is used to commence taxiing an aeroplane. The effects of wheel friction and the brakes are used to stop it.

Like all objects, an aeroplane has inertia and is resistant to change, so it requires more power to start moving than to keep moving. Once the aeroplane is rolling at taxiing speed, the power can be reduced simply to balance the frictional forces and any air resistance so that a steady speed is maintained. On a straight and smooth taxiway with no obstructions, a **fast walking pace** is a safe taxiing speed and this can be judged by looking ahead and to the left of the aeroplane. In a confined area, the ideal speed is somewhat less.

The amount of power required to maintain taxiing speed depends on the ground surface and its slope – a rough, upward-sloping grassy surface requiring much more power than a flat, sealed taxiway. High power may also be required to turn the aeroplane, especially at low speeds.

Brakes should be used gently.

To slow the aeroplane down, the power should be reduced. Friction may cause the aeroplane to decelerate sufficiently, otherwise the brakes can be used gently, but firmly.

Do not use power against brakes.

Generally speaking, power should not be used against brakes. It is a waste of energy and can lead to overheated brakes and increased brake wear. There are some aircraft, however, which have engines requiring a high idling rpm, and occasional braking may be required to avoid the taxiing speed becoming excessive.

Toe brakes are situated on top of each rudder pedal. They are individually applied using the ball of each foot. Normally, taxi with your heels on the floor and the balls of your feet on the rudder pedals, thereby avoiding inadvertent application of the toe brakes. When braking is needed, slide your feet up and, with the ball of each foot, apply the toe brakes as required. To brake the aeroplane while taxiing in a straight line, the toe brakes should be applied evenly.

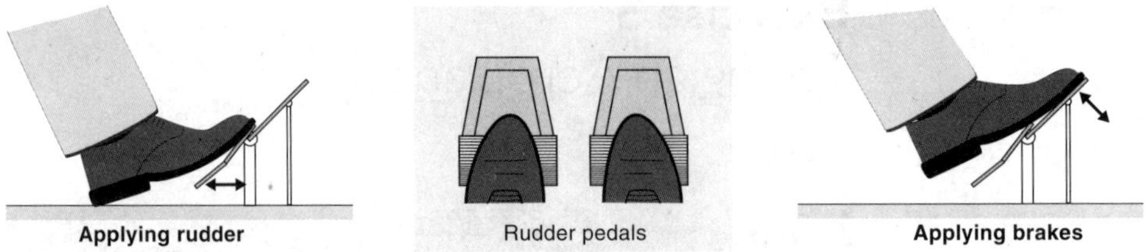

■ *Figure 5-1* ***Using rudder and using toe brakes***

Brakes should be used gently so that the aeroplane responds smoothly – harsh braking being avoided except in an emergency. For a normal stop, a good technique is to relax the braking pressure (or perhaps even release it) just as the aeroplane comes to a halt. The resulting stop will be smooth.

Differential braking is available by pressing each toe brake individually. This is useful both for turning sharply and for maintaining directional control when taxiing in a strong crosswind.

Test the brakes as you begin to taxi.

Test the brakes early. Once taxiing has commenced from the parked position, the power should be reduced and the brakes tested, but in a manner that causes the aeroplane to respond smoothly.

During extended taxiing, the brakes should be tested occasionally, and they should certainly be tested just prior to entering a congested tarmac area. Pay due attention to the ground surface, especially in wet weather when taxiways and tarmacs can become slippery. Always have an escape route in mind to avoid collisions in case the brakes fail to stop the aeroplane.

Ensure that the taxi path is clear.

Allow for the fact that the wings of an aeroplane are wide and the tail-section is well behind the main wheels. Maintain a good lookout ahead and to the sides. If the taxi path is obscured by the nose, then turning slightly left and right will permit a better view.

Should you unfortunately run into something while taxiing, stop the aeroplane, shut-down the engine, set the brakes to PARK and investigate. Do not fly!

Ground Surface Condition

Be aware of the ground surface condition.

Ensure that propeller clearance will be adequate when taxiing in long grass or over rough ground, especially if there are small ditches or holes since striking grass or the ground can seriously damage the propeller.

When taxiing on loose surfaces, avoid using high power wherever possible.

Loose stones or gravel picked up and blown back in the slipstream can also damage both the propeller and the airframe. Damage may even be caused to other aeroplanes or persons quite some distance behind. So when taxiing on loose surfaces, avoid the use of high power as much as possible.

Small ridges or ditches should be crossed at an angle so that the wheels pass across the obstruction one at a time. This will minimise stress on the undercarriage and avoid the nose pitching up and down excessively, which not only stresses the nose-wheel but also puts the propeller at risk. Large ditches or ridges should be avoided. If necessary, park the aeroplane and investigate before proceeding.

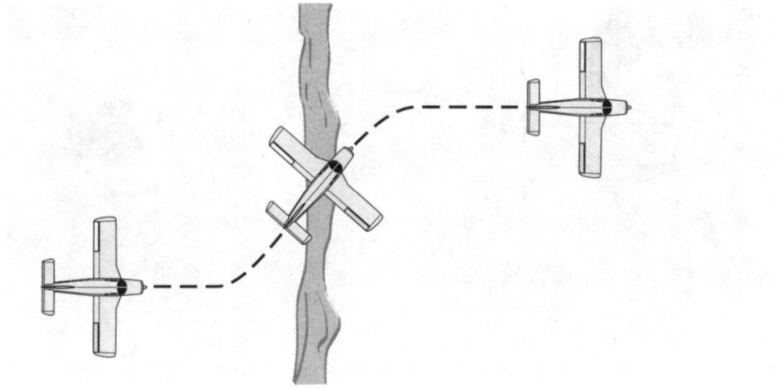

■ *Figure 5-2* ***Cross small ridges and ditches at an angle***

Wind Effect

The flight controls should be held in a position to avoid either the tail or a wing being lifted by a strong wind.

HEADWIND. When taxiing into a strong headwind, hold the control column either neutral or back. This holds the elevator neutral or up, and the tail down, and takes the load off the nose-wheel.

TAILWIND. When taxiing with a strong tailwind, hold the control column forward to move the elevator down. This stops the wind lifting the tailplane from behind.

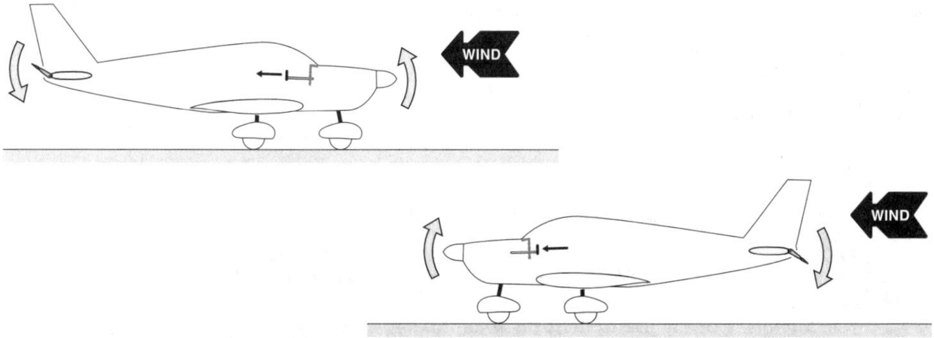

■ *Figure 5-3* ***Taxi into-wind with the control column neutral or back, and taxi downwind with the control column forward***

CROSSWIND. A crosswind will try to weathercock the aeroplane into-wind because of the large keel surfaces behind the main wheels. Using the rudder pedals, especially if nosewheel steering is fitted, should provide adequate directional control, but, if not, then use differential braking.

To avoid a crosswind from ahead lifting the into-wind wing, raise its aileron by moving the control column into-wind.

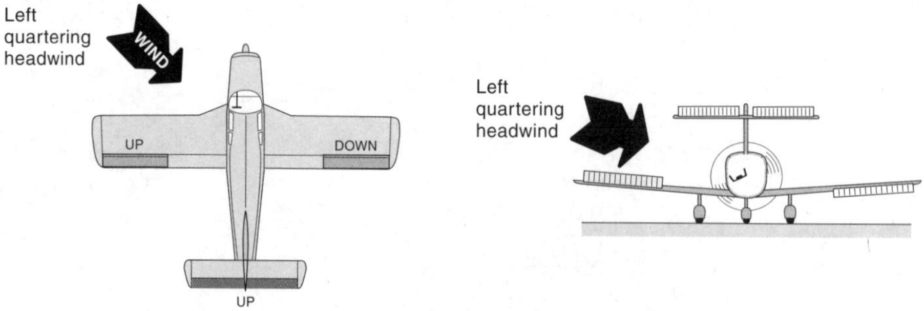
Left
quartering
headwind
WIND
UP
DOWN
UP
Left
quartering
headwind

■ *Figure 5-4* ***Taxiing with a left quartering headwind***

To avoid a crosswind from behind lifting the into-wind wing, lower its aileron so that the wind cannot get under it, by moving the control column out-of-wind.

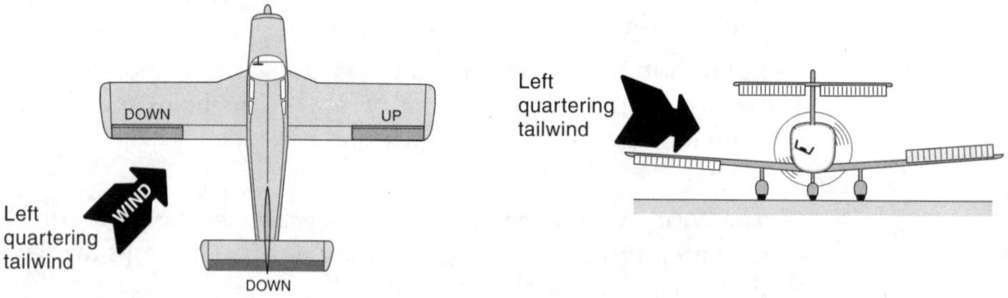
DOWN
UP
Left
quartering
tailwind
WIND
DOWN
Left
quartering
tailwind

■ *Figure 5-5* ***Taxiing with a left quartering tailwind***

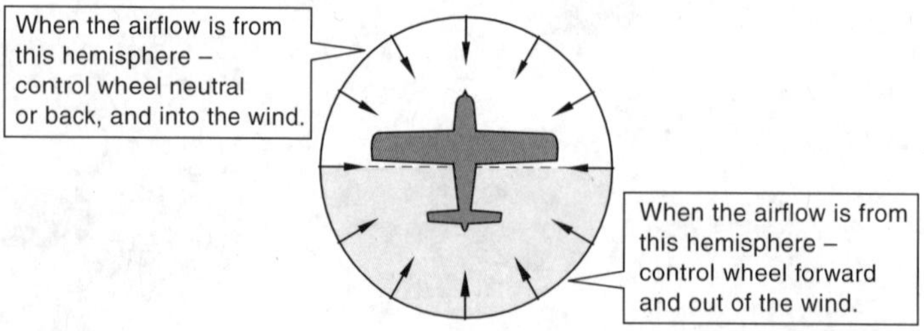
When the airflow is from this hemisphere – control wheel neutral or back, and into the wind.
When the airflow is from this hemisphere – control wheel forward and out of the wind.

■ *Figure 5-6* ***Summary of the use of controls when taxiing in windy conditions***

The propwash or jet blast of another aeroplane will produce the same affect as a wind, so always be cautious if you have to taxi close behind other aircraft, especially at an angle.

Taxiing Rules

Taxiing frequently occurs on crowded tarmacs and taxiways. Five simple rules understood and followed by all pilots make life easier for everybody.

1. Regardless of any ATC (Air Traffic Control) clearance, it is the duty of the pilot to do all possible to avoid collision with other aircraft or vehicles.
2. Aircraft on the ground must give way to aeroplanes landing or taking off, and to any vehicle towing an aircraft.
3. When two aircraft are taxiing and approaching head on or nearly so, each should turn right.
4. When two aircraft are taxiing on converging courses, the one that has the other on its right must give way, and should avoid crossing ahead of the other aircraft unless passing well clear.
5. An aircraft which is being overtaken by another has right of way. The overtaking aircraft must keep out of the way by turning left until past and well clear.

If in any doubt – STOP.

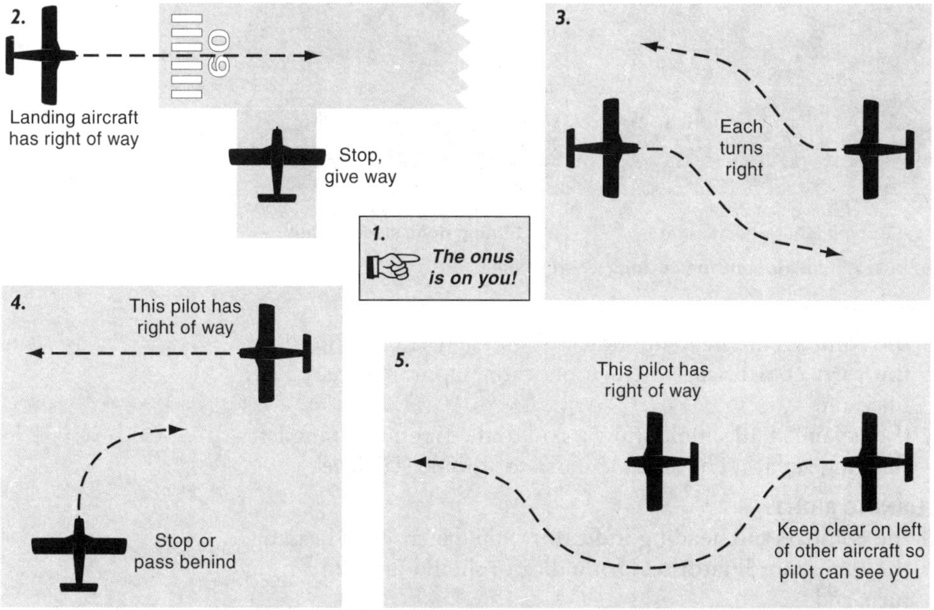

■ *Figure 5-7* ***Five rules for taxiing***

Marshalling

Although the pilot is ultimately responsible for the safety of the aeroplane on the ground regardless of who gives guidance, taxiing guidance on a tarmac area may be given by a marshaller. Some of the basic signals are illustrated below, but you should only follow them if you consider it safe to do so.

On a crowded tarmac or in very strong winds, it may be preferable to have wingtip assistance from experienced personnel, or to shut-down the engine and move the aeroplane by hand or with a tow-bar.

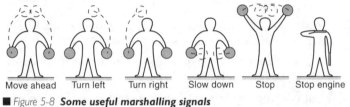

■ *Figure 5-8* ***Some useful marshalling signals***

Checks while Taxiing

Several items are checked once clear of the tarmac area and moving along on a straight taxiway. The **rudder** should be checked for full and free movement, and 'directional' **flight instruments** for correct operation:

■ *Figure 5-9* ***Instrument indications when taxiing***

TURNING LEFT:

- **the compass** and **heading indicator** should decrease in heading;
- **the turn coordinator** or turn indicator should indicate a left turn; and
- **the balance ball** should show a skid to the right: "Turning left, skidding right." (The attitude indicator should stay level.)

TURNING RIGHT:

- **the compass** and **heading indicator** should increase in heading;
- **the turn coordinator** or turn indicator should indicate a right turn; and
- **the balance ball** should show a skid to the left: "Turning right, skidding left." (The attitude indicator should stay level.)

5E. Taxiing Emergencies

Brake Failure

If the brakes fail:

- close the throttle;
- steer away from other aircraft and obstacles and towards a high-friction surface if possible (e.g. grass)

If a collision is imminent:

- Mixture control – IDLE CUT-OFF (to stop the engine by purging it of fuel);
- Fuel – OFF;
- Master switch – OFF.

When stopped, check the aeroplane. Call for assistance. Do not attempt to taxi the aeroplane.

Failure of Steering

As for brake failure consider applying differential braking to avoid obstructions. When the aircraft is stopped call for assistance. Do not attempt to taxi the aeroplane.

The Manoeuvre

Before commencing to taxi, have a reasonable idea of the path that you will follow to the take-off position, taking note of the surface and the position of other aircraft. If required, obtain a taxi clearance from ATC by radio. Ensure that tie-down ropes and chocks have been removed before releasing the park brake.

Test the brakes shortly after the aircraft starts to roll. Maintain a suitable taxiing speed for the conditions and avoid using power against brake (unless a high idling speed is required for better engine cooling). Cross ridges and small ditches at an angle, avoiding long grass and rough ground, and have an escape route in mind in case of brake failure. On the taxiing run, check the rudder and flight instruments for correct operation.

Once the aeroplane is stopped, the park brake should be applied and the engine set to idling speed.

Airmanship

Maintain a good lookout ahead and to either side. Follow the accepted taxiing rules and do not blast debris back over your aeroplane, other aeroplanes or into hangars.

Operate the throttle and brakes smoothly so that there are no sudden stops, starts or turns. Do not use power against brakes and maintain a listening watch on the radio if appropriate.

Airwork 5
Taxiing an Aeroplane

Aim *To manoeuvre the aeroplane safely on the ground.*

1. *To Commence Taxiing*

Look out:

- Survey the area around the aeroplane for obstructions and other aeroplanes. Consider the taxiing surface.
- If permission to taxi is required at your airfield, obtain this by radio prior to taxiing.
- Loosen the throttle friction nut and reduce the power to idle.
- Release the parking brake.

Moving off:

- Parking brake released.
- Apply sufficient power with the throttle to get the aeroplane moving forward.
- Reduce the power to idle and gently test the brakes.
- Apply sufficient power to recommence taxiing.
- Reduce power as necessary to maintain a safe taxiing speed (a fast walking pace).

2. *Taxiing the Aeroplane*

NOTE Steering is not possible until the aeroplane is rolling forward.

- Control direction with the rudder pedals and, if necessary, differential braking. An increased slipstream over the rudder may assist also.
- Gently test the brakes from time to time without bringing the aeroplane to a stop.
- Remember to allow plenty of clearance for the wingtips and tail.
- Hold the control column suitably to counteract any wind effect from the side or behind.
- Cross rough surfaces slowly and at an angle.
- Monitor engine pressure and temperature gauges for correct engine operation and adequate cooling.

3. *Stopping the Aeroplane*

(a) To stop the aeroplane:

- Anticipate by a few seconds.
- Close the throttle.
- Allow the aeroplane to roll to a stop with the nosewheel straight.
- If necessary, gently apply the brakes, releasing them just as the aeroplane stops so that coming to a halt is smooth.

(b) When completely stopped:

- Set the brakes to PARK and set the correct engine idling figure – usually 1,000 to 1,200 rpm.

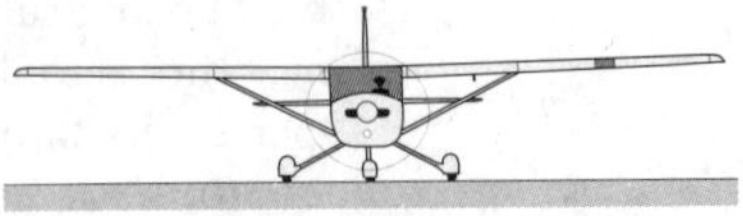

Exercise 6a
Flying Straight and Level in Balance at Constant Power

Aim

To fly straight and level in balance using a constant power setting.

Considerations

Flying **straight** means maintaining a **constant heading,** and this can be achieved by holding the wings level with the ailerons, and keeping the aeroplane coordinated with the rudder to prevent any yaw.

Flying **level** means maintaining a **constant altitude,** which can be achieved by having the correct **power** set and the nose held in the correct **attitude.** Altitude is displayed in the cockpit on the altimeter.

Steady, straight and level flight, coordinated and in trim, is desirable for both comfort and good aeroplane performance. Accurate straight and level flying is one sign of a good pilot.

The Forces that Act on an Aeroplane

There are four main forces that act on an aeroplane in flight:

- **weight;**
- **lift** generated by the wings;
- **thrust** from the propeller (using engine power); and
- **drag** (or resistance to motion of the aeroplane through the air).

In steady, straight and level flight, the aeroplane is in equilibrium with no tendency to accelerate:

- **lift opposes weight;** and
- **thrust opposes drag.**

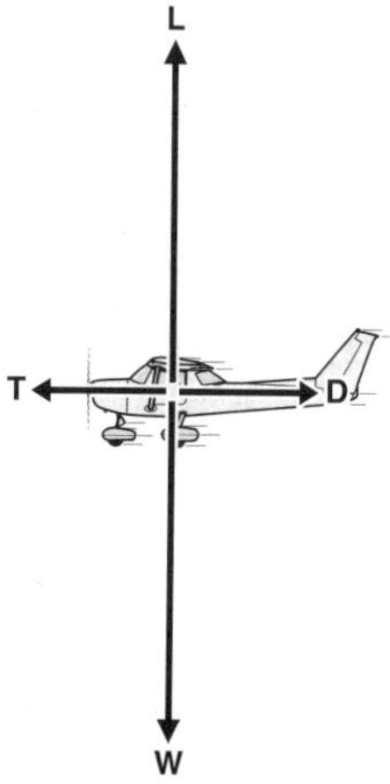

■ *Figure 6a-1*
The four main forces in steady, straight and level flight

It is unusual for the four main forces to counteract each other exactly. Almost always, a balancing force, either up or down, is required from the tailplane and elevator. Most aeroplanes are designed so that the tailplane creates a downward aerodynamic force. This balancing force is controlled by the pilot with the elevator. In normal flight, continual small adjustments of the elevator with the control column are required.

Aeroplanes are usually designed so that if **thrust is lost** through the engine failing (or the pilot reducing power), the remaining forces will automatically lower the nose into the gliding attitude, allowing a safe flying speed to be maintained. In the situation illustrated, this is achieved by having the centre of pressure (through which the lift acts) located behind the centre of gravity, so that the lift–weight couple has a nose-down effect. In normal flight, this is opposed by the thrust–drag nose-up couple. (A couple is a pair of parallel opposing forces *not* acting through the same point, and therefore causing a tendency to rotate.)

If thrust is lost, the nose-up couple is diminished, the lift–weight nose-down couple predominates and the nose drops into the gliding attitude. The same effect occurs when the pilot intentionally reduces power – the nose dropping unless back pressure is exerted on the control column.

Also, if power is reduced and the propwash airflow over the tailplane is reduced, then the downward aerodynamic force on the tail is less, and so the nose of the aeroplane will drop. (This effect does not apply to T-tail aeroplanes where the propeller slipstream passes beneath the tailplane, rather than flowing over and under its surfaces.)

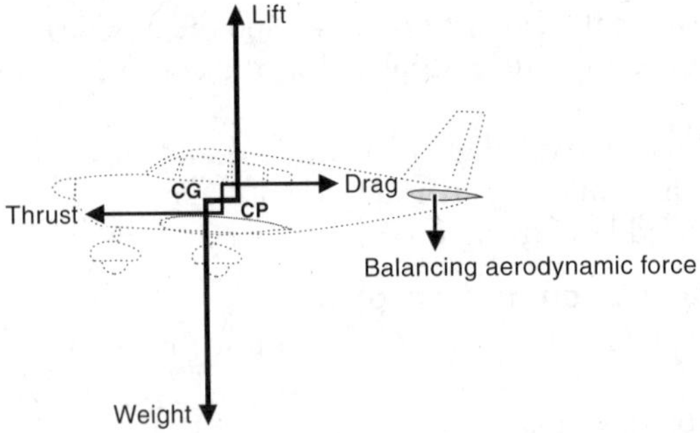

■ *Figure 6a-2* **The tailplane provides a final balancing force**

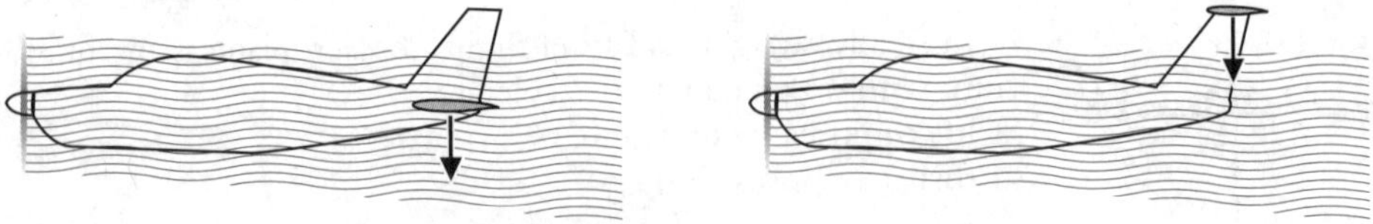

■ *Figure 6a-3* **Reduction in propwash reduces downward force on tailplane (but not for T-tails)**

Aeroplane Stability

Stability is the natural or inbuilt ability of an aeroplane to return to its original attitude following some disturbance (such as a gust) without the pilot taking any action. An inherently stable aeroplane will return to its original condition unassisted after being disturbed, and so requires less pilot effort to control than an unstable aeroplane.

Longitudinal Stability in Pitch

The tailplane (or horizontal stabiliser) provides longitudinal stability.

If, for instance, a gust causes the nose to rise, then the tailplane is presented to the airflow at a greater angle of attack. It will therefore generate a greater upward (or less downward) aerodynamic force that will raise the tail and lower the nose.

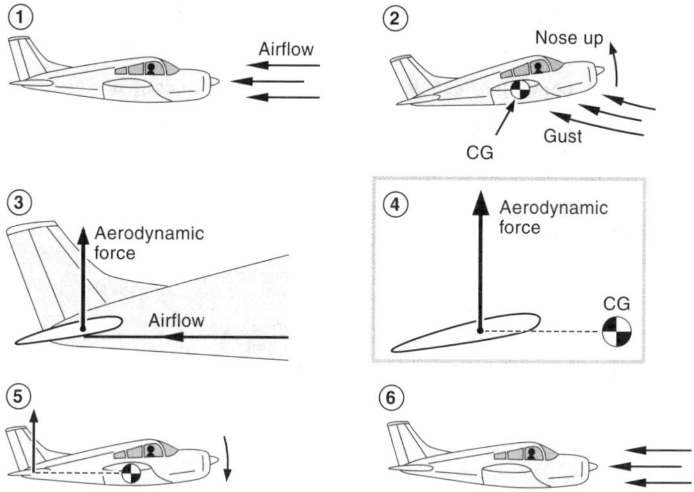

■ *Figure 6a-4* ***Longitudinal stability following an uninvited nose-up pitch***

CG POSITION AND CONTROL IN PITCH. A forward centre of gravity (CG) makes the aeroplane more stable because of the greater restoring moment from the tail due to its greater leverage.

If the aeroplane is loaded so that the **CG is too far forward:**

- **the excessive stability** will require stronger controlling forces from the elevator, which may become tiring for the pilot; and
- **during the landing,** the elevator will be less effective due to the low airspeed, and the nose-heavy moment may make it impossible to flare prior to touchdown.

If the aeroplane is loaded with the **CG too far rearward:**

- **the aeroplane** will be less stable at all airspeeds, and constant attention will have to be given to maintaining the pitch attitude; and
- **the tail-heavy moment** may cause a stall at low speeds when the elevator is less effective, and it may even be impossible to recover from stalled conditions.

*The centre of gravity must **always** be within the approved range.*

Stability and control considerations make it imperative that an aeroplane is flown only when the CG is within the approved range (as stated in the Flight Manual). It is the pilot's responsibility to ensure that this is always the case.

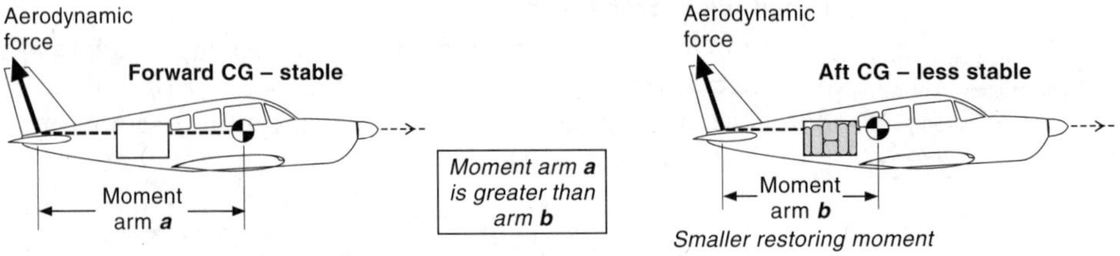

■ *Figure 6a-5* **Loading affects longitudinal stability and control**

Stability in Yaw and Roll

If the aeroplane is disturbed from a straight path (a disturbance in yaw), then the fin is presented to the airflow at a greater angle of attack and generates a restoring aerodynamic force.

The fin (or vertical stabiliser) provides directional stability.

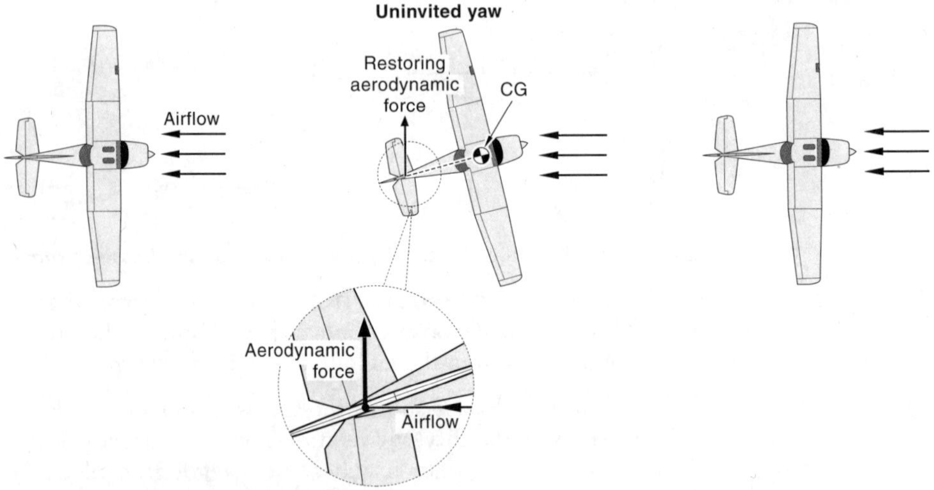

■ *Figure 6a-6* **Directional stability following an uninvited yaw**

A disturbance in roll will cause one wing to drop and the other to rise. The lift force will be tilted, causing a **slip** sideways towards the lower wing. If the aeroplane has **high keel surfaces,** such as the fin and the side of the fuselage, then the airflow striking them in the slip will tend to restore a wings-level condition.

High keel surfaces and wing dihedral provide lateral stability.

If the wings have **dihedral** (a design feature in which each wing is inclined upwards towards the wingtips), the lower wing is presented to the airflow at a greater angle of attack in the slip sideways, thereby generating a greater lift force which tends to restore a wings-level condition.

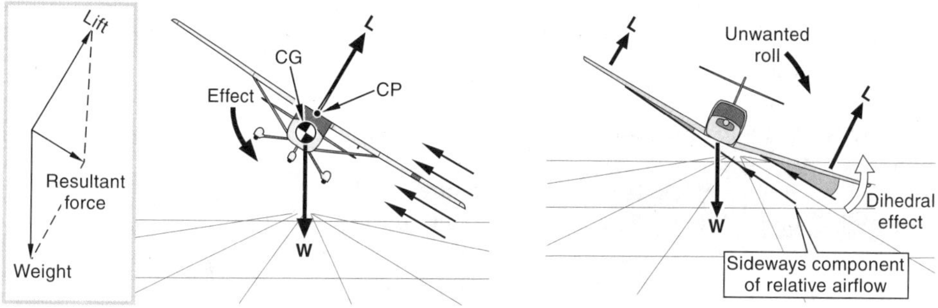

■ Figure 6a-7 ***High keel surfaces, such as the fin (left), and dihedral (right), provide lateral stability***

Compared with stability in the pitching plane, the stability of the aeroplane is not as great in the rolling and yawing planes. The interrelationship between roll and yaw (see Exercise 4b) is such that a disturbance in either roll or yaw will eventually lead to a spiral descent, unless the pilot acts to level the wings and keep the coordination ball centred.

In general terms, however, the natural stability designed into the aeroplane will assist you in maintaining straight and level flight. If the aeroplane is in trim, you can more or less let it fly itself, with only a light touch on the controls being required.

Lift

The wings generate lift.

The main wings are designed so that the airflow speeds up over their upper surface, creating a lower static pressure and an upward aerodynamic force. The vertical component is known as **lift** and the component parallel to the flightpath is called induced drag (*induced* because it is the byproduct of the production of lift).

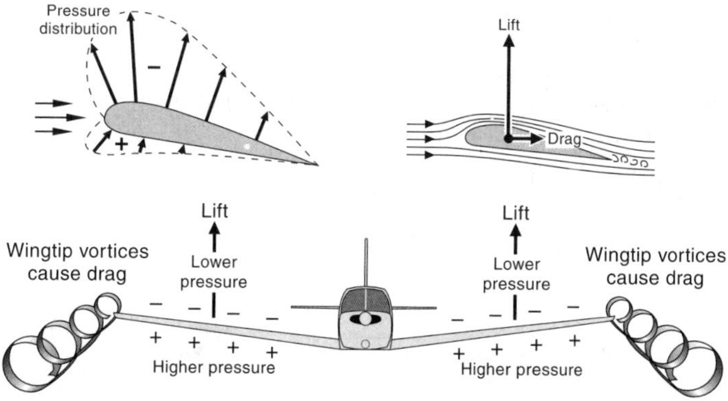

■ Figure 6a-8 ***The wings produce lift and (unfortunately) drag***

The lifting ability of a particular wing – known as the **coefficient of lift** (C_L) – depends on both the **shape** of the wing and its **angle of attack.** (The angle of attack is the angle at which the relative airflow strikes the wing.)

To fly straight and level and obtain the required lift to balance the weight:

- **at low speed,** a high angle of attack is required; and
- **at high speed,** a low angle of attack is required.

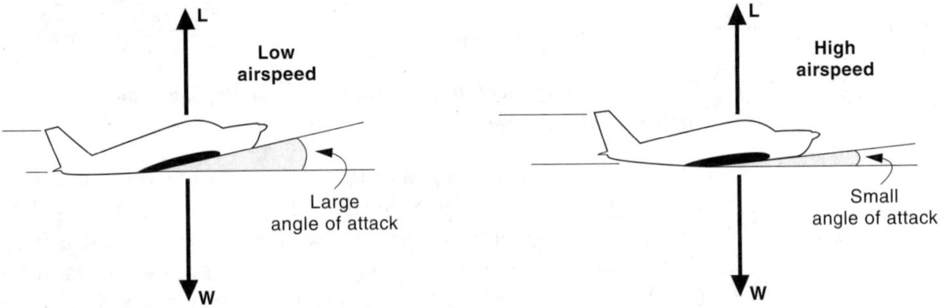

■ *Figure 6a-9* ***The lifting ability of the wings depends on the angle of attack***

NOTE The angle of attack, which is related to relative airflow, is not to be confused with the pitch attitude, which is related to the horizon.

Angle of Attack

The pilot controls angle of attack with elevator.

Backward movement of the control column raises the nose of the aeroplane. Because of the aeroplane's inertia (i.e. its resistance to any change in the flightpath), the aeroplane will continue in the same direction at the same airspeed for a brief period, but with an increased angle of attack. The wing will generate increased lift and the aeroplane will start to climb.

Conversely, moving the control column forward lowers the nose and decreases the angle of attack. Since the airspeed has not had time to alter, the wings will generate less lift, and the aeroplane will lose height.

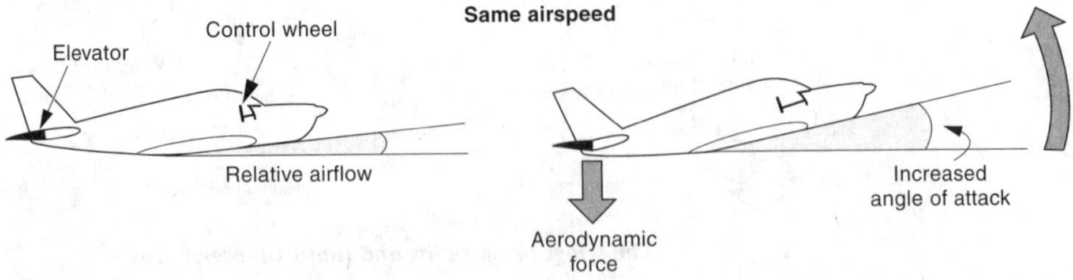

■ *Figure 6a-10* ***The elevator controls angle of attack***

The pilot cannot measure angle of attack in the cockpit, but can ensure that suitable angles of attack are being flown by setting:
- **a suitable power;** and
- **a suitable pitch attitude.**

Performance

Power plus attitude determines aeroplane performance.

Power plus attitude determines the **performance** of the aeroplane in terms of:
- **airspeed;** and
- **rate of climb** (which is, of course, zero for straight and level flight).

Flying straight and level with constant power set, there will be a particular pitch attitude for straight and level flight. If the nose is too high, the aeroplane will climb; if the nose is too low, the aeroplane will descend.

How do you know that you have set the correct pitch attitude? Because the aeroplane maintains height! You can observe this on the altimeter, with the vertical speed indicator (VSI) as a backup instrument indicating any tendency to deviate from the altitude.

Flying the Manoeuvre

Flying Straight

Keep the aeroplane in trim and relax on the controls.

Keep the wings level.

The essential elements in flying straight are to keep the wings level with aileron and to prevent yaw with rudder pressure.

The outside visual clue to the pilot of 'wings-level' is the natural horizon being level in the windscreen. If it is not level, then rotation of the control wheel or sideways movement of the control column to operate the ailerons will remedy this.

■ *Figure 6a-11* ***Level the wings with the ailerons***

Keep the balance ball centred.

Balance is achieved by keeping the balance ball centred. If it is out to the left, more left rudder pressure is required; if it is out to the right, more right rudder pressure is required.

■ *Figure 6a-12* ***Balance ball indications and corrective responses***

In straight flight, a reference point ahead on the horizon will remain in the same position relative to the nose of the aeroplane. In the cockpit, straight flight is indicated by a steady heading on the heading indicator and the magnetic compass.

If the aeroplane is deviating from straight flight, first of all stop the deviation by levelling the wings and prevent yaw with rudder. Then make a gentle turn back onto the desired reference point.

Flying Level

The essential element in **maintaining height** is to establish the correct nose attitude for the power set. The external reference is the natural horizon, which should appear at a particular position in the windscreen relative to the nose cowl or the top of the instrument panel.

Establish the correct nose attitude for the power setting.

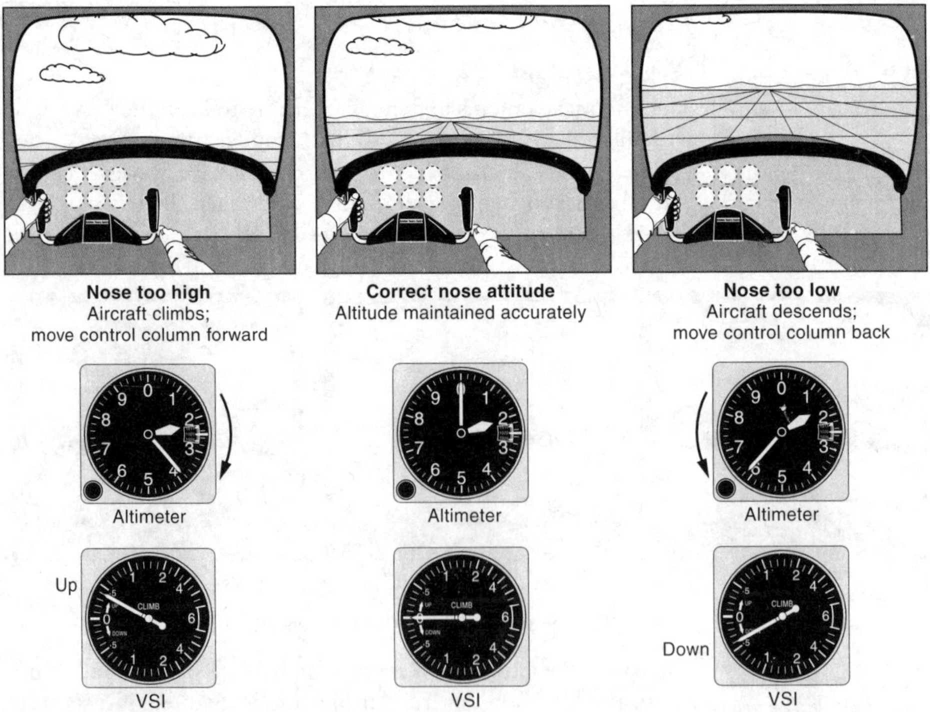

■ *Figure 6a-13* ***With cruise power set at cruise speed, maintain height with elevator***

The relationship between the horizon and the nose cowl will differ for different pilot eye-heights in the aeroplane, so you should establish a comfortable seating position and use it for every flight. This will make it easier to commit to memory the correct attitude for normal cruise. Then, with cruise power set at cruise speed, you can place the aeroplane in this attitude and be reasonably certain that level flight will result. This can be confirmed on the **altimeter** and **vertical speed indicator.**

- **If the pitch attitude is too high** and the aeroplane climbs, lower the nose slightly and regain the desired height.
- **If the pitch attitude is too low** and the aeroplane descends, raise the nose to regain the height.

Accuracy

Fly as accurately as possible.

Maintaining heading and height perfectly is almost impossible. There will inevitably be some deviations but these can be corrected so that the aeroplane flies very close to the target heading and height. More comfortable flight results from continually making small corrections rather than occasionally making large ones.

Keep the aeroplane in trim to make accurate level flight easier, the correct procedure being to hold the desired attitude and then trim off any steady control pressure.

Do not fly with **crossed controls.** It is possible to fly straight and level with one wing down and the aeroplane out of balance. For example, if the left wing is down, right rudder can be applied to stop the aeroplane turning left. This is neither comfortable nor efficient and is known as a *sideslip* or *flying with crossed controls* (since the ailerons and rudder oppose each other). It degrades performance by increasing drag and results in a reduced airspeed and/or a higher fuel consumption.

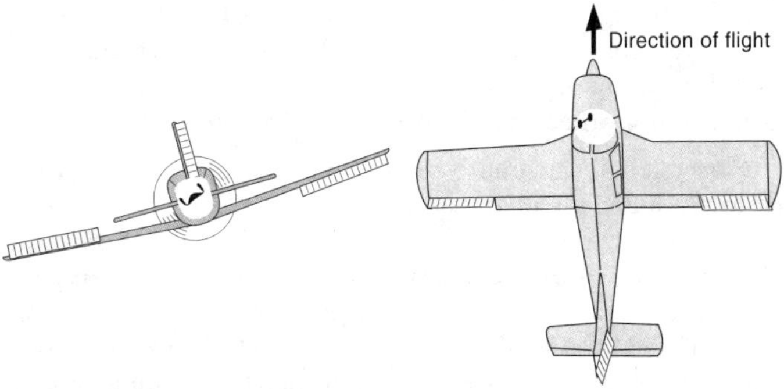

■ *Figure 6a-14* ***Crossed controls are inefficient***

An *out-of-balance* flight condition is frequently caused by a false or poor horizon – for instance when the wings are aligned with a sloping cloud base and rudder pressure is applied to suppress the subsequent yaw (turn). Such out-of-balance conditions (crossed controls) can be eliminated by moving the balance ball back into the centre with rudder pressure and flying straight with the use of ailerons towards a ground reference point.

Recovering from Slightly Unusual Attitudes

If the aeroplane is banked, level the wings with the ailerons. If the nose is too high or too low, ease it into the correct attitude with the elevator. If speed is excessively high or low, or if large alterations to height are required, some adjustment of power may be necessary.

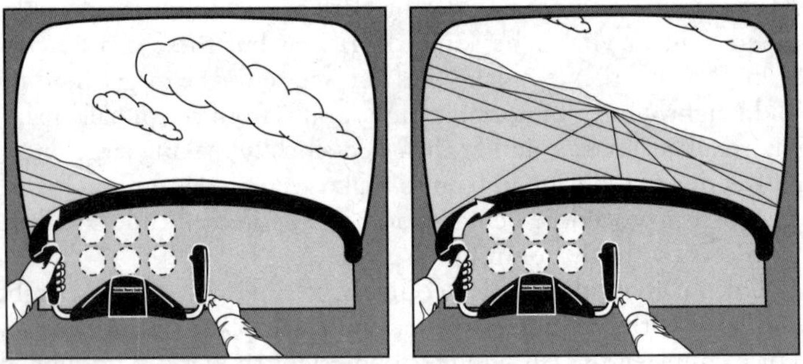

■ *Figure 6a-15* ***Nose high and turning left – lower nose and level wings. Nose low and turning left – level the wings and raise the nose***

Airmanship

Your eyes should be out of the cockpit most of the time to:
- check the correct nose position relative to the horizon;
- check the reference point on the horizon;
- look out for other aircraft above, below and to either side.

An occasional glance into the cockpit lasting only one or two seconds is sufficient to cross-check relevant instruments. Only look at the instruments from which you need information.

Maintain firm, positive and smooth control over the aeroplane and keep it well trimmed. This will decrease your workload considerably. Do not allow large deviations from the desired altitude, heading or airspeed to occur. Small and subtle movements of the controls, made sufficiently early, will avoid this, and these small movements are preferable to occasional large corrections.

Follow the basic **Rules of the Air:**

- **Give way to** airships, gliders, balloons and aircraft towing gliders or banners.
- **Give way to the right** and avoid passing over, under or ahead of other aircraft unless well clear.
- **Turn right if there is a danger** of a head-on collision.

Remain well clear of cloud.

Airwork 6a
Straight and Level in Balance at Constant Power

Aim *To fly straight and level at a constant power setting.*

- Look out.
- Select a horizon reference point on which to keep straight.
- Keep the wings level with the ailerons.
- Prevent yaw with rudder pressure.

1. With Cruise Power Set and At Desired Height

- Place the nose in the cruise attitude with elevator, and with constant power set:
  - cross-check the altimeter and vertical speed indicator;
  - make small attitude adjustments with elevator.
- Allow the airspeed to settle:
  - check the airspeed indicator for airspeed information;
  - cross-check the altimeter and vertical speed indicator for attitude information;
  - trim off elevator pressure, while holding the new pitch attitude constant.

POWER plus ATTITUDE equals PERFORMANCE

ATTITUDE

PERFORMANCE

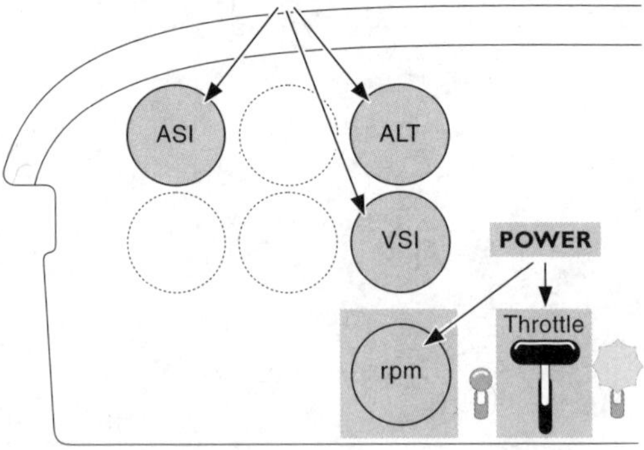

■ ***Maintain pitch attitude with elevator***

2. The Correct Trimming Technique

- Hold correct attitude with elevator pressure.
- Trim to relieve the control load.

If rudder trim is fitted, trim off rudder pressure while maintaining heading and keeping the balance ball centred.

Airwork 6a

3a. If the Aeroplane Tends to Climb

- Regain desired altitude with gentle movement of elevator.
- Hold nose attitude slightly lower than previously with elevator:
  - allow airspeed to settle;
  - check altimeter and vertical speed indicator.
- Trim off elevator pressure for the new attitude.

■ ***Climb tendency***

■ ***Regain height***

■ ***Slightly lower attitude, retrim***

3b. If the Aeroplane Tends to Descend

- Regain desired altitude with elevator (adding power if necessary).
- Hold nose attitude slightly higher than previously:
  - allow airspeed to settle;
  - check altimeter and vertical speed indicator.
- Trim off elevator pressure.

■ ***Descent tendency***

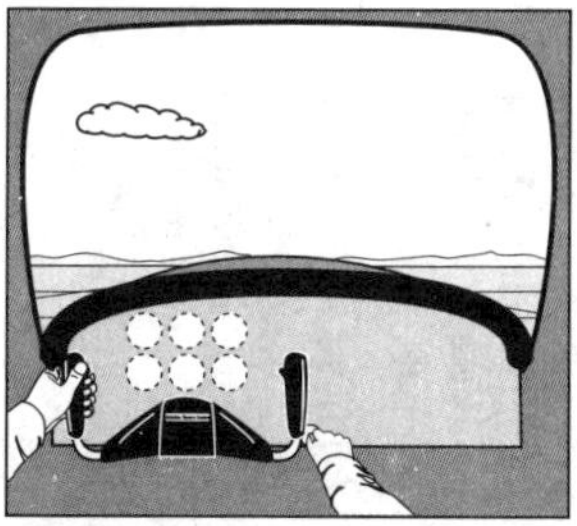

■ ***Regain height***

■ ***Slightly higher attitude, retrim***

3c. If the Aeroplane Wanders off its Reference Point

- Gently bank the aeroplane towards the desired reference point using aileron.
- Maintain height with elevator (fore or aft control column pressure).

When on desired reference point:

- Level the wings with aileron.
- Prevent yaw with rudder.
- Maintain height with elevator.

Pre-Flight Briefings

Below is the information contained in a typical pre-flight briefing. Before each flying lesson your instructor should outline the principles of the exercise to be flown. This example covers a straight and level exercise.

STRAIGHT AND LEVEL Air Exercise 6a

Aim: To learn to fly the aircraft in a constant **direction**, at a constant **altitude** and in **balance**.

Airmanship: **Lookout**, location, intro to cruise checks (fuel, mixture, temperatures and pressures, carburettor heat).

Air Exercise: Revise Effects of Controls Part 2 and Trim. Set Power (cruise) ____ to ___ rpm.

STRAIGHT

Wings level – coaming level with the horizon and establish a **reference point**.

Prevent yaw.

To maintain or regain reference point
Use about 5° bank.

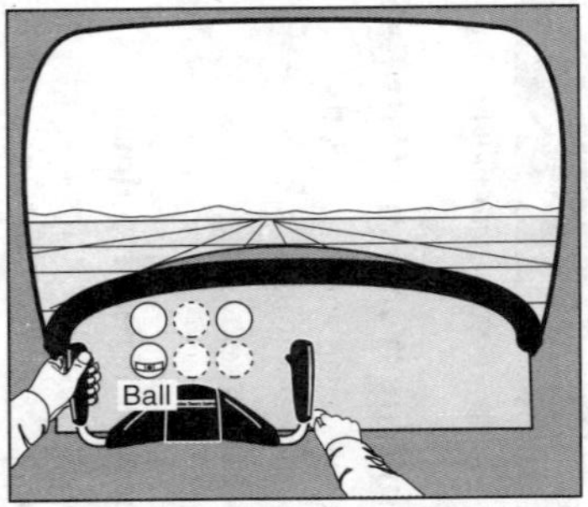

LEVEL

Select the correct pitch attitude to maintain level flight and **trim**.

Check: Altitude constant.

To maintain level flight
Change: attitude
Check: attitude
Adjust: attitude
Re-trim: attitude

To regain datum altitude
Raise or lower the nose attitude as required. Pause, then re-select. Trim. If more than ±100 ft consider using power.

BALANCE

Out-of-balance flight condition can be caused by a **false horizon**.

Demonstrate a gross out-of-balance flight condition.

Demonstrate a slight out-of-balance flight condition.

If ball out
Centre the ball with rudder and maintain straight flight with ailerons.

Work cycle: Lookout – Attitude – Instruments

Exercise 6b
Flying Straight and Level in Balance at a Selected Airspeed

Aim

To fly the aeroplane straight and level at a selected airspeed.

Considerations

Straight and level flight can be maintained over a range of speeds – from a high-speed cruise to low-speed flight just above stalling speed. While a normal cruise or high-speed cruise is suitable for cross-country flying, manoeuvring in the circuit in preparation for landing requires a low speed.

Accelerating and Decelerating

In the cruise, **thrust balances drag** – the source of the thrust being engine power. If the desired airspeed is less than that being maintained, then, by reducing power, the thrust will not balance the drag and consequently the aeroplane will slow down (i.e. decelerate). If, however, the desired airspeed is somewhat greater than that being maintained, then, by increasing power, the thrust will exceed the drag and the aeroplane will accelerate until the drag is again equal and opposite to the thrust.

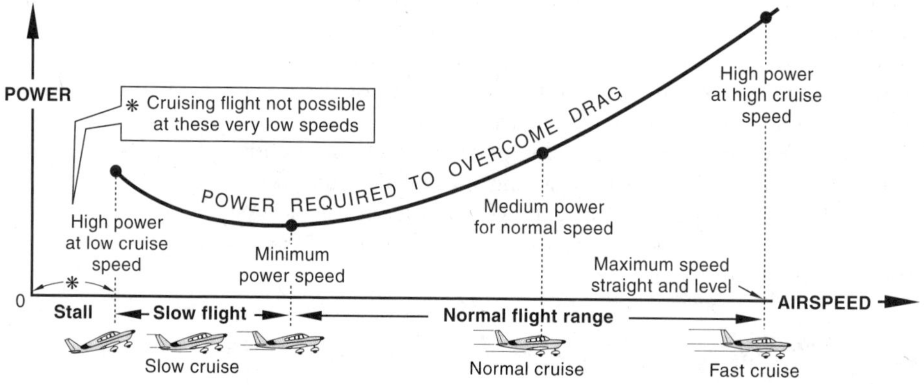

■ *Figure 6b-1* ***Vary the cruising airspeed by altering power***

Power

Once the aeroplane has accelerated or decelerated to the target airspeed, the power is adjusted to maintain it. Subsequent adjustments to the power may be required for the selected speed to be maintained accurately.

Attitude

Since the lift generated by the wings depends on both the angle of attack and the airspeed, the lift will increase as the airspeed increases and, unless the nose is lowered, the aeroplane will start to climb.

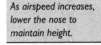

As airspeed increases, lower the nose to maintain height.

If the speed is decreasing, then the lift will decrease and the aeroplane will lose height unless the nose is raised.

As airspeed decreases, raise the nose to maintain height.

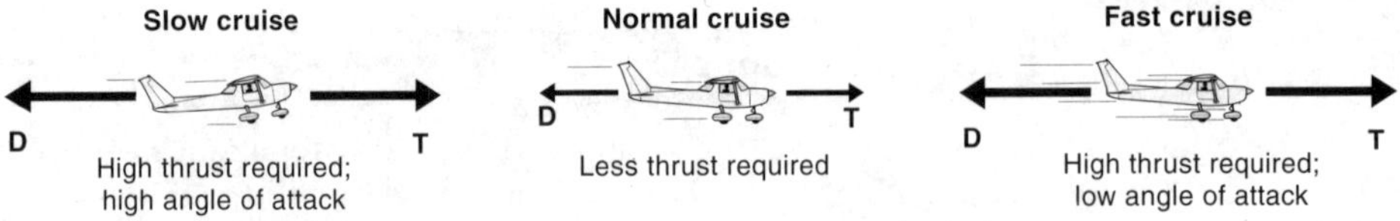

■ *Figure 6b-2* ***Maintain straight and level flight with power and attitude***

Trim

Any changes in power and/or attitude will require a trim change. Set the power, hold the desired attitude, and trim off any steady control pressures.

Flying the Manoeuvre

Prior to any significant power changes the mixture control should be in the RICH (fully in) position. Add power to increase airspeed or remove power to decrease airspeed, while maintaining height with elevator. Be prepared for the pitch/yaw tendency that occurs with power changes (nose-up and yaw as power is added, nose-down and yaw as power is reduced), counteracting it with control pressure. Once the desired airspeed is attained, adjust the power to maintain it. Then trim the aeroplane.

At very low airspeeds, where high power is required, close attention must be given to maintaining the speed using power. Frequent, and sometimes large, power adjustments may be required. The reasons for this are considered in detail in Exercises 10a and 10b of this manual.

Airmanship

Maintain a good lookout. Be positive in achieving the desired airspeed and height. Maintain them! Constant attention to power and attitude is required.

Airwork 6b
Straight and Level in Balance at a Selected Airspeed

Aim *To fly straight and level at a selected airspeed.*

1. To Increase Speed in Level Flight

- Increase power (balance with rudder pressure).
- Lower nose gradually to maintain level flight as airspeed increases.
- Adjust power to maintain desired airspeed.
- Trim off elevator pressure (nose-down).
- Make minor adjustments of power, attitude and trim as required.

■ ***Add power***

■ ***Lower nose attitude***

■ ***Adjust power and trim***

2. To Decrease Speed in Level Flight

- Decrease power (balance with rudder pressure).
- Raise nose gradually to maintain level flight as airspeed decreases.
- Adjust power to maintain desired airspeed.
- Trim off elevator pressure (nose-up).
- Make minor adjustments of power, attitude and trim as required.

■ ***Decrease power***

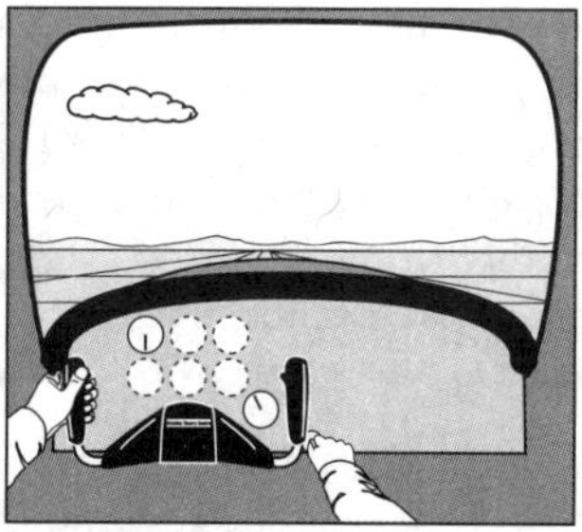

■ ***Higher nose attitude***

■ ***Adjust power and retrim***

Remember P-A-T: power–attitude–trim.

Further Points

There are sound reasons for maintaining certain selected airspeeds; for example, when the maximum range for a given quantity of fuel is desired.

Total drag, and thrust required, vary with airspeed.

Different airspeeds straight and level require different power settings. The thrust must balance the drag, which (like lift) depends on airspeed and angle of attack. At high airspeeds the drag is high; at medium speeds it is somewhat less. This is because the **parasite drag** decreases as airspeed decreases – the parasite drag being similar to the air resistance that you feel on a bicycle.

What is different with an aeroplane, however, is that, unlike a bicycle (which is supported by the ground), an aeroplane in flight must generate its own support, i.e. lift. A by-product of the production of lift by the wings is **induced drag,** and this is greatest at high angles of attack, i.e. at low airspeeds. As a result, the total drag is high when the aeroplane is flying slowly.

■ *Figure 6b-3* ***Minimum drag occurs at an intermediate airspeed***

A high power is required at both low and high airspeeds for the drag to be balanced. At intermediate speeds, the power requirement is less. The rate at which fuel is consumed depends on the power set, and an important aspect in operating an aeroplane efficiently is to obtain the maximum benefit from the fuel available.

The Best-Endurance Speed

For minimum fuel consumption, fly at the **minimum power** airspeed. This will achieve the maximum flight time for a given quantity of fuel. Since 'delaying' flight is sometimes required (for example, if holding near an aerodrome waiting for fog to clear), flying at the airspeed for **maximum endurance** provides the minimum fuel burn for a given flight time.

The **best-endurance airspeed** is nominated in the Pilot's Operating Handbook.

The Best-Range Airspeed

A more common requirement is to achieve the maximum distance for a given quantity of fuel – the **maximum range.** Since most flights are over a fixed distance, another way of expressing 'best range' is *minimum fuel burn to cover a given distance.* This occurs at the airspeed where the ratio fuel/distance is least, known as the **best-range airspeed.**

The best range airspeed is nominated in the Pilot's Operating Handbook and is higher than that for maximum endurance. The range distances published by the manufacturer **assume correct leaning of the mixture** when cruising at power settings less than 75% maximum continuous power (usually occurring when cruising above 5,000 ft amsl).

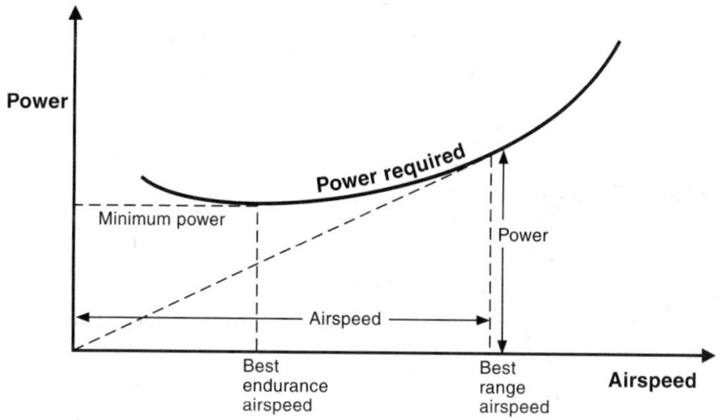

■ *Figure 6b-4* ***Airspeeds for best endurance and best range***

Best range is achieved at the airspeed where the power/speed ratio is least.

Best endurance is achieved at the airspeed where power required is least.

Referring to the best range airspeed as shown on the graph above, the *rate of fuel consumption* depends on **power.** The *rate of covering distance* is the **speed.**

Therefore the ratio of *fuel/distance* will be the same as the ratio of *power/speed,* and so the *minimum fuel consumption for a given distance* (i.e. the best range) will occur at the airspeed where the *power/speed* ratio is least, as illustrated above.

The line from the origin to any other point on the graph has a steeper gradient, i.e. the *power/speed* ratio is greater and so more fuel per mile will be burned.

Exercise 6c
Cruising with Flap Extended

Aim

To fly the aeroplane straight and level at a selected airspeed with flap lowered.

Considerations

Cruising with an early stage of flap extended is desirable when you wish to fly at a low speed: for example, when inspecting a prospective precautionary landing field or when greater manoeuvrability is required.

Avoid ballooning when lowering the flaps.

Because the lifting ability of the wings is increased as the flaps are extended, a lower nose attitude will be required to maintain height. If the nose is not lowered as the flaps are extended, the aeroplane will **'balloon'**.

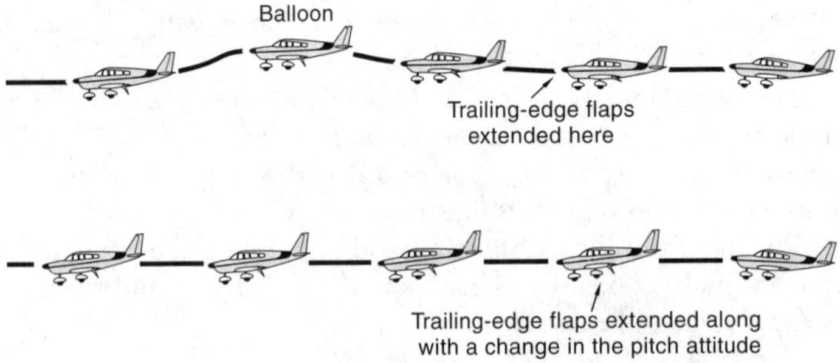

■ Figure 6c-1 **A 'balloon' can be avoided by lowering the nose as flaps extend**

Only extend flaps when the airspeed is in the flap-operating range.

The flaps should not be operated at high speeds, since this places unnecessary stress on the airframe. The maximum flap extension speed (V_{FE}) is the high-speed end of the white band on the airspeed indicator.

A low nose position improves the forward view from the cockpit – very useful, along with the low speed, when you want to inspect a potential landing field.

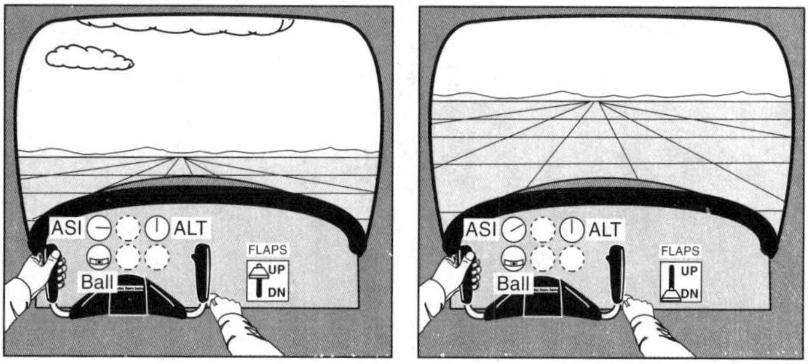

■ *Figure 6c-2* ***Lowering flaps improves the forward view (right)***

Lower speeds are possible with flap extended because of the increased lifting ability of the wings and the lower stalling speed. The stalling speed straight and level with flap extended is the low-speed end of the white band on the airspeed indicator; the stalling speed 'clean' is the low speed end of the green band. (See Figure 10a-2.)

Because extending flap increases the drag, power must be added if airspeed is to be maintained in straight and level flight. This increases the fuel consumption, making cruising with flap extended much less efficient than cruising 'clean'.

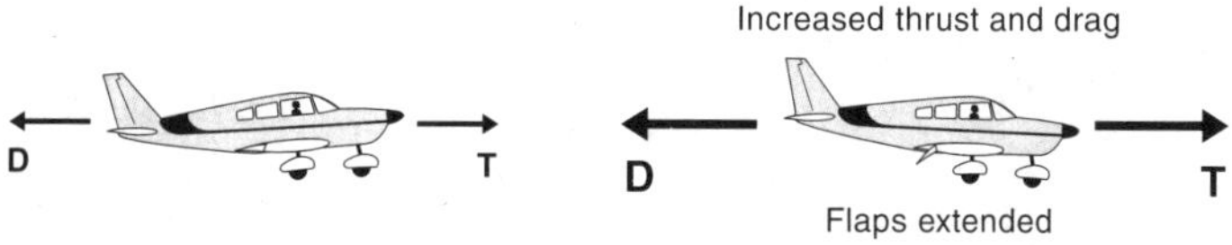

■ *Figure 6c-3* ***Flap increases drag***

Flying the Manoeuvre

As the flap position is changed, be prepared to make any necessary adjustments to power and attitude to achieve the desired performance.

- **Lowering flap** will require a lower nose position to avoid 'ballooning' and an increase in power to maintain airspeed. Once the adjustments are made, any steady control pressure should be trimmed off.
- **Raising flap** will require a higher nose position to avoid 'sinking' and an adjustment to power to maintain airspeed. Trim off any steady control pressures.

Do not operate the flaps at too high a speed: V_{FE} is the limit. Do not raise the flaps below the 'clean' stalling speed.

Airwork 6c
Cruising with Flap Extended

Aim *To fly straight and level with flap extended.*

- Reduce power.
- Establish the aeroplane in straight and level flight 'clean' (flaps fully retracted).

1. To Lower Flap, Maintaining Straight and Level Flight

- Ensure airspeed is below maximum flap extension speed (V_{FE}), i.e. in white ASI band.
- Extend flaps in stages.
- Place nose in lower attitude (to avoid 'ballooning' and maintain height).
- Adjust power to maintain desired airspeed.
- Trim off elevator pressure for each stage of flap.

2. To Raise Flap

- Check that the airspeed is suitable.
- Raise the flaps in stages, holding the nose in a higher attitude to prevent 'sink' and maintain height.
- Adjust power to maintain desired speed.
- Trim off elevator pressure.

NOTE In a go-around situation, when you want to discontinue an approach, **apply full power** first, before altering the flap position.

Exercise 7
Climbing

Aim

To enter and maintain a steady climb on a constant heading and to level off at a particular height.

Considerations

The Forces in a Climb

For an aeroplane to climb steadily the thrust must exceed the drag, otherwise it would slow down and the nose would have to be lowered to maintain airspeed. The thrust in excess of that needed to balance the drag is called the **excess thrust.**

In a climb, the vertical component of the excess thrust supports a small part of the weight and the lift generated by the wings supports the remainder – hence the surprising result that **lift is less than weight in a steady climb.**

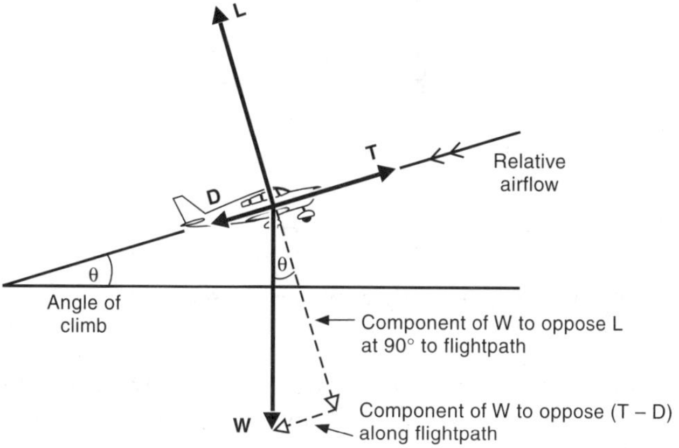

■ *Figure 7-1* ***The four forces in a steady climb***

A component of the weight acts in the direction opposite to the flightpath and opposes the climb.

Performance

Power plus attitude equals performance.

The **power** applied and the **attitude** of an aeroplane determine its **performance** in terms of:

- **airspeed;** and
- **rate of climb.**

■ *Figure 7-2* ***Climb power plus climb attitude provides climb performance***

The power in a climb is usually greater than that used for the cruise and for many training aeroplanes is in fact maximum power. The greater slipstream effect striking one side of the tail in a climb will have a yawing effect, especially at low airspeeds. Counteract the yawing tendency with rudder pressure and keep the aeroplane in balance.

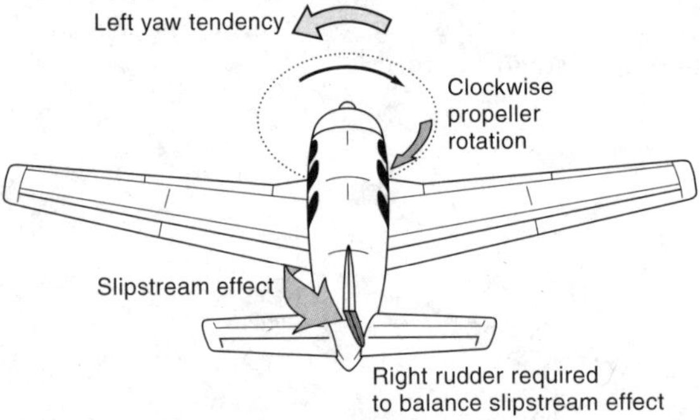

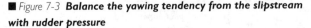

■ *Figure 7-3* ***Balance the yawing tendency from the slipstream with rudder pressure***

In a climb, the usual balance rule applies. If the ball is out to the right, for example, move it back into the centre with right rudder pressure. Most training aeroplanes have a propeller that rotates clockwise when viewed from the cockpit (see Figure 7-3).

As climb power is applied, a coordinated increase in right rudder pressure will maintain the aeroplane in balance. Some aeroplanes have a rudder trim, which may be used to relieve steady foot pressures in the climb (and at any other time).

With climb power set, **pitch attitude controls the airspeed.** Raising the nose will decrease airspeed (and vice versa). Do not 'chase' the airspeed after altering the nose attitude – allow time for the airspeed to settle before making any further (and minor) changes in attitude. If the power and attitude are correct, then climb performance will be as desired and reference to the airspeed indicator need only be made to make fine adjustments.

■ *Figure 7-4* ***The climb attitude is higher than the normal cruise attitude***

Once established in the climb, trim off any steady control pressures with the elevator trim, and the rudder trim (if fitted). An out-of-trim aeroplane is difficult to fly accurately.

Climb performance can be measured in the cockpit on the flight instruments:

- **airspeed** – primarily on the airspeed indicator;
- **rate of climb** – on the vertical speed indicator and altimeter.

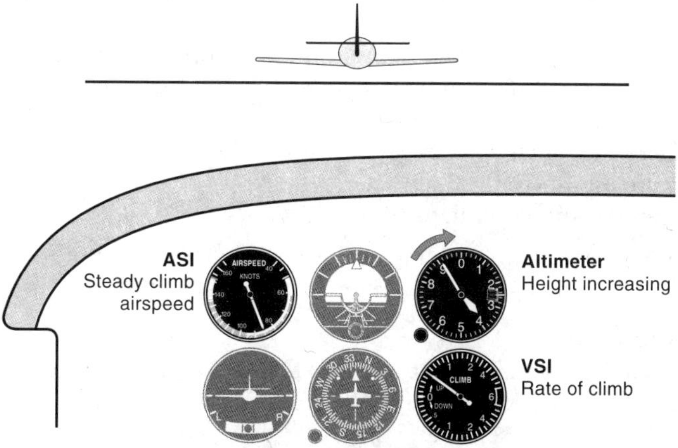

■ *Figure 7-5* ***Monitor the climb performance occasionally on the flight instruments***

Forward View in a Climb

Your forward view in a climb is restricted by the nose cowl. The restricted view ahead could mean danger – other aeroplanes may be hidden by your nose cowl. It is good airmanship to carry out a small turn left and right (or to lower the nose) every 500 ft or so in the climb to look ahead and 'clear' the area under the nose into which you are climbing. A reference point on the horizon will assist in returning to the original heading.

Periodically make small clearing turns during a climb.

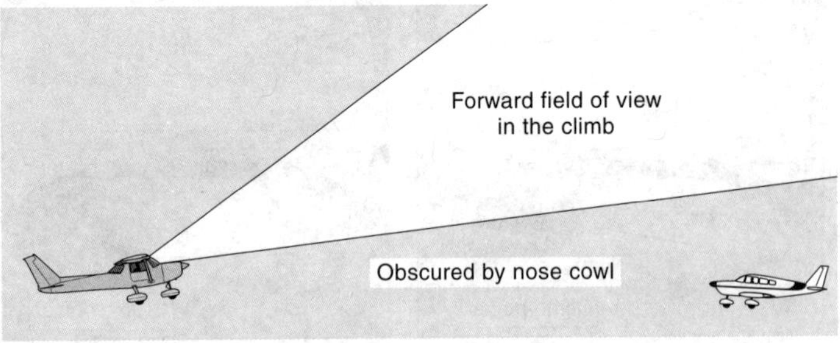

■ *Figure 7-6* ***Periodically clear the area obscured by the nose cowl***

The attitude in a normal climb will provide better forward vision than the higher nose attitudes required for best-angle and best-rate climb speeds.

Engine Considerations

During a climb using high power the engine is producing more heat energy than at lesser power settings. The lower airspeed reduces the air cooling of the engine, so there is a risk of overheating and the pilot must ensure that sufficient cooling is taking place.

Ensure that the engine is adequately cooled during a climb.

The engine instruments should be monitored periodically in the climb and, if the engine temperature is too high, better cooling may be achieved by:

- **increasing airspeed;** or
- **reducing power;** and
- **opening the cowl flaps** (if fitted).

It is usual to climb with the mixture fully RICH, because excess fuel, as it vaporises, has a cooling effect in the cylinders.

Climb Speeds

The pilot can sacrifice some airspeed for a higher rate of climb (or vice versa). The choice of airspeed on the climb depends on what the pilot wants to achieve. It may be:

There are various climb speeds to achieve different types of climb.

- **a steep angle of climb** to clear obstacles (best-angle climb, V_X);
- **a rapid climb** to gain height quickly (best-rate climb, V_Y);

- **a cruise climb** (the most usual) which provides:
  – faster en route performance;
  – better aeroplane control due to greater airflow over the control surfaces;
  – better engine cooling;
  – a more comfortable aeroplane attitude.

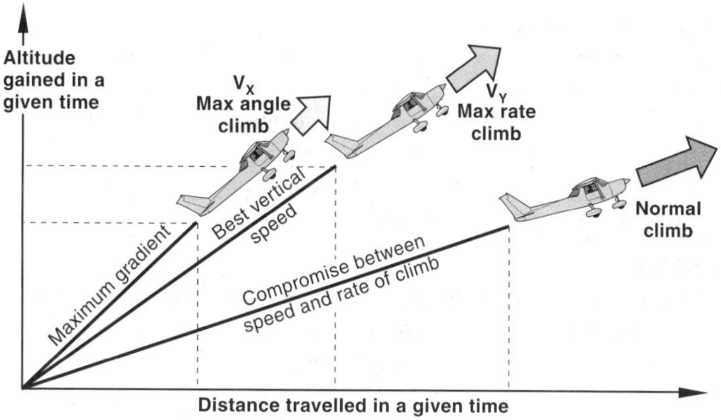

■ *Figure 7-7* ***Different types of climb***

The aeroplane can be made to climb at any of the above speeds. Their values may be found in your Pilot's Operating Handbook. With climb power set, simply fly the aeroplane at the appropriate indicated airspeed to achieve the desired type of climb – the lower the nose attitude, the higher the climb airspeed. Engine cooling will be poorer at the lower airspeeds.

■ *Figure 7-8* ***The various climb attitudes***

Flying the Manoeuvre

Before Entering the Climb

Decide on an appropriate climb speed, select a reference point well ahead and **look out** to check all clear of other aeroplanes and obstacles ahead, above, below and to either side.

To Enter the Climb

Increase **power** (first ensuring mixture RICH) by opening the throttle to climb power. Balance the unwanted yawing effect with rudder. Raise the nose to the correct climb **attitude,** allow the airspeed to settle and **trim.** An easy way to remember the sequence of events when entering a climb is P–A–T, power–attitude–trim.

To enter a climb, remember P–A–T, power–attitude–trim.

To Maintain the Climb

Maintain the wings level with aileron and the balance ball centred with rudder pressure. Maintain the desired airspeed with elevator – the higher the nose, the lower the airspeed.

Every 500 ft or so, either lower the nose or make clearing turns left and right to clear the area ahead. Periodically check engine temperatures and pressures, taking appropriate action if the engine is overheating, such as opening the cowl flaps (if fitted), increasing the airspeed and/or reducing the power.

To Level Off from a Climb

Since cruise speed is higher than climb speed, it is usual to gradually lower the nose as the intended cruise level is approached, leaving climb power set. Allow the aeroplane to accelerate until cruise speed is attained, lowering the nose gradually to maintain altitude as airspeed increases.

To level off from a climb, remember A-P-T: attitude–power–trim.

Anticipate reaching the cruise level by 20 ft or so and begin lowering the nose towards the cruise **attitude** before the cruise level is actually reached. This will make levelling off a smooth manoeuvre and avoid overshooting the cruise level. The greater the rate of climb, the more you should anticipate the level-off altitude – say by 10% of the rate of climb, e.g. if climbing at 500 ft/min, begin lowering the nose 50 ft before reaching the desired altitude.

As cruise speed is reached, reduce to cruise **power,** keeping the coordination ball centred with rudder pressure. **Trim.**

The sequence of events for levelling off is: A–P–T: attitude–power–trim.

Once established in the cruise, engine operation should be considered:

- **mixture** leaned as required;
- **carburettor heat** as required;
- **cowl flaps** (if fitted) possibly closed; and
- **engine oil** temperature and pressure checked from time to time.

Airmanship

Airmanship is looking after the engine in a climb, and keeping a good lookout – especially under the nose.

Ensure that the engine is adequately cooled during the *high power/low airspeed* climb. The mixture should be set to RICH before power is increased.

Clear the area and maintain a continuous lookout. Clear the 'blind spot' under the nose every 500 ft or so in the climb. Do not climb too close to clouds, and **do not fly into clouds** (unless you are instrument-rated and in a suitably equipped aeroplane).

Be aware of the nature of the airspace above you. For example, do not inadvertently climb into controlled airspace without a clearance to do so from ATC. Follow correct altimetry procedures – normally Regional QNH is set during training so that the altimeter reads height above mean sea level. However, if flying below an overlying portion of controlled airspace (a CTA or a TMA), aerodrome QNH should be used to ensure correct separation from aircraft operating in the lower areas of the controlled airspace above you.

Exert firm, positive and smooth control over the aeroplane.

Airwork 7
The Climb

Aims *(a) To enter and maintain a steady climb on a constant heading, and*
(b) To level off at a particular height.

1. Prior to Entry

- Decide on an appropriate climb speed.
- Select a reference point well ahead, slightly to the left of the nose.
- Look out – clear the area ahead, above, below and to either side.

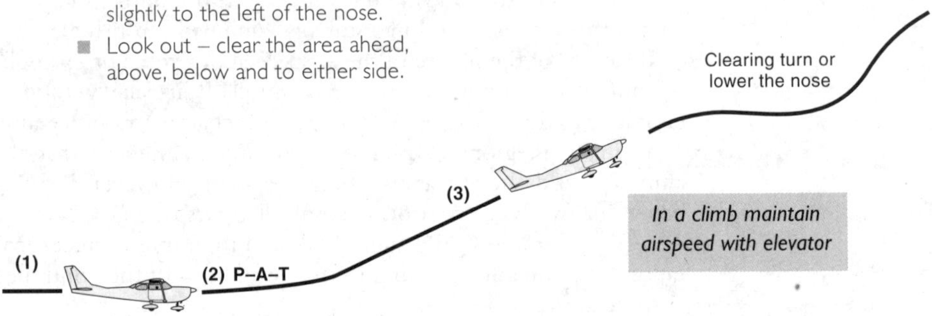

In a climb maintain airspeed with elevator

2. Entry to a Climb

Look out.

P – mixture rich;
– increase to climb **power**;
– balance with rudder.

A – raise nose to climb **attitude**;
– allow airspeed to reduce and settle;
– adjust attitude to achieve desired speed (check ASI).

T – **trim** off steady elevator pressure.

(Some instructors prefer A–P–T.)

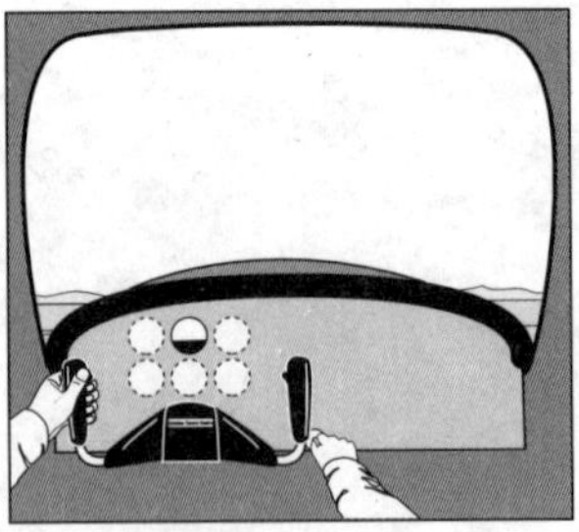

■ ***1. Set climb power.***
■ ***2. Select climb attitude.***

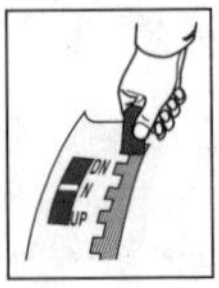

■ ***3. Trim.***

Airwork 7

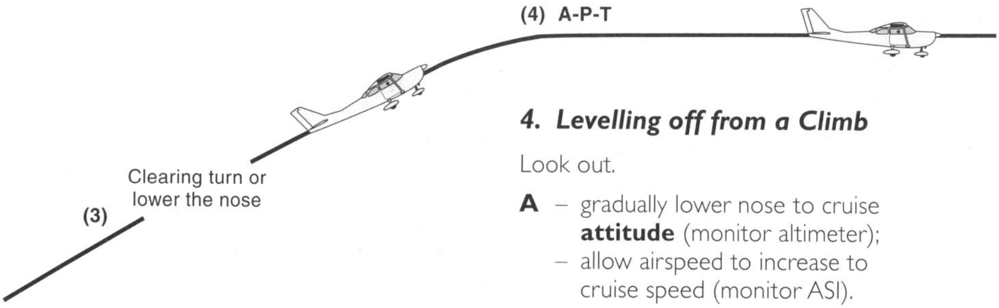

3. Maintaining a Climb

Look out.

Maintain:

- Wings level with aileron.
- Balance with rudder.
- Airspeed with elevator.

Periodically check engine temperatures and pressures.

Look out for attitude reference and for other aircraft. Make clearing turns left and right every 500 ft or so, to clear area ahead; or lower nose.

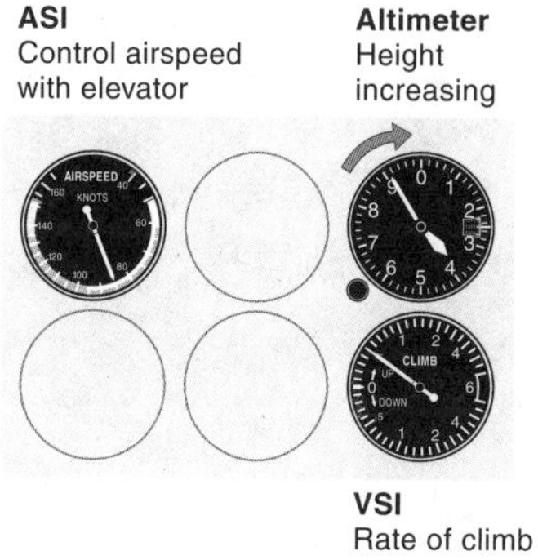

■ ***Monitor climb performance***

4. Levelling off from a Climb

Look out.

A – gradually lower nose to cruise **attitude** (monitor altimeter);
– allow airspeed to increase to cruise speed (monitor ASI).

P – at cruise speed, reduce to cruise **power**;
– relax rudder pressure to balance.

T – **trim** off steady elevator pressure.

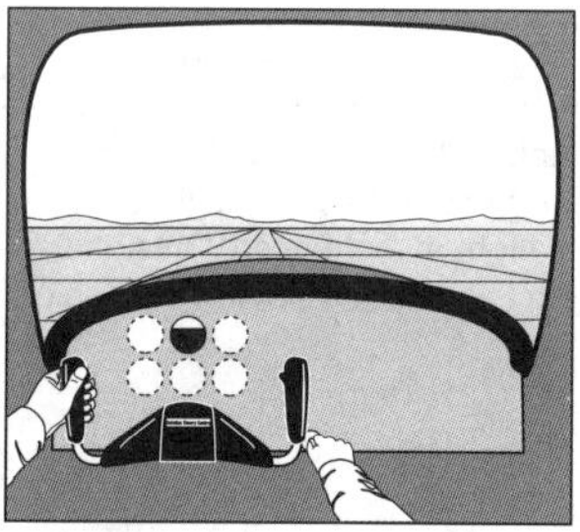

■ ***1. Select cruise attitude and accelerate.***

■ ***2. Set climb power.***

■ ***3. Trim.***

Further Points

Climb Performance

The curve below shows the power that is required for an aeroplane to maintain straight and level flight at various airspeeds. If the engine can provide power greater than this, then the aeroplane is capable of climbing at that airspeed. Power is the rate at which energy is supplied, so the **best rate of climb** will be achieved at the airspeed at which maximum *excess power* is available.

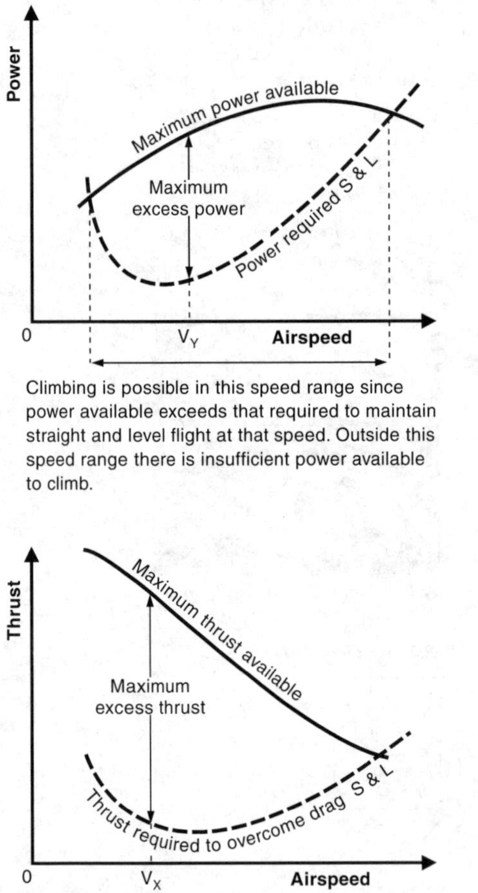

■ *Figure 7-9* ***The power curve and the thrust curve (also known as the drag curve)***

Power is defined as the product of *thrust × velocity,* so for a given power output, the higher the velocity the lower the thrust. This explains the different shapes of the power and thrust curves in the diagrams above.

The **angle of climb** depends on how much thrust is available over and above the drag (i.e. the excess thrust), and so the steepest climb, i.e. the **best-angle climb,** is achieved with maximum power set and at the airspeed where maximum *excess thrust* occurs. This is slightly lower than the best rate speed.

NOTE At low gross weights and low altitudes, the aeroplane will climb better than at high gross weights or high altitudes (where the air is less dense).

Climbing with Flap Extended

Take-off is often made with some flap extended, because it:

- **allows the same lift to be generated at a lower airspeed,** shortening the take-off run;
- **reduces the stalling speed,** allowing slower flight; and
- **may enable a steeper climb-out angle** to be achieved (depending on the aircraft type).

Use only recommended flap settings for take-off.

Full flap causes a large drag increase and greatly reduces climb performance, so always ensure that only take-off flap is set for take-off. This is typically the first stage, or 10–15°. On some aeroplanes it is zero flap.

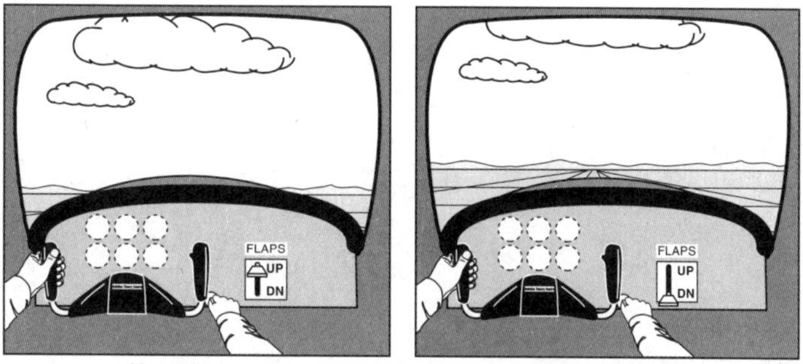

Normal climb without flap

Normal climb with take-off flap extended

■ *Figure 7-10* ***Nose position in the climb is lower with flap extended***

Raising the Flaps in the Climb-Out

When climbing out after take-off, it is usual to raise the flaps when well clear of the ground (say 200 ft above aerodrome level). To avoid any tendency for the nose to pitch or for the aeroplane to 'sink' as the flaps are raised:

- **hold the nose in the normal attitude** for a clean climb;
- **allow the airspeed to settle** at the desired airspeed;
- **trim.**

Check the airspeed indicator and adjust the nose attitude with the elevator if required (but do not 'chase' the airspeed).

Exercise 8a
The Glide

Aim

To enter and maintain a steady glide and to level off at a particular height.

Considerations

A descent without power is called a glide.

An aeroplane may be descended in two ways:

1. In a **glide,** where engine power is not used and the pilot accepts the resulting rate of descent; or
2. In a **powered descent**, where power is used by the pilot to control the rate of descent.

The Forces in a Glide

The nose must be lowered when thrust is totally removed to maintain flying speed.

If power is removed when the aeroplane is in level flight, the drag will be unbalanced and, if height is maintained, the aeroplane will decelerate. Only three forces will act on the aeroplane when the power is totally removed – drag (no longer balanced by thrust), lift and weight.

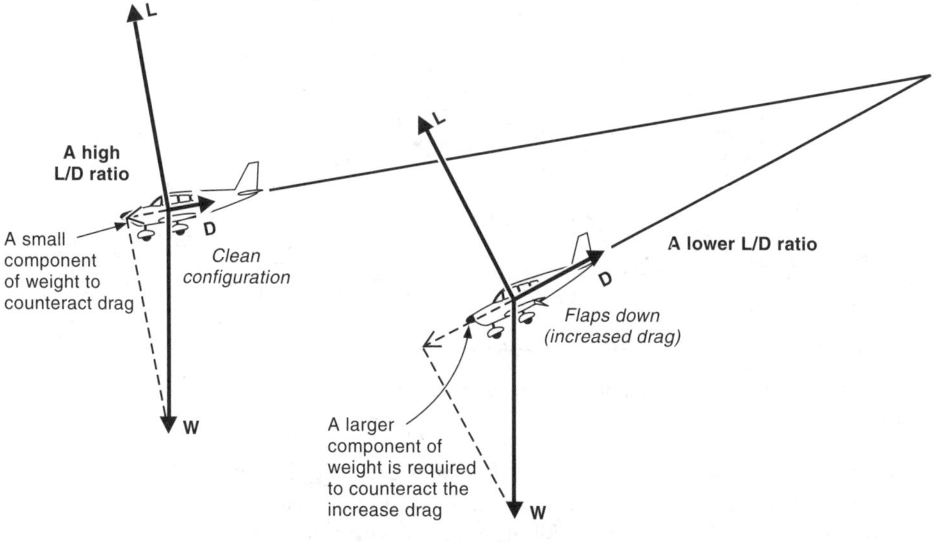

■ *Figure 8a-1* ***The forces in a glide***

To maintain flying speed when the thrust is removed, the nose must be lowered and a glide commenced. Drag (which by definition always acts in the direction opposite to the flightpath) now has a component of the weight available to balance it. A steady gliding speed will be achieved when the three forces (L, W and D) are in equilibrium.

Steepness of the Glide

High drag means a steeper glide.

If drag is increased more than lift (say by lowering flaps, sideslipping or flying at an incorrect airspeed), a greater component of the weight is required to balance it and maintain airspeed. A steeper flightpath is the result.

The gliding range through the air depends on the **lift/drag ratio.** For instance, if L:D is 6:1, for every 1,000 ft lost in height, the aeroplane will glide 6,000 ft (approximately 1 nm); if L:D is 10:1, for every 1,000 ft lost in height, the aeroplane will glide 10,000 ft (1.7 nm).

Gliding Range

Maximum glide range is achieved at the speed for best lift/drag. Low drag means a shallower glide.

Changing the angle of attack with the control column changes the airspeed and the lift/drag ratio. This will have a significant effect on the glidepath. A typical training aeroplane, flown at the best gliding speed, can achieve a lift/drag ratio of about 10:1. Flown at the wrong airspeed, the lift/drag ratio will be significantly less and consequently the glidepath will be steeper.

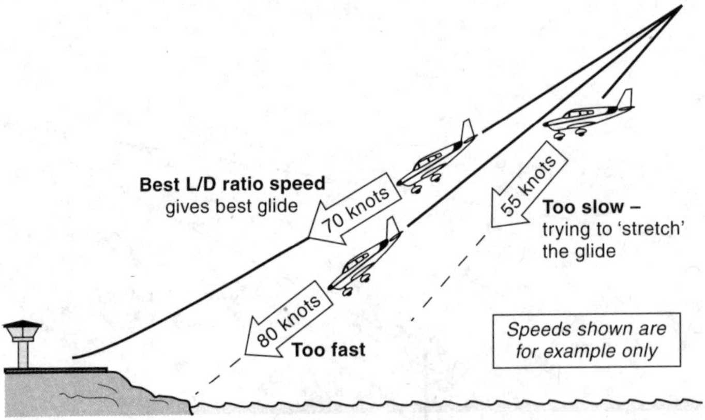

■ *Figure 8a-2* ***Glide at the recommended speed to obtain best still air range***

NOTE The Pilot's Operating Handbook specifies the best gliding speed when the aeroplane is at maximum weight. At lower weights, the best gliding speed is less but, since training aeroplanes do not have significant variations in gross weight, the one speed is generally acceptable at any weight.

Establish the target glide speed by setting the correct pitch attitude.

If the aeroplane is gliding at an airspeed below the recommended gliding speed, then, provided the aeroplane is still well above ground level, it will pay to lower the nose and gain airspeed. While the glide angle will initially steepen, the final glide angle will be flatter once the correct speed is achieved and maintained. The aeroplane will in fact glide further.

The Effect of Wind

A headwind steepens the descent over the ground; a tailwind flattens it.

At the normal gliding speed, a headwind will retard the aeroplane's passage over the ground; a tailwind will extend it.

In a tailwind, reducing the gliding airspeed slightly below the recommended gliding speed may increase the range a little by reducing the rate of descent, allowing the aeroplane to remain airborne longer and be blown further by the wind.

Conversely, the effect of a headwind can be minimised by gliding at a higher airspeed. The rate of descent will be increased, but the higher speed will allow the aeroplane to 'penetrate' further into the wind and cover more ground. Increasing speed could be an important technique to use on an undershooting gliding approach to land in a strong headwind.

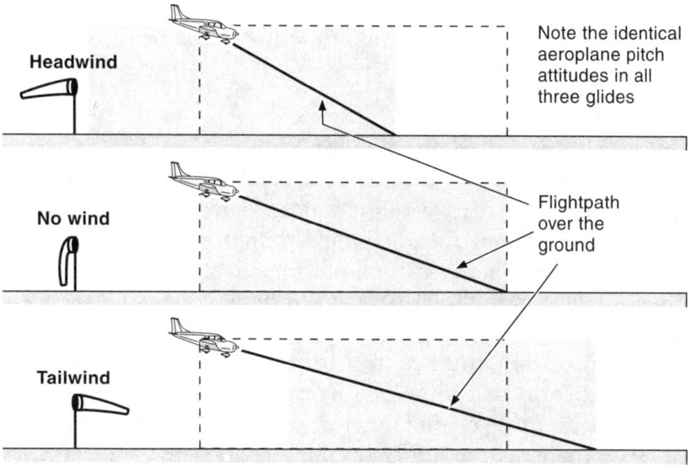

■ *Figure 8a-3* ***Compared to still air, more ground is covered when gliding with a tailwind and less with a headwind***

Estimating the Gliding Range

A practical way to estimate how far the aeroplane could glide at a constant airspeed is to note a ground feature that remains stationary in the windscreen. In the situation illustrated below, it appears that the glide will reach the trees beyond the first road, but not as far as the second road.

Raising the nose in an attempt to reach the second field may have the reverse effect. If the speed falls significantly below the best gliding speed, the glidepath will steepen and fall well short of even the first road.

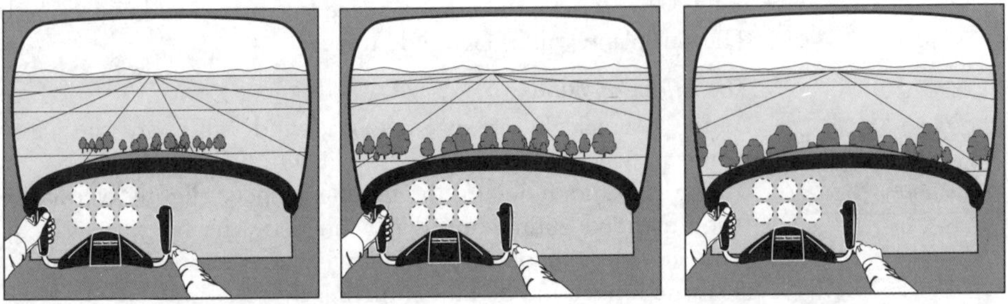

■ *Figure 8a-4* ***Estimating the gliding distance***

Cockpit Controls

Mixture Control

Move the mixture control to RICH for a glide.

It is usual to move the red mixture control to FULL RICH (i.e. fully in) before commencing the descent, so that the mixture is not too lean when power is reapplied at a lower level where the air is denser. An excessively lean mixture can cause detonation that is very damaging to an engine.

Carburettor Heat

Set carburettor heat to HOT for the glide.

The usual clues of carburettor ice forming (reduced rpm and rough running) may not be evident because of the low engine speed in a glide. Power, when it is needed, may not be available. Consequently, during the glide the carburettor heat should be set to HOT to prevent the formation of carburettor ice (but it must be the carburettor heat knob that is pulled right out and not the mixture control!).

Selecting carburettor heat HOT prior to closing the throttle is a good practice so that some hot air passes through the induction system before the engine goes to idle. Done in the reverse sequence, there may be sufficient time after closing the throttle for ice to form before HOT air is selected. Discuss the correct technique for your aeroplane with a flying instructor.

Power

Reduce power, and control airspeed with elevator and balance with rudder.

Once the mixture and carburettor heat are attended to, the power can be reduced by smoothly pulling the throttle out. Full movement of the throttle should take about the same as a slow '1-2-3' count. The reduced slipstream effect will require rudder to balance and prevent unwanted yaw. The tendency for the nose to drop too far will require back pressure on the control column.

NOTE Some aeroplanes have a rudder trim which may be used to relieve steady foot pressure in the descent. The tendency for the nose to drop as power is reduced is a safety feature that is designed into an aeroplane to ensure that it will adopt a safe gliding attitude without any help from the pilot if the engine fails.

Warm the Engine

Warm the engine periodically during a prolonged descent.

Every 1,000 ft or so on a prolonged descent, the pilot should apply approximately 50% power for a few seconds to:

- **keep the engine and oil warm;**
- **avoid carbon fouling** on the spark plugs; and
- **ensure that the carburettor heat** is still supplying warm air.

Monitor Descent Rate

The rate of descent is a measure of how fast height is being lost (in ft/min) and can be monitored on either:

- **the vertical speed indicator;** or
- **the altimeter** and **clock** combined.

The Best Endurance Glide

Generally, the aim in a glide is to achieve the maximum range (i.e. the greatest distance over the ground) and this is the situation that we have addressed so far. Occasionally, time in flight (rather than distance covered) becomes important, say if the engine has stopped at 5,000 ft directly over an airfield and you want as long as possible to restart it.

The **best endurance glide** is achieved at the speed which results in the minimum rate of descent as indicated on the vertical speed indicator. Typically, it is some 25% less than the more common gliding speed used for maximum range.

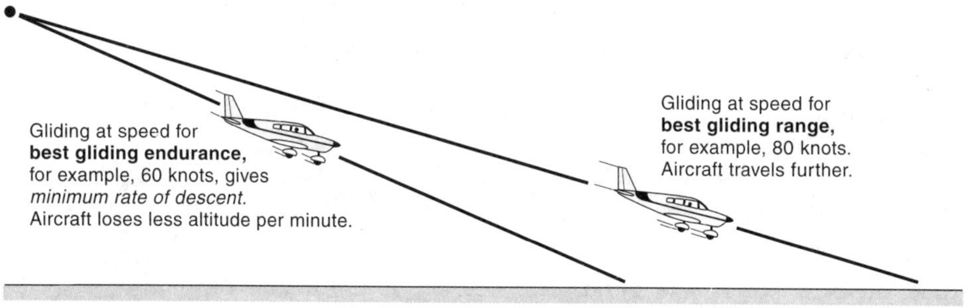
Gliding at speed for
best gliding endurance,
for example, 60 knots, gives
minimum rate of descent.
Aircraft loses less altitude per minute.
Gliding at speed for
best gliding range,
for example, 80 knots.
Aircraft travels further.

■ *Figure 8a-5* ***Select the best gliding speed for range or for endurance***

Flying the Manoeuvre

Prior to commencing the descent, decide on an appropriate gliding speed, select a reference point well ahead and **look out** to check all clear of other aeroplanes and obstacles ahead, below and to either side. A clearing turn to view under the nose may be advisable.

To Commence the Glide

Reduce the power by placing the mixture control to RICH (i.e. fully in), carburettor heat to HOT (i.e. fully out, so do not confuse it with the mixture control) and closing the throttle (i.e. fully out). This removes the thrust. Back pressure on the control column and rudder pressure will be required to counteract the 'pitch/yaw' tendencies as the power is changed.

Hold the nose up and maintain height, allowing the airspeed to decrease. When at the desired gliding speed, lower the nose to the gliding attitude and maintain airspeed with fore and aft pressures as required on the control column. Trim.

An easy way to remember the sequence of events when beginning a descent is P–A–T, which stands for: **power–attitude–trim.**

To Maintain the Glide

Maintain the wings level with ailerons and the balance ball centred with rudder pressure. Control airspeed with elevator – a higher nose attitude for a lower speed.

Maintain a good lookout in the descent, possibly with clearing turns left and right every 500 ft to clear the area hidden by the nose. To enable you to maintain the original direction, select a reference point on the horizon or use the heading indicator and/or the magnetic compass. Another means of achieving a good lookout, and without changing heading, is to lower the nose.

Warm the engine periodically. Also, remain very aware of your height above the ground at all times, and of the height still to be descended to your selected level. Ensure that the altimeter subscale is set correctly.

To Level Off

Anticipate by about 10% of the descent rate, e.g. at 400 ft/min RoD, commence raising the nose 40 ft above the desired level and start increasing the **power** (mixture should already be rich, throttle smoothly forward to cruise rpm, carburettor heat COLD).

Gradually allow the nose to rise to the cruise **attitude.** The yawing and pitching effects of adding power should be counteracted with rudder pressure and forward pressure on the control column to stop the nose rising too far. Once the cruise speed is achieved, trim.

An easy way to remember this sequence is P–A–T, **power–attitude–trim.**

To Climb Away

To climb away from a descent, such as in a go-around, P–A–T still applies.

Climbing away hardly differs from levelling off, except that you:

- **smoothly apply full power** (mixture RICH, a silent '1-2-3' for correct timing, carburettor heat COLD); there will be a greater 'pitch/yaw' tendency which you can counteract with pressures on the rudder and control column.
- **hold the higher pitch attitude for climb,** maintaining climb airspeed; and
- **trim.**

Airmanship

Airmanship is knowing exactly where you are in the air, and keeping a good lookout.

Maintain a high visual awareness and clear the area under the nose every 500 ft or so in the descent. Maintain a listening watch on the radio if appropriate.

Remain very conscious of your height above the ground when descending. Set the altimeter subscale correctly so that you can level off exactly at the desired altitude. QNH will normally be set in training so that height **above mean sea level (amsl)** is displayed.

Airwork 8a
The Glide

Aim *To enter and maintain a steady glide on a constant heading and to level off at a particular height.*

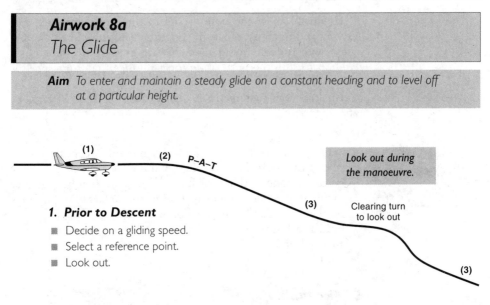

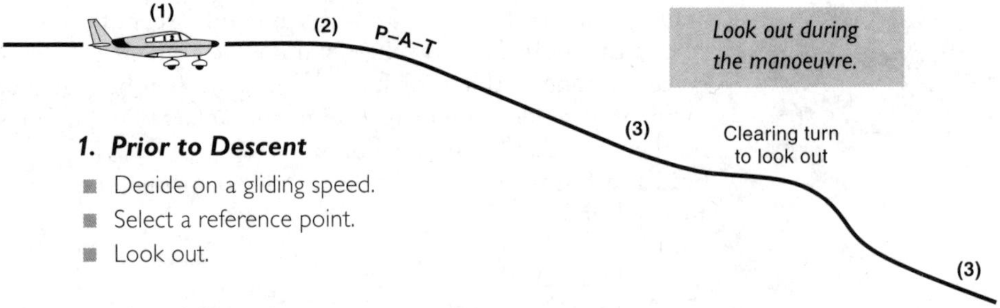

1. *Prior to Descent*

- Decide on a gliding speed.
- Select a reference point.
- Look out.

2. *To Commence a Glide*

Look out.

P – **power** off: mixture RICH, throttle CLOSED (carburettor heat HOT);
– balance with rudder;
– maintain height and allow speed to reduce to chosen gliding speed.

A – (when speed reached) lower nose to glide **attitude**;
– maintain airspeed with elevator.

T – **trim**.

■ ***1. Reduce power, maintain height.***

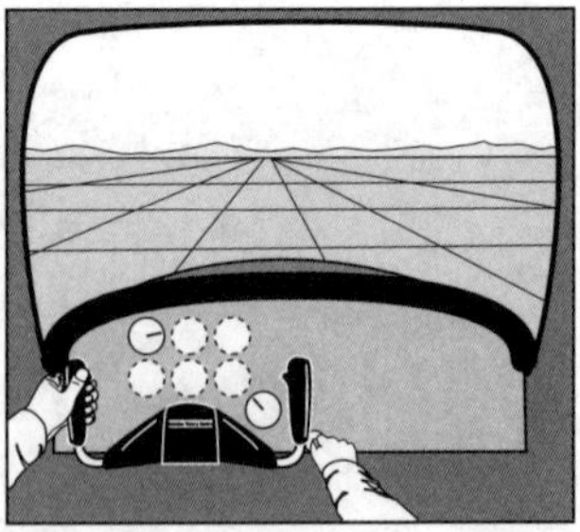

■ ***2. Select the glide attitude.***

■ ***3. Trim.***

Airwork 8a

3. To Maintain the Glide

- Look out – make clearing turns if necessary.
- Maintain:
  - wings level with ailerons;
  - balance with rudder pressure;
  - airspeed with elevator;
- Monitor engine instruments and warm engine periodically.

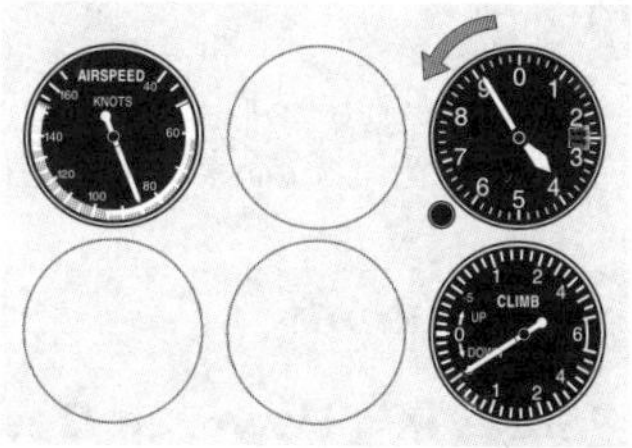
ASI
Monitor airspeed, and control it with elevator
Altimeter
Monitor descent
AIRSPEED
KNOTS
CLIMB
UP
VSI
Monitor descent

■ ***Do not attempt to stretch the glide by raising the nose. It will not work. Maintain gliding airspeed.***

4a. To Level Off

Look out.

Anticipate desired level-off height.

P – set cruise **power** with throttle (carb heat COLD);
– balance with rudder.

A – raise nose to straight and level **attitude**.

T – **trim**.

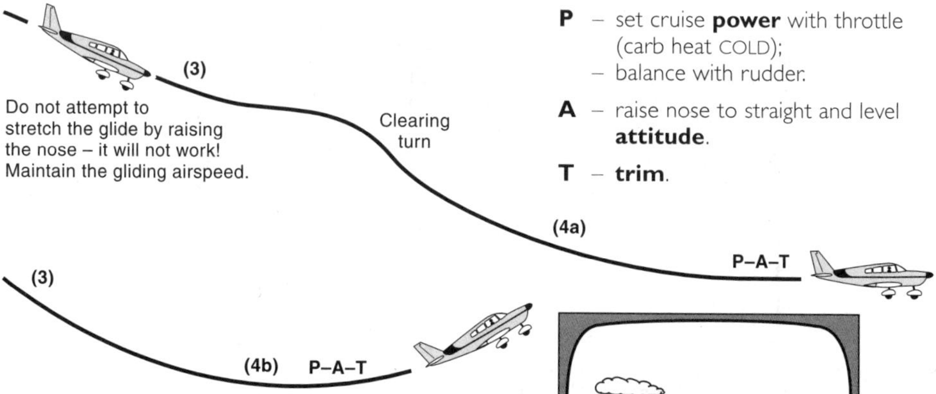
(3)
Do not attempt to stretch the glide by raising the nose – it will not work! Maintain the gliding airspeed.
Clearing turn
(4a)
P–A–T
(3)
(4b)
P–A–T

■ ***1. Set power.***

■ ***2. Set attitude.***

■ ***3. Trim.***

4b. To Establish a Climb from the Glide

P – apply climb **power** (as in step 4a).

A – set climb **attitude**.

T – **trim**.

Exercise 8b
The Powered Descent

Aim

To control the rate of descent and the flightpath using power, while maintaining a constant airspeed.

Considerations

The Forces in a Powered Descent

If power is applied in a descent, the resulting thrust will balance some of the drag. Consequently, the component of weight acting along the flightpath need not be as great for the same airspeed to be maintained. The pitch attitude will be higher and the rate of descent less, resulting in the descent being shallower.

The pitch attitude for a powered descent is not as low as for the glide.

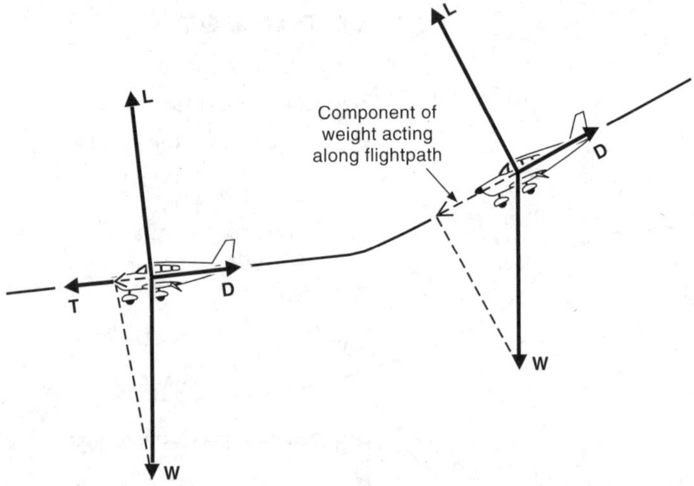

■ *Figure 8b-1* ***Adding power flattens the descent***

Performance

Power plus attitude equals performance. The performance achieved by an aeroplane depends both on the **power** selected and the **attitude.** To alter the rate of descent and the flightpath, while maintaining a constant airspeed, both power and attitude must be adjusted – power with the throttle and attitude with the control column. This is precisely what happens on a normal approach to land and on a cruise descent.

The **cruise descent** is used to save time, say at the end of a long cross-country flight, by commencing descent to the destination airfield from the cruise level some miles out by reducing the power slightly and lowering the nose to maintain the same speed as on the cruise.

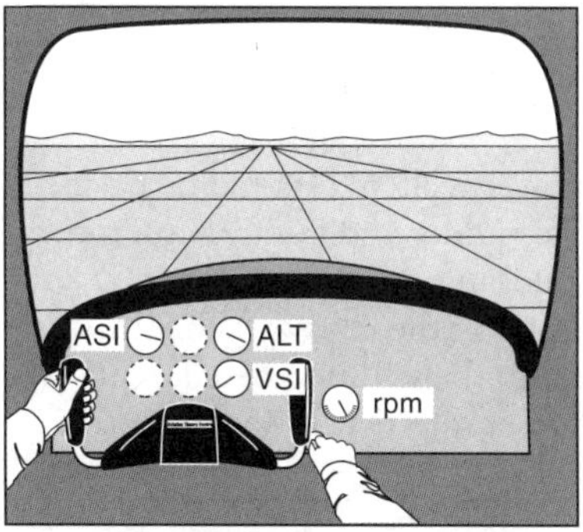

■ *Figure 8b-2* ***Control airspeed with elevator and rate of descent with power***

The Aiming Point

The aiming point on the ground during descent stays fixed in the windscreen.

A practical means of estimating where the descent would reach ground level is to note the particular ground feature which remains 'stationary' in the cockpit windscreen while a constant nose attitude is maintained. This becomes particularly important when you are on an approach to land, and adjusting your flight-path to arrive at the chosen aiming point on the runway.

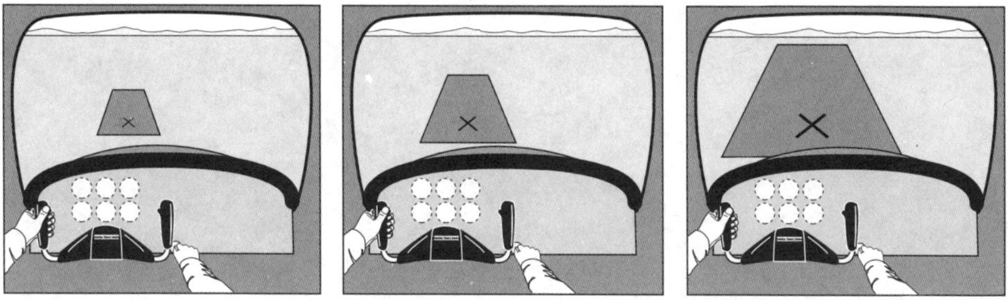

■ *Figure 8b-3* ***The aiming point stays 'fixed' in the windscreen***

Flying the Manoeuvre

You can monitor the rate of descent on:

- the vertical speed indicator; or with
- the altimeter and a clock.

To decrease the rate of descent and flatten the descent flightpath:
- increase power;
- raise the nose to maintain airspeed;
- trim.

To increase the rate of descent and steepen the descent path:
- decrease power;
- lower the nose to maintain airspeed;
- trim.

The pitch/yaw tendency as power is altered should be balanced with appropriate pressures on the rudder and control column.

On an approach to land, the pilot monitors the descent by constantly referencing the aiming point on the runway and estimating whether his flightpath will take him there. If not, he takes positive action with power and attitude to ensure that it does.

Airmanship

Take positive action to achieve the desired airspeed and rate of descent. If on approach to land, firmly control the airspeed and the flightpath.

Airmanship is positively controlling your flightpath and airspeed.

Consider the engine. Warm it periodically on a prolonged descent and use the carburettor heat as required.

Maintain a good visual awareness.

Airwork 8b
The Powered Descent

Aim *To control the rate of descent and the flightpath using power, while maintaining a constant airspeed.*

1. If the Descent Rate is Too High

- Add power with throttle – balance with rudder.
- Hold a higher nose attitude to maintain airspeed (monitor airspeed indicator: power + attitude = performance).
- Trim.

Rate of descent will decrease (monitor vertical speed indicator and altimeter), and the descent flightpath will be shallower (more distant ground aiming point).

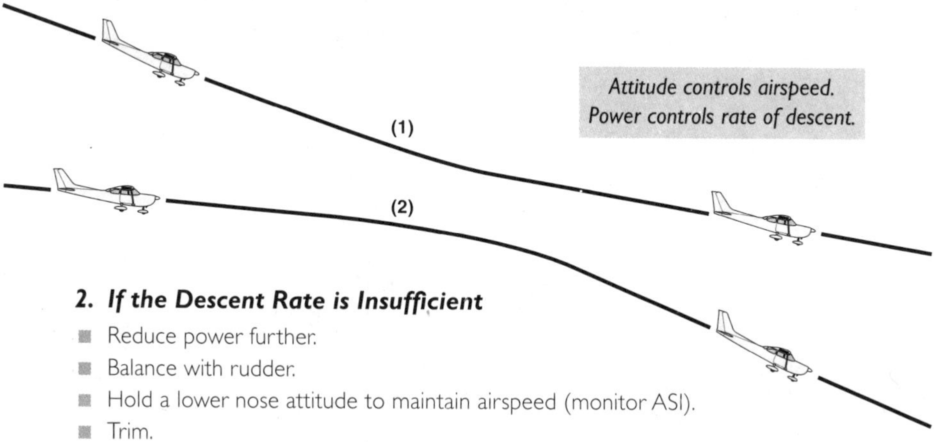
(1)
(2)
Attitude controls airspeed.
Power controls rate of descent.

2. If the Descent Rate is Insufficient

- Reduce power further.
- Balance with rudder.
- Hold a lower nose attitude to maintain airspeed (monitor ASI).
- Trim.

The rate of descent will increase (monitor VSI and altimeter), and the descent flightpath will steepen (closer ground aiming point).

ASI
VSI
rpm

■ **Descent attitude with higher power and lower rate of descent**

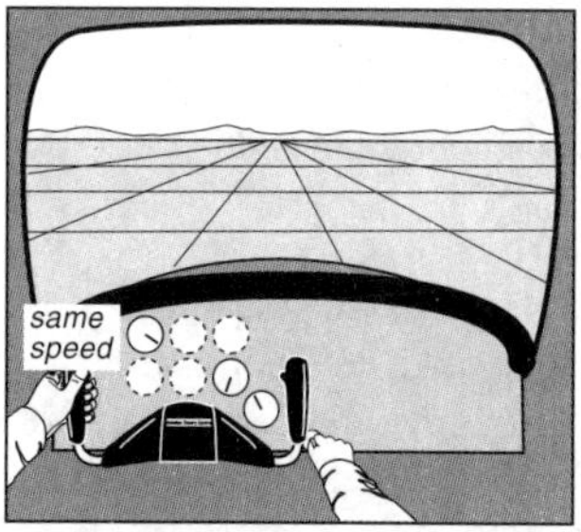
same
speed

■ **Descent attitude with less power and high rate of descent**

Exercise 8c
Use of Flap in the Descent

Aim

To use flap to steepen the descent.

Considerations

Flaps, Drag and Glide Angle

Extending the flaps causes a small increase in lift and a greater proportional increase in drag, i.e. the L/D ratio is decreased. If maintaining a constant airspeed in the glide, the flightpath will be progressively steeper following the extension of each stage of flap.

Flaps increase drag and steepen the glidepath.

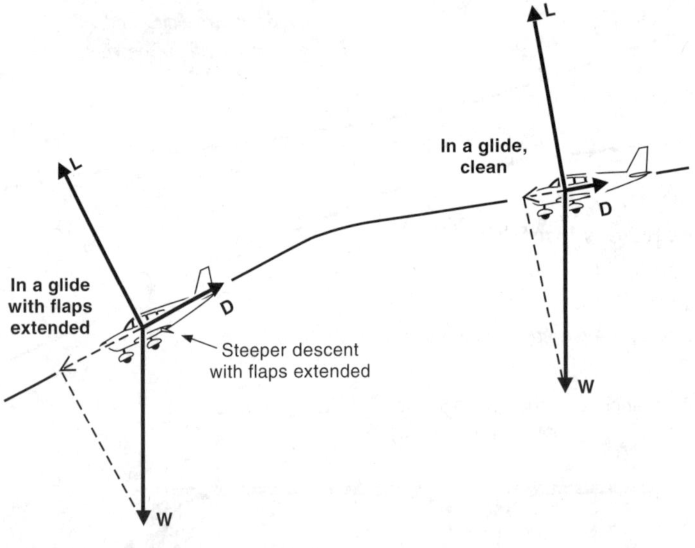

■ *Figure 8c-1* ***Flaps steepen the glide***

Nose Attitude

The increased drag as the flaps extend requires a lower pitch attitude if airspeed is to be maintained. The lower nose position affords a better view through the windscreen in a flapped descent. This is a significant advantage, especially on an approach to land. The greater the flap extension, the lower the nose position.

With flap extended, a lower nose attitude is required.

The desired airspeed is maintained by adjusting the pitch attitude with elevator, trimming off any steady control column pressure.

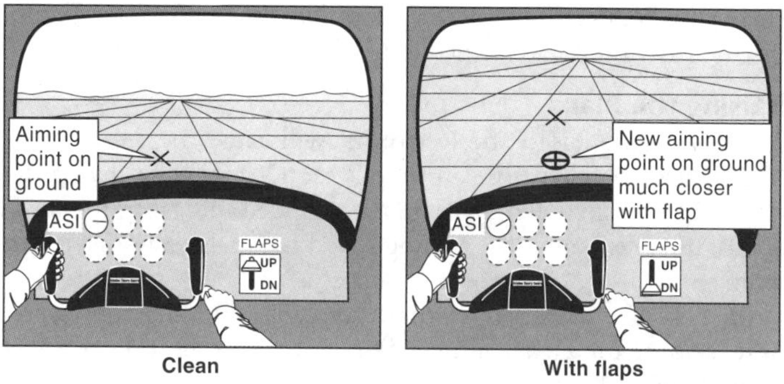

■ *Figure 8c-2* ***A lower nose attitude is required to maintain speed with flaps extended***

Stalling Speed

Flap lowers the stalling speed.

Extending the flaps alters the shape of the wing and increases its lifting ability. The stalling speed is reduced and so safe flight at a (slightly) lower airspeed is possible, retaining an adequate safety margin above the stall.

Flap Extension and Retraction

Operate the flaps at a suitable airspeed and be prepared for a pitch change.

As flap is lowered, the changing shape of the wing and the different aerodynamic forces produce extra stress on the airframe structure. For this reason, flap should only be extended when the airspeed does not exceed the maximum flap operating speed (known as V_{FE}).

The flap range is shown on the airspeed indicator as a white band. V_{FE} is at the high-speed end of this white arc; stalling speed with full flap extended and wings level is at the low-speed end (see Figure 10a-2).

There may be a pitching tendency as the flaps are lowered due to the centre of pressure (through which lift acts) moving its position fore or aft on the wing. This can be counteracted with movements of the control column to hold the desired nose attitude.

Flying the Manoeuvre

Extending the Flaps

With the aircraft established in a normal descent, check that the airspeed is below V_{FE} (i.e. in the white band). Extend the flaps in stages as required, holding the desired pitch attitude for each stage of flap and controlling the airspeed with elevator. Trim.

The more flap that is extended, the lower the required nose position. Retrimming will be required after each stage of flap is extended to relieve control column pressures. If the original airspeed is maintained, a higher rate of descent will occur. If the airspeed is reduced slightly (e.g. as on an approach to land), then the increase in the rate of descent will not be quite as much.

Raising the Flaps

As the flaps are raised, the loss of lift will cause the aeroplane to 'sink' unless a higher nose attitude is set. Do not raise the flaps at speeds below the green band on the airspeed indicator; the lower end of the green arc is the stalling speed wings-level with a 'clean' wing.

To raise the flaps, retract them in stages, holding the desired nose attitude for each configuration and controlling the airspeed with elevator. Trim.

The flaps are generally used on an approach to land, so it is not a common procedure to raise flap in a continued descent once having lowered it if the landing is to proceed. It is, however, necessary to raise the landing flap in a 'go-around' from a discontinued approach because the high drag would compromise the ability to climb out.

There is a very strong pitch-up tendency as maximum power is applied to go-around, and this has to be resisted with forward pressure on the control column.

Full flap generates too much drag for a good climb-away and should be retracted in stages at a safe speed. This very important manoeuvre (the go-around) is covered in detail in Exercise 13b.

Airmanship

Do not exceed the maximum speed for flap extension (V_{FE}) and do not raise flap at airspeeds below the 'clean' stalling speed.

Fly the aeroplane smoothly as flap is extended or raised; hold the desired pitch attitude, changing it smoothly as required when the flap position is changed.

Be aware of your airspeed.

Avoid ballooning as flap is lowered, and avoid sinking as flap is raised.

Airmanship is flying the aeroplane within its limitations.

Airwork 8c
Use of Flaps in the Descent

Aim *To extend the flaps in a descent.*

To Lower the Flaps

(a) Check at desired speed – speed must be definitely below maximum flap extension speed – $\mathbf{V_{FE}}$ (high-speed end of white band on ASI).

(b) Lower the flaps in stages.

(c) Hold a lower nose attitude and control airspeed with elevator.

(d) Trim off any steady elevator pressure.

Note the increased rate of descent resulting from the flap extension in the descent.

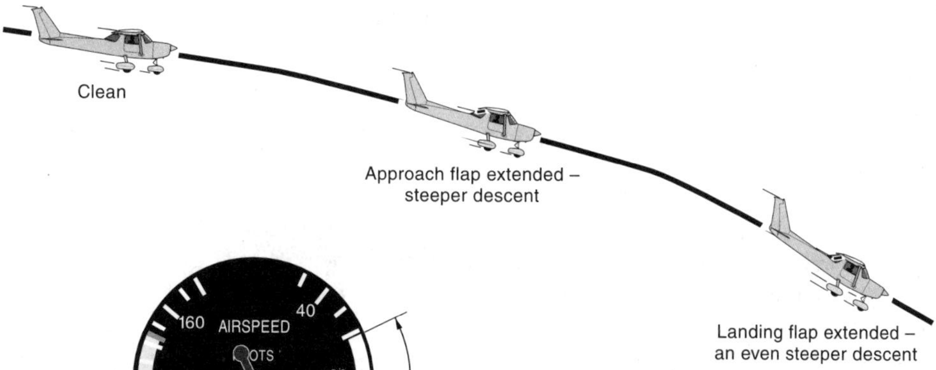

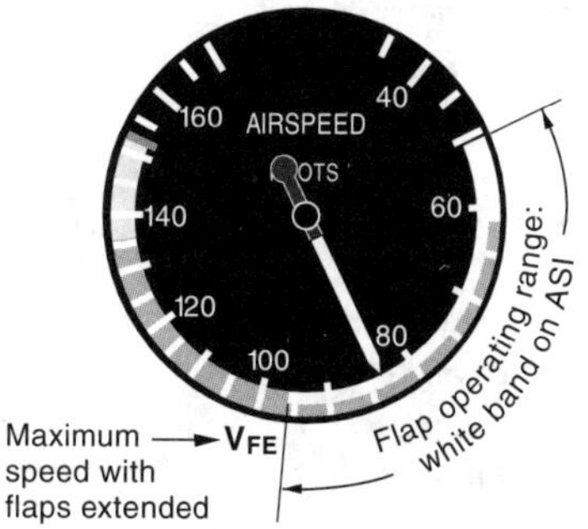

Exercise 8d
The Sideslip

Aim

To increase the rate of descent and steepen the descent flightpath at a constant airspeed by sideslipping using 'crossed controls' and without using flap.

Considerations

What is a Sideslip?

The sideslip is an out-of-balance flight condition. In days gone by, it was mainly used to steepen the glide without gaining airspeed in aeroplanes not fitted with flaps. A sideslip is an especially valuable manoeuvre when too high on an approach to land in such aeroplanes. Nowadays, of course, flap is generally used to increase the steepness of the flightpath.

When an aeroplane is banked using the ailerons alone, it will slip towards the lower wing and (due to its large keel surfaces, especially the fin) the nose will yaw towards the lowered wing. This yaw can be prevented by applying opposite rudder (sometimes referred to as 'top rudder'). If the bank is to the left, right rudder would be applied – the greater the bank angle, the greater the opposite rudder.

The aeroplane will be out of balance with the balance ball on the low wing side. You will have 'crossed controls' – the control column one way and the rudder the other. This is a sideslip.

A sideslip is flown with crossed controls.

Pitch attitude and airspeed control can be maintained with back pressure on the control column, but do not rely heavily on the airspeed indicator since it may not give a reliable reading due to the unusual airflow around the pitot tube and static vent(s) in a sideslip.

A Sideslip Steepens the Descent

Presenting the wing-down side of the aeroplane to the airflow causes a large increase in drag and therefore the L/D ratio is significantly decreased. This causes the rate of descent to increase, resulting in a steeper flightpath. The greater the bank angle and top rudder used, the steeper the descent.

Aircraft Limitations

The sideslipping manoeuvre is restricted for some aeroplanes when flap is extended. This is to avoid high rates of descent developing and situations where the elevator and rudder, which are used in the sideslip, lose their effectiveness through 'blanketing' of the airflow over them. The aeroplane Flight Manual or the Pilot's Operating Handbook will contain this restriction if it applies. There may also be a placard in the aeroplane itself.

Sideslipping is not an approved manoeuvre for all aeroplanes.

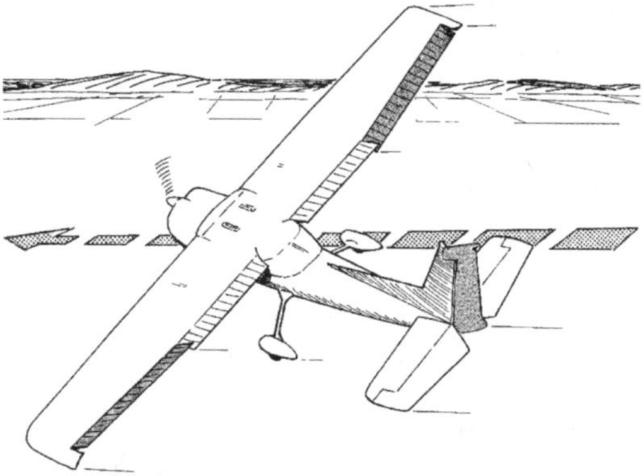

■ *Figure 8d-1* ***The sideslip***

Flying the Manoeuvre

To Enter a Sideslip

To enter a sideslip, ensure that you have adequate height above the ground to recover, since a high rate of descent can be achieved in a sideslip. Close the throttle, bank the aeroplane and apply opposite rudder to stop the yaw. The nose may want to drop and back pressure on the control column may be required. Do not trim, since sideslipping is a transient manoeuvre.

To Maintain a Sideslip

To maintain the sideslip, maintain the bank angle with ailerons and control the heading with opposite rudder. The greater the bank angle and rudder used, the steeper the flightpath. Airspeed is controlled with the elevator, but bear in mind that the airspeed indicator may be unreliable.

To Recover from a Sideslip

To recover from a sideslip, level the wings with ailerons and centralise the balance ball by removing the excess rudder pressure. Resume a normal, in-balance descent.

Airmanship

Maintain a good visual awareness of other aircraft and your proximity to the ground due to the very high descent rates. Do not sideslip in non-approved configurations.

Airwork 8d
The Sideslip

Aim *To increase rate of descent and steepen the descent flightpath at a constant airspeed by sideslipping using 'crossed controls' and without using flap.*

1. *To Enter the Sideslip*

From a normal descent:

- Apply bank with ailerons.
- Maintain heading with coarse use of opposite rudder.
- Hold nose attitude and maintain airspeed with elevator.

2. *To Maintain the Sideslip*

- Maintain bank angle with ailerons – (the steeper the bank, the greater the rate of descent).
- Control heading with opposite rudder.
- Maintain airspeed with elevator.

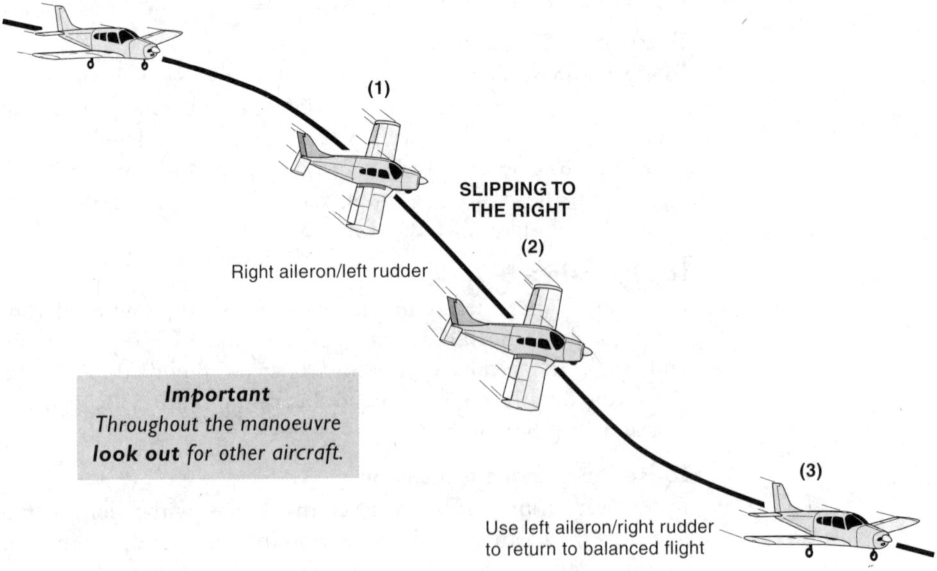

Important
Throughout the manoeuvre ***look out*** *for other aircraft.*

3. *To Remove the Sideslip*

- Level wings with aileron.
- Remove opposite rudder – balance normally.
- Maintain desired airspeed with elevator.

Exercise 9a
The Medium Level Turn

Aim

To enter, maintain and roll out of a medium level turn, using constant power.

Considerations

What is a Medium Level Turn?

A medium level turn is a turn performed:

- **at a constant height;** with
- **a medium angle of bank** (30° or less);
- **at constant power;** and
- **in balance.**

Apart from the medium level turn, other turns which you will master in the course of your training are:

- **climbing turns;**
- **descending turns;**
- **rate 1 turns** (a rate of turn to achieve 360° in 2 minutes);
- **steep turns** (bank angle 45° or greater).

The Forces in a Turn

A turn is achieved by banking the aeroplane.

Banking the aeroplane tilts the lift, which provides a horizontal turning force (known as the *centripetal force*). Since there is no other horizontal force to counteract it, the aeroplane is no longer in equilibrium and will be pulled into a turn. The greater the bank angle, the greater the turning force.

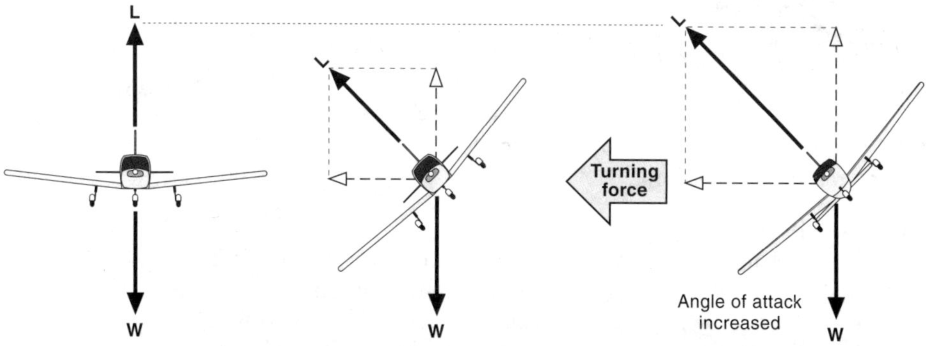

■ *Figure 9a-1* ***Banking an aeroplane creates a turning force***

Maintaining Altitude

Tilting the lift reduces its vertical component which will result in a height loss unless the pilot increases the lift generated by the wings. By applying the correct amount of back pressure on the control column as the aeroplane is banked, a vertical component of the lift sufficient to balance the weight can be retained.

To maintain altitude in a level turn, you must apply back pressure to increase the lift.

Airspeed

Airspeed tends to decrease in a turn, due to increased drag. The lift is increased by increasing the angle of attack, which also results in increased induced drag. As a consequence of this **increased drag,** the aeroplane will tend to slow down, usually by 5 kt or so in a medium level turn. At normal flight speeds, this small airspeed loss at medium bank angles is acceptable.

Airspeed decreases in a turn.

Stalling Speed

The stalling speed increases in a turn. The wings are at a higher angle of attack in a turn than when the aeroplane is flying straight at the same speed. They carry an extra load (i.e. they generate increased lift) and so experience a **higher load factor.** The stalling angle will therefore be reached at a higher speed in a turn than when straight and level. It is about 7% higher in a 30° banked turn, increasing a stall speed of 50 kt to 54 kt.

Stall speed increases in a turn.

For medium level turns at normal flight speeds, the small drop in airspeed (due to the increased drag) still allows an adequate speed range for safe flight above the new and slightly increased stalling speed.

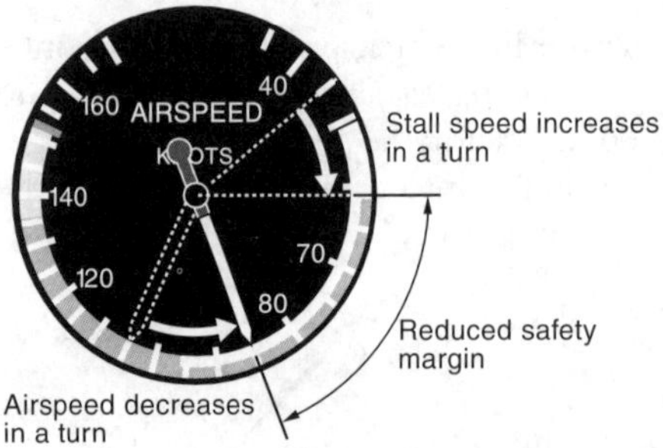

■ *Figure 9a-2* ***Airspeed decreases and stalling speed increases in a level turn***

Bank Angle

Estimate the bank angle using the natural horizon. A specific bank angle can be flown quite accurately by estimating the angle between the nose cowl of the aeroplane and the natural horizon. This is referred to as the **bank attitude.** It can be verified in the cockpit on the attitude indicator using either the angle between the index aeroplane and the artificial horizon, or by using the bank pointer at the top of the instrument.

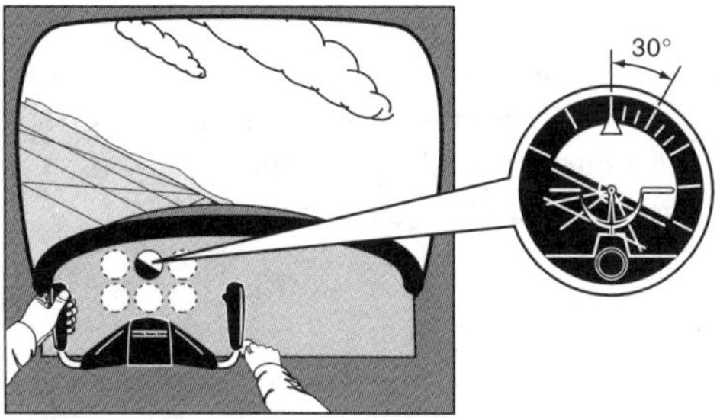

■ Figure 9a-3 **Estimate the bank angle**

Pitch Attitude

The pitch attitude is higher in a level turn.

Lift is increased in a turn by applying back pressure on the control column to increase the angle of attack. For this reason, the nose attitude of the aeroplane will be higher in a level turn than when flying straight and level.

Estimating the correct pitch attitude against the natural horizon requires a little experience, especially if you are flying in a side-by-side cockpit, as is the case in most modern training aeroplanes. The pitch attitude for a given bank angle and airspeed will be correct if the aeroplane neither gains nor loses height.

Nose Cowl and the Horizon

The nose cowl/horizon relationship appears different in left and right turns.

These remarks apply to a side-by-side cockpit. **In a left turn,** the pilot in the left seat will be on the low side of the aeroplane's longitudinal axis and the position of the centre of the nose cowl will appear to be higher relative to the natural horizon. Conversely, **when turning right,** the centre of the nose cowl should appear lower against the horizon. After one or two turns left and right, you should have these attitudes fixed in your mind.

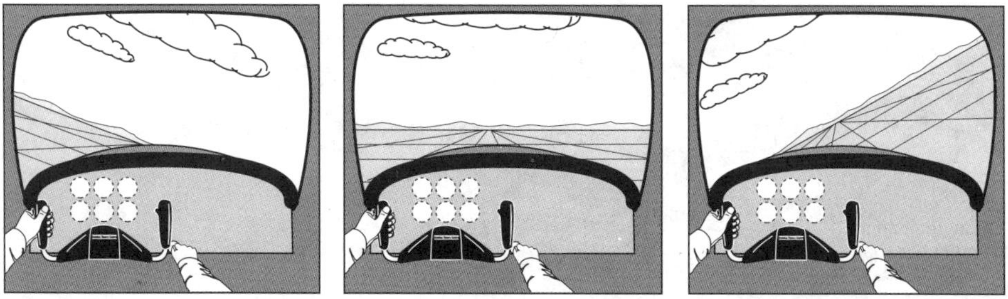

■ Figure 9a-4 **Different nose positions for left and right turns**

Turning Performance

The two aspects of turning performance are:

- **the rate at which the heading changes;** and
- **the radius of the turn** (its 'tightness').

Turning performance increases at steeper bank angles. The steeper the bank angle (for a constant airspeed), the better the turning performance – the rate of heading change increasing and the radius of turn decreasing as bank angle is increased.

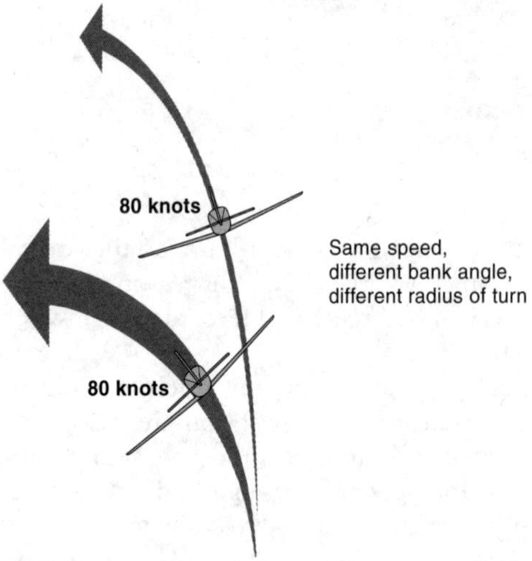

■ *Figure 9a-5* ***A steep bank angle increases turning performance***

Turning performance increases at lower airspeeds. For the same bank angle, a lower airspeed will give a smaller radius of turn and a greater rate of heading change.

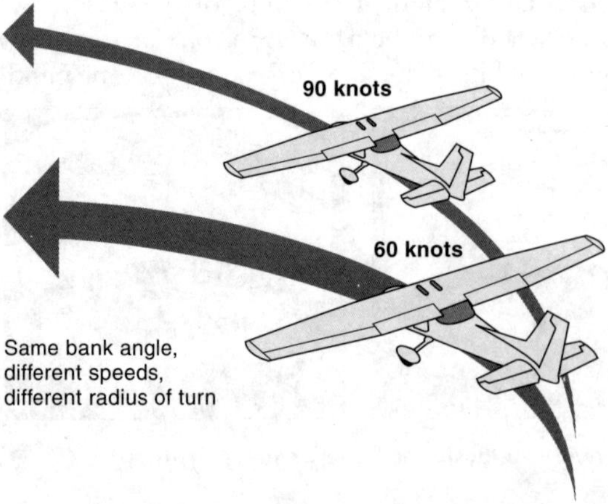

■ *Figure 9a-6* ***Turning performance is increased at low airspeeds***

Rate 1 Turns

Changing heading at **3° per second** is known as a **rate 1 turn** and is marked on the turn coordinator (or turn indicator). It is the *standard rate of turn* commonly used in instrument flying (IF) and will achieve a turn of 180° in 1 minute or 360° in 2 minutes (hence the label '2 MIN' shown on many turn coordinators).

■ *Figure 9a-7* ***Rate 1 turn indications***

To achieve rate 1 turning performance at different airspeeds, different bank angles will be required. These are easily estimated using a simple rule of thumb:

Divide the airspeed by 10, and add one-half the answer.

EXAMPLES:

- **At 80 knots,** to achieve a rate 1 turn: bank angle = 80/10 (which is 8) + one-half of 8 (which is 4) = 8 + 4 = 12°.
- **At 100 knots,** bank angle = 100/10 (10) + one-half of 10 (5) = 10 + 5= 15°.
- **At 120 knots,** required bank angle is (12 + 6) = 18°.
- **At 150 knots,** required bank angle is 22°.

The estimate gives you a target bank angle to achieve a rate 1 turn, which can be verified in the turn by checking either:

- **the turn coordinator** (or turn indicator); or
- **the heading indicator** and **clock** combined.

Overbanking

There is a tendency to overbank in a level turn.

The higher speed of the outer wing in a level turn will create extra lift on that wing, which tends to increase the bank angle. There is no need for you to be particularly conscious of this – simply maintain the desired bank angle using the control column.

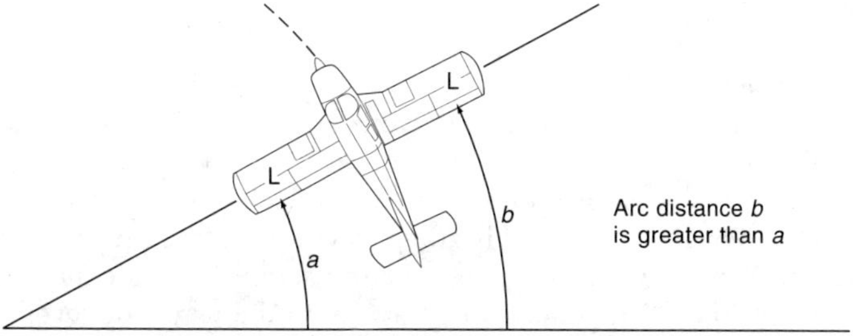

■ *Figure 9a-8* ***There is a tendency to overbank in a level turn***

Flying the Manoeuvre

Trim the Aeroplane

Be in trim before entering a turn.

Unless an immediate turn is necessary, trimming the aeroplane properly for steady, straight and level flight makes it easier to maintain height before and after the turn. Do not trim during the turn since it is only a transient manoeuvre.

There is no need to trim during a turn.

Prior to applying bank, glance at the cockpit instruments and ensure that you are flying at the desired:

- **indicated airspeed;** and
- **altitude** (altimeter reading desired height; VSI zero, or fluctuating about zero, indicating no tendency to climb or descend).

Scanning for Traffic

Always look out and clear the area.

Develop a thorough scanning technique from side to side and both up and down before turning, remembering that aeroplanes move in three dimensions.

A good sky-scanning technique is:

- **first look in the direction of turn,** raising/lowering the wing to give you a view above and below;
- **look in the direction opposite to the turn** and as far behind as cockpit vision allows; then
- **commence a steady scan** from that side of the windscreen both up and down until you are again looking in the direction of turn.

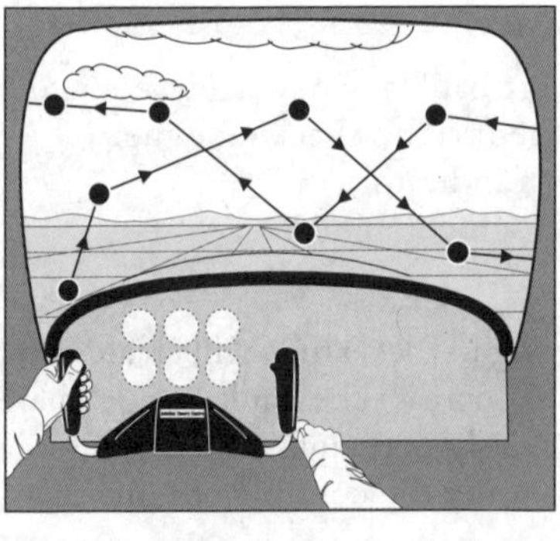

■ *Figure 9a-9* ***A suitable scan before a left turn***

Reference Point

Select a reference point on which to roll out.

While scanning for other aircraft, you can note visible landmarks helpful for orientation (i.e. knowing where you are). Select a landmark as a reference point on which to roll out following the turn. Anticipate the desired heading by commencing the roll-out about 10° prior to reaching it, since the aeroplane will continue turning (although at a decreasing rate) until the wings are level.

The Controls

Control bank angle with ailerons.

ROLL INTO THE TURN with a coordinated use of 'stick and rudder'. Apply bank with ailerons and balance with same-side rudder pressure (keeping the ball in the centre). Back pressure on the control column will be needed to maintain height, which can be checked on the altimeter and VSI. Estimate the bank angle against the horizon, checking it on the attitude indicator if desired.

Hold altitude with elevator.

TO MAINTAIN THE TURN, control the bank angle with ailerons, balance with rudder and height with elevator. Do not forget to look out for other aircraft. **If gaining height,** either the bank angle is too shallow or the back pressure is too great – increase bank angle and/or lower the nose. **If losing height,** either the bank angle is too steep or the back pressure is insufficient – decrease bank angle and/or raise the nose.

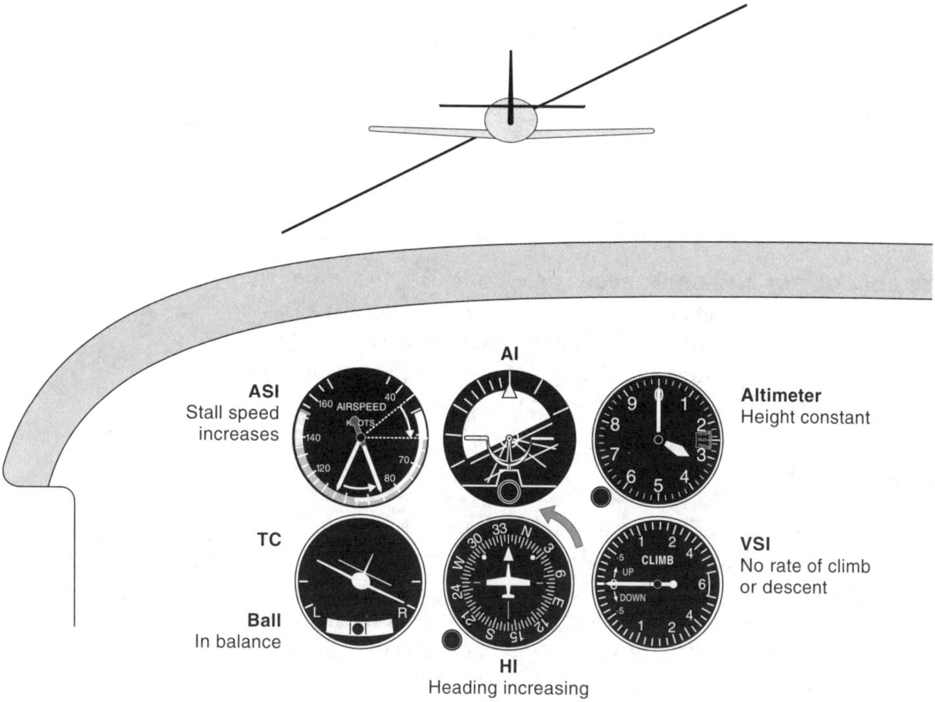

■ *Figure 9a-10* ***Flight instrument indications in a medium level turn***

Keep the ball centred with rudder pressure.

KEEP IN BALANCE using rudder pressure. Rolling right requires more right rudder pressure, rolling left requires more left rudder pressure. The balance ball indicates the precise balance of the aeroplane – if the ball is out to the right, more right rudder is needed (and vice versa). Aim to keep the ball centred throughout the turning manoeuvre.

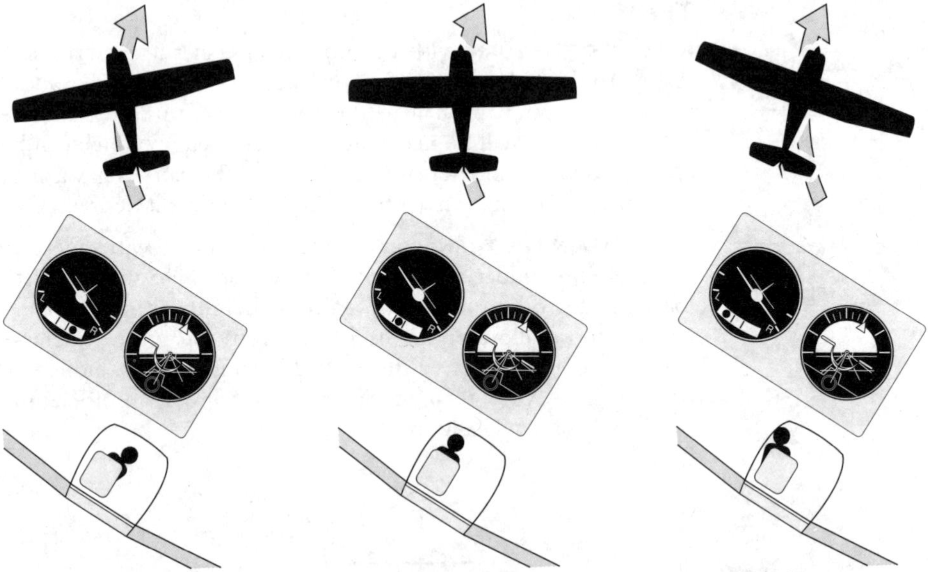
Slipping turn
Pilot slips into turn – more right rudder required to balance the turn
Balanced turn
Skidding turn
Pilot skids out of turn – too much right rudder has been applied

■ *Figure 9a-11* ***Keep the aeroplane in balance with rudder pressure***

TO ROLL OUT OF A MEDIUM LEVEL TURN, anticipate reaching the reference point by about 10° and start removing bank with aileron, balancing with same-side rudder pressure. Gradually release the back pressure and lower the nose to the straight and level position. Adjust the heading and height as required.

Airmanship

Remain aware of landmarks and keep yourself orientated with respect to the airfield.Your aeroplane will be changing heading in a turn, so maintain a good **lookout.**

Airmanship is scanning the sky before beginning a turn.

Since a constant power will be set, you can concentrate on placing the nose just exactly where you want it on the horizon. Become familiar with these attitudes for both left and right turns. Do not trim in the turn since it is only a transient manoeuvre. Develop an awareness of balance and use rudder pressure to keep the ball in the centre at all times. Aim for smoothly coordinated use of controls.

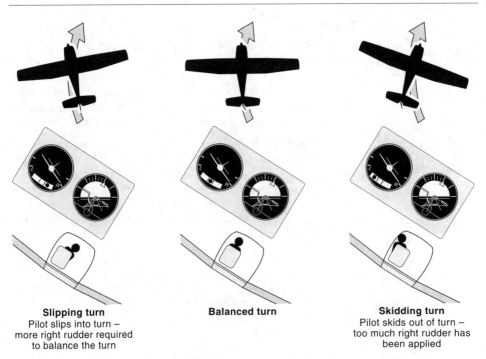

Airwork 9a
The Medium Level Turn

Aim *To enter, maintain and roll out of a medium level turn, using constant power.*

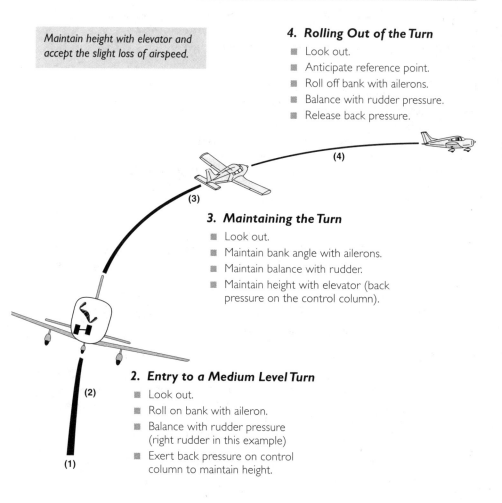

Maintain height with elevator and accept the slight loss of airspeed.

4. Rolling Out of the Turn

- Look out.
- Anticipate reference point.
- Roll off bank with ailerons.
- Balance with rudder pressure.
- Release back pressure.

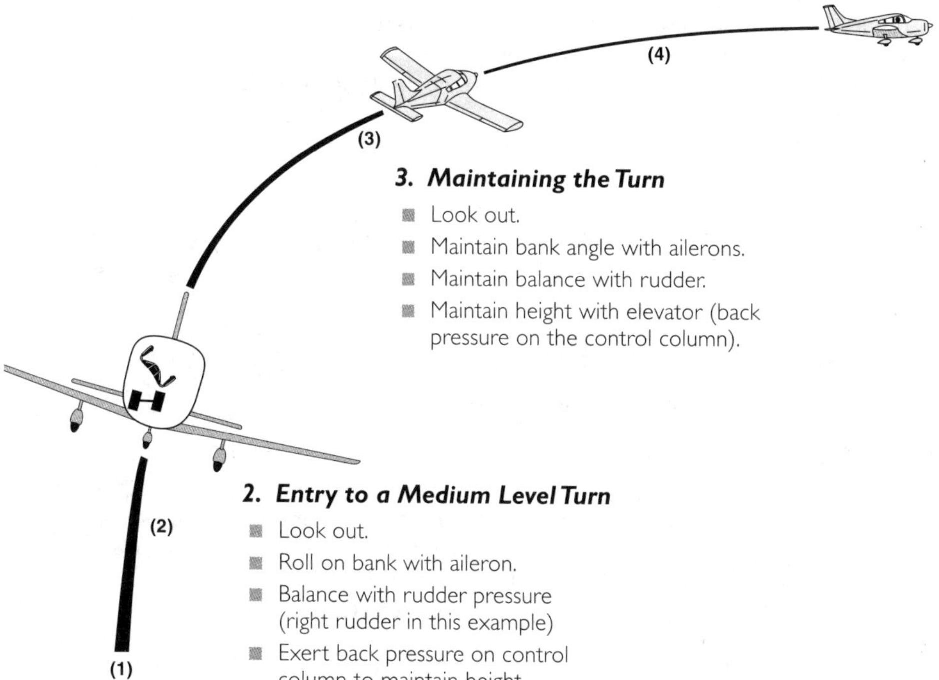

3. Maintaining the Turn

- Look out.
- Maintain bank angle with ailerons.
- Maintain balance with rudder.
- Maintain height with elevator (back pressure on the control column).

2. Entry to a Medium Level Turn

- Look out.
- Roll on bank with aileron.
- Balance with rudder pressure (right rudder in this example)
- Exert back pressure on control column to maintain height.

1. Prior to Entry

- At desired height and airspeed.
- In trim.
- Look out for other aircraft.
- Select reference point for roll out.

NOTE Trim is not used during this transient manoeuvre.

START HERE

Exercise 9b
The Climbing Turn

Aim

To change heading while climbing at a constant airspeed.

Considerations

The Forces in a Climbing Turn

The forces in a climbing turn are similar to those in a straight climb except that, because the lift is tilted to turn the aeroplane, its contribution to supporting the weight is reduced. The result is a decreased climb performance (reduced rate of climb) if airspeed is maintained.

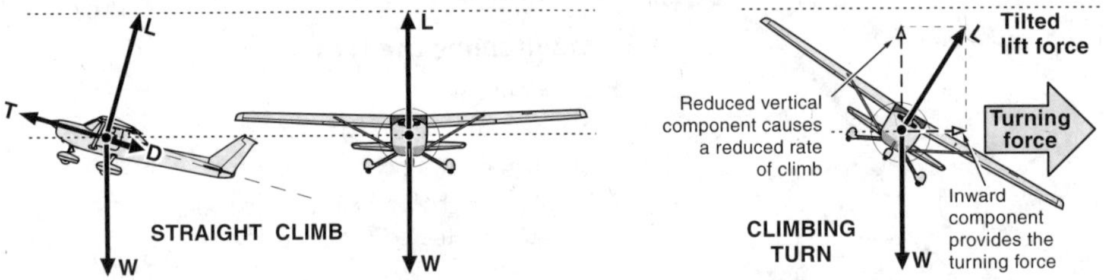

■ *Figure 9b-1* ***A straight climb and a climbing turn***

Rate of Climb

The rate of climb decreases in a climbing turn.

The rate of climb depends on the excess power, i.e. the amount of power available in excess of that required to overcome the drag. Tilting of the lift and the increased drag in a climbing turn reduces the excess power available for climb performance. The result is a decreased rate of climb in a turn, as indicated on the vertical speed indicator and the altimeter.

Limit the bank angle in a climbing turn.

The steeper the bank angle in a climbing turn, the poorer the rate of climb. To retain a reasonable rate of climb, the bank angle in climbing turns should be limited to 15° or 20°.

Airspeed

Maintain airspeed in a climbing turn by lowering the nose.

Climb performance depends on the correct climb speed being flown with climb power set. For many training aeroplanes, climb power is maximum power, so the tendency to lose airspeed cannot be overcome by adding extra power (since there is no more). To maintain the correct climb speed in a turn it is therefore necessary to lower the nose.

There is a natural tendency for the nose to drop too far as bank is applied in a climbing turn, but this can be checked with slight back pressure on the control column. Hold the desired pitch attitude with elevator and monitor the airspeed with an occasional glance at the airspeed indicator.

■ *Figure 9b-2* ***Maintain airspeed in a climbing turn by lowering the nose***

Slipstream Effect

Keep the ball centred with rudder pressure.

Most aeroplanes are designed so that slipstream effect is balanced at cruise speed with cruise power set. Climbs are carried out with high power at an airspeed less than the cruise, with the result that steady rudder pressure is usually required to balance the slipstream effect on the tail.

The usual rules for maintaining balance apply, no matter what the manoeuvre involved, i.e. move the balance ball back into the centre with same-side rudder pressure. The balance ball tells you which rudder pressure is needed.

Overbanking

Control bank angle with ailerons.

The higher speed and greater angle of attack of the outer wing in a climbing turn creates a tendency for the bank angle to increase. Bank may have to be held-off in a climbing turn, but this will occur naturally as you monitor the bank angle against the horizon.

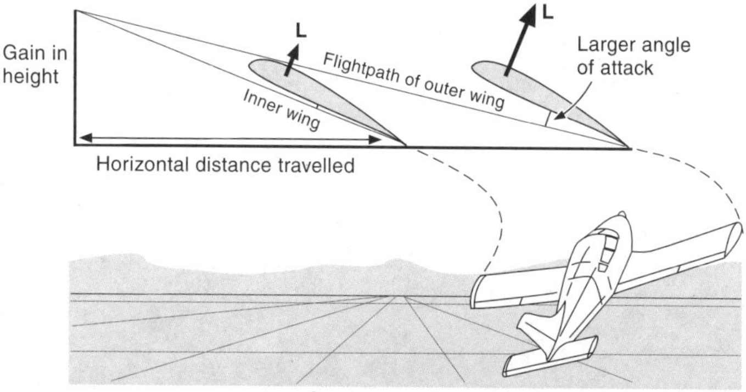

■ *Figure 9b-3* ***There is an overbanking tendency in a climbing turn***

Flying the Manoeuvre

To enter a climbing turn, establish the aeroplane in a straight climb at the desired airspeed and in trim. **Look out** and **select a reference point** on which to roll out. Roll into the turn by applying bank in the direction of turn, using sufficient rudder to keep the ball in the centre. Limit the turn to 15–20° bank angle and hold the nose in a slightly lower position to maintain airspeed.

To maintain the climbing turn, control bank angle with ailerons, balance with rudder pressure and maintain the desired airspeed with nose attitude. Keep a constant airspeed throughout the climbing turn, even though the rate of climb will decrease. Continue a steady lookout.

To roll out of a climbing turn, commence removing the bank some 10° before reaching your reference point. Roll off bank with aileron, balance with rudder pressure and raise the nose to the normal climb attitude. Level the wings and keep the balance ball centred, adjusting the heading and airspeed as required.

Airmanship

Limit the bank to 15–20° and maintain a constant airspeed with elevator. Exert firm, positive and smooth control over the aeroplane. Maintain a **lookout.**

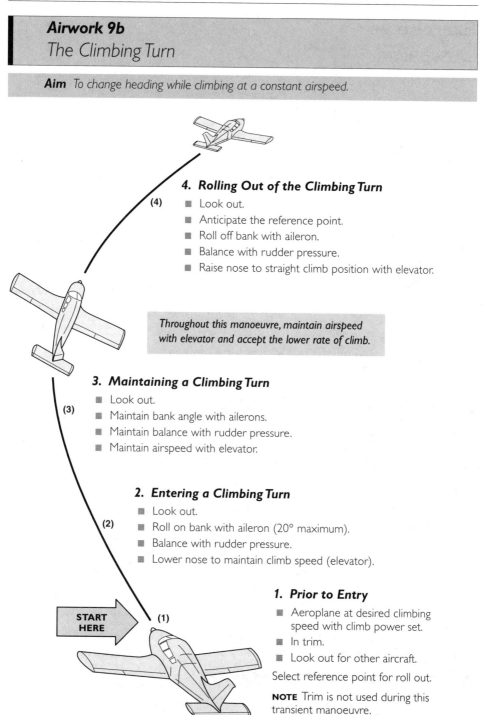

Airwork 9b
The Climbing Turn

Aim *To change heading while climbing at a constant airspeed.*

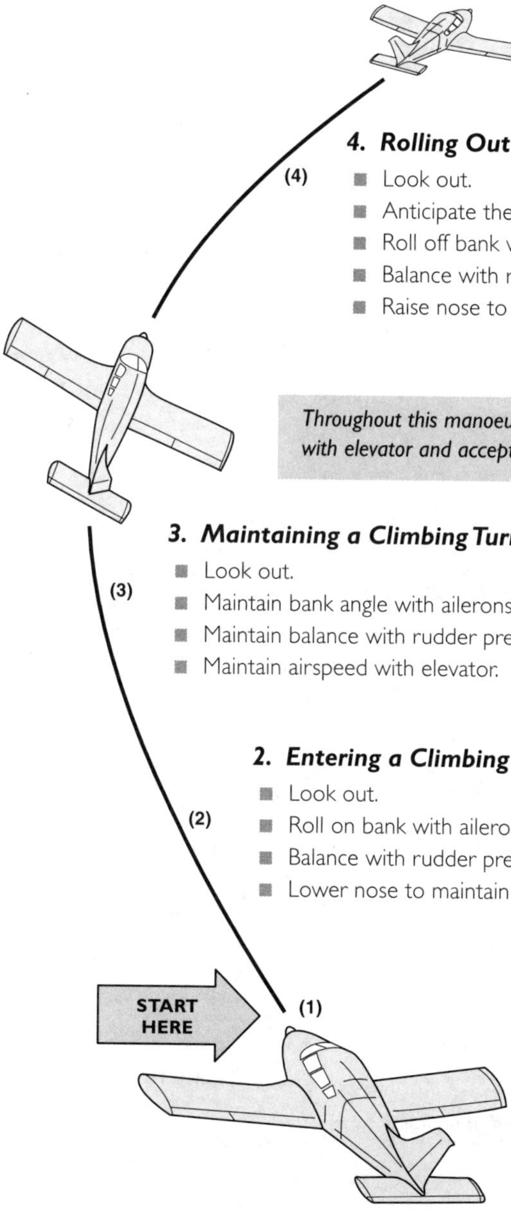

4. Rolling Out of the Climbing Turn

- Look out.
- Anticipate the reference point.
- Roll off bank with aileron.
- Balance with rudder pressure.
- Raise nose to straight climb position with elevator.

Throughout this manoeuvre, maintain airspeed with elevator and accept the lower rate of climb.

3. Maintaining a Climbing Turn

- Look out.
- Maintain bank angle with ailerons.
- Maintain balance with rudder pressure.
- Maintain airspeed with elevator.

2. Entering a Climbing Turn

- Look out.
- Roll on bank with aileron (20° maximum).
- Balance with rudder pressure.
- Lower nose to maintain climb speed (elevator).

1. Prior to Entry

- Aeroplane at desired climbing speed with climb power set.
- In trim.
- Look out for other aircraft.

Select reference point for roll out.

NOTE Trim is not used during this transient manoeuvre.

Exercise 9c
Descending Turns

The four types of descending turn covered are:

(i) The gliding turn.

(ii) The descending turn using power.

(iii) The descending turn with flap extended.

(iv) Sideslipping in a descending turn.

Part (i)
The Gliding Turn

Aim

To enter, maintain and roll out of a gliding turn, while maintaining airspeed.

Considerations

The Forces in a Gliding Turn

The forces acting on an aeroplane in a gliding turn are similar to those in a straight glide, except that the aeroplane is banked and the lift is tilted.

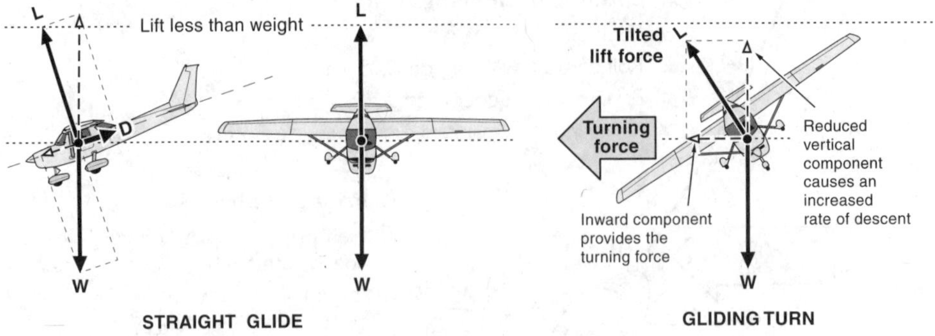

■ *Figure 9c-1* ***The forces in a straight glide and in a gliding turn***

Banking the aeroplane to create a turning force:

- **reduces the amount of lift** available to oppose the weight force – resulting in an **increased rate of descent** and a steeper glide; and
- **increases the drag** – resulting in a tendency to **decrease the airspeed** (undesirable since an aeroplane's stalling speed increases in a turn).

Airspeed

Maintain airspeed in a gliding turn by lowering the nose.

The increased drag in a turn will tend to decrease airspeed, so, to maintain the desired airspeed in a gliding turn, the nose should be held in a lower attitude.

As in all turns, there will be a tendency for the nose to drop, requiring back pressure to stop it dropping too far. Simply hold the attitude that gives the desired airspeed. For side-by-side cockpits, the position of the nose cowl relative to the horizon will differ for left and right turns.

■ *Figure 9c-2* ***Entering a gliding turn, lower the nose to maintain airspeed***

Rate of Descent

The rate of descent in a glide increases in a turn.

Tilting of the lift in a gliding turn, and the lower nose position to maintain airspeed, result in an increased rate of descent and a steeper flightpath. The steeper the turn, the greater the effect, so be careful near the ground!

Limit the rate of descent in a gliding turn by restricting the bank angle. In a gliding approach to land, the turn to join final 500 ft above aerodrome level (aal) should be flown at about 20° and certainly should not exceed 30°.

Overbanking

Hold desired bank angle with aileron.

Two effects tend to cancel each other out in descending turns, both when gliding and when using power. They are:

- **an overbanking tendency** due to the outer wing travelling faster; and
- **an underbanking tendency** due to the inner wing in a descending turn having a higher angle of attack.

There is no need to be conscious of this when flying – simply maintain the desired bank angle with aileron.

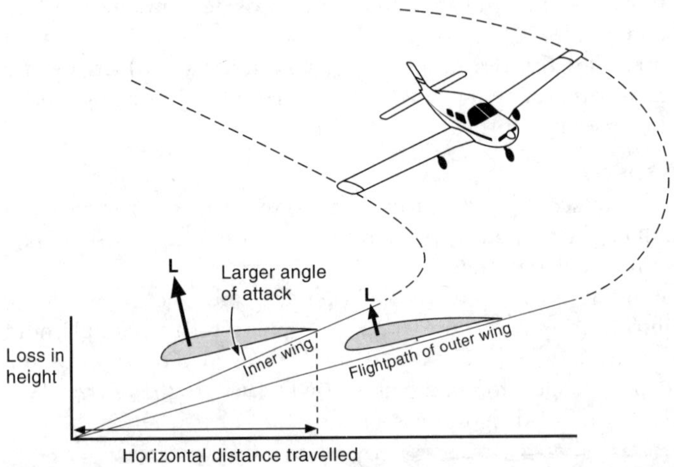

■ *Figure 9c-3* **There is less tendency to overbank in a descending turn**

Slipstream Effect

Keep the ball centred with rudder pressure.

Most aeroplanes are designed to be in balance and require no rudder pressure when cruising. In a glide (in which there is no slipstream effect) rudder pressure may be required for balance, i.e. to keep the balance ball in the centre.

For an aeroplane fitted with a propeller that rotates clockwise as seen from the cockpit, the lack of slipstream effect in the glide will require steady left rudder pressure. If the aeroplane has a rudder trim, then make use of it to relieve this steady pressure. Normal balance rules apply. If the ball is out to the left, apply left rudder pressure. Left rudder pressure should be increased when rolling left in a descent and decreased when rolling right.

Engine Temperature

Keep the engine warm in a prolonged glide.

As in a normal straight glide, apply power from time to time if the gliding turn is prolonged. This will keep the engine and its oil supply warm and clear any spark plug fouling that may have built up while the engine was idling in the glide.

Flying the Manoeuvre

To enter a gliding turn, establish the aeroplane in a straight glide at the desired airspeed and in trim. Look out for other aircraft and select a reference point on which to roll out. Roll into the turn with aileron and apply sufficient rudder pressure to keep the balance ball centred.

Lower the nose slightly to maintain airspeed (back pressure may be required to stop it dropping too far). Do not exceed a bank angle of 30°.

To maintain the gliding turn, control bank angle with aileron, balance with rudder pressure and airspeed with elevator. Accept the higher rate of descent and maintain the desired airspeed. Keep a good lookout.

To roll out of the gliding turn, anticipate reaching the reference point by 10° or so and commence removing bank with aileron, balancing with rudder pressure. Hold the nose in the straight glide attitude (slightly higher than in the turn). Level the wings and then make minor adjustments to maintain the desired heading and airspeed.

Airmanship

Airmanship is keeping a good lookout in descending turns, and being very aware of your height above the ground.

Maintain a good **lookout** – especially important in any turn. Be aware of your altitude, since descent rates in descending turns can be high. Maintain airspeed with elevator and exert firm, positive and smooth control over the aeroplane. There is no need to trim, since the turn is a transient manoeuvre.

Airwork 9c, Part (i)
The Gliding Turn

Aim *To enter, maintain and roll out of a gliding turn, while maintaining airspeed.*

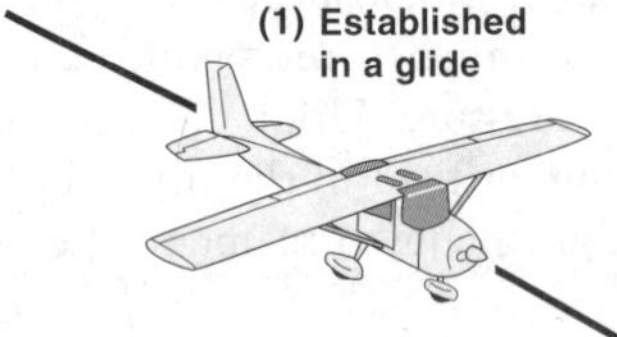

1. *Prior to Entry*

- At desired descent speed.
- In trim.
- Look out for other aircraft.
- Select reference point for roll out.

2. *Entry to a Gliding Turn*

- Look out.
- Roll on bank with aileron (30° maximum).
- Balance with rudder pressure.
- Lower nose to maintain descent speed (elevator).

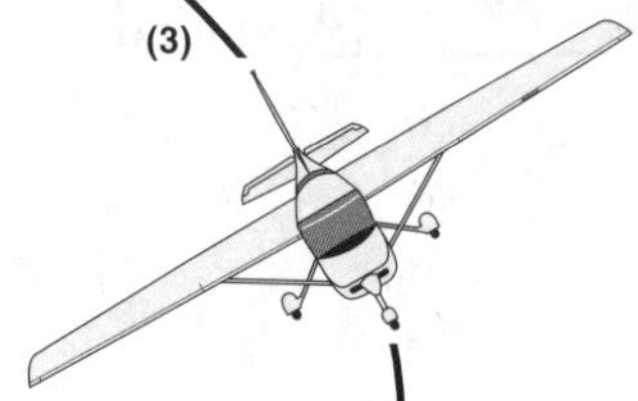

3. *Maintaining a Gliding Turn*

- Look out.
- Maintain bank angle with ailerons.
- Maintain balance with rudder.
- Maintain airspeed with elevator.

4. *Rolling Out of the Gliding Turn*

- Look out.
- Anticipate the reference point.
- Roll off bank with ailerons.
- Balance with rudder pressure.
- Raise nose slightly to straight ahead descent position.

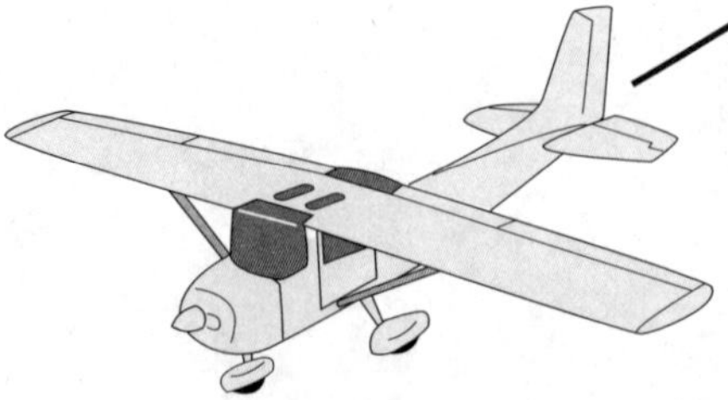

Throughout this manoeuvre maintain airspeed with elevator and accept the higher rate of descent.

Part (ii)
The Descending Turn Using Power

Aim

To alter heading in a descent at a constant airspeed with a controlled rate of descent.

Considerations

Descent Performance

The rate of descent can be controlled with power.

A descent may be either a glide with the throttle closed, or a powered descent in which power is used to control both the rate of descent and the flightpath.

Descent performance is controlled by power and attitude – control **airspeed** with the elevator and the **rate of descent** and **flightpath** with power. The nose attitude in a powered descent is higher compared to that in a glide at the same airspeed.

Flying the Manoeuvre

Establish the aircraft in a powered descent at a steady airspeed and a specific rate of descent (e.g. 300 ft/min) using power as required, with the wings level and in trim.

Enter the turn normally, adding power to maintain the desired rate of descent and controlling airspeed with elevator.

The steeper the bank angle in a descending turn, the greater the additional power required to keep the rate of descent constant.

To reduce the rate of descent and flatten the descent path:
- **add power;** and
- **raise the nose** to a slightly higher attitude to maintain airspeed.

To increase the rate of descent and steepen the flightpath:
- **reduce power;** and
- **lower the nose** to a slightly lower attitude to maintain airspeed.

Rolling out of the turn, gradually reduce the power to maintain the desired descent rate and adjust the pitch attitude to maintain the airspeed.

Airwork 9c, Part (ii)
The Descending Turn Using Power

Aim *To alter heading in a descent at a constant airspeed, with a controlled rate of descent.*

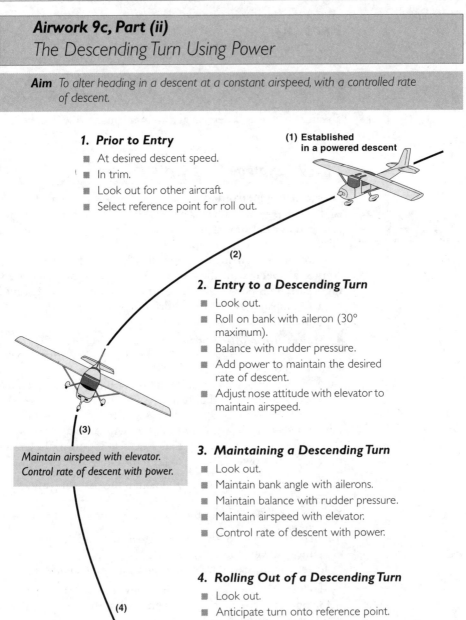

1. Prior to Entry

- At desired descent speed.
- In trim.
- Look out for other aircraft.
- Select reference point for roll out.

(2)

2. Entry to a Descending Turn

- Look out.
- Roll on bank with aileron (30° maximum).
- Balance with rudder pressure.
- Add power to maintain the desired rate of descent.
- Adjust nose attitude with elevator to maintain airspeed.

(3)

Maintain airspeed with elevator.
Control rate of descent with power.

3. Maintaining a Descending Turn

- Look out.
- Maintain bank angle with ailerons.
- Maintain balance with rudder pressure.
- Maintain airspeed with elevator.
- Control rate of descent with power.

(4)

4. Rolling Out of a Descending Turn

- Look out.
- Anticipate turn onto reference point.
- Roll off bank with ailerons.
- Balance with rudder pressure.
- Reduce power to maintain constant rate of descent.
- Adjust nose attitude to maintain airspeed with elevator.

Part (iii)
The Descending Turn with Flap Extended

Aim

To alter heading in a descending turn with flap extended.

Flying the Manoeuvre

Turning with flap extended is a very common manoeuvre when making an approach to land. Flying with flap extended:

- **allows the required lift** to be generated at a lower airspeed;
- **reduces the stalling speed,** making slower flight and shorter landing distances possible;
- **requires a lower nose attitude** for the same airspeed.

A descending turn with flaps extended is flown exactly the same as a clean descending turn except that the **nose position is lower.** Because such manoeuvres are made during the approach to land it is important that suitable airspeeds and rates of descent are maintained. In general, do not exceed 30° bank angle.

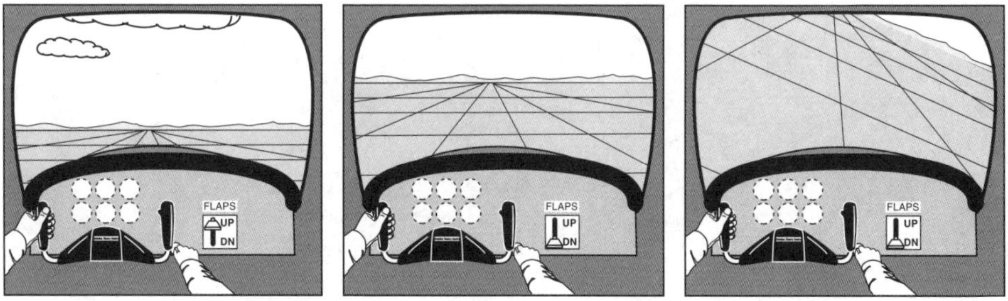

■ *Figure 9c-4* ***With flap extended, the nose position is lower***

As in all turns:

- maintain the bank angle with ailerons;
- maintain balance with rudder pressure;
- maintain airspeed with elevator; and
- (if desired) control rate of descent with power.

Airwork 9c, Part (iii)
The Descending Turn with Flap Extended

The same procedure as in the previous exercise, 9c Part (ii), applies, except that the nose attitude is lower with flap extended.

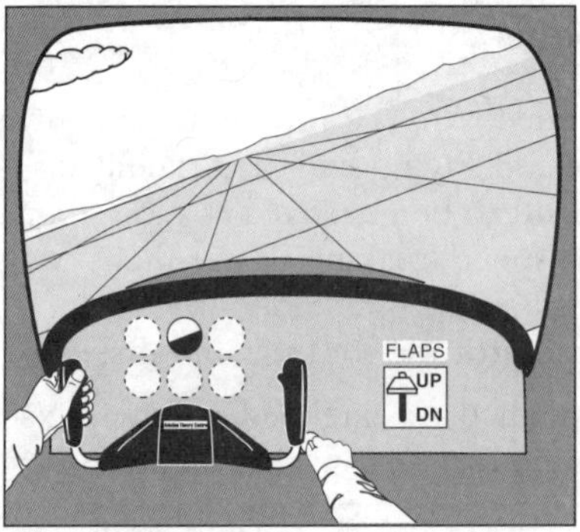

■ ***Typical horizon view in a descending turn clean***

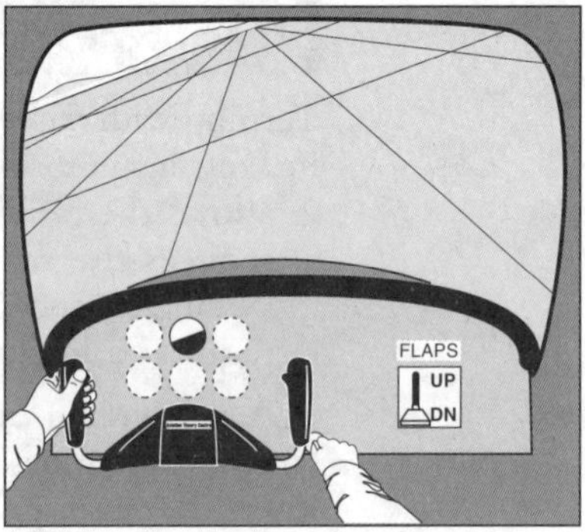

■ ***Typical horizon view in a descending turn with full flap extended***

Practise these turns in both directions.

Part (iv)
Sideslipping in a Descending Turn

Aim

To lose excess height in a gliding turn at a constant airspeed by sideslipping the aeroplane in the turn using **crossed-controls.**

NOTE Refer to the Pilot's Operating Handbook to determine if sideslipping is an approved manoeuvre for your particular aeroplane type and, if so, in which configurations. For instance, some aeroplanes are not to be sideslipped with flap extended because of the disturbed airflow around the wings.

Considerations

Flightpath

Slipping can steepen the flightpath.

The rate of descent and the steepness of the flightpath can be increased dramatically by sideslipping, while the airspeed is kept constant. This manoeuvre is especially useful in an aeroplane not fitted with flaps when too high on approach to land.

The Importance of Slipping

Slipping is not as important as it once was. The means of steepening the glide in most modern aeroplanes is to use the flaps, which will provide a steeper glide angle than a slip. The power of the rudder determines the amount of slip that can be achieved and, since effective flaps have removed the need for the large and powerful rudder deflections required to slip the aeroplane, modern aircraft in general will not slip as well as some older types.

The Forces in a Gliding Turn when Sideslipping

Drag increases dramatically in a slipping, descending turn, causing a high rate of descent.

These are similar to the forces in a normal gliding turn, except that drag is increased dramatically to steepen the descent. This is achieved by applying significant rudder pressure opposite to the turn, i.e. 'top rudder', causing the large keel surfaces of the aeroplane to be presented to the airflow. The sideslip can only occur in the direction of the turn, e.g. if turning to the left, apply right rudder to sideslip to the left.

The aeroplane is out of balance in a slipping turn.

The aeroplane will be out of balance in the sideslipping turn and this is indicated by the balance ball being on the 'downside' of the slip, i.e. to the inside of the slipping turn. The imbalance can also be felt by the occupants of the aeroplane. The rudder actually opposes the turn and so the rate of turn will decrease unless the bank angle is increased.

To maintain airspeed, the nose attitude must be lower than in a straight descent. With a large keel surface presented to the airflow, there may be a tendency for the nose to drop, and so back pressure on the control column may be required to stop the nose dropping too far. Do not rely too greatly on the airspeed indicator, as the sideways airflow over the pitot tube and static vent may cause indication errors. A safe airspeed must still be maintained.

Back pressure may be needed.

The result of a sideslip is an increased rate of descent at a constant airspeed and a steeper descent angle. The greater the bank angle and rudder pressure, the steeper the flightpath. It is not usual to use power during this manoeuvre since the purpose of a sideslip is to increase the steepness of the flightpath.

Do not use power in a slip.

Since a sideslip, and especially a sideslipping turn, are transient manoeuvres, do not trim.

Do not trim in a slip.

Flying the Manoeuvre

Establish the aeroplane in a gliding turn, and maintain a good lookout for other aircraft.

To establish a sideslip in the gliding turn apply 'top rudder' and control bank angle with aileron and airspeed with the nose position. The rate of descent and the steepness of the flightpath can be increased by using a greater bank angle and more top rudder.

To stop the sideslip in the turn, centralise the balance ball with the rudder, maintain the desired bank angle with aileron and the airspeed with elevator.

Airmanship

Only sideslip in approved aeroplanes and configurations (refer to your Pilot's Operating Handbook).

Airmanship is being aware of your height above the ground.

Be aware that high rates of descent and steep flightpaths can result from sideslipping, so allow sufficient height to recover balanced flight at the end of the manoeuvre.

Airwork 9c, Part (iv)
Sideslipping in a Gliding Turn

Aim *To lose excess height in a gliding turn at a constant airspeed by sideslipping the aeroplane in the turn using crossed controls.*

NOTE Refer to the Pilot's Operating Handbook to determine if sideslipping is an approved manoeuvre for your particular aircraft type.

1 & 2. Enter a Gliding Turn

As per Exercise 9c, Part (i).

During the sideslip, maintain airspeed with elevator, and control rate of descent with bank angle and out-of-balance rudder.

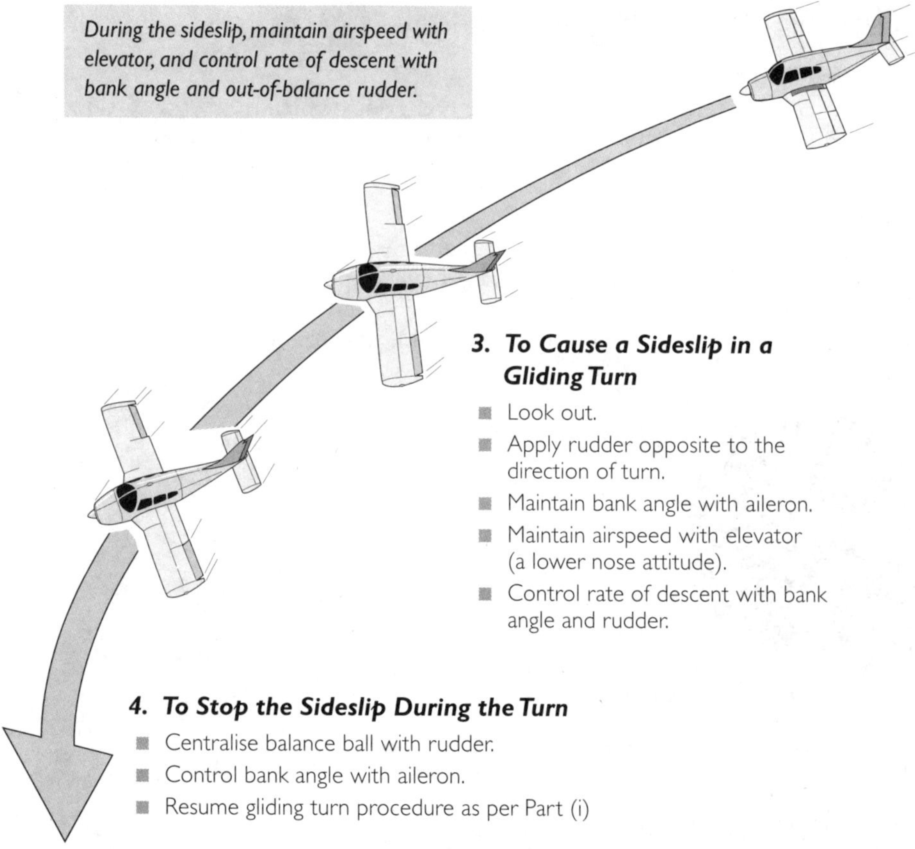

3. To Cause a Sideslip in a Gliding Turn

- Look out.
- Apply rudder opposite to the direction of turn.
- Maintain bank angle with aileron.
- Maintain airspeed with elevator (a lower nose attitude).
- Control rate of descent with bank angle and rudder.

4. To Stop the Sideslip During the Turn

- Centralise balance ball with rudder.
- Control bank angle with aileron.
- Resume gliding turn procedure as per Part (i)

Exercise 9d
Turning onto Selected Headings

Aim

To turn onto a selected magnetic heading using:

1. The heading indicator; or
2. The clock and the turn coordinator; or
3. The magnetic compass.

Flying the Manoeuvres

Reference Point

Whenever possible, select a distant reference point onto which to turn. This acts as a back-up to the instrument indications as well as aiding you in orientation.

Select a visual reference point as a guide.

1. Using the Heading Indicator

The heading indicator (HI) is easier to use and more accurate in a turn than a magnetic compass because it is a gyroscopic instrument and consequently does not suffer acceleration and turning errors. It must, however, be correctly aligned with the magnetic compass in steady flight.

■ *Figure 9d-1* ***The heading indicator***

To turn onto a specific heading using the heading indicator (HI):

1. Fly at a steady speed, straight and level.
2. Align the HI with the magnetic compass (uncaging the HI if necessary).
3. Decide the shorter way to turn (left or right) to reach the desired heading (e.g. from 090°M, to 240°M, turn right 150°);

4. Look out and clear the area.
5. Carry out a normal turn with occasional reference to the HI.
6. Commence the roll-out approximately 10° prior to reaching the desired heading on the HI.
7. Make minor adjustments to maintain the desired heading.

2. Using the Clock and the Turn Coordinator

The turn coordinator allows you to turn at a constant rate and the clock can be used to time the turn. A **rate 1 turn** (3° per sec) for 30 seconds will alter the heading by 90°.

To turn onto a specific heading using a rate 1 timed turn:

1. Divide the change in heading by 3 to obtain the number of seconds (e.g. from 090°M to 300°M is 150° to the left, which, at 3°/sec, will take 50 seconds).
2. Carry out a normal rate 1 turn with reference to the turn coordinator (at say 120 kt, this will require an angle of bank of ⅒ of 120 kt plus half of that = 12 + 6 = 18°).
3. Time the turn using the second hand on the clock.

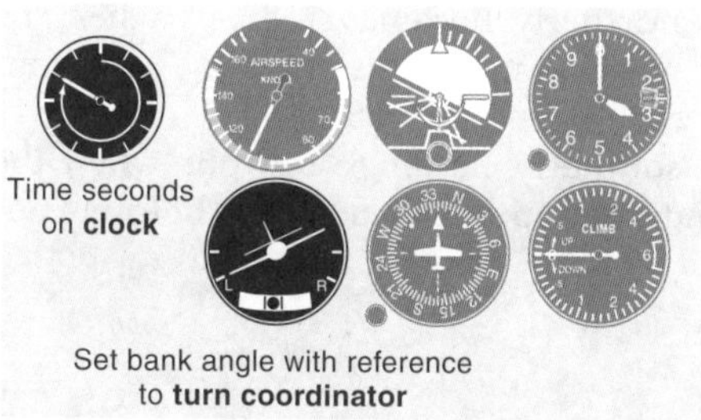
Time seconds on **clock**
Set bank angle with reference to **turn coordinator**
For example:
A turn from 090°M to 300°M is 150°.
150° at rate 1 (3°/sec) = 50 seconds.

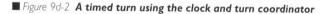

■ *Figure 9d-2* ***A timed turn using the clock and turn coordinator***

3. Using the Magnetic Compass

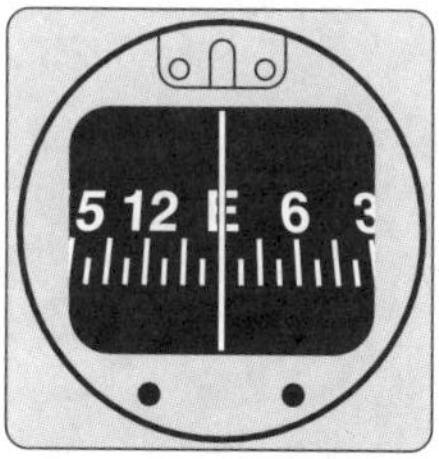
Heading 090°M

■ *Figure 9d-3* ***Magnetic compass***

This is the least-preferred method since the magnetic compass suffers considerable indication errors in a turn. It can, however, be used to verify heading once the aeroplane has settled into steady wings-level flight and the compass oscillations have ceased.

The construction of a magnetic compass is such that, when an aeroplane is turning (especially through north or south), it will give false indications of magnetic heading. To allow for this in the **northern hemisphere** observe the following:

- When turning onto **northerly headings,** roll out when the magnetic compass indicates approximately 30° **before** your desired heading.
- When turning onto **southerly headings,** roll out when the magnetic compass has passed approximately 30° **past** your desired heading.

An easy way to remember this is UNOS:

***U**ndershoot on **N**orth. **O**vershoot on **S**outh.*

The above allowances should be reduced:

- when turning with bank angles less than 30°; and
- when turning onto headings well removed from north and south – in fact, when turning onto due east or due west, no allowances need be made.

NOTE The allowances described above only apply to the magnetic compass because of the turning and acceleration errors associated with it. They do not apply to the heading indicator because it is a gyroscopic device which does not suffer from these errors and hence is easier to use.

If the aeroplane has an unserviceable heading indicator, perform a timed rate 1 turn (using the turn coordinator and the clock), using the magnetic compass as a back-up.

In the **southern hemisphere,** the allowances required when turning onto particular headings using the magnetic compass are reversed.

- When turning onto **northerly** headings, roll out when the magnetic compass indicates approximately 30° **past** your desired heading.
- When turning onto **southerly** headings, roll out when the magnetic compass indicates approximately 30° **before** your desired heading.

Exercise 10a
Stalling

Aim

To recognise the stall, and to recover from it with a minimum loss of altitude.

Considerations

What is Stalling?

Stalling occurs when the critical angle of attack is exceeded, irrespective of airspeed.

Streamline flow over the wings breaks down and becomes turbulent when the critical (or stalling) angle of attack is exceeded. This causes:

- **buffeting** (shaking or shuddering) of the airframe, felt through the controls;
- **a marked decrease in lift,** resulting in sinking;
- **rearward movement of the centre of pressure** (through which the lift acts), resulting in the nose dropping;
- **a marked drag increase.**

Stalling will occur whenever the critical angle of attack is exceeded, irrespective of airspeed. The only way to recover is to decrease the angle of attack (i.e. relax the back pressure and/or move the control column forward).

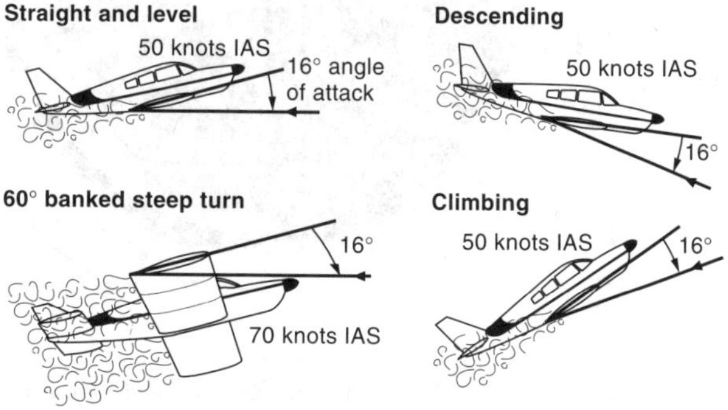

■ *Figure 10a-1* ***Stalling occurs at the critical angle of attack***

The pilot can increase the angle of attack (and reduce airspeed) by pulling the control column back. This happens in many manoeuvres such as:

- **establishing slow flight;**
- **turning (especially steep turns);**

- pulling out of a dive; and
- landing.

Also, an upward gust of wind encountering the wing will increase its angle of attack.

What is Stalling Speed?

The basic stalling speed is considered to be the speed at which the aeroplane stalls when it is at maximum weight, with the wings 'clean' (i.e. no flap) and flying straight and level with the power removed. The stall is made to occur by the pilot progressively raising the nose.

The basic stalling speed is called V_{S1}. It is published in the Pilot's Operating Handbook and shown on the airspeed indicator as the lower end of the green arc. V_{S1} for your aeroplane should be memorised as it is a valuable guide.

The stalling speed with full flap extended (at maximum weight, straight and level, and idle power) is called V_{S0}. It is also found in the Pilot's Operating Handbook and at the lower end of the white arc on the airspeed indicator. The V_{S0} speed should also be memorised.

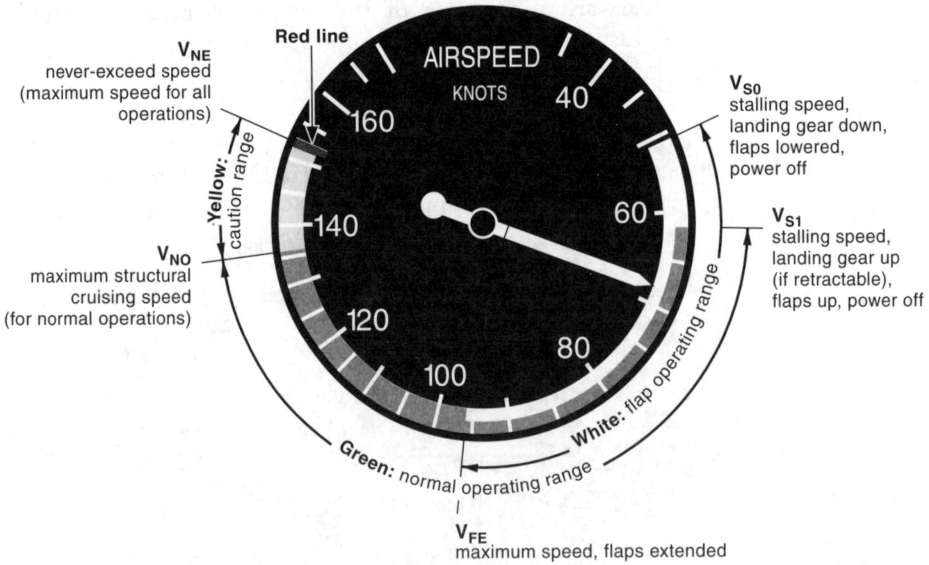

■ *Figure 10a-2* ***Colour coding on the ASI***

Treat published stalling speeds as a guide only.

The published stalling speeds are only a guide, since stalling always happens at the same angle of attack and not the same indicated airspeed. Turns, pulling out of dives and contaminated wing surfaces (e.g. frost or snow) will increase the stalling speed; high power and decreased weight will reduce it.

The Flight Controls in the Stall

The flight controls are less effective near the stall.

A reduced airflow over the controls will cause them to become less effective as speed reduces and the stall is approached. Control pressures will decrease and larger movements of the elevator and rudder will be required.

It is the main wing that stalls. The fin and the tailplane remain unstalled (by design) so that during the stall the elevator and rudder remain effective. The ailerons may or may not remain effective during a stall, depending on the aeroplane type.

The Ailerons

Be careful using ailerons near the stall.

A dropping wing can normally be 'picked-up' by moving the control column in the opposite direction. This causes the aileron on the dropping wing to deflect downwards, increasing the angle of attack, and producing more lift on that wing. If the wing is near the stalling angle, the aileron deflection could cause the critical angle to be exceeded on that wing and, instead of rising, the loss of lift would cause the wing to drop further. With any yaw, a spin could develop.

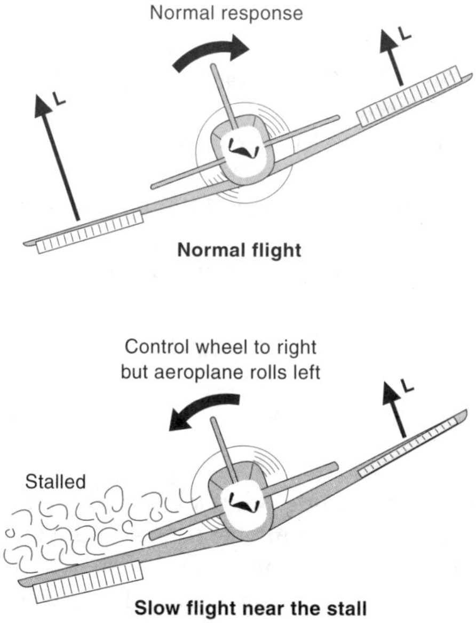

■ *Figure 10a-3* ***Near the stall, use of aileron may not pick-up the wing***

The ailerons on some more recently designed aeroplanes are effective right through the stall and their use, coordinated with rudder, may be possible. This point should be discussed with your flying instructor.

The Rudder

Near the stall, any tendency for a wing to drop or for the aeroplane to yaw can be prevented with opposite rudder.

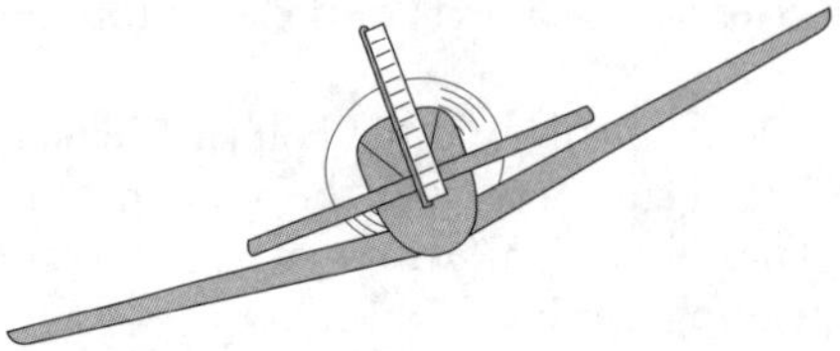

■ *Figure 10a-4* **Near the stall, prevent wing drop and further yaw with opposite rudder**

Flying the Manoeuvre

Stalling in Straight and Level Flight

Stalling is first practised in straight and level flight by reducing power and raising the nose to maintain height. The angle of attack will gradually increase.

Warnings of an impending stall include:

- **a reducing airspeed** and air noise level, decreasing control effectiveness and a 'sloppy' feel;
- **operation of a pre-stall warning** (such as a horn, buzzer, light or whistle);
- **the onset of buffet,** felt in the airframe and through the control column;
- **a high nose attitude** for the manoeuvre being flown.

The actual stall may be recognised by:

- **the nose dropping** (caused by the centre of pressure moving rearwards);
- **a high sink rate.**

Stall Recovery

Stall recovery requires decreasing the angle of attack.

To recover from a stall **reduce the angle of attack** by moving the control column centrally forward (releasing the back pressure may be sufficient) until the buffet or stall warning stops.

Once the wings are unstalled buffeting ceases, the airspeed increases, and the aeroplane can be eased out of the slight dive back into normal flight. The height loss will be of the order of 200 ft. Power can be added to regain or maintain height, otherwise flying speed should be maintained in a glide.

Height loss during a stall can be minimised with power.

Height loss during the stall can be minimised with power. Adding power is not required to recover from the stall; however, height loss will be minimised if full power is applied as back pressure is released and the nose is lowered. Recovery can be achieved with a height loss of less than 50 ft.

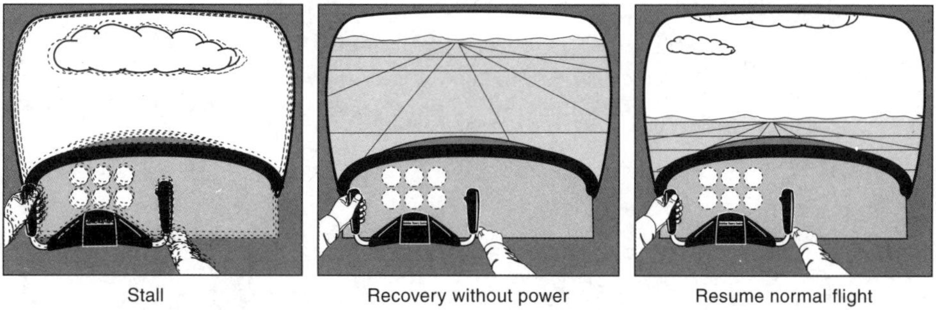

■ *Figure 10a-5* ***Stall and recovery attitudes***

After Stalling

Avoid entering a secondary stall during a stall recovery.

Following stall recovery, ease the aeroplane into normal flight by gently raising the nose and applying power as the nose passes through the horizon.

The inertia of an aeroplane causes it to follow the original flightpath for a brief time before the change in attitude and resulting change in forces move it into a new flightpath. Pulling the nose up too sharply during the stall recovery may not give the aeroplane time enough to react and ease out of the dive, but may merely increase the angle of attack beyond the stalling angle again. A **secondary stall** will be induced, and a second recovery from the stall will be necessary.

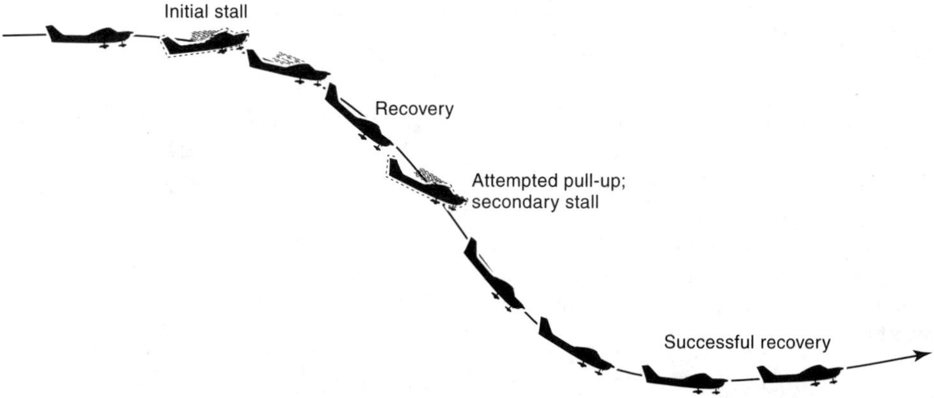

■ *Figure 10a-6* ***Raising the nose too sharply during recovery may induce a secondary stall***

Stalling with Flap Extended

When the trailing-edge flaps are lowered, the effective angle of attack of the wings is increased. This allows the aeroplane to fly at a slower speed with a lower nose attitude. The stall with flap extended will occur with a much lower nose attitude and a lower airspeed than when the wings are clean. With full flap extended on an approach to land, for instance, the stall could occur with the nose well below the horizon.

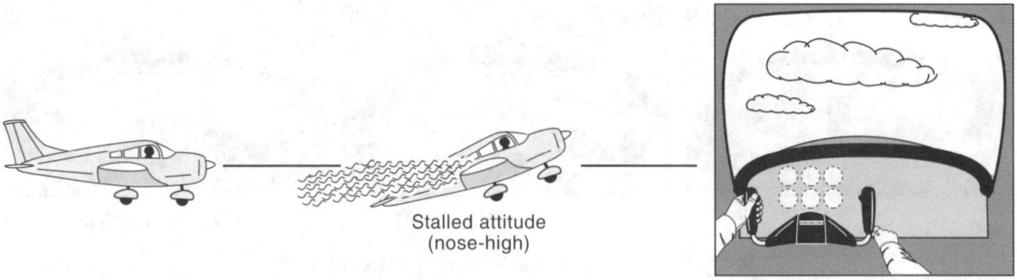

■ *Figure 10a-7* ***The clean stall***

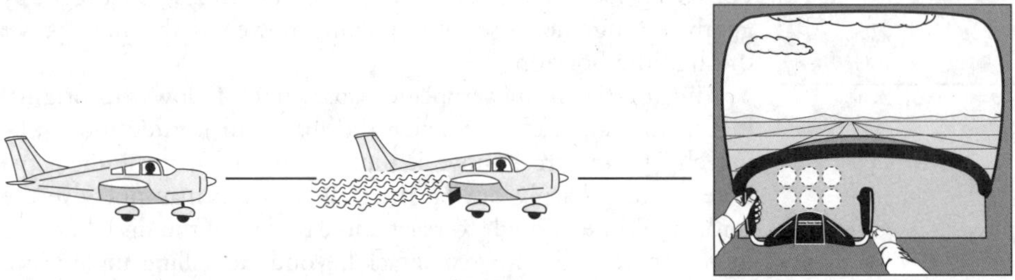

■ *Figure 10a-8* ***The pitch attitude in a flapped stall – nose much lower***

Airmanship

Unexpected stalls should never occur.

Carry out the HASELL check (page 165) prior to practising stalls and stall recovery.

Exert smooth, but firm and positive control over the aeroplane.

Be particularly conscious of any other aircraft in the vicinity, your height above ground level and the area over which you are flying. Ensure that stalling is only practised at altitude. Note landmarks and the direction to the airfield. Maintain a high visual awareness.

Airmanship is never allowing a stall to develop inadvertently – but knowing how to recover, just in case.

The Pre-Aerobatic HASELL Checklist

Stalling is the first aerobatic-type manoeuvre that you will perform.

Prior to doing any aerobatics, it is usual to carry out a series of checks to ensure safe operation. The Pilot's Operating Handbook will contain a suitable check covering items such as those in the HASELL check below. The items it contains start with these letters.

PRE-AEROBATIC 'HASELL' CHECKLIST	
H	***Height*** *Sufficient to recover by 3,000 ft above ground level.*
A	***Airframe*** *Flaps and landing gear as desired, brakes off, in trim.*
S	***Security*** *– hatches and harnesses secure;* *– no loose articles in the cockpit (e.g. fire extinguishers, tie-down kits, etc.);* *– gyros caged (if necessary).*
E	***Engine*** *– normal engine operation;* *– fuel contents and selection checked (fullest tank selected, fuel pump on if appropriate);* *– Mixture and carburettor heat as required.*
L	***Location satisfactory*** *– away from controlled airspace, towns, active aerodromes and other aircraft, and in visual conditions.*
L	***Look out*** *– make an inspection turn (of at least 180°, preferably 360°) to clear the area around and below you. Begin the manoeuvre immediately on completion of the clearing turn.*

NOTE Realign the heading indicator with the magnetic compass once the manoeuvre is completed.

Airwork 10a
The Standard Stall and Recovery Procedure

Aim *To fully stall the aeroplane and then recover with a minimum loss of height.*

1 Prior to Entry

Pre-aerobatic check (see also expanded version on previous page):

H – Height sufficient to recover by 3,000 ft agl.

A – Airframe (flaps AS DESIRED, in trim).

S – Security:
hatches and harnesses secure;
no loose articles;
gyros CAGED (if applicable).

E – Engine:
operating normally;
fuel contents and selection checked;
mixture and carburettor heat as required.

L – Location satisfactory.

L – Look out: clearing turn to check for any other aircraft.

Begin the manoeuvre as soon as area is clear.

2. Stall Entry

- Power OFF – throttle CLOSED (carburettor heat HOT).
- Prevent yaw and maintain balance with rudder.
- Maintain height with elevator.
- Ailerons neutral.
- Continue bringing control column fully back.

3. Symptoms of an Approaching Stall

- Decreasing airspeed and noise level.
- Controls less firm and less effective.
- Pre-stall warning (light, horn or buzzer).
- Shuddering airframe.
- A relatively high nose-up attitude.

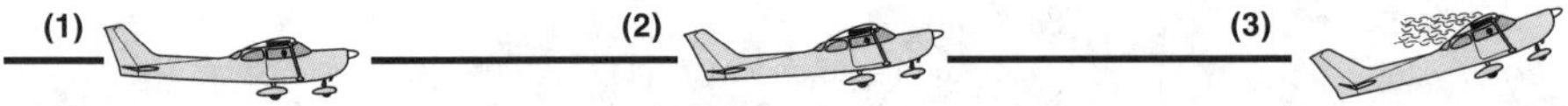

***Look out** and clear the area.*

During the stall use rudder only to prevent further yaw.

Recognise the actual stall:

- nose drop
- sink rate

Practise stalls in various configurations:
Clean, power off
Clean, power on
Flapped, power off
Flapped, power on
Climbing, descending and turning

Airwork 10a

4a. Stall Recovery without Power

- Move the control column centrally forward to unstall the wings.
- Prevent further yaw with rudder.
- Level wings with aileron if necessary.
- Attain safe flying speed.
- Resume normal flight and regain altitude as required.

Height loss approximately 200 to 300 ft.

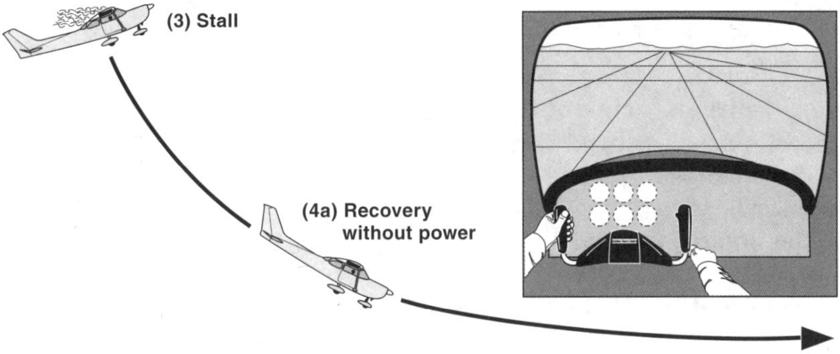

4b. Standard Stall Recovery with Power (SSR)

Simultaneously:

- Move the control column centrally forward to unstall the wings.
- Add full power – throttle smoothly FULLY OPEN (carb heat COLD).
- Prevent further yaw with rudder.
- Level wings with aileron if necessary.
- Attain safe flying speed and regain altitude.

Should the wing *not* drop at the point of stall, maintain aircraft balance on application of power with rudder.

Height loss approximately 50 ft.

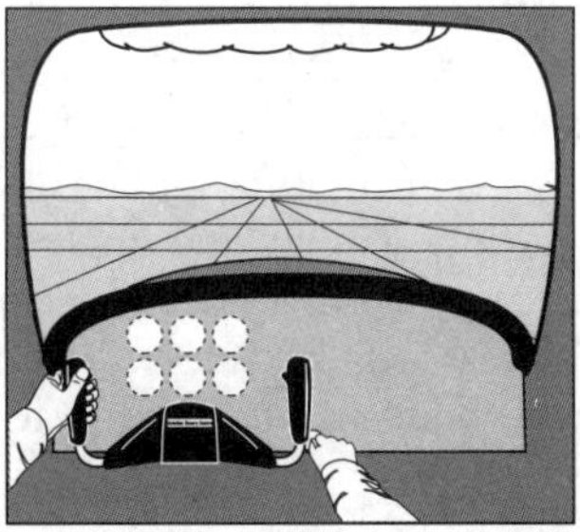

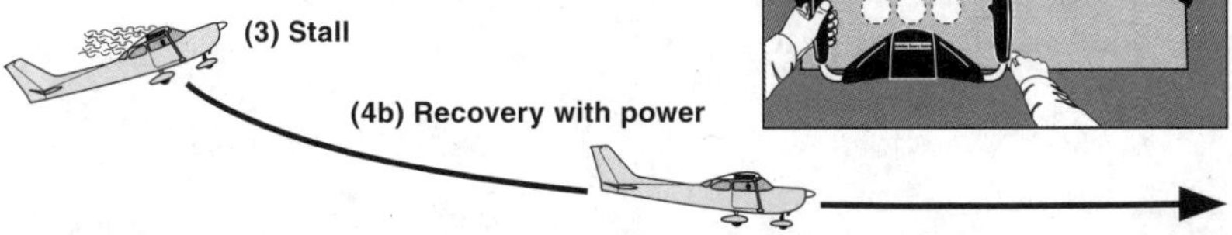

Variations on the Basic Stall

Recovery at the Incipient Stall Stage

Recover immediately at the first sign of an inadvertent stall.

The term incipient stall means the beginning stages of a stall. It precedes the actual stall. If ever an unwanted stall appears imminent, then recover at the incipient stage. This is especially applicable if the aeroplane is near the ground, say during take-off, approach to land, going around or low-level flying.

The recovery from an incipient stall is simply:

- **move the control column centrally forward** (relaxing the back pressure may be sufficient); and simultaneously
- **apply power smoothly;** and
- **use the controls normally** (i.e. the ailerons), since the wing is not stalled.

Recovery from an Incipient Spin

The recovery from a stall with a wing drop (i.e. the initial stages of a spin) is really the same as for an incipient stall with a wing drop. Simultaneously:

- **ease the control column forward** sufficiently to unstall the wings;
- **apply sufficient rudder** to prevent further yaw;
- **apply maximum power;**
- **when the airspeed increases** as the wings become unstalled, **level the wings** with coordinated use of rudder and ailerons, **ease out of the descent** and resume the desired flightpath.

Wing Surface

Contaminated or damaged wings increase stalling speed.

If ice, frost, insects or any other contaminant is on a wing or if the wing is damaged (especially its upper leading edge), the airflow could become turbulent at a lesser angle of attack than normal. Stalling will then occur sooner and at a higher airspeed. **Always check the surface condition of the wings** (especially the upper leading edges) in your pre-flight inspection.

Stalls during Manoeuvres

Stalling speed increases in manoeuvres.

To turn or pull out of a dive, the wings must produce more lift. This is achieved by the pilot using back pressure on the control column to increase the angle of attack. The relative air flow striking the wings at a greater angle causes the **stalling angle** to be reached at a *higher* indicated airspeed. For example, the stalling speed increases by 7% at 30° bank angle and by 40% when pulling 2g in a 60° banked turn or dive recovery.

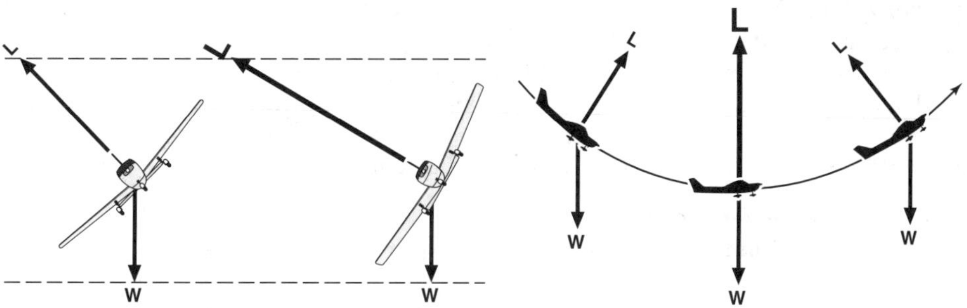

■ *Figure 10a-9* ***Increased wing loading (g-factor) means increased stall speed***

You can physically recognise an increased load factor by the increased g-loading, so any time your *apparent weight* is increased in manoeuvres, the stall speed is increased.

When the aeroplane approaches a stall in manoeuvres (say in a steep turn or pulling out of a dive), releasing back pressure is usually sufficient to prevent the stall occurring.

Stalling in a Turn

Accelerated stalls – at a higher stalling speed than straight and level – can occur with the higher g-loading in manoeuvres such as turns.

Back pressure on the control column increases the angle of attack and may cause a stall. Since the load factor is increased in a turn, the stall will occur at a higher speed than in straight and level flight – by how much depends on the g-loading. Stalls at a higher speed than normal are called **accelerated stalls.**

Follow the standard recovery of moving the control column centrally forward (relaxing the back pressure may be sufficient), and when the wings are unstalled, use coordinated rudder and ailerons to roll the wings level. Apply power as required and resume the desired flightpath.

The Effect of Flaps

Extending flap lowers the stalling speed and affects the stall characteristics.

The stall with flaps extended will differ somewhat from the clean stall. For a start, flaps increase the lifting capability of the wings, allowing the required lift to be generated at a lower speed. The stalling speed will be lower. The increased drag will cause the aeroplane to decelerate more rapidly when power is reduced and the lower speed may make the controls feel very 'sloppy'. Also, the changed distribution of lift on the wings may cause a greater tendency for a wing to drop.

With flaps extended, the nose attitude will be lower in each phase of flight, therefore stalling will occur at a lower pitch attitude than when 'clean'.

The recovery from a stall with flaps extended is standard. Height loss can be minimised by applying full power as the control column is moved centrally forward, but be prepared to hold forward pressure on the control column so that the nose does not rise too far with the strong pitch-up moment that full power produces. Do not use ailerons to roll the wings level until the wings are unstalled. If full flap is used, a climb-away may be difficult unless some flap is raised once a safe speed is attained.

Stalling on Final Approach

Do not stall on final approach.

Initiate a recovery immediately you suspect an impending stall on approach to land. Lower the nose and apply power to minimise height loss.

Never allow a stall to occur near the ground.

It is worthwhile practising the developed stall in the approach configuration at altitude so as to familiarise yourself with it. This should ensure that you never allow a stall to occur near the ground.

A situation in which a stall might occur could be an approach that has got out of hand: for example, full flap extended and a tendency to undershoot, with the pilot raising the nose (instead of adding power). The airspeed will decrease and the undershoot will worsen. If the pilot continues to pull the control column back, a stall could occur. With full flap and possibly high power applied, the stall could be fairly sudden and with a wing drop.

The standard recovery technique would be used. The control column may have to be moved well forward to unstall the wings, and care should be taken to avoid using ailerons until the wing is unstalled. The substantial drag from full flap may make a climb-away difficult; gain speed in level flight or a slight climb, reduce the flap in stages and then climb away as desired.

Power-On Stalls

Power decreases the stalling speed.

With power on, the propeller creates a slipstream over the inner sections of the wings which may delay the stall. This will occur at a higher nose position. The slipstream makes the elevator and rudder more effective, but not the ailerons. The increased airflow may delay the stall on the inner sections of the wing – the stall occurring first on the outer sections, perhaps leading to a greater wing-dropping tendency. Standard recovery technique is used, any further yaw being prevented with opposite rudder to prevent a spin developing.

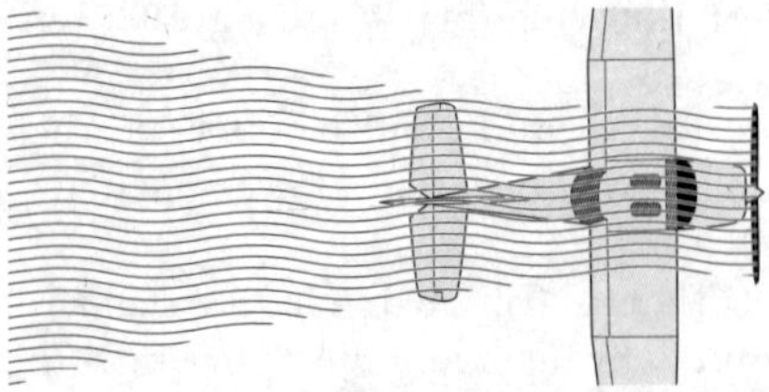

■ *Figure 10a-10* **Power reduces stalling speed**

The Effect of Weight

Stalling speed decreases as weight decreases.

The lighter the aeroplane is, the less lift the wings must generate for straight and level flight, and so the smaller the required angle of attack at a given speed. Therefore a light aeroplane can be flown at a slower airspeed before the stalling angle of attack is reached.

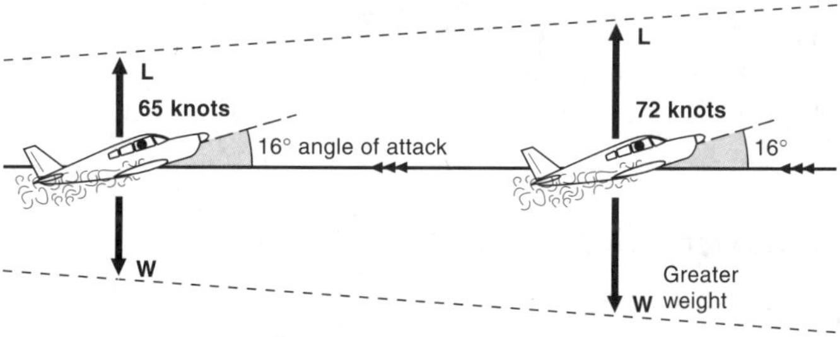

■ *Figure 10a-11* ***Stalling speed is less at lower weights***

Centre of Gravity Position

A forward centre of gravity increases the stalling speed.

In many aircraft, the tailplane generates a small downward force to balance the four main forces and prevent the aeroplane pitching. The lift from the main wings in straight and level flight will therefore have to support both the weight and this downward aerodynamic force on the tail.

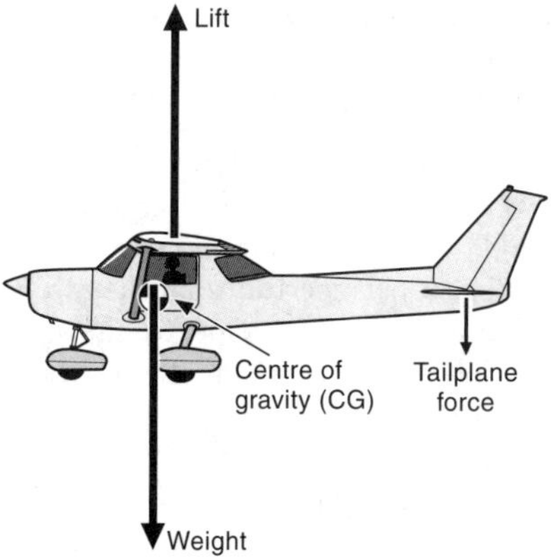

The position of the CG is shown in diagrams with a centroid symbol: ⊕

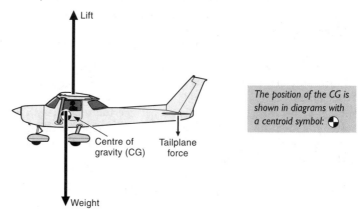

■ *Figure 10a-12* ***The forces straight and level***

The further forward the CG, the greater the downward tailplane force and so the greater is the lift required from the main wings. This requires a greater angle of attack at a given airspeed, therefore the stalling angle will be reached at a higher airspeed. This is one very good reason why the aeroplane must be correctly loaded with the CG within approved limits.

Exercise 10b
Slow Flying

Aim

To develop an awareness of the aeroplane's handling characteristics at abnormally low airspeeds, and to return the aeroplane to a safe flying speed.

Considerations

Slow Flight

This exercise is designed to provide exposure to flight at abnormally low airspeeds so that the pilot can:

Slow flying is an awareness exercise.

- **recognise an inadvertent approach to the stall;**
- **experience how the aeroplane handles** at an abnormally low airspeed; and
- **take recovery action** by returning the aeroplane to a safe flying speed.

The exercise also provides handling practice for those brief periods of low airspeed that do occur in normal flight, when the aeroplane is accelerating to climbing speed immediately after lift-off, and during the landing flare as the airspeed decreases prior to touchdown.

Power Required for Steady Flight

To maintain a steady airspeed, engine power must produce enough thrust from the propeller to balance the total drag. The power-required curve is therefore similar in shape to the drag curve. It shows that high power is required for steady flight at both high and low speeds, with minimum power occurring at a specific speed in between.

Minimum power will give minimum fuel consumption and consequently maximum endurance, so this speed is often listed as the endurance speed in the Pilot's Operating Handbook.

Flight at speeds less than the best endurance speed is slow flight.

Power Handling

At normal cruising speeds, higher speeds require higher power settings. Also, any minor speed variations due to gusts will automatically correct themselves in the normal flight range – a slight increase in speed causing a drag increase that will slow the aeroplane down.

Conversely, a slight decrease in speed reduces drag, allowing the aeroplane to regain speed. An aeroplane is *speed stable* in the normal flight range.

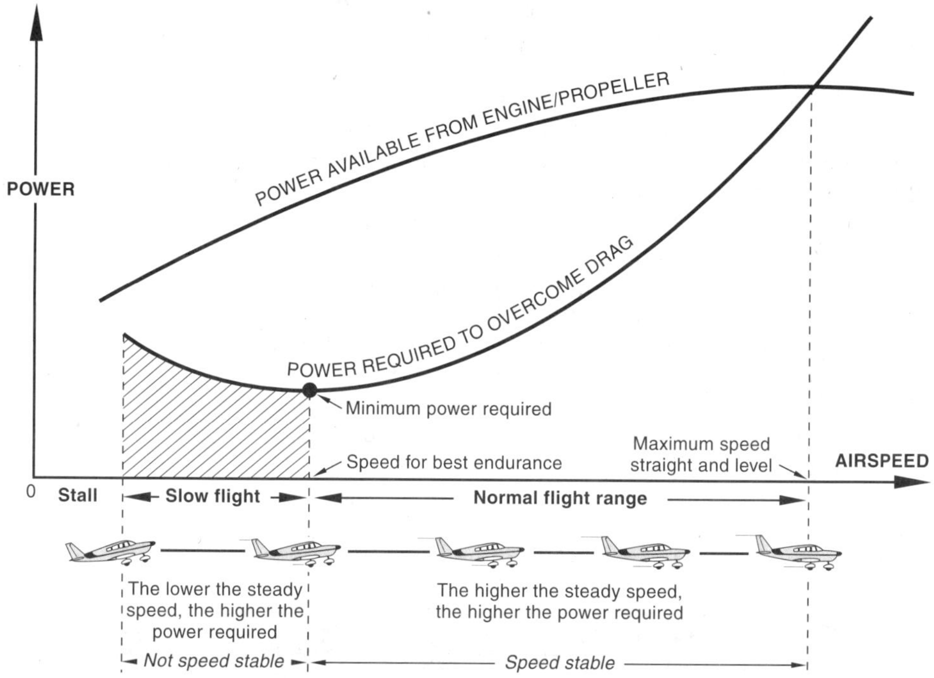

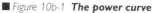

■ *Figure 10b-1* ***The power curve***

The slower the steady speed you want to maintain, the more power you require.

In the slow flight range the situation is reversed, i.e. the lower the speed, the higher the power required. This is because at low speeds a high angle of attack is needed to produce the required lift, greatly increasing the induced drag. The increase in total drag will slow the aeroplane down unless power is applied. The lowest steady speed that can be maintained by an aeroplane may be limited either by the maximum power that the engine/propeller can deliver, or by the stall.

In the slow-speed range, the aeroplane is *not* speed stable because an airspeed loss due to a gust will result in an increase in total drag which will slow the aeroplane down further (and continue to do so) unless the pilot takes corrective action by adding power. An airspeed gain, conversely, will reduce the total drag and the aeroplane will accelerate unless the pilot reduces power.

Control Effectiveness

The effectiveness of the flight controls depends on the airflow over them.

At low airspeeds, the controls will feel 'sloppy' and less effective. Large control movements may be required to obtain the desired response. Since the elevator and rudder are in the propeller slipstream, they may be somewhat more effective when high power is set. The ailerons will not be affected by the slipstream.

A high power and a low airspeed will lead to a strong **slipstream** effect, which may require significant rudder deflection to balance the yawing tendency. At very low speeds and high power, the large rudder deflection might require extra aileron movement to hold the wings level, i.e. **crossed-controls.**

The 'feel' of the aeroplane becomes very important in slow flight. The low speed, the less-effective controls, the high nose attitude, the high power required and the large rudder deflection are all clues that the stalling angle is not far away. Slow flight at 10 kt above the stall (and then possibly only 5 kt above) will be practised. Stalling speeds straight and level at maximum weight are delineated on the airspeed indicator: V_{S1} at the lower end of the green band for a clean wing and V_{S0} at the lower end of the white band for full flap.

The airspeed needs to be monitored closely in slow flight. It should be controlled accurately with power and attitude changes due to the proximity of the stall. The tendency to lose speed in a turn should be counteracted with additional power. Do not attempt steep turns at slow speeds near the stall – the stalling speed will increase to meet your actual airspeed!

Flying the Manoeuvre

1. To Attain Slow Flight

To reduce airspeed to the selected value (5 or 10 kt above the stall):

- **reduce power and gradually raise the nose** to maintain height;
- **when the desired airspeed is reached,** increase power and continually adjust both power and attitude to maintain that speed;
- **retrim** and check the balance ball for correct balance.

2. Manoeuvring in Slow Flight

To maintain speed and height, be prepared to work the throttle vigorously and to readjust the attitude as necessary. The longer you leave corrections, the greater they will have to be. As always: **power + attitude = performance.**

TO CORRECT SPEED VARIATIONS:

- if speed increases – raise the nose and reduce power;
- if speed decreases – lower the nose and add power.

TO CORRECT HEIGHT VARIATIONS:

- if the aeroplane climbs – reduce power and lower the nose;
- if the aeroplane sinks – add power and raise the nose.

The use of elevator, power and rudder must be coordinated. Every time power changes there will be a pitch/yaw tendency that you will have to counteract. Slow flight is very good practice for your coordination.

TO ENTER A SLOW-SPEED CLIMB:
- increase power;
- slowly adjust attitude to maintain airspeed;
- trim.

TO LEVEL OFF FROM A SLOW-SPEED CLIMB:
- lower the nose;
- slowly reduce power;
- trim.

TO COMMENCE A DESCENT:
- reduce power;
- lower the pitch attitude to maintain airspeed;
- trim.

TO LEVEL OFF FROM A DESCENT:
- add power;
- gradually raise the nose to cruise attitude to maintain airspeed;
- trim.

TO TURN AT A LOW AIRSPEED:
- add power to maintain speed as bank angle is applied.

MAXIMUM PERFORMANCE CLIMB:

To make a maximum performance climb away from a descent:
- open the throttle fully (and balance with rudder);
- allow the nose to rise and hold it in the climb attitude;
- control airspeed with elevator;
- trim.

TO APPROACH THE STALL:
- raise the nose until a stall is imminent;
- recover by easing the control column forward and applying power.

TO RETURN TO NORMAL CRUISE SPEED:
- increase power;
- lower the pitch attitude to maintain height;
- adjust power as desired speed is attained;
- trim.

These manoeuvres should be practised both clean and with flap extended.

Airmanship

Exert firm, positive and smooth control over the aeroplane, being prepared to make large and prompt power changes when required.

Maintain airspeed in level turns at a low airspeed with the use of additional power. Coordinate the use of power/elevator/rudder.

Airmanship is flying the aeroplane accurately and positively, especially at the critically slow airspeeds, and keeping a good lookout.

Monitor the engine instruments to confirm adequate cooling of the engine at the high power and low airspeed.

Maintain a safe height above ground level and obstacles if the slow flying is associated with low flying.

Remember that a continuing lookout is important in all phases of visual flight.

Airwork 10b
Slow Flying

Aim *To develop an awareness of the aeroplane's handling characteristics at abnormally low airspeeds, and to return the aeroplane to a safe flying speed.*

1. Establishing Slow Flight, Flaps Up

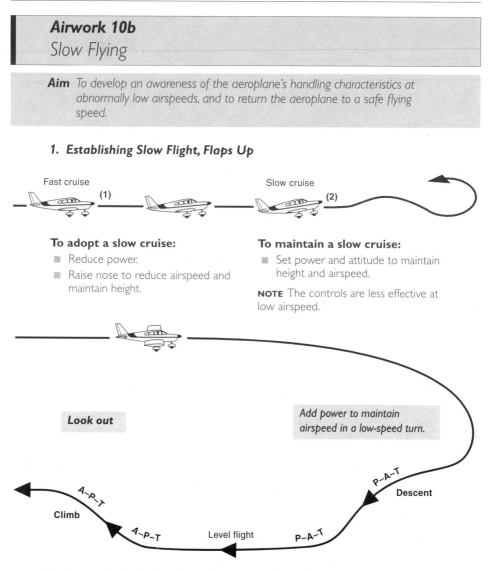

To adopt a slow cruise:

- Reduce power.
- Raise nose to reduce airspeed and maintain height.

To maintain a slow cruise:

- Set power and attitude to maintain height and airspeed.

NOTE The controls are less effective at low airspeed.

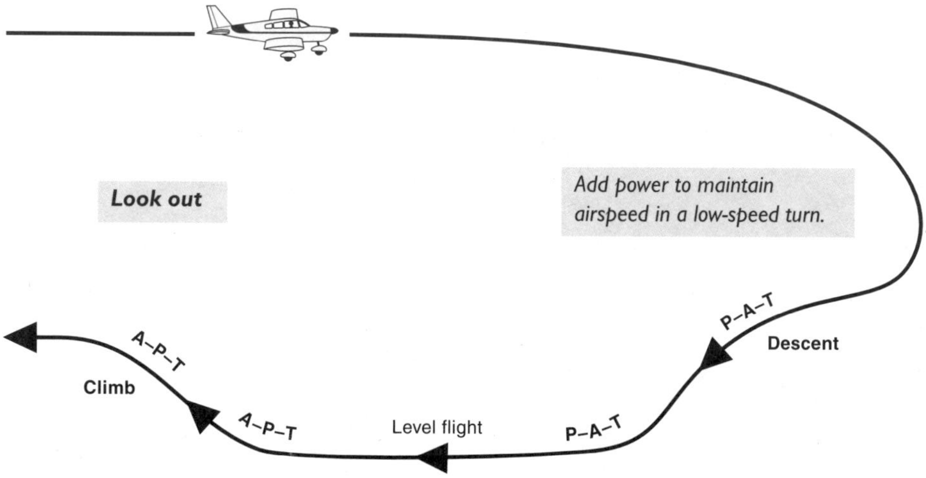

Practise gentle climbs, descents and turns at a constant airspeed.

2. Recovering from Slow Flight

- Increase power.
- Lower pitch attitude to maintain height.
- Adjust power as desired airspeed is approached.
- Trim.

Repeat the above procedure with flap extended.

Exercise 11a ⁂ Ex. 11b JAR-FCL
Full Spins

Aim

To enter, maintain and recover from a fully-developed spin (provided it is an approved manoeuvre for the aeroplane).

NOTE Spinning is an optional instructional exercise.

Considerations

What is a Spin?

A spin is a condition of stalled flight in which the aeroplane describes a spiral descent.

As well as the aeroplane being in a stalled condition, one wing is producing more lift than the other (caused by yaw) and this results in a roll. Greater drag from the stalled lower wing results in further yaw, further roll, etc., etc. Pitching of the nose may also occur.

The aeroplane is in motion about all three axes. In other words, lots of things are happening!

In a spin, the aeroplane is:

- **stalled;**
- **rolling;**
- **yawing;**
- **pitching;**
- **sideslipping; and**
- **rapidly losing height,** even though the airspeed may not be increasing.

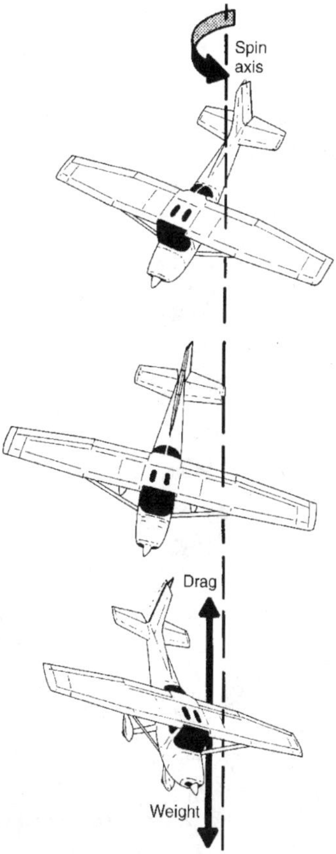

■ *Figure 11a-1* ***The spin***

In a spin the wings will not produce much lift, since they are stalled. The aeroplane will accelerate downwards until it reaches a vertical rate of descent where the greatly increased drag balances the weight. The height loss will be rapid as the aeroplane spins downwards about the vertical spin axis.

Characteristics of a developed spin include a **low indicated airspeed** (which does not increase until recovery action is initiated) and a **high rate of descent.** A vital part of the spin recovery is to unstall the wings by moving the control column centrally forward (which reduces the angle of attack), and to build up flying speed.

A well-flown spin will not stress a properly certificated aeroplane any more than a normal stall.

Spin Rotation

If the aeroplane adopts a higher nose attitude and the spin flattens:
- **the rate of rotation will decrease;** and
- **the rate of descent will reduce** (due to increased drag from the higher angle of attack).

The flatness of the spin determines the rate of rotation.

A spinning ice-skater moves her arms in and out from her body to alter the rate of rotation. The same effect occurs in an aeroplane. In a steep nose-down attitude, the mass of the aeroplane is close to the spin axis and the rate of rotation is high. If the spin flattens, some of the aeroplane's mass is distributed further from the spin axis and the rate of rotation decreases.

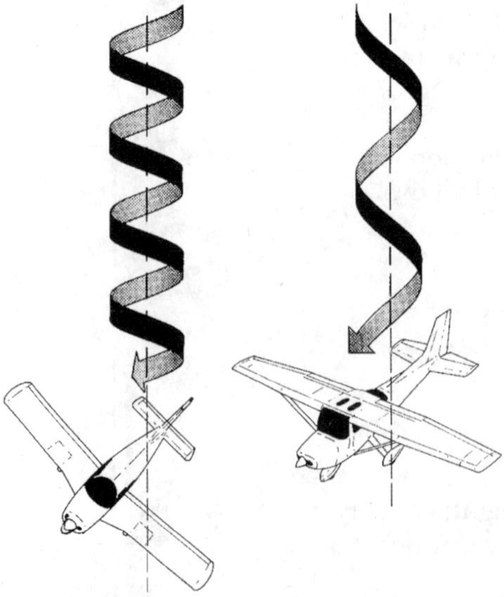

■ *Figure 11a-2* ***A steep spin (left) and a flat spin***

If the nose pitches up and down in the spin, the rate of rotation will vary – becoming slower when the spin is flatter and faster when the nose position is steeper. Since the nose is purposely lowered in the recovery from a spin, you can expect a temporary increase in the rate of rotation until the recovery is complete.

A rearward CG will encourage a flatter spin and it will be more difficult to lower the nose in the recovery. This is one (very important) reason for ensuring that you never fly an aeroplane loaded outside its approved weight and balance limits.

Conversely, **a forward CG** normally results in a steeper spin with a higher rate of descent and a higher rate of rotation. It may make recovery much easier and, in fact, may even prevent a spin occurring.

Spiral Dives

Do not confuse a spin (stalled) with a spiral dive (not stalled).

A manoeuvre that must not be confused with a spin is the spiral dive, which can be thought of as a steep turn that has gone wrong. In a spiral dive the nose attitude is low, the wing is not stalled, the airspeed is high and rapidly increasing and the rate of descent is high. Because the wing is not stalled, there is no need, in the recovery from a spiral dive, to move the nose forward. Spiral dives are considered in Section 15 on Advanced Turning.

Practising Spins

During your first spin, you will probably be a little overcome by the sensations and not really know exactly what is happening. After a few practice spins, however, you will become reasonably comfortable and the whole manoeuvre will seem to slow down enough for you to recognise the characteristics, count the turns, recognise landmarks and so on.

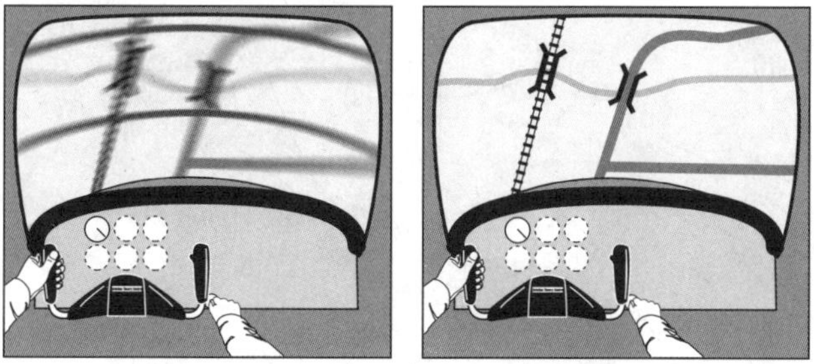

■ *Figure 11a-3* ***The spin as you first see it and as you will see it***

The Three Stages in a Spin Manoeuvre

The spin manoeuvre can be considered in three stages:

1. **The incipient spin** (or the beginning of the spin), which is an unsteady manoeuvre in which the entry path of the aeroplane is combined with a phenomenon called autorotation.
2. **The fully-developed spin,** in which the aeroplane has settled into a comparatively steady rate of rotation and a steady rate of descent at a low airspeed and a high angle of attack.

3. The recovery from a spin, initiated by the pilot who:
– opposes the autorotation with rudder;
– unstalls the wings with forward control column; and
– eases out of the ensuing dive.

How a Spin Develops

A spin is a condition of stalled flight, so the first prerequisite is that the wings be at a high angle of attack. This is achieved by moving the control column progressively back, as in a normal **stall entry.**

A **wing drop** is essential to enter a spin and this may occur by itself or (more likely) be induced by the pilot yawing the aeroplane with rudder or 'misusing' the ailerons just prior to the aeroplane stalling.

Autorotation will commence through the dropping wing becoming further stalled, with a consequent decrease in lift and increase in drag. The aeroplane will roll, a sideslip will develop and the nose will drop. If no corrective action is taken, the rate of rotation will increase and a spin will develop. It will be an unsteady manoeuvre with the aeroplane appearing to be very nose-down. The rate of rotation may increase quite quickly and the pilot will experience a change of g-loading.

An aeroplane will not usually go straight from the stall into a spin. There is usually a transition period which may vary from aeroplane to aeroplane, typically taking two or three turns in the unsteady and steep autorotation mode, before settling into a fully-developed and stable spin.

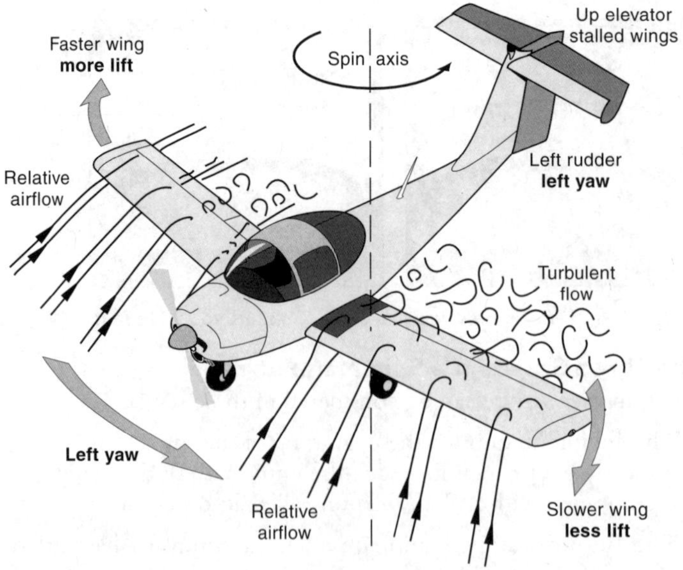

■ *Figure 11a-4* ***The aeroplane in a spin***

Misuse of Ailerons

Misuse of ailerons can cause a spin.

Trying to raise a dropped wing with opposite aileron may have the reverse effect when the aeroplane is near the stall. If, as the aileron goes down, the stalling angle of attack is exceeded, instead of the wing rising it may drop quickly, resulting in a spin. This is the spin entry technique on some aircraft types.

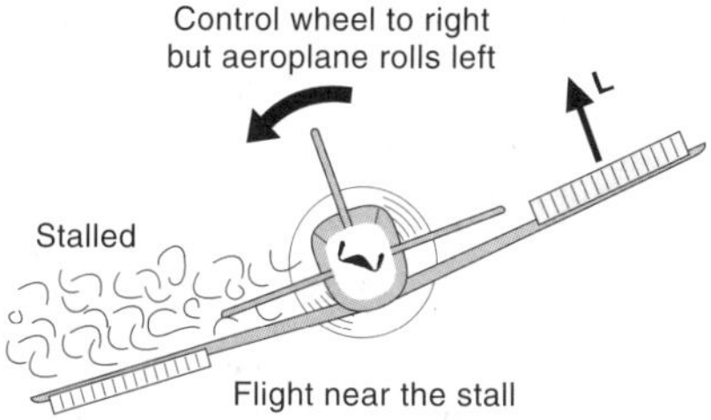

■ *Figure 11a-5* ***Inducing a spin with opposite aileron***

Use of Power

Power may destabilise an aeroplane before and during a spin

At the incipient (early) stage of a stall, having power on may cause a greater tendency for a wing to drop, which could lead to a spin. Once the aeroplane is in a spin, power may destabilise it as the slipstream will tend to flow across the outer wing, increasing its lift and consequently increasing the rate of roll. If power is applied, the entire spin manoeuvre will be speeded up.

It is essential, therefore, to remove power by closing the throttle either before or during the spin recovery.

Flaps

The flaps should be raised for spinning.

The flaps tend to decrease the control effectiveness of the elevator and rudder and so should be raised either before or during the spin recovery. For many aircraft, practising spinning with flaps down is not permitted, since the aerodynamic loads on the flap structure may cause damage.

Flying the Manoeuvre

Entering a Spin

It is usual to enter a spin by yawing with rudder just prior to the stall.

About 5 to 10 kt prior to the aeroplane stalling, with the control column being progressively moved back, a smooth and firm large-scale deflection of the rudder will speed up one wing and cause it to generate more lift. The aeroplane will begin to roll and a spin will develop.

The spin entry may require full travel of the rudder. If the left rudder pedal is pushed fully forward, the aeroplane will yaw and roll to the left and a spin to the left will develop. If the right rudder is pushed fully forward, the aeroplane will yaw and roll to the right and a spin to the right will develop.

Maintaining the Spin

To allow a steady spin to develop and continue:

- hold the control column fully back;
- hold on full rudder;
- keep ailerons neutral.

Recognition of a Spin

You can recognise a spin by the following characteristics:

- a steep nose-down attitude;
- continuous rotation;
- buffeting (possibly);
- an almost constant low airspeed;
- a rapid loss of height at a steady rate of descent.

The gyroscopes may topple in a spin, so information from the attitude indicator will be of no value. Some aircraft have gyroscopic instruments (e.g. the AI) which should be caged (locked) prior to performing any aerobatic manoeuvre in order to protect them.

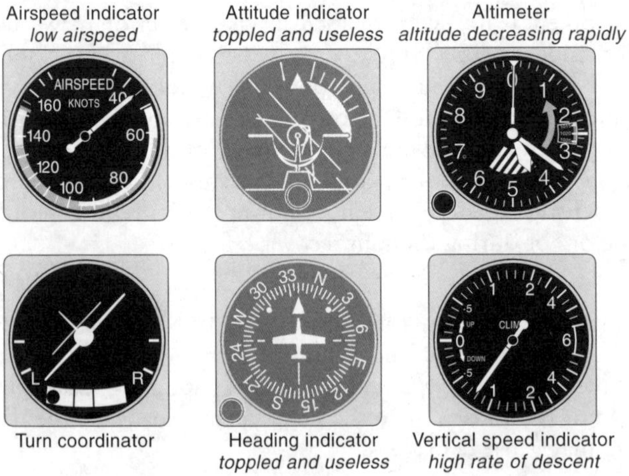

■ *Figure 11a-6* ***The flight instruments in a spin***

The precise spin recovery depends on the **spin direction.** In practice, of course, you will know the direction of the spin that you have induced. In an inadvertent spin, however, where the direction of spin may not be obvious, it can be obtained from the turn coordinator indicating left or right. Pay no attention to the balance ball in a spin. Your outside view of the ground may also assist you, but the turn coordinator is the best clue to spin direction.

The turn coordinator is the best clue to spin direction.

Recovery From a Spin

The technique is:

- **check throttle closed and flaps up;**
- **verify direction of spin** on the turn coordinator;
- **apply full opposite rudder;**
- **pause** (to allow the rudder to become effective and stop the yaw, which turns a stall into a spin);
- **move the control column centrally forward** to unstall the wings (full forward if necessary);
- **as soon as the rotation stops, centralise the rudder** (it may take one, two or more complete turns for the rotation to stop);
- **level the wings** and ease out of the ensuing dive;
- **as the nose comes up** through the horizon **add power** and **climb** to regain height.

In the process of unstalling the wings, the nose attitude will become steeper and the mass of the aeroplane will move closer to the spin axis. The result may be a noticeable increase in the rate of rotation just before recovery.

Airmanship

Airmanship is knowing how to recover from a spin, even though you may never have to do it.

Ensure that your aeroplane is certified for spins and that weight and balance aspects are correct.

Ensure that you know the correct spin recovery technique for your aeroplane type (found in the Pilot's Operating Handbook).

The spin is an aerobatic manoeuvre and so the pre-aerobatic HASELL check should be performed prior to practising. A proper aerobatic harness should be worn. A thorough **lookout** is essential as a spin and recovery will consume a lot of height (possibly 500 ft per rotation). Commence your practice at a height that will allow you to **recover by 3,000 ft agl.**

Exert firm control over the spin entry and recovery. You should fly the aeroplane – not vice versa. Never spin inadvertently! When climbing away after each spin recovery, reorientate yourself using familiar landmarks.

Airwork 11a
Full Spins

Aim *To enter, maintain and recover from a fully developed spin (provided that it is an approved manoeuvre for the aeroplane).*

NOTE Recovery from the spin should be made by 3,000 ft agl.

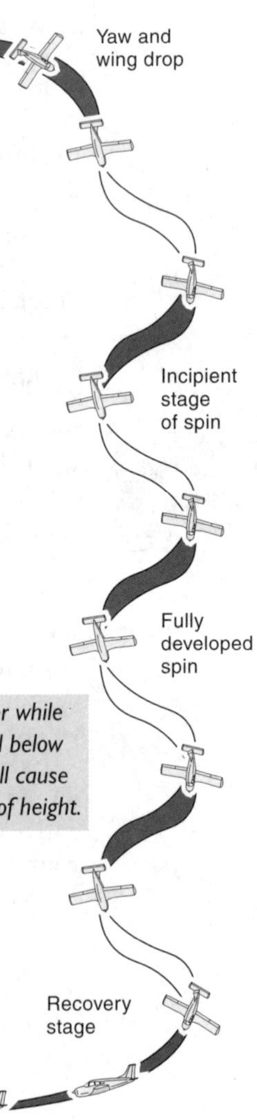

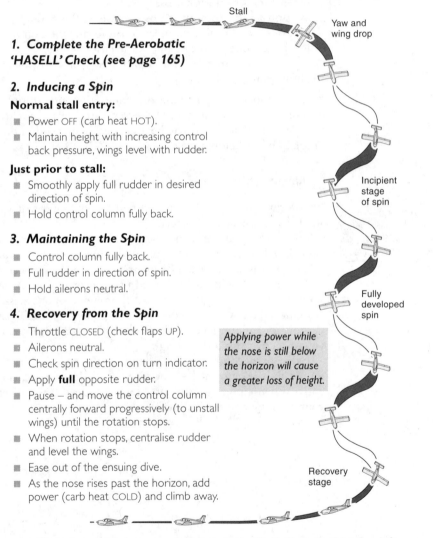

1. Complete the Pre-Aerobatic 'HASELL' Check (see page 165)

2. Inducing a Spin

Normal stall entry:

- Power OFF (carb heat HOT).
- Maintain height with increasing control back pressure, wings level with rudder.

Just prior to stall:

- Smoothly apply full rudder in desired direction of spin.
- Hold control column fully back.

3. Maintaining the Spin

- Control column fully back.
- Full rudder in direction of spin.
- Hold ailerons neutral.

4. Recovery from the Spin

- Throttle CLOSED (check flaps UP).
- Ailerons neutral.
- Check spin direction on turn indicator.
- Apply **full** opposite rudder.
- Pause – and move the control column centrally forward progressively (to unstall wings) until the rotation stops.
- When rotation stops, centralise rudder and level the wings.
- Ease out of the ensuing dive.
- As the nose rises past the horizon, add power (carb heat COLD) and climb away.

Applying power while the nose is still below the horizon will cause a greater loss of height.

NOTE The spin entry and recovery technique in the Pilot's Operating Handbook for your aircraft may differ slightly from this procedure. Use the technique recommended for your aeroplane.

Exercise 11b ⁘ Ex. 11a JAR-FCL Incipient Spins

Aim

To recognise the onset of a spin and recover before a full spin develops.

Considerations

Incipient spin means the beginning or onset of a spin. It is, if you like, a recovery from a spin before the spin actually occurs – with a minimum loss of height.

While spinning is not permitted in many training aeroplanes, the incipient spin is. Recovery should be made before the wings go through a bank angle exceeding 90°.

Flying the Manoeuvre

An incipient spin can be induced from almost any flight conditions by flying slowly, continually bringing the control column back and then, when almost at the stall, applying full rudder to generate yaw in the desired spin direction.

To recover from an incipient spin, simultaneously:

- **move the control column centrally forward** sufficiently to unstall the wings;
- **apply sufficient rudder** to prevent further yaw;
- **apply maximum power** (see note below); and
- **as airspeed increases, level the wings** with coordinated use of rudder and ailerons, **ease out of the descent** and resume desired flightpath.

NOTE If the nose has dropped below the horizon, do not apply power until after the recovery is complete and the nose rises above the horizon.

Airwork 11b
The Incipient Spin

Aim *To recognise the onset of a spin and recover before a full spin develops.*

1. To Induce an Incipient Spin

- Fly slowly, bringing the control column progressively back, maintaining height as the speed reduces.
- Just prior to the stall, apply full rudder in the desired spin direction.

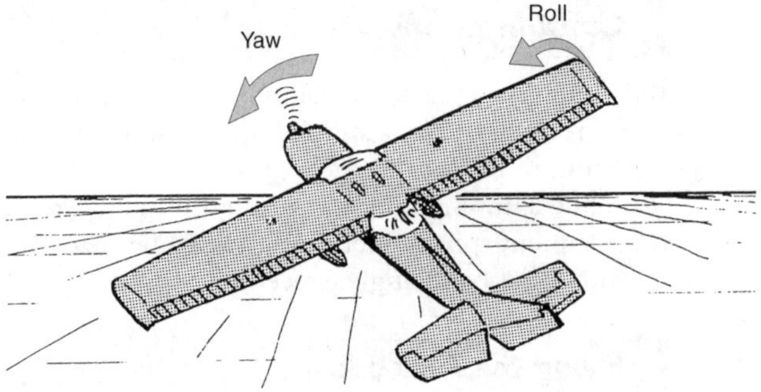

2. Recovery Procedure

As the spin commences, simultaneously:

- Move the control column centrally forward sufficiently to unstall the wings.
- Apply sufficient rudder to prevent further yaw.
- Apply maximum power (see note below).
- As the airspeed increases when the wings are unstalled, level the wings with coordinated use of rudder and ailerons, ease out of the descent and resume desired flightpath.

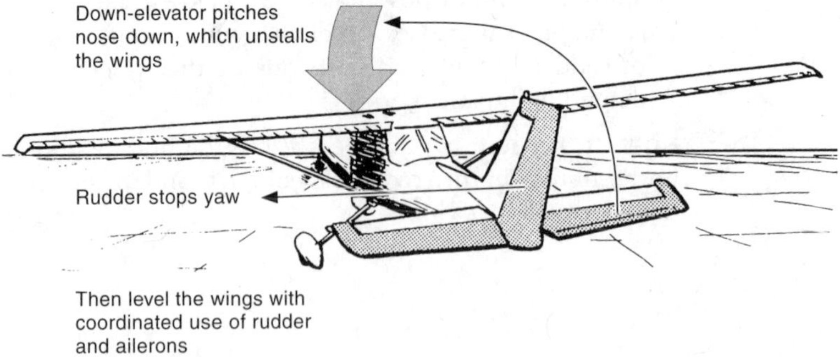

NOTE If the nose has dropped below the horizon, do not apply power until after the recovery is complete and the nose rises above the horizon as you ease out of the dive.

Exercise 12
Standard Take-Off and Climb to Downwind Leg

Aim

To take off into wind and climb out in the circuit pattern to downwind leg.

Considerations

This manoeuvre involves:
- **flying the aeroplane off the ground** and clearing any obstacles;
- **a climb to circuit altitude;** and
- **positioning the aeroplane on downwind leg.**

The Take-Off

Take-off into wind if possible.

During the take-off, the aeroplane must be accelerated to an airspeed at which it is capable of flying. Having a headwind component on a runway 'gives' you airspeed even before you have started rolling. For example, a 10 knot headwind component gives you 10 kt of airspeed over and above the groundspeed on take-off.

Taking off into wind is good airmanship because it gives:
- **the shortest ground run;**
- **the lowest groundspeed** for the required take-off airspeed;
- **the best directional control,** especially at the start of the ground run, when there is not much airflow over the control surfaces;
- **no side forces** on the undercarriage (as in a crosswind);
- **the best obstacle clearance** because of the shorter ground run and the steeper flightpath over ground;
- **the best position in the climb-out** from which to make an into-wind landing straight ahead (or slightly to one side) in the case of engine failure immediately after take-off.

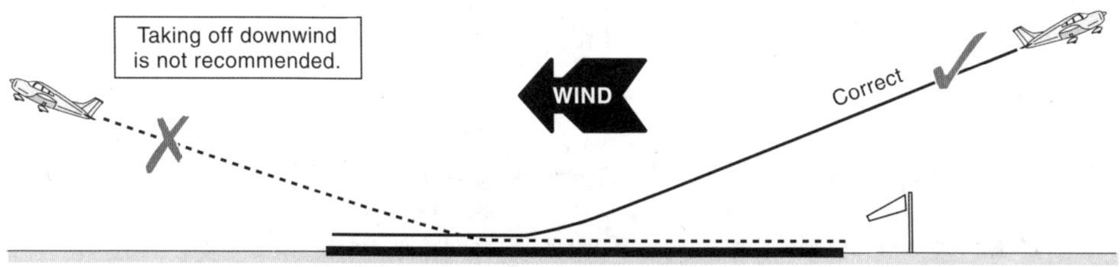

■ *Figure 12-1* ***Take-off into wind***

Wind Direction

Always be aware of the surface wind direction.

The circuit direction will normally be into wind, since this benefits both take-offs and landings. Knowing the wind, you can choose the most suitable runway and work out what the circuit pattern will be. You can determine the wind direction:

- **as you walk out** to the aeroplane;
- **from the wind direction indicator** (i.e. the windsock);
- **from other clues** such as smoke being blown away from a chimney;
- **by asking Air Traffic Control** (ATC), who will advise you of the (magnetic) direction from which the wind is blowing and its strength, e.g. 360/25 is a north wind at 25 kt.

Runway Distance

Ensure that the runway is adequate.

The take-off performance chart should be consulted if you are not certain that the runway is adequate in all respects. High-elevation aerodromes and high temperatures will increase the runway distances required, because of the decreased air density which degrades both engine and aerodynamic performance. Runway upslope and a tailwind component will also degrade the take-off.

Flaps

Use of take-off flaps shortens the take-off run. Most training aircraft use either zero flap or an early stage of flap for take-off. Extending take-off flap increases the lifting ability of the wings, enabling the aeroplane to take off at a lower airspeed and with a shorter ground run.

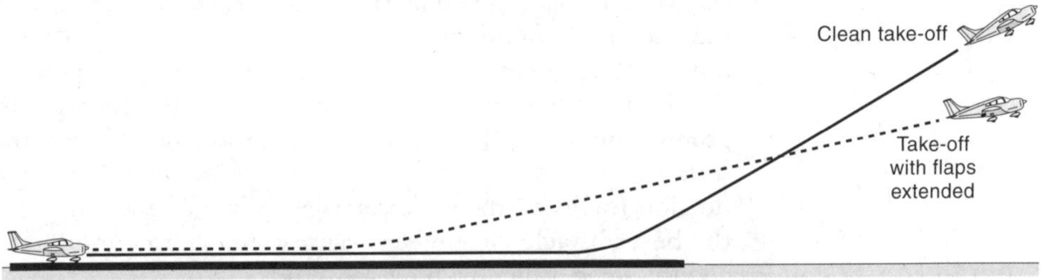

■ *Figure 12-2* ***Flap allows a shorter take-off ground run***

Do not use landing flap for take-off, because the significant increase in drag will degrade the take-off and climb-out performance. Do not exceed the recommended flap settings for take-off!

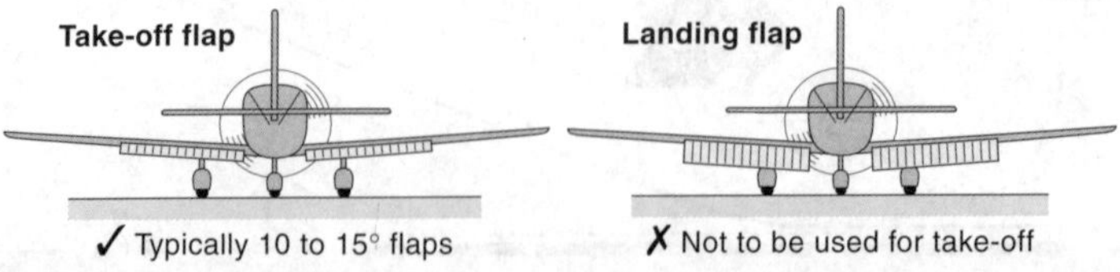

■ *Figure 12-3* ***Flap for take-off is less than that used for landing***

The Standard Circuit

To maintain some form of safe and orderly flow of traffic at an aerodrome, and to allow easy and safe access to the active runway, aircraft are flown in the standard circuit pattern. For good operational reasons, the preferred direction of take-off and landing is into wind, hence the same direction will generally be used by aircraft both taking off and landing.

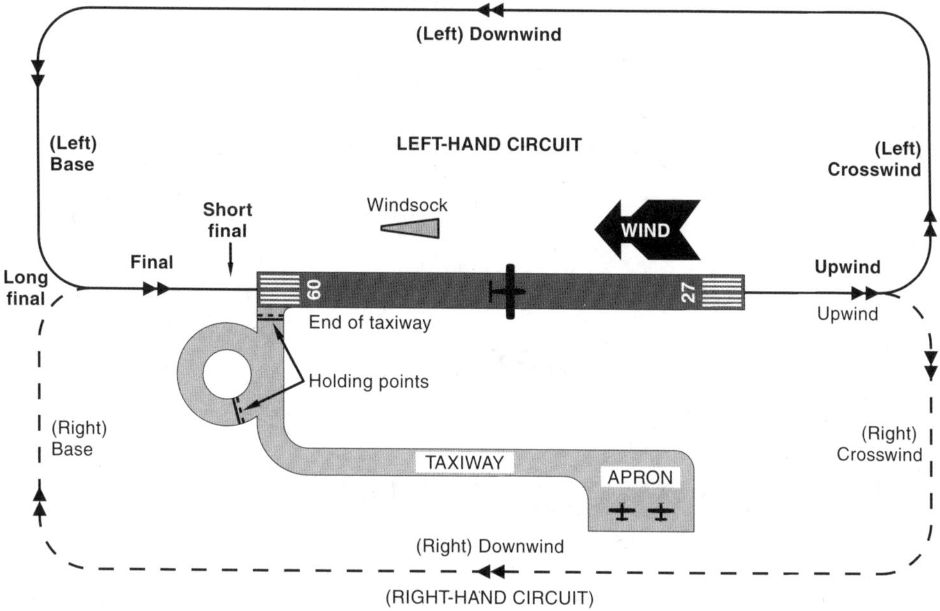

■ *Figure 12-4* ***The circuit pattern is rectangular***

The standard circuit pattern is left-handed.

The circuit is a rectangular pattern, based on the runway in use. The standard circuit is left-handed, with all turns being made to the left. This gives a better view from the captain's seat than turns to the right. At some aerodromes and on some particular runways, however, the circuits are right-handed to avoid built-up areas, high terrain, restricted airspace, etc.

The circuit is referred to the runway on which it is based, e.g. "join the circuit for 36" refers to the circuit based on Runway 36. The '36' indicates that the runway heading is somewhere in the range 355° to 360° to 005°M.

The Legs of a Circuit

Following take-off, climb straight ahead on the **upwind leg** to at least 500 ft above aerodrome level (aal).

At 500 ft, commence a turn onto the **crosswind leg** and continue the climb to circuit height, which for most aerodromes is 1,000 ft aal, and level out.

Circuit height at some aerodromes may be different for various reasons (to avoid terrain or remain beneath certain airspace), but will almost certainly lie in the range of 750 ft to 1,250 ft aal.

A turn is made onto **downwind** leg and the aeroplane is flown at circuit height parallel to the runway. A 'downwind' radio call as you fly abeam the upwind (i.e. take-off) end of the runway is often made to alert other aircraft and Air Traffic Control to your position.

At a suitable point on downwind a turn onto **base** leg is made and a descent commenced. Ideally, a turn onto **final approach** should be completed by 500 ft above aerodrome level (aal).

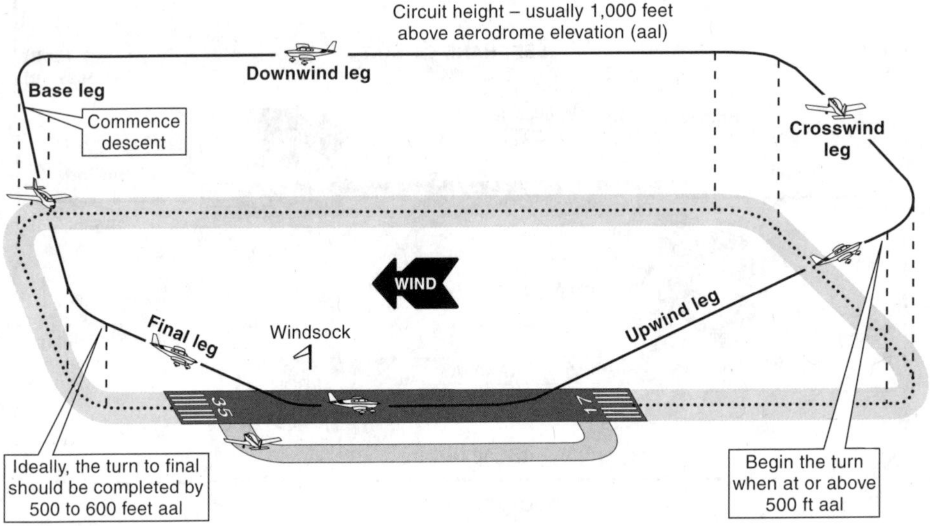

■ *Figure 12-5* ***The normal circuit pattern is flown at 1,000 ft aal***

Wind

Allow for wind effect in the circuit.

While flying in the circuit, you should aim to fly a rectangular pattern over the ground. This means that, on any leg where there is a crosswind component, drift should be laid off to compensate for the wind effect. This is most easily achieved by selecting a reference point on the ground well ahead of the aeroplane and making sure that the aeroplane tracks directly towards it.

The wind at circuit height may differ from that on the ground – simply adjust your heading so that the track over the ground is correct.

Flying the Manoeuvre

Before Take-Off

Taxi to a suitable position for the pre-take-off checks.

Taxi towards the runway and position the aircraft clear of the runway (or in a run-up bay if provided) to carry out your engine run-up and pre-take-off checks. Ensure that:

- **the slipstream** will not affect other aircraft;
- **a brake failure** will not cause you to run into other aircraft or obstacles;
- **loose stones** will not damage the propeller or be blown rearwards.

A suitable position is usually at 90° to the runway, giving you a good view in either direction, although, in strong winds, it is better to face into wind. This ensures adequate cooling of the engine and avoids spurious rpm fluctuations due to wind gusts during the run-up.

Set the brakes to PARK and set idling rpm (typically 1,000 to 1,200 rpm). This allows the engine to continue warming-up, yet be adequately cooled.

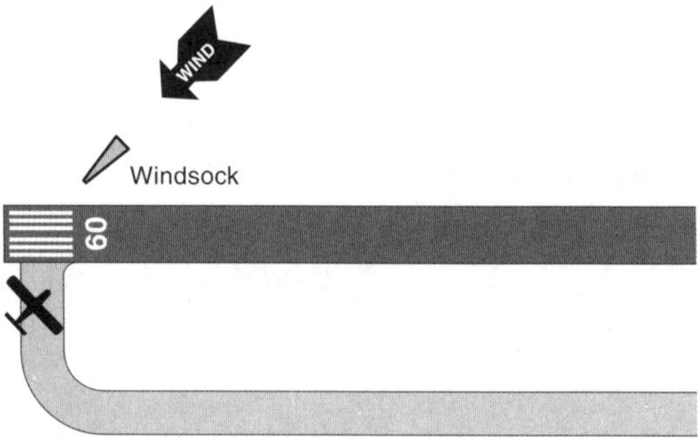

■ Figure 12-6 ***Position aircraft for pre-take-off check, preferably into wind***

Vital Actions

The pre-take-off check contains vital actions. Set the brakes to PARK and complete the pre-take-off vital actions. You are just about to take the aeroplane off the ground and into the air, so it is vital that everything is as it should be. The pre-take-off check should confirm this.

A Typical Pre-Take-Off Check

Use the pre-take-off check in your Pilot's Operating Handbook. The mnemonic TMPFISCH covers the pre-take-off items well; but still read the checklist! It will probably contain such items as those shown on the following pages.

TYPICAL TMPFISCH CHECKLIST

T **Trim:** *set for take-off.*

Throttle Friction Nut: *sufficiently tight (to prevent the throttle slipping once it has been set), but not so tight that the throttle is difficult to move.*

M **Mixture:** *RICH.*

P **Primer:** *fuel primer in and locked.*

F **Fuel:** *correct fuel tank selected and contents sufficient for flight.*

Fuel Pump: *ON (if fitted – most likely in low-wing aeroplanes) and fuel pressure adequate.*

Flaps: *set for take-off.*

I **Instruments:** *flight instruments checked for correct settings and indications and engine instruments checked for correct indications. Follow a systematic scan around the instrument panel.*

Flight Instruments

Airspeed indicator: *indicating zero or well below the stalling speed.*

Attitude indicator: *set the model aeroplane against the artificial horizon.*

Altimeter: *set Aerodrome QNH and check that correct elevation is indicated (or vice-versa, i.e. set the known aerodrome elevation and confirm that a reasonable QNH is displayed in the subscale); or set QFE so that the altimeter indicates zero.*

Vertical speed indicator: *showing zero (neither a climb nor a descent).*

Heading indicator: *align with the magnetic compass (which you also check).*

Turn coordinator: *previously checked with left and right turns during the taxi (if it is driven electrically or by an engine-driven vacuum pump – if venturi-driven, it cannot be tested prior to flight).*

Balance ball: *tested during the taxi with left and right turns.*

Clock: *wound (yes, the clock is a flight instrument); check that the correct time is set.*

Engine and Other Instruments

Tachometer: *rpm remaining steady as set (at idling rpm, typically 1,000 to 1,200 rpm).*

Oil pressure: *normal.*

Oil temperature: *normal.*

Fuel pressure: *already checked if a fuel pump (or boost pump or auxiliary pump) is fitted.*

Ammeter: *to indicate that the electrical system is charging.*

Suction gauge: *for correct 'suction' from engine-driven vacuum pumps (if a vacuum-driven gyroscopic attitude indicator and/or heading indicator is fitted).*

This seems a lot but, if you work your way around the panel systematically, you will cover them all.

TYPICAL TMPFISCH CHECKLIST

S ***Switches***

Magnetos: *confirm that there are no aircraft behind you and run the engine up (typically to 1,800 or 2,000 rpm).*

While at high rpm, the carburettor heat can be tested at HOT, which should cause the rpm to drop by about 100 rpm. This indicates that the system is working, the warm air entering the engine being less dense and causing a drop in the power produced. An rpm increase during the 10 seconds or so you leave the carburettor heat HOT indicates that carburettor ice was present and has been melted. At the end of this test, return carburettor heat to COLD. The magnetos can now be checked knowing that the carburettor is free of ice. If you think carburettor ice may re-form prior to take-off, take appropriate action (see later).

Switch from BOTH to LEFT (and note an rpm drop, typically between 75 rpm and 175 rpm, due to the right magneto system being earthed and only the left spark plug in each cylinder firing, then back to BOTH, when the rpm should return to that set).

Switch from BOTH to RIGHT (and note an rpm drop, typically between 75 rpm and 175 rpm, due to the left magneto system being earthed and only the right spark plug in each cylinder firing, then back to BOTH, when the rpm should return to that set).

No rpm drop, a 'dead cut' (i.e. the engine stops firing) or an imbalance in the two rpm drops (exceeding 75–100 rpm) indicates a problem.

If you inadvertently go to OFF when testing the magnetos, allow the engine to stop. An experienced pilot will be able to keep the engine going, but quick action is needed, otherwise backfiring and possible damage could occur. It is no problem to stop the engine and then restart it again normally.

Close the throttle and check rpm (typically 600 to 700 rpm); then return to 1,000 or 1,200 rpm.

Other Switches: *as required (including pitot heaters, rotating beacon, if fitted).*

C **Controls:** *full and free movement.*

Carburettor heat: *COLD (or as advised by the Pilot's Operating Handbook if you are in conditions where the formation of carburettor ice is likely).*

Cowl flaps: *set for take-off (if fitted);*

H **Hatches:** *doors secure, and no loose articles in the cockpit.*

Harness: *secure, seat firmly locked in place on the floor, passengers briefed.*

Hydraulics: *as required (if appropriate).*

NOTE 'TMPFISCH' is only one mnemonic to help pilots remember the items in the pre-take-off check. There are others such as 'TTMFGHH' and so on. The important thing is that you learn the check as described in your own Pilot's Operating Handbook. Checks are a vital part of safe flying.

Line-Up

ATC and Radio Procedures

Consider Air Traffic Control (ATC) and radio procedures before lining up on the runway. The category of the aerodrome will determine whether take-off clearances are required. Consider this and other ATC aspects before entering the runway, checking 'all clear left' and 'all clear right' along the runway and on final approach before you do. Aircraft already taking off or landing have right of way over a taxiing aeroplane.

Straighten the Nosewheel

Line up and ensure that the nosewheel is straight. Make full use of the runway length available (within reason). One of the most useless things in aviation is runway behind you!

The take-off run should be along the centreline of the runway, and the easiest way to achieve this is to line up with one main wheel either side of the centreline markings (if the runway has them). Roll forward a metre or two, thereby ensuring that the nosewheel is straight (before applying brakes if used); but do not waste runway length.

Have a good look out. Scan the runway and circuit area for other aircraft that could conflict with you. Maintain an awareness of other circuit traffic, both visually and aurally (by listening to the radio). It is good habit to check the windsock at this time, just before you roll.

The Take-Off Roll

Release the Brakes and Open the Throttle Smoothly

Select a reference point at the end of the runway (or beyond) on which to keep straight. In side-by-side cockpits, you should view this reference point straight ahead (parallel with the longitudinal axis of the aeroplane), and not over the propeller spinner.

Select a distant reference point.

Release the brakes and smoothly apply full power. A mental count of "one-two-three" will occupy the time required to advance the throttle to full power. Glance at the tachometer early in the take-off run to confirm that the correct rpm has been achieved. Have your heels on the floor with the balls of your feet on the rudder pedals to control steering (and not high enough to apply the toe brakes).

Keep straight and accelerate smoothly in the first few seconds of the ground roll.

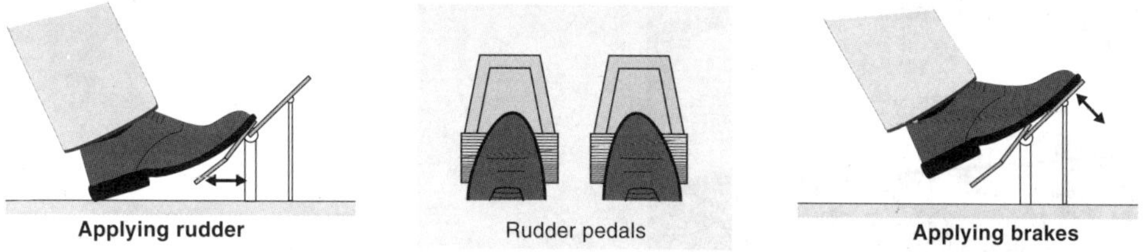

■ *Figure 12-7* ***Heels on the floor (and no pressure on brakes)***

Keep Straight with Rudder

Use your reference point at or beyond the far end of the runway centreline to assist you in keeping straight. Even though you are focusing well ahead, the edges of the runway in your peripheral vision and the runway centreline disappearing under the nose provide supporting guidance.

With the application of power, there may be a tendency to yaw because of the:

- **slipstream effect** on the tail-fin; and
- **torque reaction** pressing one wheel down.

For an aeroplane whose propeller rotates clockwise as seen from the cockpit, the tendency is to yaw left on take-off. If the propeller rotates anti-clockwise, the tendency is to yaw right.

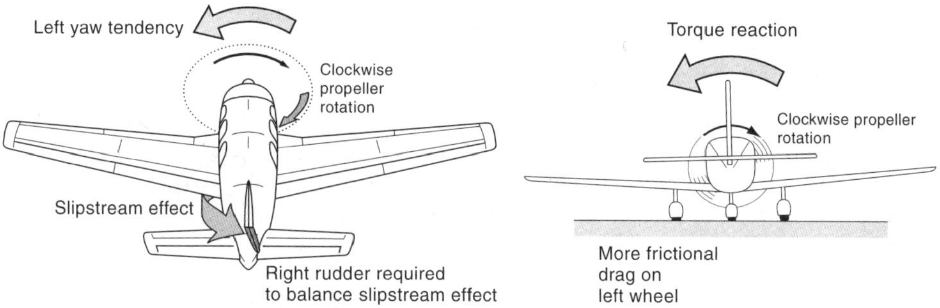

■ *Figure 12-8* ***There is a tendency to yaw on the take-off run***

Any yawing tendency should be counteracted with rudder. If yawing left, apply right rudder (and vice versa). Large rudder pedal movements may be required early in the take-off run but, as the airflow over the rudder increases, smaller movements will be sufficient. Just look ahead and keep the aeroplane tracking straight down the centreline. Steer the aeroplane with your feet (and not your hands). Keep straight with rudder.

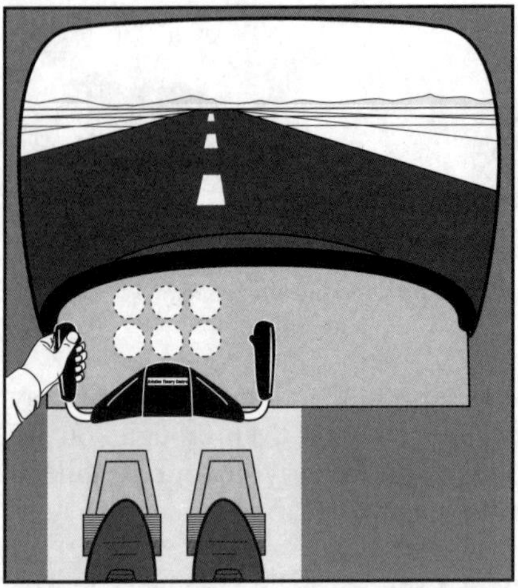

■ *Figure 12-9* ***Keep straight using your feet on the rudder pedals***

NOTE A brief mention of crosswinds (which are covered more fully in Exercise 13) in case an into-wind runway is not available. Any significant crosswind will tend to lift one wing. The wings can be kept level by holding the control column sufficiently into wind (by a large amount at the start of the take-off run, reducing the amount as speed is gained and the ailerons become more effective). Keep the wings level with aileron.

Protect the Nosewheel

Protect the nosewheel by holding the weight off it.

On the ground, the nosewheel carries a fair load, especially if the take-off surface is rough or soft. During the normal take-off roll of a tricycle-gear aeroplane, hold a little back pressure on the control column. This takes some of the weight off the nosewheel and protects it somewhat.

Back pressure also prevents 'wheelbarrowing' – a situation where the nosewheel is held on the ground after sufficient lift has been generated for flight. 'Wheelbarrowing' is bad news for the nosewheel!

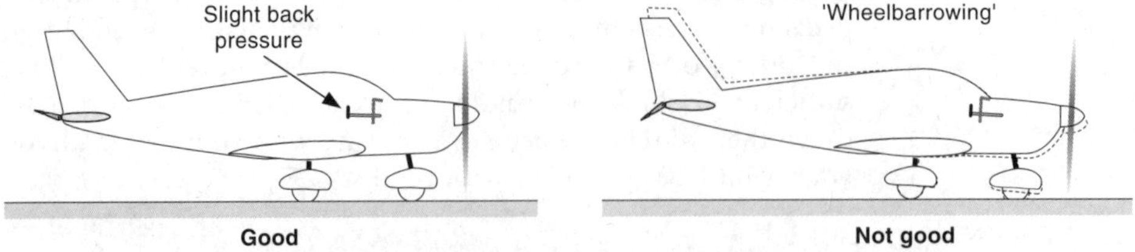

■ *Figure 12-10* ***Protect the nosewheel by holding the weight off it***

Check the Power

Check the power early in the take-off run.

After maximum power has been set and tracking down the runway centreline is under control, glance at the engine instruments to check that full power is indeed being delivered. Engine rpm should be as expected. Oil pressure and temperature should both be within limits. This glance should take no more than one or two seconds.

Lift-Off

Lift the aeroplane off the ground when you reach flying speed.

When flying speed is reached, take the aeroplane off the ground with elevator. A gradual backward movement of the control column will allow the aeroplane to become airborne when flying speed is reached.

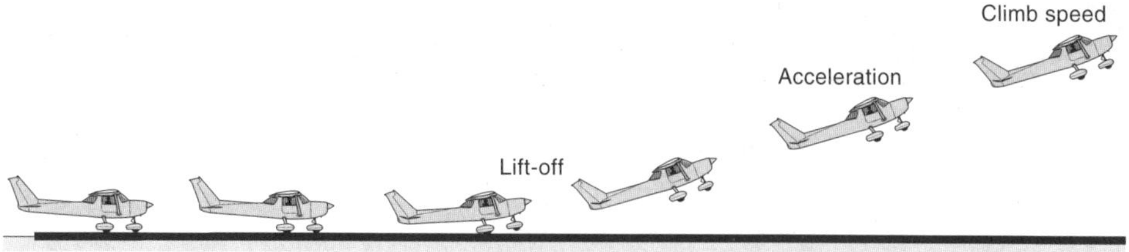

■ *Figure 12-11* ***When flying speed is reached, lift off gently with elevator***

If you lift off too soon, the aeroplane may not fly and will settle back onto the ground; if you lift off too late, the wheels and tyres will have been subjected to extra stress, the airspeed will be excessive and the take-off will have been unnecessarily lengthened. Obstacle clearance might also be a problem.

■ *Figure 12-12* ***Gradually assume the climb attitude with elevator***

The 'cushioning' of ground effect when the aeroplane is flying close to the ground allows flight at lower speeds than when the aeroplane is well clear of the ground. It is important that the aeroplane accelerates to the correct climbing speed soon after lift-off to avoid 'sink'.

The Climb-Out

Initial Climb-Out

When airborne and climbing, check attitude and tracking, and look out for other traffic.

- **Look out,** both at the horizon to check your attitude and your tracking, and to look for other aircraft.
- **Keep the wings level** with ailerons.
- **Maintain balance** with rudder pressure.
- **With the elevator,** hold the nose attitude in the correct position relative to the horizon for the climb-out, glancing at the airspeed indicator to confirm that climb speed has been achieved.
- **Trim.**

At a safe height (say 200 or 300 ft aal) raise the take-off flaps (if used). During the climb following take-off, look out to check your attitude and to check for other aircraft. Confirm that you have achieved the desired climb speed and adjust the attitude if necessary. After the aeroplane has settled into a steady climb, trim-off any steady control pressure.

The procedure for aircraft that have a fuel pump switched on for take-off is to switch it off at a safe height (say 500 ft aal). Then check that fuel pressure remains satisfactory.

NOTE In more advanced aeroplanes with a retractable undercarriage, the wheels will be raised once a positive climb is established after lift-off. Most training aeroplanes have fixed landing gear and so this is not a consideration.

If your Pilot's Operating Handbook calls for an after-take-off check (with respect to flaps and fuel pump for instance), then it would be appropriate to perform this check when you are established in the climb-out (say at about 600 ft aal).

Climb-Out to Circuit Height

As you climb-out following take-off:

- **Look out** to check your attitude and scan ahead, above and to either side. Check your reference point to confirm that you are tracking on the extended centreline of the runway and not drifting to one side.
- **At 500 ft aal,** first scan the area into which you will be turning and then turn (usually left) onto the crosswind leg using a 7normal climbing turn (bank angle 20° or less). Balance with rudder pressure and maintain climbing speed with elevator. Selecting a new reference point will assist you to track correctly on this crosswind leg. Allow for any drift due to wind effect.
- **Complete the after-take-off check** (if required).

Anticipate reaching circuit height and, as you approach it, start lowering the nose to the cruise attitude. To level off from a climb, use A–P–T:

- **A ATTITUDE** – lower the nose to the straight and level attitude;
  – allow the speed to increase to the desired airspeed.
- **P POWER** – reduce power to maintain the desired airspeed.
- **T TRIM.**

Downwind Leg

At (or approaching) circuit height, check 'all clear' for other traffic and turn onto downwind leg, selecting a reference point well ahead on which to parallel the runway. You may be required to call "Downwind" on the radio as you pass abeam the upwind end of the runway (i.e. the climb-out end of the runway).

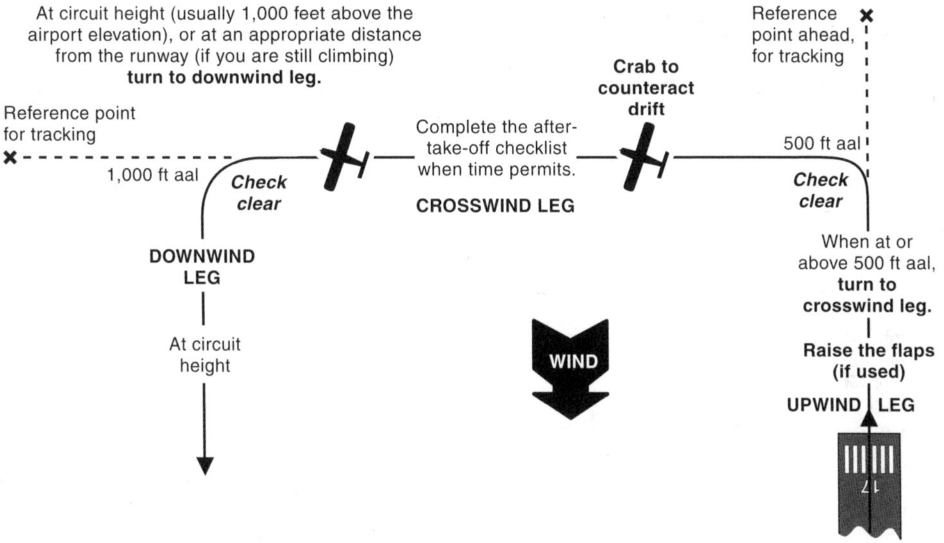

■ *Figure 12-13* ***Take-off to downwind***

Airmanship

Maintain a good lookout prior to entering the runway and in the circuit area.

The take-off roll, lift-off and climb-out to circuit height is one continuous manoeuvre that you should endeavour to fly smoothly, with firm control over the aeroplane. Hold your heading accurately, and adjust the pitch attitude to hold the climb-out speed as closely as possible, but certainly within 5 kt.

Fly an accurate circuit and follow the basic Rules of the Air.

Airwork 12
Standard Take-Off and Climb to Downwind Leg

Aim *To take off into wind and climb out in the circuit pattern to downwind leg.*

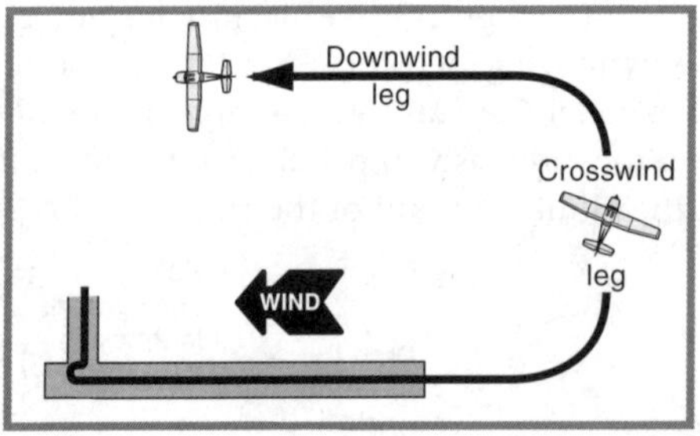
Downwind
leg
Crosswind
leg
WIND

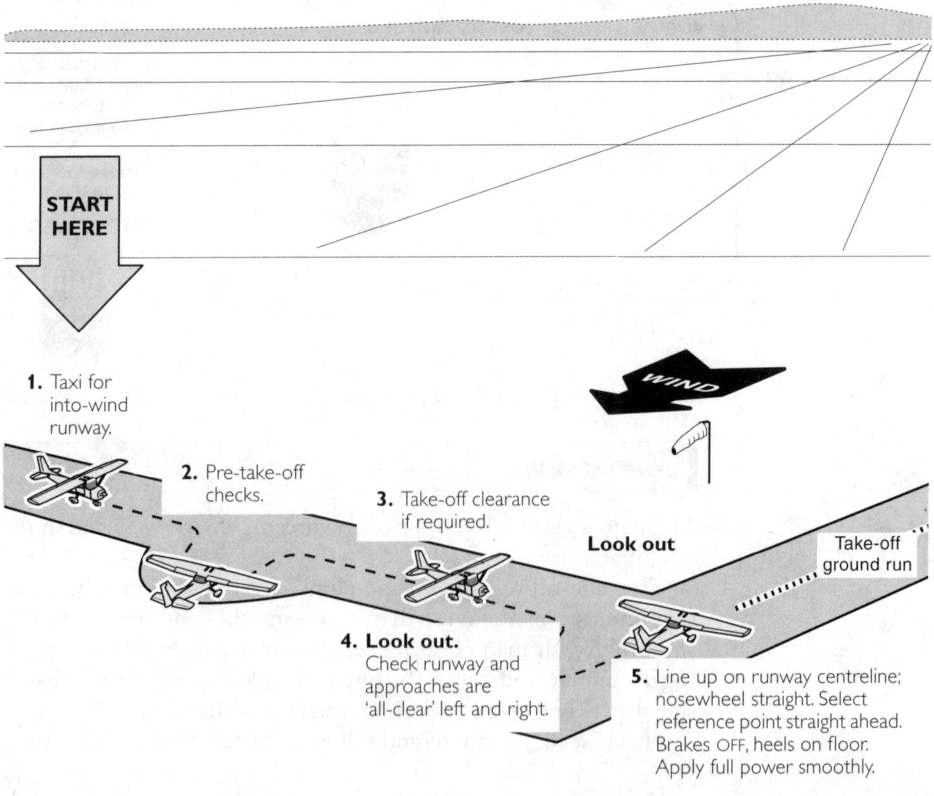
START
HERE
1. Taxi for into-wind runway.
2. Pre-take-off checks.
3. Take-off clearance if required.
WIND
Look out
Take-off ground run
4. Look out. Check runway and approaches are 'all-clear' left and right.
5. Line up on runway centreline; nosewheel straight. Select reference point straight ahead. Brakes OFF, heels on floor. Apply full power smoothly.

Airwork 12

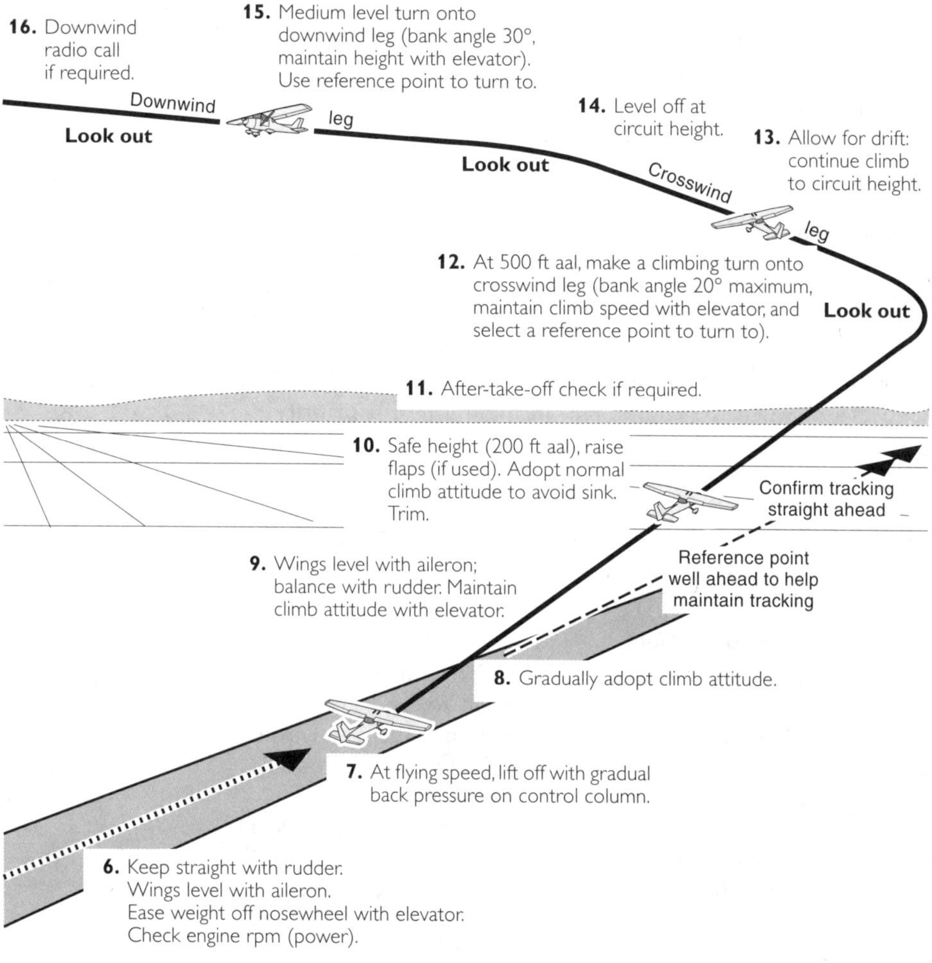
16. Downwind radio call if required.
15. Medium level turn onto downwind leg (bank angle 30°, maintain height with elevator). Use reference point to turn to.
Downwind
leg
Look out
14. Level off at circuit height.
13. Allow for drift: continue climb to circuit height.
Look out
Crosswind
leg
12. At 500 ft aal, make a climbing turn onto crosswind leg (bank angle 20° maximum, maintain climb speed with elevator, and select a reference point to turn to).
Look out
11. After-take-off check if required.
10. Safe height (200 ft aal), raise flaps (if used). Adopt normal climb attitude to avoid sink. Trim.
Confirm tracking straight ahead
Reference point well ahead to help maintain tracking
9. Wings level with aileron; balance with rudder. Maintain climb attitude with elevator.
8. Gradually adopt climb attitude.
7. At flying speed, lift off with gradual back pressure on control column.
6. Keep straight with rudder. Wings level with aileron. Ease weight off nosewheel with elevator. Check engine rpm (power).

12E. Emergencies During the Take-Off

There are two emergencies in the take-off for which you should be prepared (even though they may never happen):

> Under the JAR-FCL1, Emergencies during Take-off and Landing are numbered Exercises 12E and 13E.

1. **Engine failure after take-off** (fortunately not as common these days as it once was!).
2. **The discontinued take-off** while still on the ground (pilot-initiated).

Prior to opening the throttle on each take-off, it is a good idea to run through both of these procedures in your mind.

Engine Failure After Take-Off

If engine power is lost in the climb-out following take-off, the options open to the pilot will vary according to how high the aeroplane is, the nature of the terrain ahead, the wind conditions and so on. An event such as engine failure close to the ground requires prompt and decisive action by the pilot.

> *Immediately lower the nose to the gliding attitude to maintain flying speed.*

No matter when the engine fails in flight, the first priority is to maintain flying speed. Immediately lower the nose to the gliding attitude to maintain flying speed.

A controlled descent and landing, even on an unprepared surface, is preferable by far to an unwanted stall in the attempted climb-out. Close the throttle, in case the engine comes back to life at an inopportune time.

Do Not Turn Back to the Field

> *Land straight ahead.*

The height at which the failure occurs determines how you manoeuvre but, in general, you should plan to land fairly well straight ahead. Height is rapidly lost in descending turns and, from less than 500 ft aal, it is doubtful if you would make the runway. Look for a landing area ahead and within range.

Make yourself familiar with suitable emergency landing areas in the vicinity of your aerodrome, so that in the unlikely event of engine failure you already have a plan of action in mind.

Following engine failure, and having established the glide, quickly select the best landing area from the fields available ahead and within approximately ±30° if possible, otherwise ±60°. Make only gentle turns (say 15° angle of bank maximum).

Gliding turns at low level can be dangerous due to:
- **high rates of descent;** and
- **a tendency** for the pilot to raise the nose to stop a high rate of descent and inadvertently stalling or spinning the aeroplane.

Complete checks and make a Mayday call if time permits. Any attempt to switch fuel tanks and/or to restart the engine depends on time being available.

Maintaining flying speed is vital, more important than any radio call or even starting the engine. If the selected field looks rough and you think damage may result, then, when committed to carrying out the landing:

- **Ignition** OFF.
- **Fuel** OFF.
- **Doors** – unlocked (or as advised in the Pilot's Operating Handbook) in anticipation of a quick evacuation.

After landing:

- **Stop the aeroplane** and set the brakes to park.
- **Stop the engine** (if it is still running).
- **Check fuel** OFF/**ignition** OFF/**electrics** OFF.
- **Evacuate.**

After lift-off on a long runway, you may have sufficient runway remaining to land on. This is one reason why it is good airmanship to start such a take-off using the full length of the runway. One of the most useless things in aviation is runway behind you!

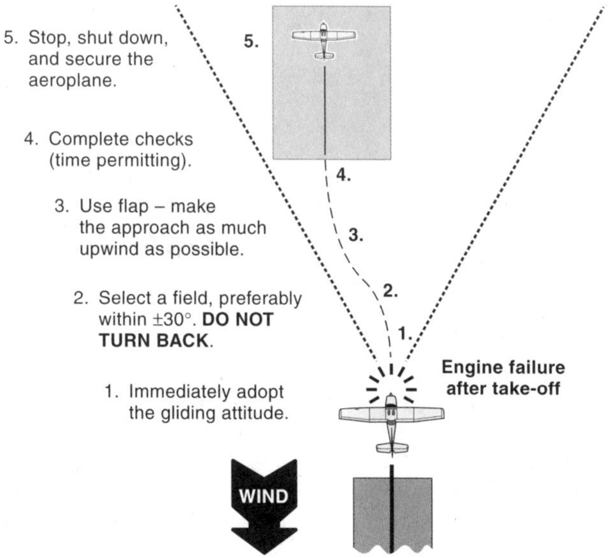

5. Stop, shut down, and secure the aeroplane.
4. Complete checks (time permitting).
3. Use flap – make the approach as much upwind as possible.
2. Select a field, preferably within ±30°. DO NOT TURN BACK.
1. Immediately adopt the gliding attitude.
5.
4.
3.
2.
1.
Engine failure after take-off
WIND

■ *Figure 12-14* ***Engine failure after take-off***

The Discontinued Take-Off

A pilot may decide to abort a take-off during the ground run for many reasons, such as:

- **an obstruction** on the runway;
- **engine failure** or loss of power;
- **engine** or **fuel** problems;
- **faulty instrument indicators** (e.g. airspeed indicator zero);

- **a doubt** that the aeroplane is capable of flying;
- **an insecure seat** that feels as if it might slip backwards; or
- **any other condition** that may, in your opinion, make the take-off inadvisable.

This 'accelerating-and-then-stopping' manoeuvre is known by various names, including **accelerate-stop, discontinued take-off, aborted take-off** or **abandoned take-off.**

Aborting the Take-Off

You must make a firm and conscious decision to abort the take-off, and then act positively:

- **Close the throttle fully.**
- **Keep straight** with rudder.
- **Brake firmly** (immediate maximum braking if required), avoiding skidding or slipping, while maintaining directional control.
- **Stop the aeroplane**, set the brakes to PARK, and establish the cause of the problem.
- **Shut down the engine** if necessary (preferably clear of the runway).
- **Notify the ATS unit** and seek assistance if required.

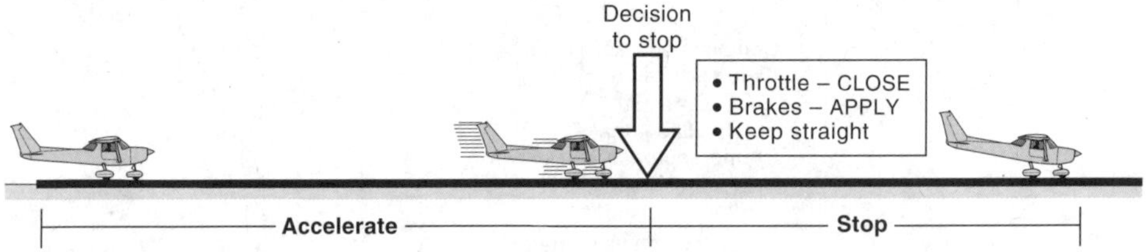

■ *Figure 12-15* ***The aborted take-off***

Variations on the Standard Take-Off

A restricted runway length, a soft surface, and a runway crosswind component, are all variables which require the pilot to adopt a slightly different technique on take-off, compared to the basic technique covered in this exercise.

To avoid interrupting the flow of learning to fly a standard circuit by describing these variations now, they are covered in the next section, within the relevant Exercises:

- **The crosswind take-off** – Exercise 13f, *Crosswind Operations.*
- **The short-field take-off** – Exercise 13g, *Short-Field Operations.*
- **The soft-field take-off** – Exercise 13h, *Soft-Field Operations.*

However, in the UK these take-offs actually form part of Exercise 12 for the purpose of standard Flying Training Records.

Exercise 13a
The Circuit, Powered Approach and Normal Landing

Aim

To continue a normal circuit for a powered approach and landing into wind.

Considerations

Continuing from Exercise 12, this manoeuvre involves:
- flying an accurate circuit based on the runway used;
- making a powered descent, an approach; and
- an into-wind landing.

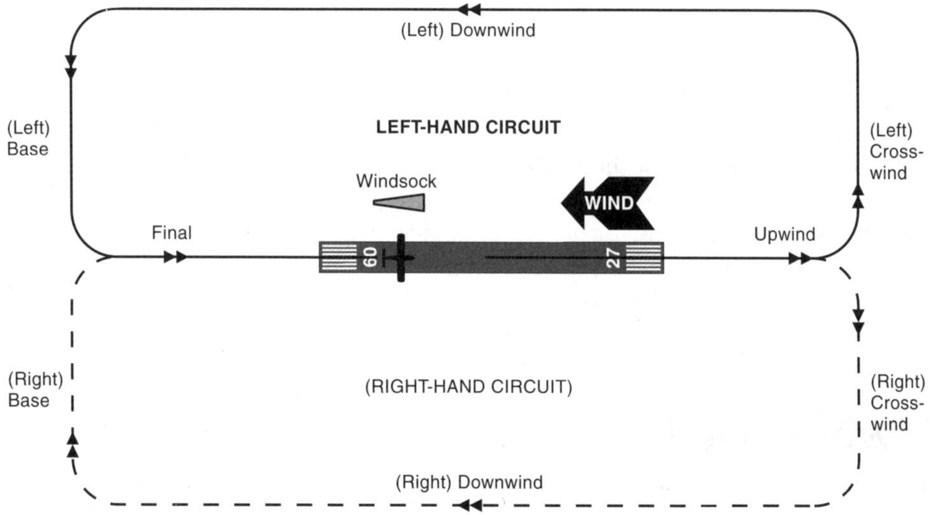

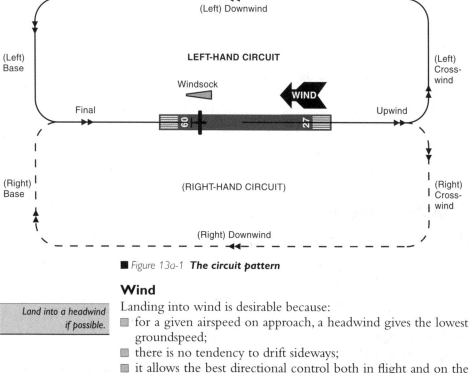

■ *Figure 13a-1* **The circuit pattern**

Wind

Land into a headwind if possible.

Landing into wind is desirable because:
- for a given airspeed on approach, a headwind gives the lowest groundspeed;
- there is no tendency to drift sideways;
- it allows the best directional control both in flight and on the ground; and
- the landing distance required is least.

Landing Distance

If necessary, consult the landing chart to confirm that the runway is adequate for the conditions and aeroplane weight. High elevations and high temperatures decrease air density and increase the landing distance required, as does a tailwind component, a downslope, or a contaminated runway.

Ensure that the landing distance available is adequate.

Power

An engine-assisted approach is the normal procedure, since:

- **you can control the rate of descent** and approach flightpath in varying winds;
- **the engine is kept warm** (ensuring power is available for a go-around); and
- **the change of attitude** in the round-out from a powered approach to the landing attitude is less compared with that for a glide approach.

Use power in the approach and landing.

Flap

Using flap provides:

- **a lower stalling speed,** thus permitting a lower approach speed while retaining an adequate margin over the stall;
- **a steeper flightpath** at a given airspeed, because of the increased drag;
- **a lower nose attitude** at a given airspeed, providing a better view of the approach and landing path;
- **a shorter hold-off** and a shorter landing run because of the increased drag and the lower airspeed.

Use flap in the approach and landing.

NOTE The amount of flap used will depend on the aeroplane and the wind conditions actually prevailing. In strong and gusty winds it may be preferable to use less than full flap (possibly no flap at all) for better controllability and power response. Your flying instructor will advise you.

Flying the Manoeuvre

Flying the Circuit

A good landing is most likely following a good approach. Fly an accurate circuit and get set-up early. Make a "Downwind" call abeam the take-off end of the runway, complete the pre-landing drills and keep a good lookout, both for other aircraft and to check your position relative to the runway.

The Pre-Landing Check

Completing the pre-landing check by about the mid-point on the downwind leg allows you to concentrate fully on your base turn, approach and landing.

The pre-landing check should be completed on downwind leg.

Know the pre-landing drill for your aeroplane. It will include such items as:

- **Brakes** OFF;
- **Mixture** RICH;
- **Fuel:** correct tank(s) selected, contents sufficient, fuel pump on (if fitted) and fuel pressure normal, fuel primer locked;
- **Flaps** as required (and consider what flap you will use on approach, since this may affect where you turn onto base leg);
- **Hatches** (doors) and **harnesses** (seatbelts): SECURE.

Turning Base

A medium level turn from downwind onto base leg is made when the touchdown point on the runway lies approximately 30° behind. This is the 8 o'clock position from the track of the aeroplane. In a strong wind, the turn should be commenced earlier to keep base leg closer to the aerodrome boundary.

Allow for drift on base leg so that the wind does not carry the aeroplane too far from the field and to maintain the rectangular circuit pattern. The amount of drift can assist you in estimating wind strength – the greater the drift angle on base, the stronger the headwind on final.

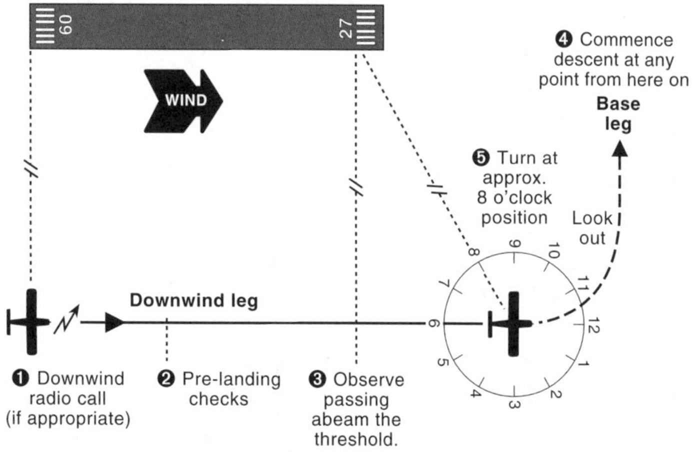

■ *Figure 13a-2* ***Positioning in the circuit and turning base***

Commencing Descent on Base Leg

An approximate descent point for a normal engine-assisted approach to the aiming point on the runway lies at 45° to the aeroplane's track on base leg. In strong winds, when base is usually flown closer to the aerodrome boundary, the descent point at 45° will still be suitable.

The descent should be judged so that you roll out on final no lower than 500 ft above aerodrome level (aal). This means that the turn onto final should be commenced not below 600 ft aal. With a little experience, you will get a feel for just where to commence descent to achieve this. Judgement develops with experience. The availability of power and flap also gives you the ability to control your descent flightpath as you wish.

Flap for the approach and landing should be used as recommended in the Pilot's Operating Handbook and as advised by your flying instructor.

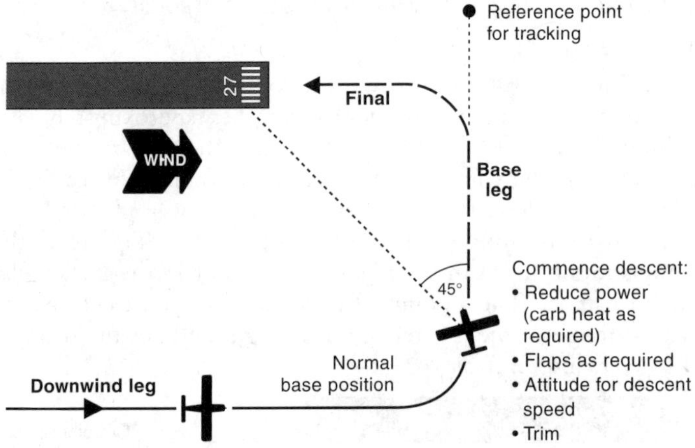

■ *Figure 13a-3* ***Commencing descent on base leg***

Final Approach

The turn onto final is a medium descending turn in which you should:

- **limit the bank angle to 30°** or less (ideally about 15–20°), maintaining balance with rudder pressure;
- **aim to be lined up** on final at or above 500 ft aal;
- **maintain airspeed** with elevator.

Aim to be lined up on final by at least 500 ft above aerodrome level.

The runway perspective as seen from the cockpit will indicate whether you are in line with the runway or not. If not, then do something about it!

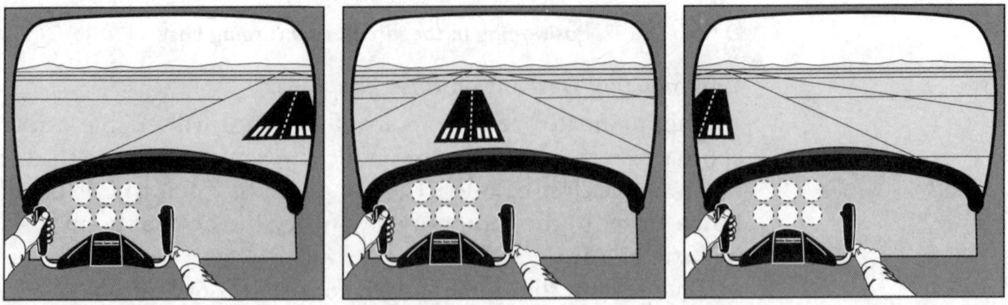

■ *Figure 13a-4* ***Runway perspective on final approach***

Steep turns near the ground should be avoided. If you overshoot the turn onto final, rather than steepen the turn, fly through final and rejoin it from the other side without exceeding a medium bank angle.

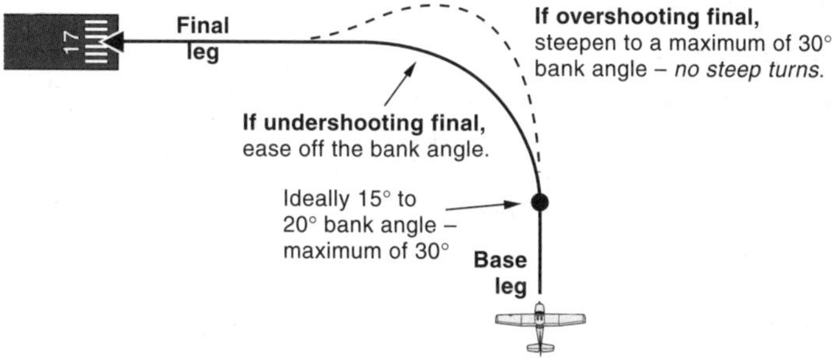

■ *Figure 13a-5* ***Turning onto final approach***

Wind Effect

Allow for wind effect when turning final.

A tailwind on base will increase the aeroplane's speed over the ground and the turn should be commenced a little early to avoid flying through final. Conversely, if there is a headwind on base, the turn onto final can be delayed. If any crosswind exists on final, then lay-off drift so that the aeroplane tracks along the extended centreline of the runway, ensuring that the aeroplane is in balance.

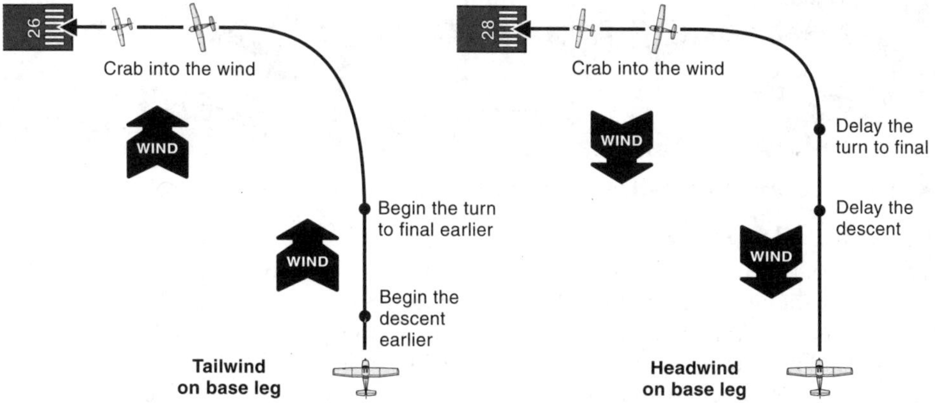

■ *Figure 13a-6* ***Allow for wind effect when turning final***

Windshear and Turbulence on Final

The wind often changes in strength and direction near the ground.

It is usual for the wind to change in strength and direction near the ground due to friction and other causes. A sudden reduction in the headwind component will cause a reduction in indicated airspeed, which can result in an increased sink rate. Turbulence on final also causes airspeed and descent rate fluctuations.

If a strong wind gradient is suspected, then consider flying the approach using a lower flap setting (or no flap at all) and a higher approach speed than normal. The aeroplane will be more stable and more responsive compared to when full flap is lowered and a slow airspeed flown.

Runway Perspective

The perspective of the runway seen on approach will depend on the position of the aeroplane. If it is too high, then the runway will appear longer and narrower than usual and a steep flightpath will be required to arrive near the aiming point for round-out. If the aeroplane is too low, then the runway will appear shorter and wider than usual and the aeroplane will have to be 'dragged in' with power.

Either of these situations can be remedied and the earlier the better! Adjust the rate of descent and the flightpath (using power and attitude) so that the runway assumes its normal perspective as soon as possible. This may require firm and positive action, but the sooner you do it, the more likely you are to make a good landing.

*Take positive action with **power** and **attitude** to stay on slope and on speed.*

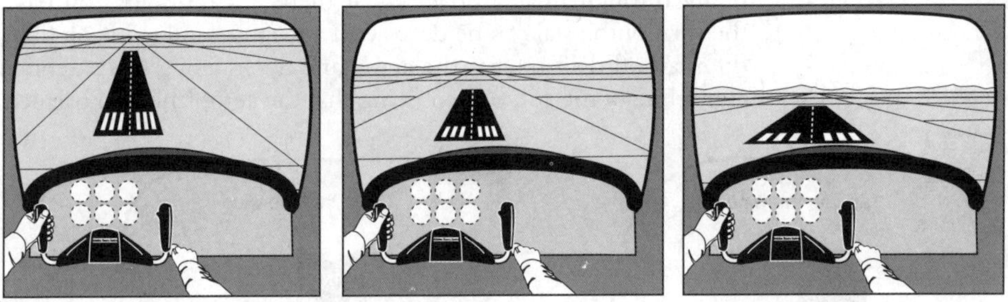

■ *Figure 13a-7* ***Runway perspective on approach***

Fly a Stabilised Approach

The approach path to the runway is three-dimensional. A good approach requires tight control of the flightpath and of the airspeed (i.e. a stabilised approach), and this will set the scene for a good landing. Landing flap should be selected by at least 300 ft aal and the aeroplane retrimmed.

A stable approach sets you up for a good landing.

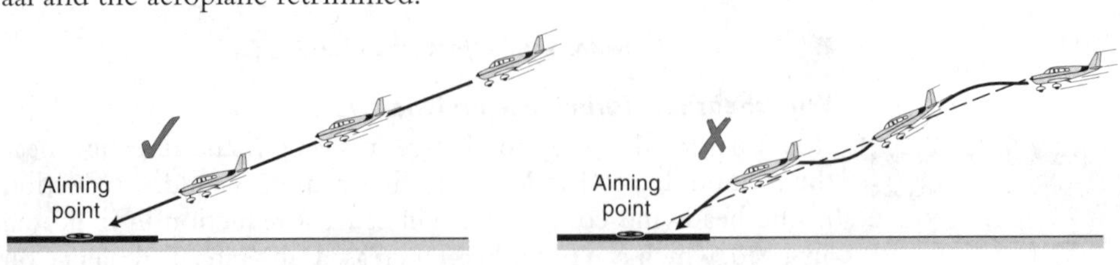

■ *Figure 13a-8* ***Fly a stabilised approach***

Approach at the selected indicated airspeed (IAS) on a suitable slope and remain aligned with the extended runway centreline. This will require positive and firm action on your part. The approach speed chosen will depend on the flap selected and the prevailing conditions (wind strength and direction, or the suspected presence of gustiness, windshear, turbulence or wake turbulence).

The Aiming Point

Ideally, the aiming point should remain fixed in the windscreen – the runway appearing larger and larger as it is approached, without its perspective changing.

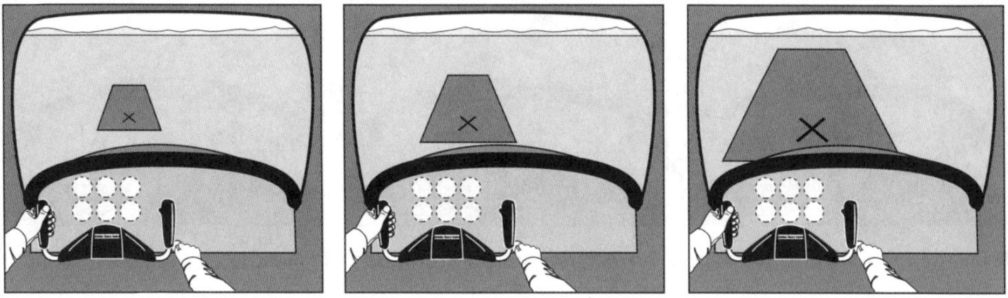

■ *Figure 13a-9* ***Ideally, the aiming point remains fixed in the windscreen***

If the aiming point moves progressively up the windscreen, then the aeroplane is undershooting. Conversely, if the aiming point moves progressively down the windscreen, then the aeroplane is overshooting. In either case, you must take positive action to modify the approach path.

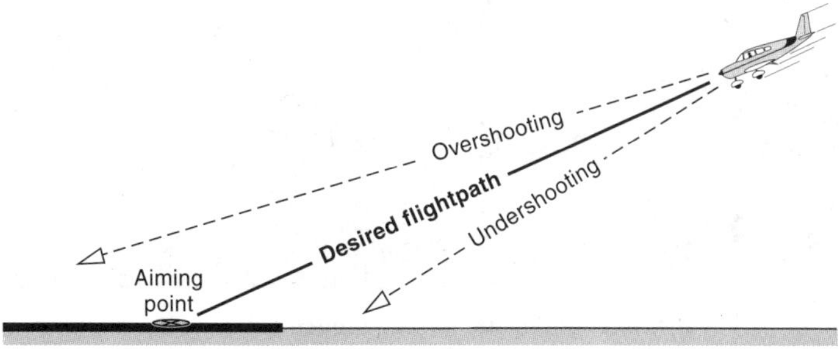

■ *Figure 13a-10* ***Fly the aeroplane down the desired approach path***

Airspeed Control

Control airspeed with elevator and flightpath with power.

Power plus attitude equals performance. Any change in power will require a change in pitch attitude if the same airspeed is to be maintained.

- **If power is added,** raise the nose to maintain airspeed.
- **If power is reduced,** lower the nose to maintain airspeed.

Keeping the aeroplane in trim during the approach will make you task considerably easier.

Undershooting

If the actual approach path projects to a point short of the aiming point (indicated by the aiming point moving up the windscreen and the runway appearing shorter and wider), then regain the desired flightpath by adding power and raising the nose to maintain airspeed.

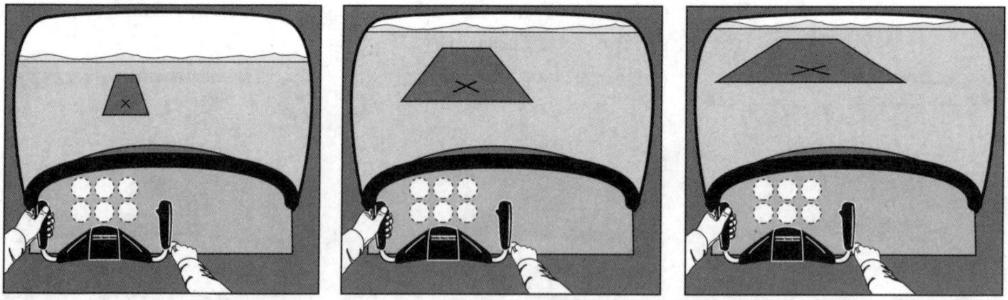

■ *Figure 13a-11* ***Undershooting: to correct, add power and raise the nose***

Overshooting

If the actual approach path projects beyond the aiming point (indicated by the aiming point moving down the windscreen and the runway appearing longer and narrower), steepen the descent by:

- **increasing flap** and adjusting the pitch attitude; or
- **reducing power** and lowering the nose to maintain airspeed.

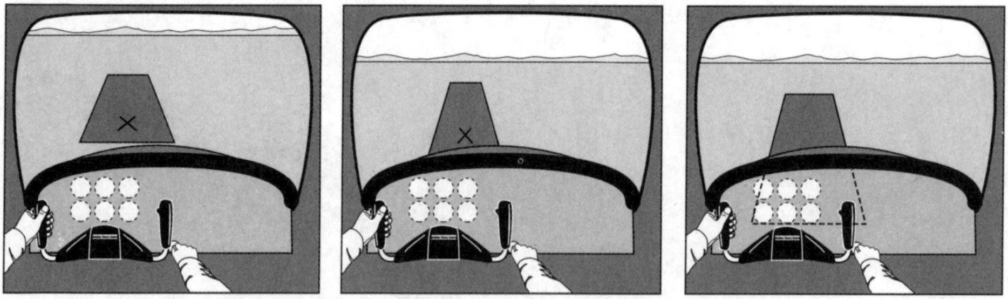

■ *Figure 13a-12* ***Overshooting: to correct, reduce power and lower the nose, or increase flap***

Flightpath Corrections

You will make many corrections to the approach flightpath. Most flightpaths fluctuate between a slight overshoot and a slight undershoot and continual minor corrections are required. Ideally, of course, you will always be on the perfect slope.

Short Final

A good landing is most likely following a good approach, so aim to be well established in a stabilised approach, with the aeroplane nicely trimmed, by the time you reach short final. *Short final* for a training aeroplane may be thought of as the last 200 ft. Do not allow significant deviations in flightpath, tracking or airspeed to develop and destabilise the approach.

Carburettor heat will normally be returned to COLD on short final in case maximum power is required for a go-around; however, if icing conditions exist, follow the guidance provided in your Pilot's Operating Handbook.

Throughout the final approach and landing, have your:

- **left hand** on the control column to control attitude; and
- **right hand** on the throttle to control power.

The Landing

The landing starts with a round-out commencing at about 20 feet above the runway and does not finish until the end of the landing run. Once you reach the round-out height, forget the aiming point because you will fly over and well past it before the wheels actually touch down. It has served its purpose and you should now look well ahead.

A normal landing is similar to a power-off stall, with touchdown just prior to the moment of stall. This method of landing allows the lowest possible touchdown speed (significantly less than the approach speed), with the pilot still having full control.

The landing consists of four phases:

1. The flare (or round-out).
2. The hold-off.
3. The touchdown.
4. The landing run.

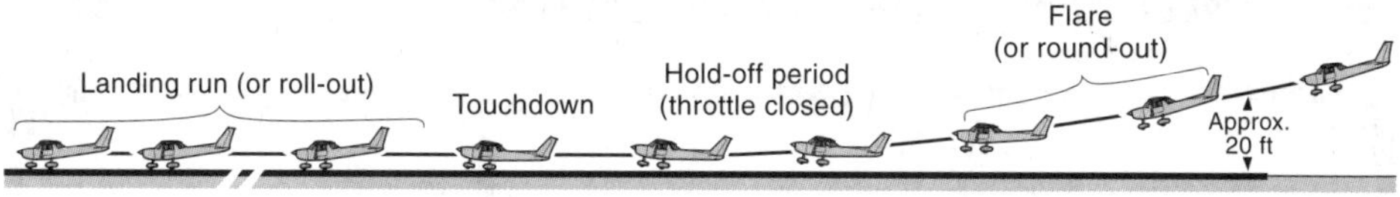

■ *Figure 13a-13* ***The landing***

1. The Flare

Break the rate of descent as you near the ground.

During the flare (or round-out) the power is reduced and the nose is gradually raised to break the rate of descent. The rate of sink is checked with the control column – a high rate of sink requiring a greater backward movement to check it.

2. The Hold-Off

The hold-off should occur with the aeroplane close to the ground (within a foot or so). The throttle is closed and the control column progressively brought back to keep the aeroplane flying level with the wheels just off the ground. If sinking, apply more back pressure; if moving away from the ground, relax the back pressure. The airspeed will be decreasing to a very low figure, but this is of no concern to you. You should be looking well ahead from the beginning of round-out until touchdown. Any sideways drift caused by a slight crosswind can be counteracted by lowering the into-wind wing a few degrees and keeping straight with rudder.

Hold the aeroplane off for as long as possible, just above the runway.

3. The Touchdown

In the touchdown, the main wheels should make first contact with the ground (which will be the case following a correct hold-off). The nosewheel is kept off the ground using the control column while the speed decreases.

Touch down on the main wheels.

4. The Landing Run

During the landing run the aeroplane is kept rolling straight down the centreline using rudder and the wings kept level with aileron. The nosewheel is finally lowered to the ground before elevator control is lost. Brakes (if required) may be used once the nosewheel is on the ground. Remember that the landing is not complete until the end of the landing run when the aeroplane is stationary or at taxiing speed.

Keep on the runway centreline during the ground roll using rudder, and keep the wings level with aileron.

■ Figure 13a-14 **Some typical attitudes in the approach and round-out**

Judgement in the Flare and Landing

To assist in judging the height of the wheels above the ground and the rate at which the aeroplane is 'sinking', your eyes should remain 'outside the cockpit' from shortly before commencing the flare (when airspeed is no longer important) until the end of the landing run.

To achieve the best depth perception and develop a feel for just where the main wheels are in relation to the ground, it is best to look ahead and to the left of the aeroplane's nose. If you look too close, the ground will be blurred as it passes by; too far and your depth perception will suffer.

Avoid looking directly over the nose. This makes it difficult to raise the nose in the flare and still retain depth perception, as well as causing a tendency to fly the aeroplane into the ground, resulting in a heavy touchdown (possibly nosewheel first) and even a bounce.

The After-Landing Check

Once clear of the runway, stop the aeroplane, set idle rpm (1,000 to 1,200 rpm as recommended) and complete the after-landing check as specified in the Pilot's Operating Handbook. It will contain such items as:

- **Flaps** RETRACT;
- **Carburettor heat** check COLD (hot air may be unfiltered);
- **Fuel pump** OFF (if fitted);
- **Throttle friction nut** LOOSEN.

Airmanship

Airmanship involves flying accurately and smoothly, and exercising good judgement.

Fly a neat circuit pattern, **on height** and **on speed.** Commence descent once on base leg to position the aeroplane for a turn that will have you lined up on final at or above 500 ft aal. Use flap as appropriate.

Fly a stabilised approach **on slope, on the extended centreline** and **on speed.** Maintain firm, positive and tight control of all three.

Although you will be very busy, remain aware of other aircraft. Keep a good lookout.

Airwork 13a

Powered Approach and Normal Landing

Aim *To make an approach with power and land into wind.*

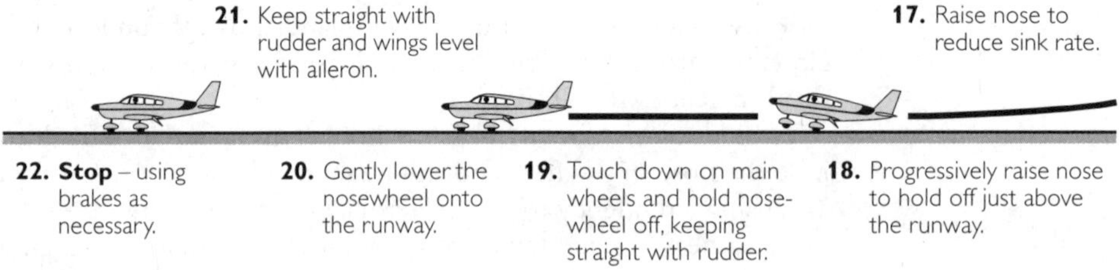

21. Keep straight with rudder and wings level with aileron.
17. Raise nose to reduce sink rate.
22. Stop – using brakes as necessary.
20. Gently lower the nosewheel onto the runway.
19. Touch down on main wheels and hold nose-wheel off, keeping straight with rudder.
18. Progressively raise nose to hold off just above the runway.

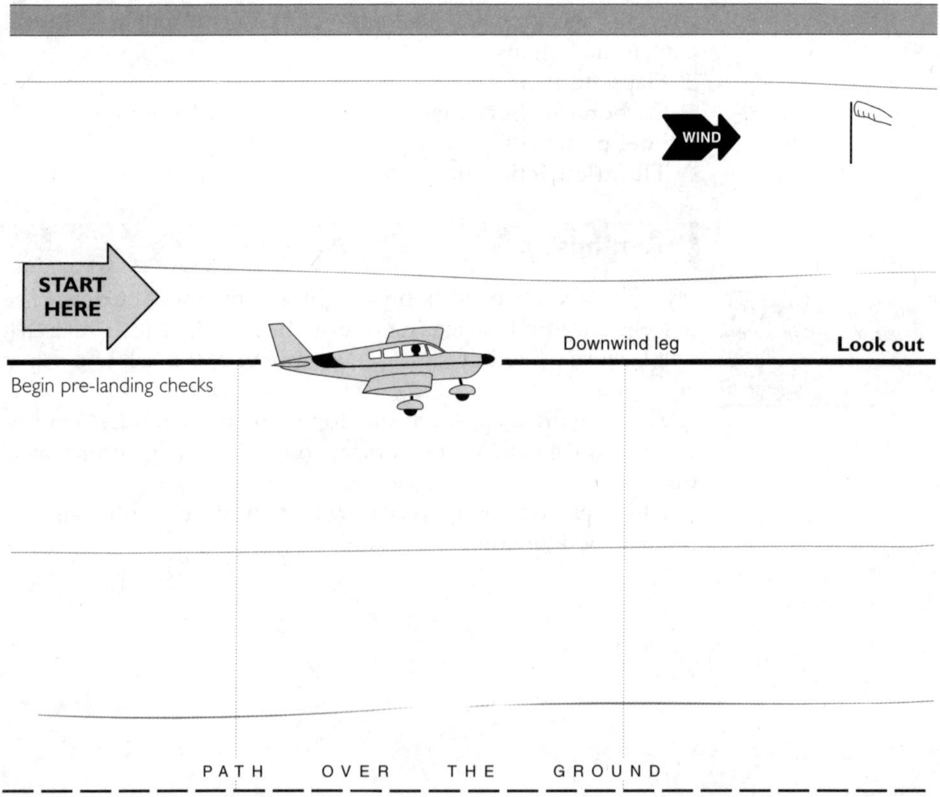

WIND
START HERE
Downwind leg
Look out
Begin pre-landing checks
PATH OVER THE GROUND

Airwork 13a

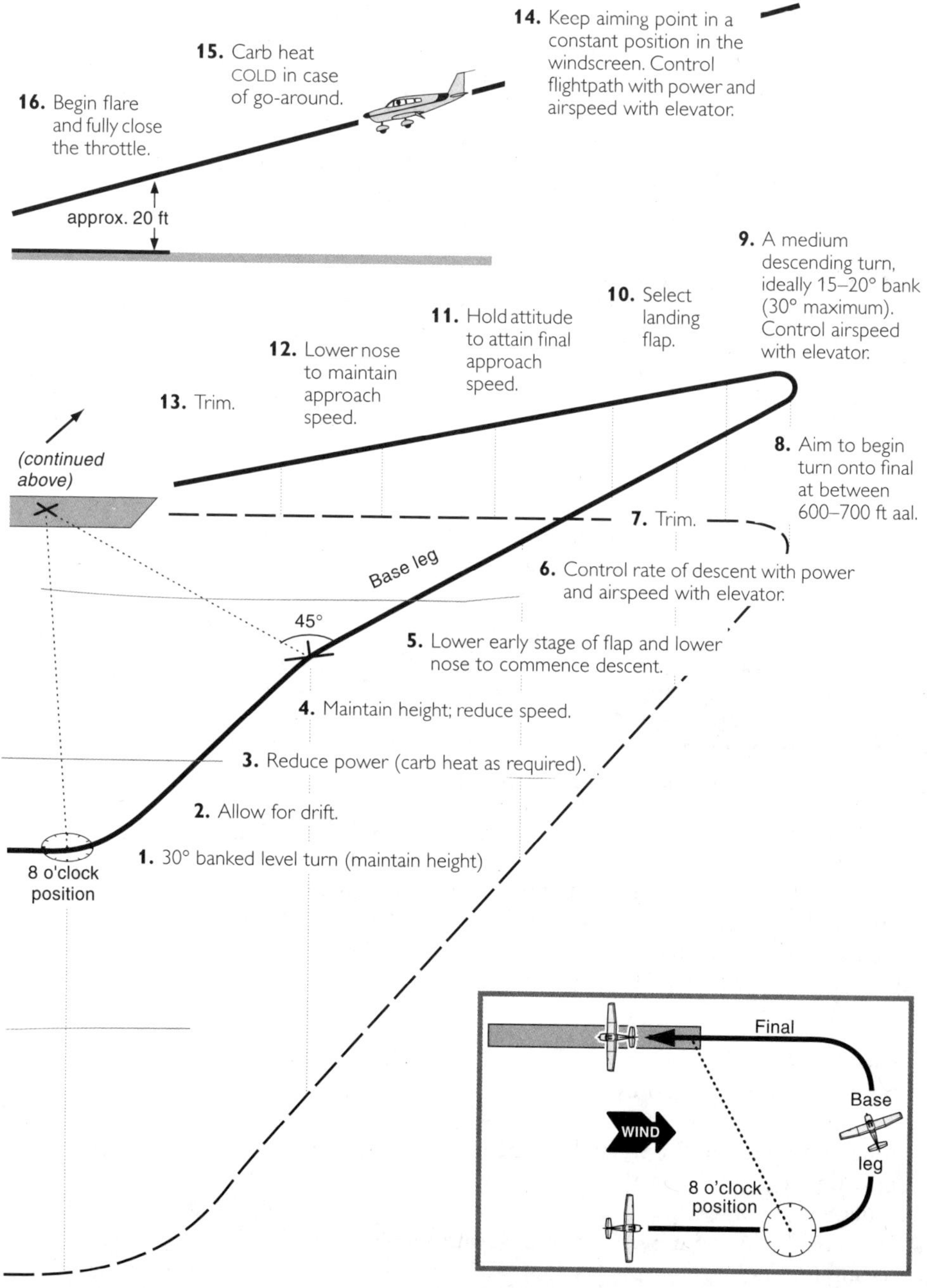
14. Keep aiming point in a constant position in the windscreen. Control flightpath with power and airspeed with elevator.
15. Carb heat COLD in case of go-around.
16. Begin flare and fully close the throttle.
approx. 20 ft
9. A medium descending turn, ideally 15–20° bank (30° maximum). Control airspeed with elevator.
10. Select landing flap.
11. Hold attitude to attain final approach speed.
12. Lower nose to maintain approach speed.
13. Trim.
(continued above)
8. Aim to begin turn onto final at between 600–700 ft aal.
7. Trim.
Base leg
6. Control rate of descent with power and airspeed with elevator.
45°
5. Lower early stage of flap and lower nose to commence descent.
4. Maintain height; reduce speed.
3. Reduce power (carb heat as required).
2. Allow for drift.
1. 30° banked level turn (maintain height)
8 o'clock position
Final
Base
leg
WIND
8 o'clock position

Further Points

Common Faults in the Landing

Every pilot learns how to land through experience. It is inevitable that many landings will be far from perfect, but progress will be made when you can recognise faults and correct them. Three very common faults are the balloon (when the aeroplane moves away from the ground before touchdown), the bounced landing (when it moves away from the ground after touchdown, perhaps after several touchdowns) and rounding out too high.

The Balloon

A balloon can be caused by either:

- too much back pressure on the control column; and/or
- too much power left on; and/or
- too high an airspeed; and/or
- a gust of wind.

To correct for a small balloon:

- relax some of the back pressure on the control column;
- allow the aeroplane to commence settling (sinking) again;
- when approaching the hold-off height, continue the backward movement of the control column; and
- complete the landing normally.

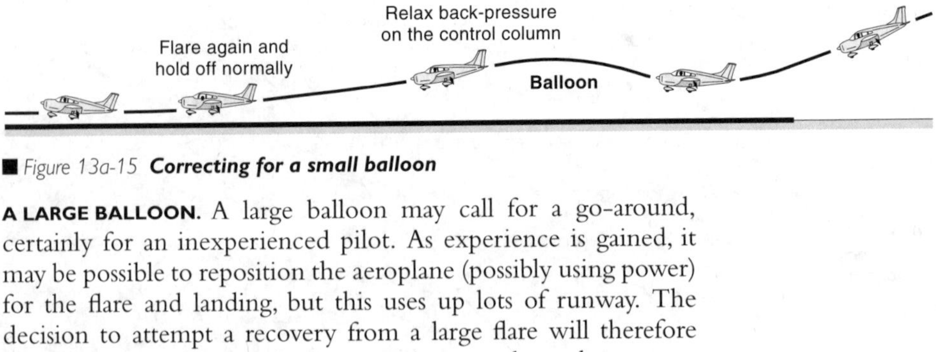
Relax back-pressure
on the control column
Flare again and
hold off normally
Balloon

■ *Figure 13a-15* ***Correcting for a small balloon***

A LARGE BALLOON. A large balloon may call for a go-around, certainly for an inexperienced pilot. As experience is gained, it may be possible to reposition the aeroplane (possibly using power) for the flare and landing, but this uses up lots of runway. The decision to attempt a recovery from a large flare will therefore depend on the extent of your experience and on the runway length remaining.

The Bounced Landing

A bounce can be caused by:

- a failure to round out sufficiently;
- touching down on the nosewheel (possibly caused by looking over the nose);
- touching down too fast;
- excessive backward movement of the control column; or
- flaring too high.

An inexperienced pilot should consider an immediate go-around following a bounce. With experience, however, a successful recovery from a bounce can be made (provided that the runway length is adequate) by relaxing the back pressure and adding power if necessary to reposition the aeroplane suitably to recommence the landing. Avoid pushing the nose down as a second bounced landing may result.

Avoid a second touchdown on the nosewheel – a series of kangaroo hops down the runway is not a desirable way to land an aeroplane! Prior to touchdown, make sure that the aeroplane is in the correct nose-high attitude (even if it is the second touchdown).

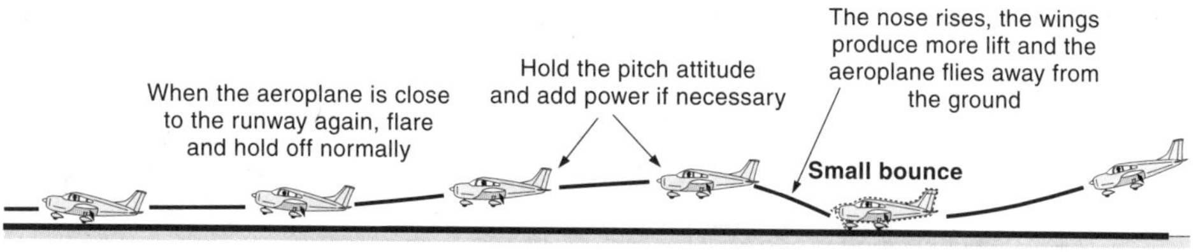
When the aeroplane is close to the runway again, flare and hold off normally
Hold the pitch attitude and add power if necessary
The nose rises, the wings produce more lift and the aeroplane flies away from the ground
Small bounce

■ *Figure 13a-16* ***Recovery from a bounced landing***

Rounding Out and Holding Off Too High

The hold-off is best completed within a foot or so of the ground. Any more than this and a landing somewhat heavier that usual will result.

If you recognise before 'impact' that you are too high, add power; this will break the descent rate somewhat and allow a less heavy touchdown. Immediately the wheels touch the ground, close the throttle, otherwise the aeroplane may not decelerate.

Holding off too high usually results from either:

- not looking far enough into the distance, with the result that the ground rushing by is blurred and depth perception is poor; or
- a second attempt to land following a balloon or bounce.

NOTE The more experienced you become, the less likely you are to find yourself bouncing, ballooning or rounding out too high. It is part of the average student pilot's lot to become somewhat of an expert at recovering from misjudged landings, but this phase will not last too long.

The Go-Around or Baulked Approach

If at any stage during the approach or landing you feel uncomfortable about the situation, carry out a go-around (also known as a baulked approach, overshoot or discontinued approach). This manoeuvre is covered fully in Exercise 13b.

Touch-and-Go Landings

The number of practice circuits per hour can be greatly increased by doing touch-and-go landings. This involves a normal approach and landing and then, when established in the landing run and after the nosewheel has been gently lowered onto the ground (and with sufficient runway length remaining):

- **move the flap** to the take-off setting;
- **apply full power** and perform a normal take-off without having stopped.

In a touch-and-go take-off, the trim may not be set for take-off and so there will be a reasonable amount of forward pressure required on the control column to hold the nose in the climb attitude. Once established in the climb away from the ground, this pressure can be trimmed off.

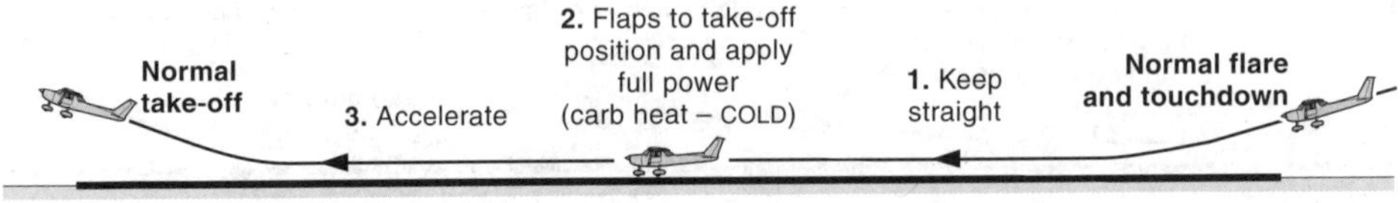

■ *Figure 13a-17* ***The touch-and-go landing***

If the landing is misjudged and excessive runway is used, then bring the aeroplane to a stop as in a normal landing, rather than continue with a doubtful take-off on possibly insufficient runway with a degraded obstacle clearance in the climb-out.

Turbulence in the Circuit Area

Friction affects the air flowing over the earth's surface, leading to the wind at ground level being different to that at circuit height and higher. Any change in wind speed and/or direction is called **windshear,** and it can cause turbulence.

Uneven heating of the earth's surface will cause vertical convection currents, also leading to turbulence. You experience this as a bumpy ride with a fluctuating airspeed.

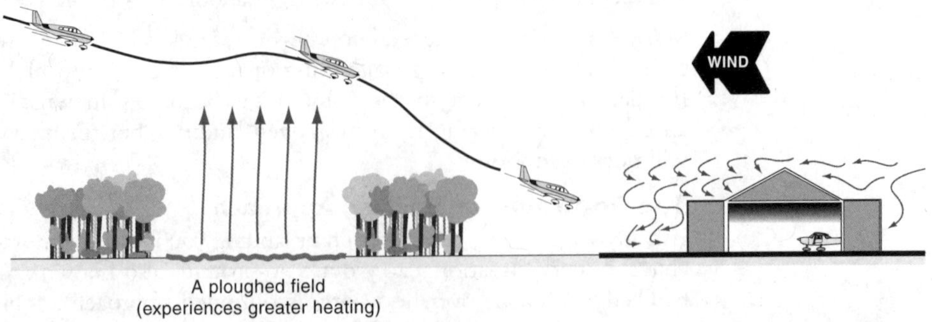

■ *Figure 13a-18* ***Turbulence has various causes***

In turbulent conditions, it is advisable to carry a few extra knots on the approach to give you better controllability. A flapless approach should be considered, since it will make the aeroplane more responsive to a power increase (due to the lower drag).

Wake Turbulence

Significant wake turbulence can form behind the wingtips of large aeroplanes flying at high angles of attack (e.g. during take-off and landing). The vortices that cause the turbulence drift downwards and with the wind. They are best avoided! Never be afraid to delay a take-off or approach if you suspect that wake turbulence from another aircraft (fixed-wing or rotary) could be a problem. For more about wake turbulence see Volume 4 of *The Air Pilot's Manual*.

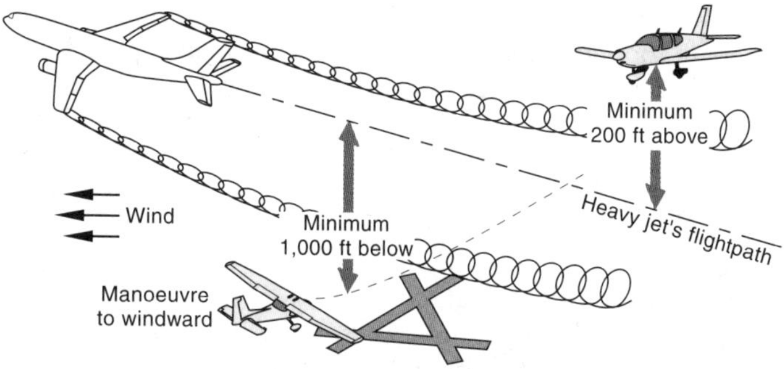

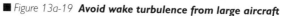

■ Figure 13a-19 **Avoid wake turbulence from large aircraft**

Exercise 13b
The Go-Around

Aim

To enter a climb from a flapped approach.

Considerations

Why Go-Around?

It may be necessary to perform a go-around for various reasons:

The go-around is a climb-away from a discontinued approach to land.

- the runway is occupied by an aeroplane, a vehicle or animals;
- you are too close behind an aeroplane on final approach that will not have cleared the runway in time for you to land;
- the conditions are too severe for your experience (turbulence, windshear, heavy rain, excessive crosswind, etc.);
- your approach is unstable (in terms of airspeed or flightpath);
- you are not aligned with the centreline or directional control is a problem;
- the airspeed is far too high or too low;
- you are too high at the runway threshold to touch down safely and stop comfortably within the confines of the runway;
- you are not mentally or physically at ease;
- following a balloon or bounced landing.

The Effect of Flap

Full flap makes a climb-away difficult.

Full flap causes a significant increase in drag. This has advantages in the approach to land – it allows a steeper descent path, the approach speed can be lower and the pilot has a better forward view.

Full flap has no advantages in a climb – in fact establishing a reasonable rate of climb may not be possible with full flap extended. For this reason, when attempting to enter a climb from a flapped descent, consideration should be given to raising the flap. It should be raised in stages to allow a gradual increase in airspeed as the climb is established.

Flying the Manoeuvre

Establish a Descent

Follow the usual descent procedures and lower an appropriate stage of flap. Initially, it may be desirable to practise the go-around manoeuvre with only an early stage of flap extended (or perhaps none at all), as would be the case early in the approach to land.

A go-around with full flap requires more attention because of the aeroplane's poorer climb performance.

Initiating a Go-Around

A successful go-around requires that a positive decision be made and positive action taken. A sign of a good pilot is a decision to go around when the situation demands it – the manoeuvre being executed in a firm, but smooth manner.

The procedure to use is similar to that already practised when entering a climb from a 'clean' descent. **P–A–T: power–attitude–trim.** The additional consideration is flap, which will be raised when the descent is stopped and the climb (or level flight) is initiated.

Keep the aeroplane straight and the wings level.

TO INITIATE A GO-AROUND smoothly **apply full power** (counting "one–two–three" fairly quickly is about the correct timing to achieve full power) and move the carburettor heat to COLD.

Be prepared for a strong pitch-up and yawing tendency as the power is applied. These tendencies can be counteracted with forward pressure on the control column and rudder pressure. Hold the nose in the desired climb **attitude** for the flap that is set, and then **trim.** The initial pressure and trim required may be quite significant, especially with full flap.

Full flap creates a lot of drag and only a poor climb performance at a suitable airspeed may be possible. In this case level flight might be necessary while the flap setting is initially reduced. If only an early stage of flap is extended, a reasonable climb can be entered without delay.

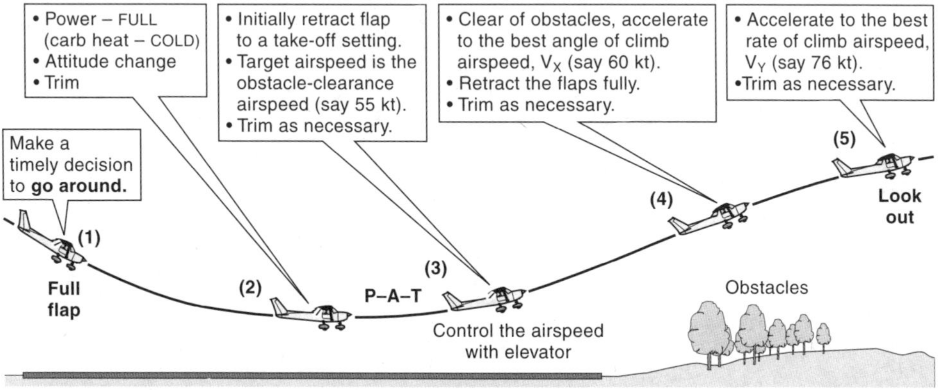

• Power – FULL (carb heat – COLD)
• Attitude change
• Trim
• Initially retract flap to a take-off setting.
• Target airspeed is the obstacle-clearance airspeed (say 55 kt).
• Trim as necessary.
• Clear of obstacles, accelerate to the best angle of climb airspeed, V_X (say 60 kt).
• Retract the flaps fully.
• Trim as necessary.
• Accelerate to the best rate of climb airspeed, V_Y (say 76 kt).
•Trim as necessary.
Make a timely decision to go around.
(1)
Full flap
(2)
P–A–T
(3)
Control the airspeed with elevator
(4)
(5)
Look out
Obstacles

■ *Figure 13b-1* ***The go-around***

As the aeroplane accelerates to an appropriate speed, raise the flap in stages and adjust the pitch attitude to achieve the desired speeds and climb performance. Trim as required.

Airmanship

Make a positive decision to go-around, then perform it decisively. Exert firm, positive and smooth control over the aeroplane. Firm pressure must be held on the control column and rudder pedals when the power is applied. Correct trimming will assist you greatly.

Airmanship is being decisive.

Ensure that a safe airspeed is reached before each stage of flap is raised. Once established comfortably in the climb-out, advise the Air Traffic Service unit (and the other aircraft in the circuit) by radio that you are going around.

It is usual, once established in the go-around, to move slightly to one side of the runway so that you have a view of aeroplanes that may be operating off the runway and beneath you. The 'dead-side' away from the circuit direction is preferred.

Following the go-around, delay turning onto crosswind leg until at least at the upwind end of the runway to avoid conflict in the circuit.

Airwork 13b
The Go-Around

Aim *To enter a climb from a flapped descent.*

With the Aeroplane Established in a Flapped Descent

1. Make a firm decision to go around.
2. P–A–T:

   P – power – throttle OPEN FULLY (carb heat COLD);

   A – attitude – raise nose to appropriate pitch attitude;

   T – trim.
3. Raise the flaps slowly, in stages.
4. Adjust pitch attitude (higher as flaps are retracted), and maintain speed with elevator.
5. Retrim for the climb-out.

Look out during the manoeuvre, especially in a real go-around situation.

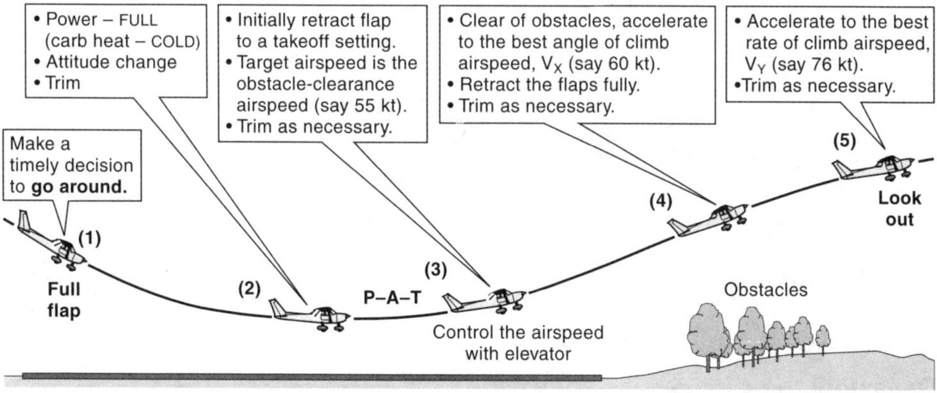

• Power – FULL (carb heat – COLD)
• Attitude change
• Trim
• Initially retract flap to a takeoff setting.
• Target airspeed is the obstacle-clearance airspeed (say 55 kt).
• Trim as necessary.
• Clear of obstacles, accelerate to the best angle of climb airspeed, V_X (say 60 kt).
• Retract the flaps fully.
• Trim as necessary.
• Accelerate to the best rate of climb airspeed, V_Y (say 76 kt).
•Trim as necessary.
Make a timely decision to **go around.**
(1)
Full flap
(2)
P–A–T
(3)
Control the airspeed with elevator
(4)
(5)
Look out
Obstacles

Exercise 13c
Departing and Joining the Circuit

Aim

The aim of this Exercise is to become familiar with standard procedures and considerations when:

1. Departing from the circuit after take-off on a flight to the training area or on a cross-country flight; and
2. Returning to the aerodrome from outside the circuit area with the intention of joining the circuit for an approach and landing.

Considerations

A lot of your early training will be carried out away from the airfield and this gives you a chance to develop good habits in departing from and rejoining the circuit. It should be noted that procedures for circuit departure and circuit joining vary between countries and, if flying overseas, you should ask to be briefed on them. The procedures here refer to the United Kingdom.

For flights away from the circuit area, you need to be confident of your:

- **local area knowledge** (landmarks and airspace restrictions);
- **circuit departure and rejoining procedures** for your particular aerodrome;
- **altimetry procedures;**
- **radio procedures;**
- **en route or regular checks** to ensure satisfactory operation of the aeroplane;
- **ability to fly a particular heading** using the magnetic compass.

Departing the Circuit

Follow any Air Traffic Control instructions given. If ATC is not active at your field, then you should plan a circuit departure that will not conflict with other aircraft in the circuit or joining it. Also, follow any special procedures applicable to your field.

An efficient means of departing an uncontrolled field is to extend the upwind leg as you climb out after take-off and then, when clear of other circuit traffic, manoeuvre to set heading for the local training area (or the first leg of your cross-country flight).

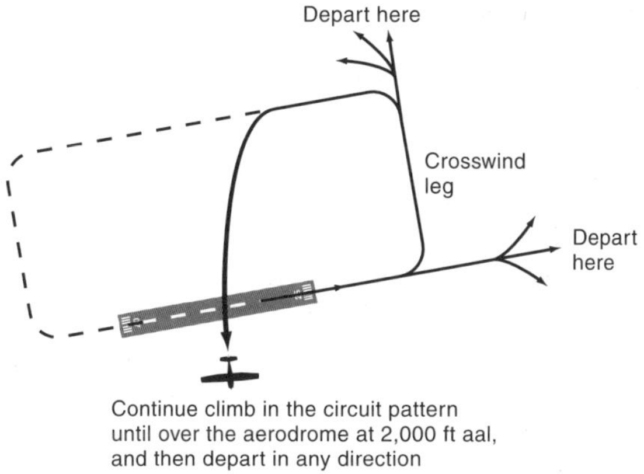

■ *Figure 13c-1* ***Departing the circuit***

Once outbound to the local training area, ensure that QNH is set in the subscale so that the altimeter will read height above mean sea level (amsl). Heights of mountains, radio masts, etc., are shown as heights amsl on charts.

Joining the Circuit

You should always have prior knowledge of the **elevation** of the aerodrome you intend to use.

Approaching the circuit, set the altimeter subscale to QNH or QFE (as advised by the ATS unit) according to your normal procedure. With QNH set the altimeter will read height above mean sea level; with QFE set the altimeter will read height above aerodrome level (aal).

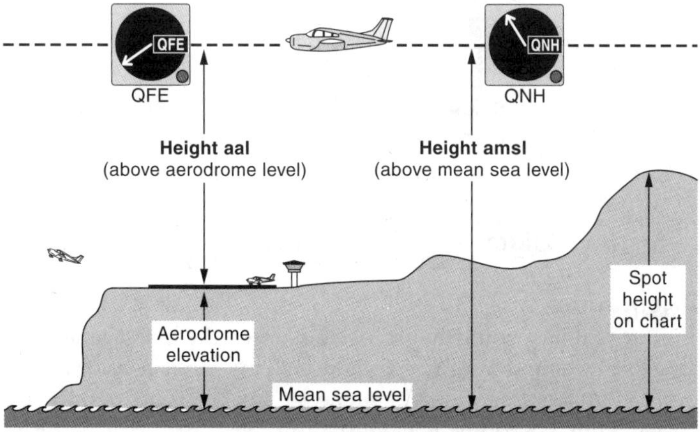

■ *Figure 13c-2* ***The altimeter reads height amsl with QNH set; height aal with QFE set***

When arriving at an aerodrome, follow any Air Traffic Control instructions given. If ATC is not active at your field, then you should plan an arrival that will not conflict with other aircraft in the circuit and follow any special procedures applicable to the field.

The usual methods of entering the circuit pattern are to either:

- join on downwind leg at circuit height, provided you know the circuit in use; or
- overfly at 2,000 ft above aerodrome level, determine the circuit direction (if not already known) from the windsock or signals area, descend to circuit height on the inactive ('dead') side and then join the circuit by crossing the upwind end of the runway.

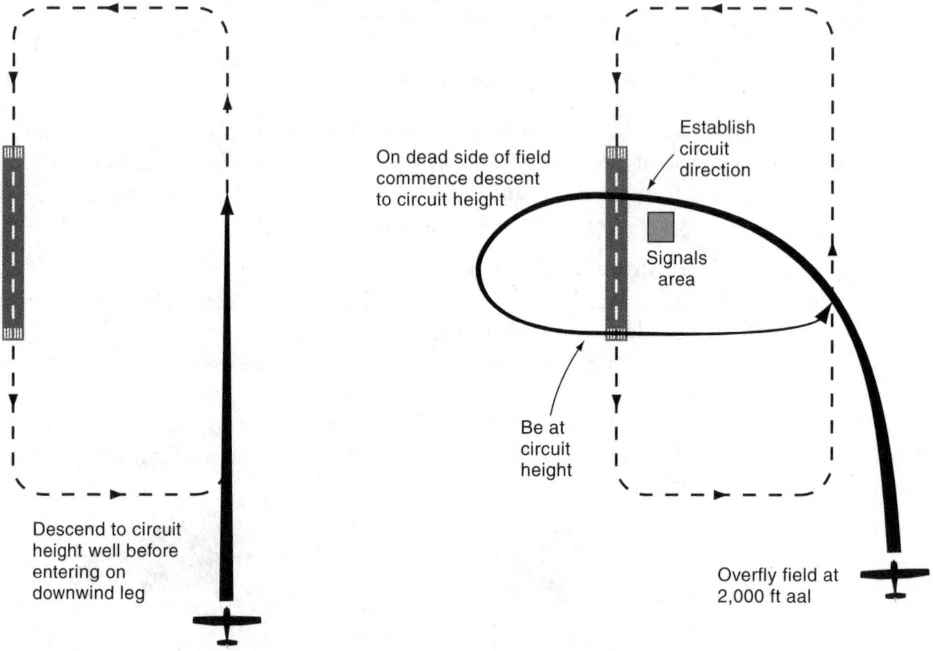
On dead side of field commence descent to circuit height
Establish circuit direction
Signals area
Be at circuit height
Descend to circuit height well before entering on downwind leg
Overfly field at 2,000 ft aal

■ *Figure 13c-3* ***Joining the circuit***

Further Points

Orientation

In poor visibility you may not be able to see the aerodrome from your local training area. You should become familiar with all the local landmarks (e.g. reservoirs, railway lines, motorways, towns, villages, churches, other airfields, radio towers, etc.) that will lead you to your home field. You should also know the approximate magnetic heading to steer to return home.

Flying magnetic headings can assist your orientation in the vicinity of the aerodrome.

The magnetic compass suffers errors when the aeroplane is turning or otherwise accelerating. It gives accurate headings only when the aeroplane is in straight flight at a steady airspeed. Therefore, to maintain an accurate magnetic heading, fly straight at a constant speed, making use of external reference points on the horizon if you can.

If a turn is needed, select a new external reference point and turn onto it. Allow the compass to settle down and then check the heading. If you use the heading indicator, ensure that it is aligned with the magnetic compass during straight and steady flight. Being a gyroscopic instrument, the HI (once aligned correctly) is easier to use than the compass.

QDM

Some ATS units are able to determine the position of an aircraft from its radio transmissions. This is a useful facility if you are lost and request navigation assistance.

In such a situation, the ATS unit will advise you of the magnetic track to the station, known as QDM. You can then steer a suitable heading to allow for drift due to the wind to make good this track. The QDM may be revised by the ATS unit, if necessary, as the return to the field progresses.

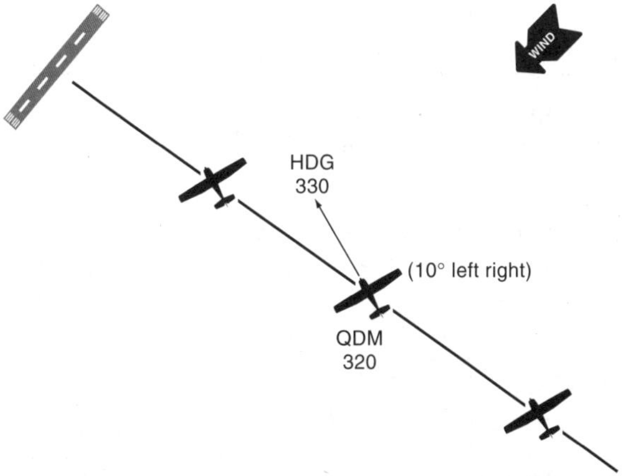

■ *Figure 13c-4* ***An ATS unit can provide a QDM (magnetic track) to the aerodrome***

In-Flight Checks

In-flight checks of the aeroplane should be made regularly.

While flying the aeroplane for long periods, either en route, in the local training area, or for prolonged periods in the circuit area, periodic checks (say every 15 minutes or so) should be made of the various systems that are vital to safe flight.

Your flying instructor will ensure that you perform the appropriate check, but it will contain items such as are included in this FREHA check:

FREHA IN-FLIGHT CHECK

F	***Fuel*** *Fuel on and sufficient.* *Fuel tank usage monitored.* *Mixture rich or leaned as required.* *Fuel pump on (if fitted and if required) and fuel pressure checked.*
R	***Radio*** *Radio frequency correctly selected, volume and squelch satisfactory.* *Make any necessary radio calls.*
E	***Engine*** *Engine oil temperature and pressure; mixture set correctly; carburettor heat if required; check of other systems (ammeter for electrical system; suction gauge for air-driven gyroscopes if installed).*
H	***Heading*** *Heading indicator aligned with magnetic compass (only realign the HI with the magnetic compass in steady straight and level flight).*
A	***Altitude*** *Altitude checked and subscale setting correct (normally Regional QNH en route, and Aerodrome QNH or QFE if joining a circuit).*

It is good airmanship to perform these checks at regular intervals on every flight and also just prior to entering the circuit area (where your workload generally increases).

Important Emergency Radio Transmissions

As well as the more usual traffic-type radio calls, you may occasionally hear **distress** or **urgency** signals. If ever you have to make an emergency call or a distress call, you should also squawk 7700 on your transponder. This will alert the radar controller.

Example of a **distress call:**

Mayday Mayday Mayday
Golf Alpha Bravo Charlie Delta – Cessna one seven two
Engine failed
Losing height
Intend to land five miles south of Ponteland
Passing two thousand feet
Heading two eight zero
Student pilot

The use of the word **Mayday** (an anglicised version of the French *m'aidez* – 'help me') signifies a **distress signal** and it takes priority over all other calls. It informs ATC that the pilot of the aeroplane registered G-ABCD has a serious problem.

While ATC may offer helpful suggestions, the pilot in distress must not be distracted from his main duty, which is to fly the aeroplane as safely as possible. Remember that an aeroplane does not need a radio to fly.

Example of an **urgency call:**

> *Pan-Pan Pan-Pan Pan-Pan*
> *Golf Bravo Charlie Delta Echo – Piper Warrior*
> *Unsure of position in poor visibility north of Airdrie*
> *Cruising two thousand feet*
> *Heading three four zero*
> *Student pilot*

The use of the term **Pan-Pan** signifies that this is an **urgency signal.** It informs ATC that the pilot of G-BCDE is requesting assistance, but the use of Pan-Pan indicates that the aeroplane is in no immediate danger. A Pan-Pan call is also appropriate if you wish to report another aeroplane or ship in difficulty.

Hopefully, you will never have to make a distress or urgency call of this nature but, if you do, remember to fly the aeroplane first and make radio calls second. If you hear another pilot make such a call, then impose a temporary radio silence on yourself for a suitable period to avoid jamming these important transmissions and ATC responses.

Light Signals from the Tower

If radio contact cannot be maintained at a towered aerodrome, the tower controller can pass instructions to the pilot by means of **light-gun signals.** Figure 13c-5 summarises the meanings of these light signals. Refer to CAA CAP 85, *Meaning of Lights and Pyrotechnic Signals,* for a full description.

If ever you experience radio failure, you should squawk 7700 on your transponder for 1 minute, then 7600 for 15 minutes; and repeat. This will alert the radar controller to your radio communications failure.

For more about emergency radio calls and radio failure procedures, see Vol. 7 of *The Air Pilot's Manual – Radiotelephony.*

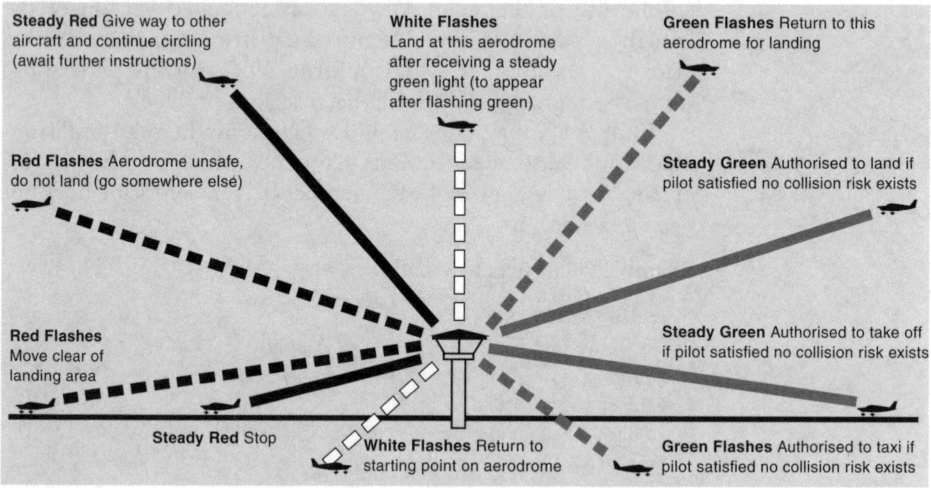
Steady Red Give way to other aircraft and continue circling (await further instructions)
White Flashes Land at this aerodrome after receiving a steady green light (to appear after flashing green)
Green Flashes Return to this aerodrome for landing
Red Flashes Aerodrome unsafe, do not land (go somewhere else)
Steady Green Authorised to land if pilot satisfied no collision risk exists
Red Flashes Move clear of landing area
Steady Green Authorised to take off if pilot satisfied no collision risk exists
Steady Red Stop
White Flashes Return to starting point on aerodrome
Green Flashes Authorised to taxi if pilot satisfied no collision risk exists

■ *Figure 13c-5* ***Light signals that can be beamed to aircraft***

Exercise 13d
The Flapless Approach and Landing

Aim

To approach and land without the use of flaps.

Considerations

A flapless approach will be necessary if a failure of any part of the flap system occurs (a rare event), and is advisable in strong and gusty winds. Crosswind landings are often made in such conditions.

Compared to a normal approach and landing with flap, the main features of a flapless approach and landing are:

- **a flatter flightpath** requiring an extended circuit;
- **a higher approach speed** (due to the higher stalling speed);
- **a higher nose attitude** and poorer forward vision;
- **almost no round-out** and a longer float (due to less drag) if the hold-off is prolonged before the aeroplane touches down;
- **a risk of scraping the tail** if the nose is raised too high on touchdown; and
- **a longer landing run.**

It is most important to control the flightpath and airspeed fairly tightly on a flapless approach. As usual, airspeed is controlled with elevator and flightpath with power. If too high, reduce power and lower the nose slightly – if the power is already at idle, consider a sideslip to increase the rate of descent and lose height.

A 'clean' wing has less drag than a flapped wing, which means that excess speed takes longer to 'wash-off', i.e. a flapless aeroplane is 'slippery'. This can lengthen the hold-off and float considerably. To avoid using too much runway and also to avoid the risk of scraping the tail, do not prolong the hold-off, particularly on a short runway.

Once the nosewheel is on the ground, brakes can be used if required.

Airwork 13d
The Flapless Approach and Landing

Aim *To approach and land without the use of flaps.*

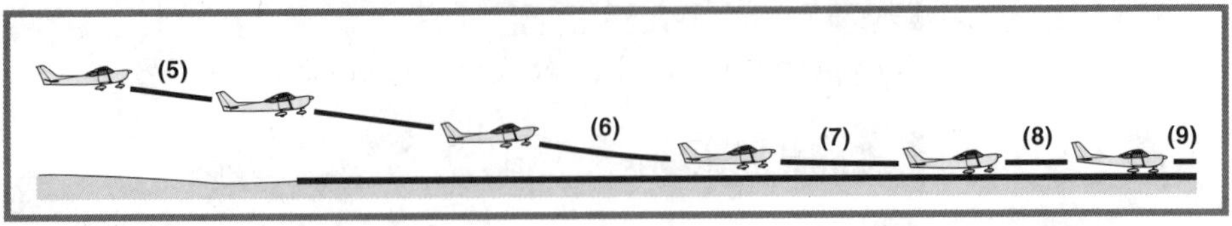
(5)
(6)
(7)
(8)
(9)

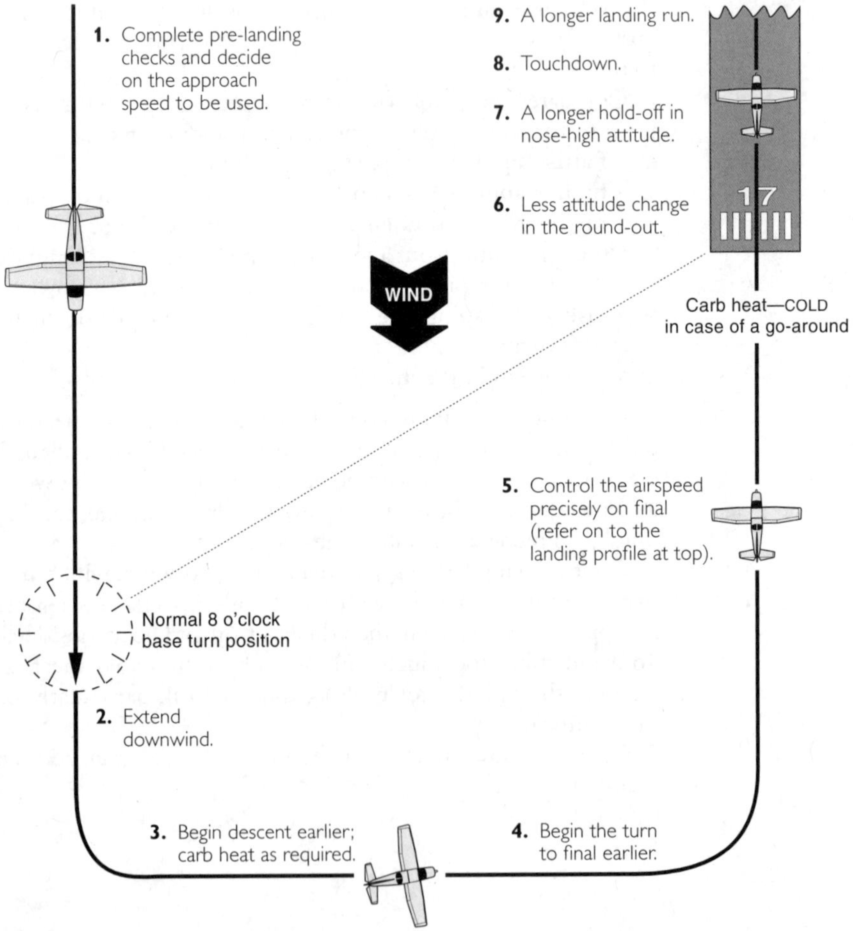
1. Complete pre-landing checks and decide on the approach speed to be used.
9. A longer landing run.
8. Touchdown.
7. A longer hold-off in nose-high attitude.
6. Less attitude change in the round-out.
17
WIND
Carb heat—COLD in case of a go-around
5. Control the airspeed precisely on final (refer on to the landing profile at top).
Normal 8 o'clock base turn position
2. Extend downwind.
3. Begin descent earlier; carb heat as required.
4. Begin the turn to final earlier.

Exercise 13e
The Glide Approach and Landing

Aim

To carry out an approach and landing without using power.

Considerations

Why Not Use Power?

The glide approach and landing made without the assistance of power is very good for developing your judgement and is good practice for emergency forced landings following an engine failure. On a glide approach, the flightpath angle to the runway is controlled mainly by the use of flaps to steepen it.

The Approach Flightpath

The flightpath on a glide approach is steep and the round-out more pronounced.

On a normal, engine-assisted approach, power is used to control the rate of descent and the flightpath to the aiming point on the runway. Without power, the descent rate is greater and the pitch attitude of the aeroplane must be lower to maintain the desired approach speed. The result is a steeper approach path to the runway on a glide approach and so the aeroplane must be positioned higher on final than normal. The lower nose position in the glide, especially with full flap, will mean that the change of pitch attitude required in the round-out will be greater.

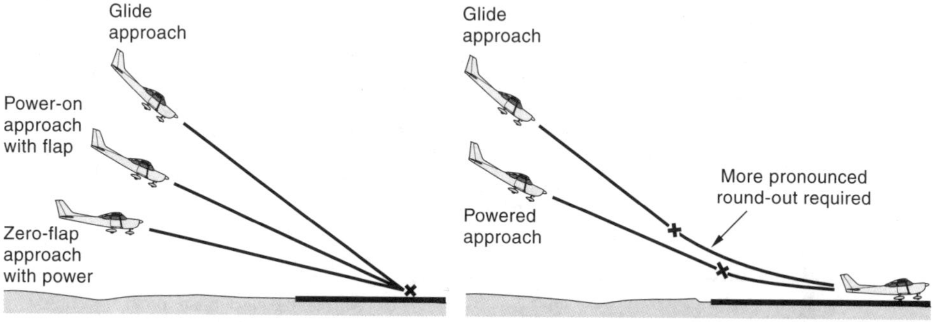

■ *Figure 13e-1* ***A glide approach is steep and the round-out more pronounced***

Flying the Manoeuvre

Base Leg Position

To achieve a steeper approach path to the aiming point on the runway, make the downwind leg shorter than normal, with base leg flown closer to the field than in the normal power-assisted approach. In strong wind conditions, the base leg should be flown even closer to the field to ensure that you do not undershoot.

Fly a closer base leg for a glide approach, especially in strong winds.

Descent Point

Descent point on base leg should be carefully chosen since the aim is, once power is removed, not to have to use it again. Use the amount of drift required on base to estimate the wind strength on final.

Delay the descent from circuit height on a glide approach.

Ideally, if you have judged the closer base leg correctly, descent may be commenced when the runway is at 45° (as for a normal engine-assisted approach, except that the closer base leg means that you are closer to the runway). Initially, aim well down the runway (say 200 metres) so that the aeroplane is definitely higher than normal on approach. The approach can later be steepened with flap, whereas it cannot be flattened without the use of power.

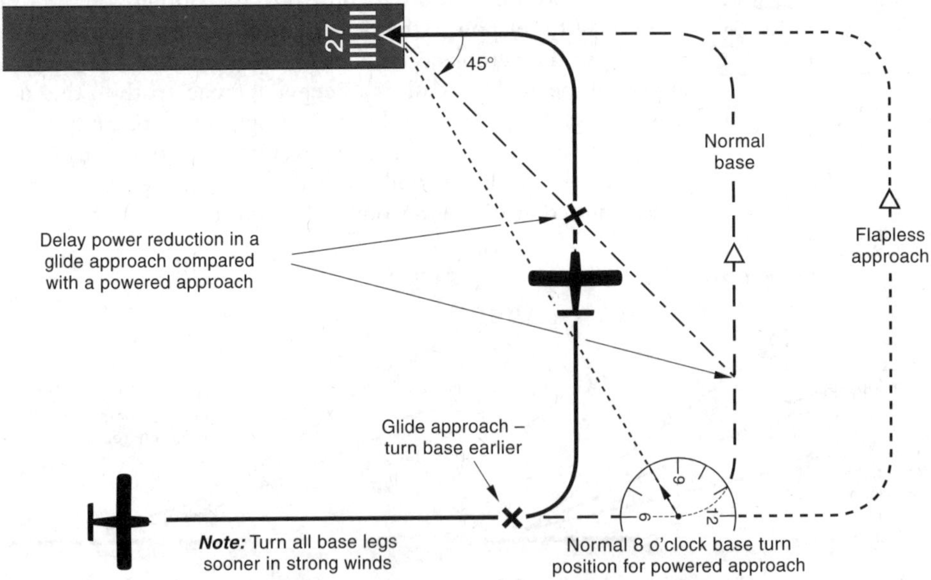
27
45°
Normal
base
Flapless
approach
Delay power reduction in a glide approach compared with a powered approach
Glide approach – turn base earlier
Note: Turn all base legs sooner in strong winds
Normal 8 o'clock base turn position for powered approach
6
9
12

■ Figure 13e-2 **Turn base earlier and delay descent for a glide approach**

Controlling the Flightpath

Use flap and tracking modifications to control the flightpath.

Use of the flaps in stages will steepen the glidepath and bring the aiming point nearer the threshold. It is preferable to be high on approach rather than too low.

If you are high on approach:
- **extend some flap,** lower the nose to achieve the correct airspeed, and retrim; or
- **widen out the base leg** a little; or
- **fly S-turns on final** (but these can lead to an unstable approach and so are best avoided).

If you are low on approach:
- **delay the selection of flap;** and/or
- **cut in on base leg** to shorten final.

If hopelessly low, use power to reposition the aeroplane on the glidepath or to go around and start again.

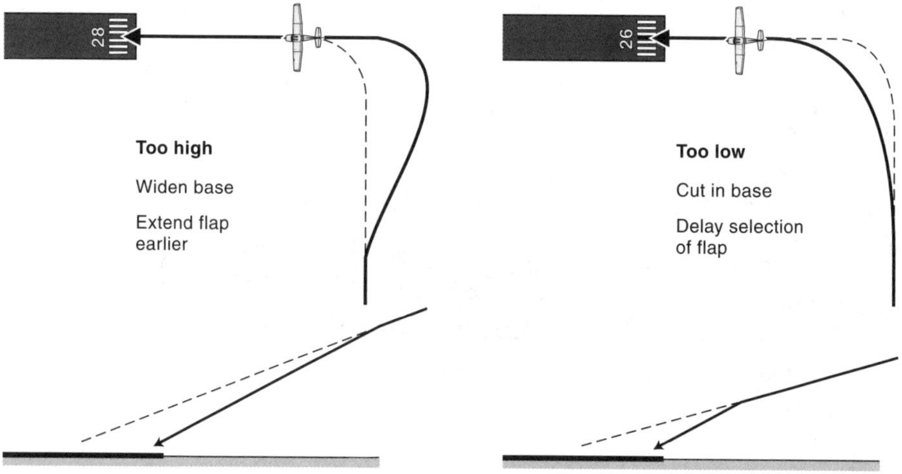

■ *Figure 13e-3* ***Use flap to control flightpath, backed-up by tracking modifications***

Turns

The glidepath will steepen in a turn.

Avoid *steep* gliding turns, since the descent rate will increase significantly and stalling speed will increase. Be prepared for an increased rate of descent and a steepening of the glidepath in the medium turn onto final.

Glide Distance

Do not allow airspeed to get too low by trying to 'stretch' the glide – it will not work! At very low airspeeds the flightpath will steepen even though the nose position is high. Raising the flaps is not advisable, since it will initially cause the aeroplane to sink. In a strong headwind, a slightly higher approach speed may give the aeroplane more 'penetration' even though the descent rate is increased. Apply power and go around if the approach has been badly misjudged.

Do not try to 'stretch' the glide.

Landing Flap

If the aiming point with partial flap is 200 metres down the runway, selection of more flap will give you a new aiming point nearer the threshold. Progressively lower the flap as required, but delay the selection of landing flap until you are absolutely certain that the runway will be reached comfortably. In a glide approach, a slight overshoot of the aiming point is preferable to an unrecoverable undershoot.

Delay the selection of landing flap until certain of reaching the field.

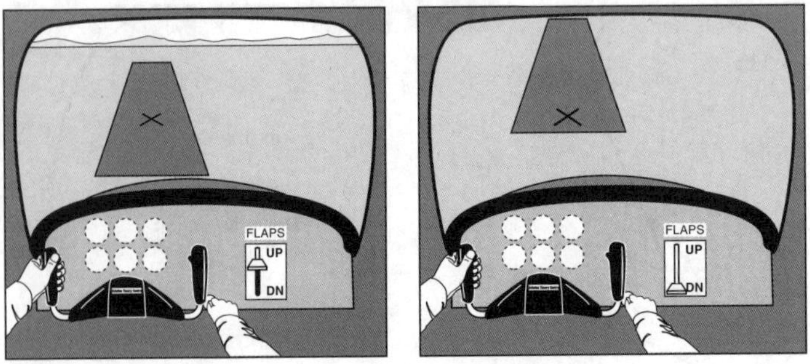

■ *Figure 13e-4* **Bringing the aiming point closer by lowering additional flap**

The Flare

With full flap and no power, the glidepath will be steep and the nose attitude will be quite low to achieve the desired approach speed. The change of attitude in the round-out will be quite pronounced and a gentle flare should be commenced a little higher than normal. Make the appropriate type of landing applicable to the conditions (crosswind, short-field, soft-field, etc.).

In a glide approach, commence the flare slightly higher than normal.

Airwork 13e
The Glide Approach and Landing

Aim *To carry out an approach and landing without the use of power.*

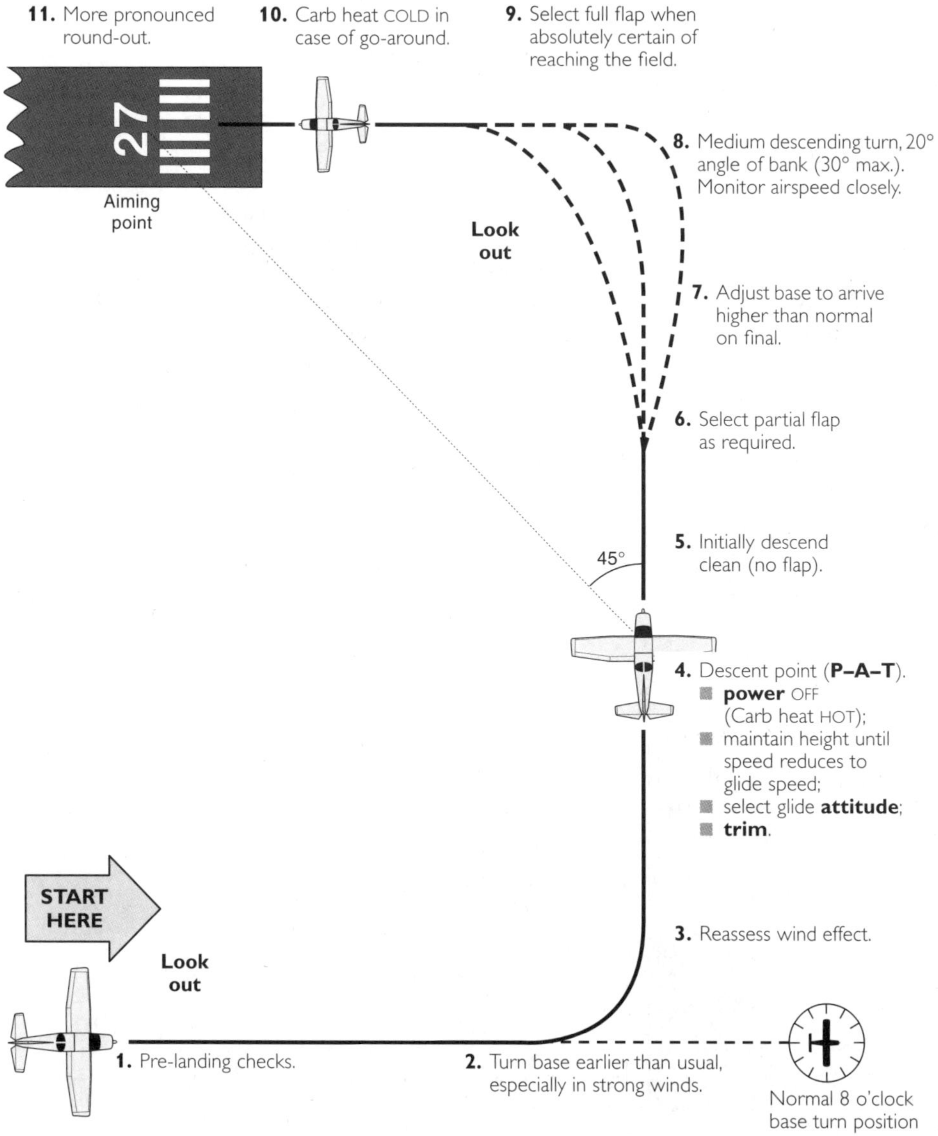

11. More pronounced round-out.
10. Carb heat COLD in case of go-around.
9. Select full flap when absolutely certain of reaching the field.
27
Aiming point
8. Medium descending turn, 20° angle of bank (30° max.). Monitor airspeed closely.
Look out
7. Adjust base to arrive higher than normal on final.
6. Select partial flap as required.
45°
5. Initially descend clean (no flap).
4. Descent point (**P–A–T**).
power OFF (Carb heat HOT);
maintain height until speed reduces to glide speed;
select glide **attitude**;
trim.
START HERE
Look out
3. Reassess wind effect.
1. Pre-landing checks.
2. Turn base earlier than usual, especially in strong winds.
Normal 8 o'clock base turn position

Exercise 13f
Crosswind Operations

Aim

To take off, fly a full circuit and land using a runway which is experiencing a significant crosswind component.

Considerations

Not all aerodromes have a runway which is facing into wind on a given day. For this reason, take-offs and landings on runways where there is a crosswind component are frequent events.

Every aeroplane type (from the smallest trainer up to the Airbus A340 and Boeing 747) has a maximum crosswind component specified in the Flight Manual and Pilot's Operating Handbook. If the actual crosswind component on the runway exceeds the limit for the aeroplane and/or what you feel is your own personal limit, then use a different runway (which may even mean proceeding to a different aerodrome).

Do not operate in crosswind conditions that exceed aircraft or personal limits.

Crosswind Strength

The crosswind component on a runway can be estimated from the wind strength and the angle that the wind direction makes with the runway.

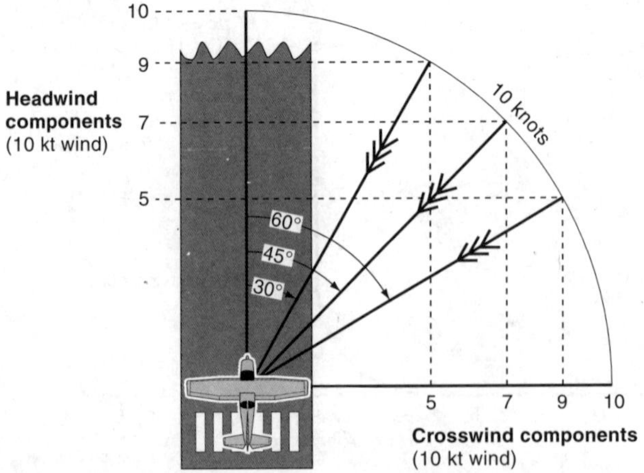

■ *Figure 13f-1* ***Estimating crosswind component***

As a rough guide:

- a wind 30° off the runway heading has a crosswind component of ½ the wind strength;
- a wind 45° off the runway heading has a crosswind component of ⅔ the wind strength;
- a wind 60° off the runway heading has a crosswind component of ⅞ the wind strength;
- a wind 90° off the runway heading is all crosswind.

The Crosswind Circuit

The crosswind circuit is a rectangular pattern over the ground and is based on the runway used. The standard names are given to the various legs of the crosswind circuit, even though the actual wind effect experienced on each of those legs may differ from what the name of the leg suggests.

Adjustments should be made to allow for the wind effect in the circuit, such as laying off drift and modifying the turns. Since the wind at circuit height may differ in direction and strength from that at ground level, make use of ground features to assist in correct tracking around the circuit.

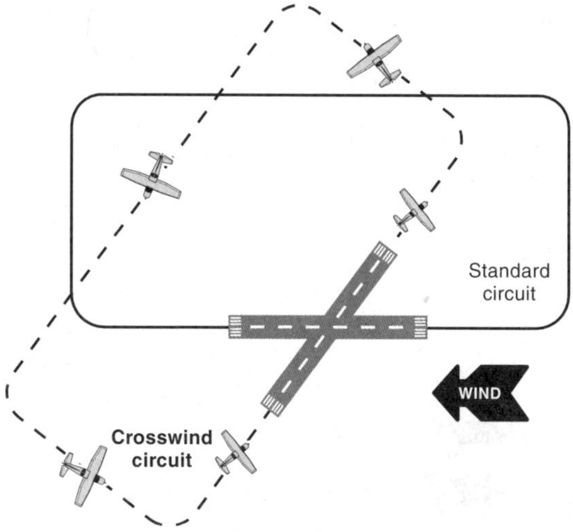

■ *Figure 13f-2* ***Lay-off drift to maintain a rectangular circuit pattern***

When flying in a crosswind circuit, be aware that other aircraft may be operating in a standard into-wind circuit and that their traffic pattern may conflict with yours.

Aeroplanes in the standard circuit will generally have right of way, so the main responsibility for avoiding conflict is with the pilot in the crosswind circuit. A crosswind circuit might sometimes be flown at a different level to avoid conflict with the standard circuit.

Part (i)
Crosswind Take-Off

Flying the Manoeuvre

Weathercocking

In a crosswind, an aeroplane will tend to weathercock into wind because of the large keel surfaces behind the main wheels.

Keep straight with rudder control.

Provided that the crosswind limit for your aeroplane is not exceeded, it will be possible to keep straight on the ground with rudder without too much difficulty. A crosswind from the right will require left rudder to counteract its effect – more rudder at slow speeds and less as the airflow over the rudder increases. Use whatever rudder is required to keep straight. Holding the nose-wheel firmly on the ground until lift-off will assist in directional control.

Lift on the Wings

A crosswind blowing under the into-wind wing will tend to lift it. Counteract this effect and keep the wings level with aileron, i.e. move the control column into wind. While full deflection might be required early in the take-off run, this can be reduced as the faster airflow increases control effectiveness. You do not have to consciously think of aileron movement; just concentrate on keeping the wings level.

Keep the wings level with aileron control.

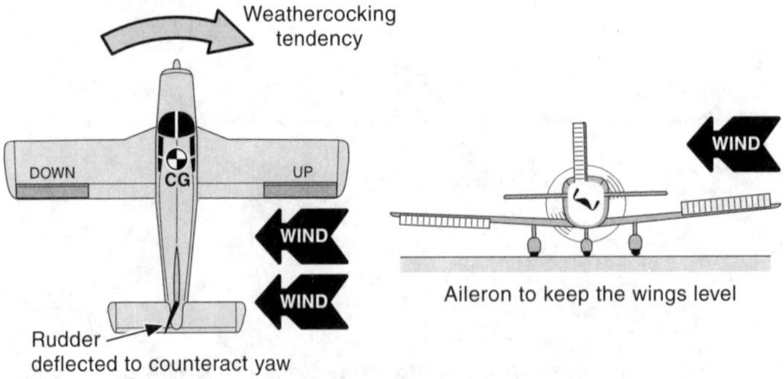

■ *Figure 13f-3* ***Keep straight with rudder; and wings level with ailerons***

Crossed Controls

A right crosswind, for example, requires right control column and left rudder, i.e. crossed controls. A glance at the windsock before you open the throttle for the take-off run will allow you to anticipate this and position the controls correctly.

The controls are crossed in a crosswind take-off.

As speed increases, the amount of aileron and rudder required will reduce until, at lift-off, there will probably be some rudder still applied, but little or no aileron. There is no need to consciously think about this; just:

- **keep straight** with rudder; and
- **keep the wings level** with the ailerons.

Drift after Take-Off

As the aeroplane enters the air mass after lift-off, it will tend to move sideways with it. Any tendency to sink back onto the ground should be resisted to avoid the strong sideways forces that would occur on the undercarriage.

Hold the aeroplane firmly on the ground during the take-off run.

For this reason it is usual, in a crosswind take-off, to hold the aeroplane firmly on the ground during the ground run (with slight forward pressure on the control column) and then **lift off cleanly and positively** with a backward movement of the control column.

Lift off cleanly.

It may be advisable to delay lift-off until 5 kt or so past the normal rotation speed to achieve a clean lift-off.

After lift-off, establish balanced flight and apply a wind correction angle.

Once well clear of the ground, turn into wind sufficiently to counteract the drift and climb out normally on the extended centreline of the runway. Any remaining crossed-control should be removed once airborne by centralising the balance ball and keeping the wings level.

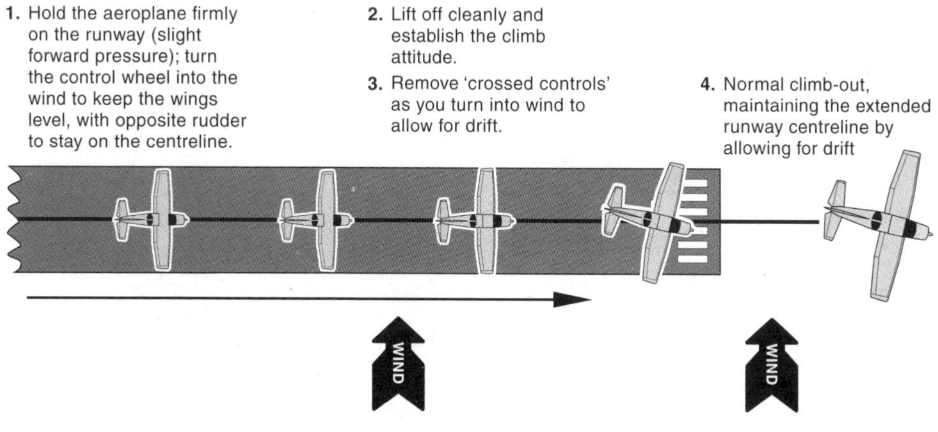

1. Hold the aeroplane firmly on the runway (slight forward pressure); turn the control wheel into the wind to keep the wings level, with opposite rudder to stay on the centreline.
2. Lift off cleanly and establish the climb attitude.
3. Remove 'crossed controls' as you turn into wind to allow for drift.
4. Normal climb-out, maintaining the extended runway centreline by allowing for drift
WIND
WIND

■ *Figure 13f-4* ***The crosswind take-off***

Airmanship

Maintain an exceptionally good lookout and give way to aeroplanes using the into-wind runway and standard circuit, which may conflict with your circuit.

Exert firm, positive control during this manoeuvre and ensure a clean lift-off.

Airwork 13f, Part (i)
Crosswind Take-Off

Aim *To take off on a runway with a crosswind component that is below the limit for the aeroplane.*

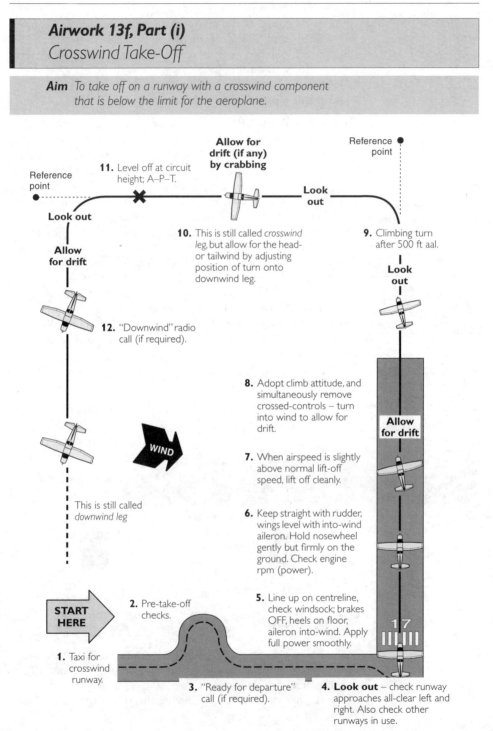

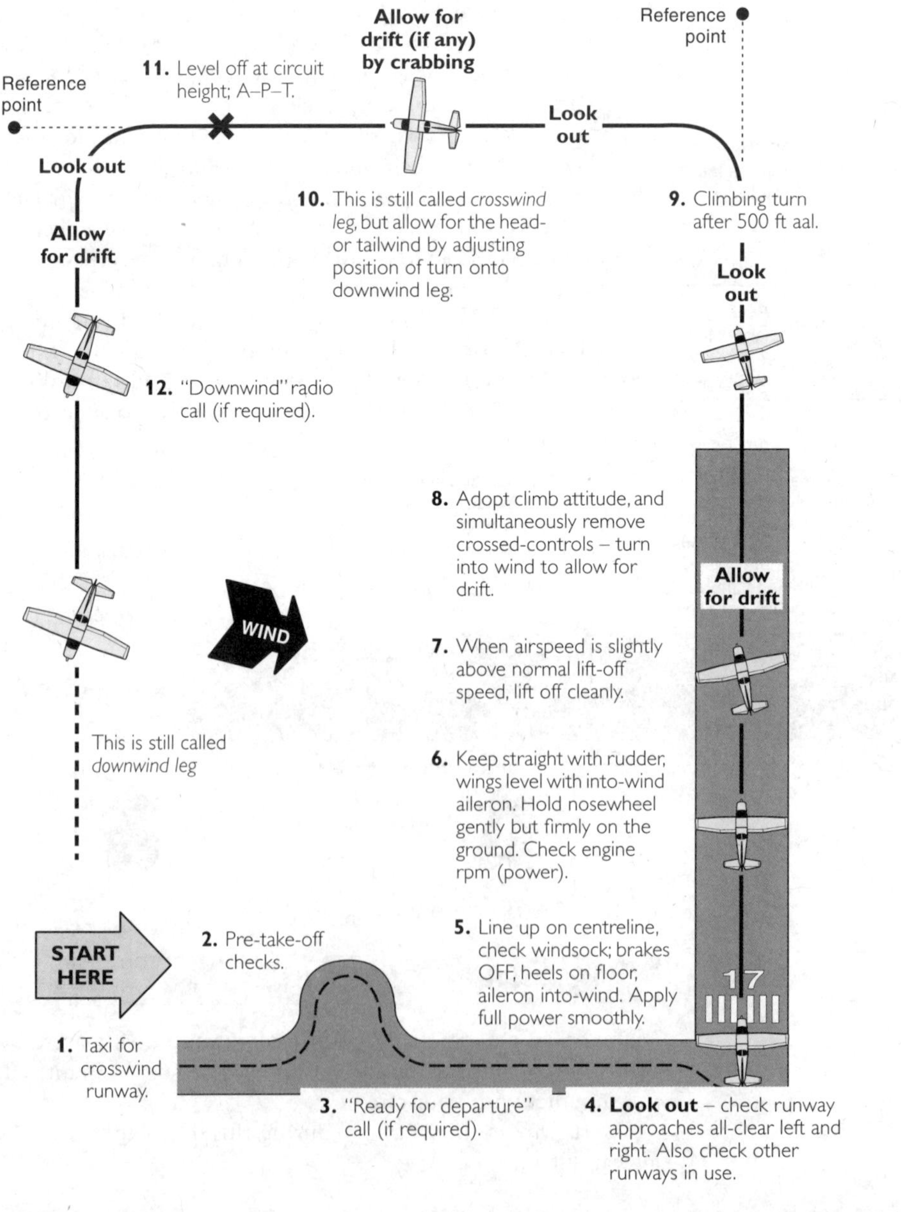
START HERE
1. Taxi for crosswind runway.
2. Pre-take-off checks.
3. "Ready for departure" call (if required).
4. **Look out** – check runway approaches all-clear left and right. Also check other runways in use.
5. Line up on centreline, check windsock; brakes OFF, heels on floor, aileron into-wind. Apply full power smoothly.
6. Keep straight with rudder, wings level with into-wind aileron. Hold nosewheel gently but firmly on the ground. Check engine rpm (power).
7. When airspeed is slightly above normal lift-off speed, lift off cleanly.
8. Adopt climb attitude, and simultaneously remove crossed-controls – turn into wind to allow for drift.
Allow for drift
17
Look out
9. Climbing turn after 500 ft aal.
Reference point
Look out
Allow for drift (if any) by crabbing
10. This is still called *crosswind leg*, but allow for the head- or tailwind by adjusting position of turn onto downwind leg.
11. Level off at circuit height; A–P–T.
Reference point
Look out
Allow for drift
12. "Downwind" radio call (if required).
WIND
This is still called *downwind leg*

Part (ii)
Crosswind Approach and Landing

Flying the Manoeuvre

Ensure that the crosswind component on the selected runway does not exceed the limit for the aeroplane (or your own personal limit).

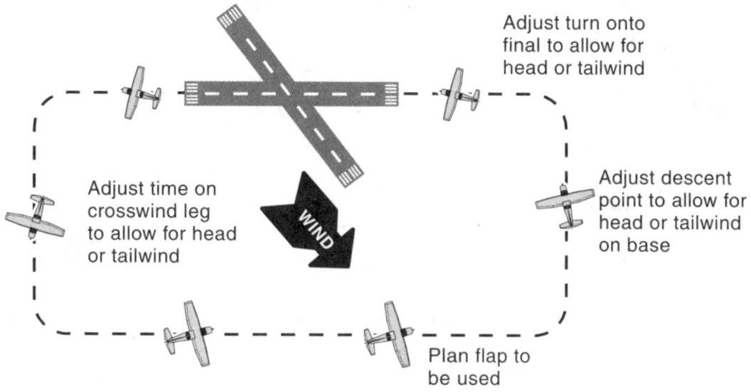
Adjust turn onto final to allow for head or tailwind
Adjust time on crosswind leg to allow for head or tailwind
WIND
Adjust descent point to allow for head or tailwind on base
Plan flap to be used

■ *Figure 13f-5* ***Flying the crosswind circuit***

Crosswind Circuit

Fly the crosswind circuit according to the wind.

Planning for the crosswind approach and landing starts early in the circuit, even as you turn onto the crosswind leg shortly after take-off. A tailwind on the crosswind leg will tend to carry you wide; a headwind will hold you in too close. Adjust each leg of the circuit to position the aircraft suitably with respect to the runway.

Tailwind on Base Leg

Anticipate the effect of a tailwind on base leg.

A tailwind on base leg will increase your speed over the ground and tend to carry you past the runway. For this reason, you should show some anticipation and:

- **commence descent early;**
- **begin the turn onto final early;** and
- **continue the turn onto final** beyond the runway heading to allow for drift.

NOTE If you fly through final, avoid any tendency to overbank (30° bank angle is a reasonable maximum). Simply rejoin final from the other side.

Headwind on Base Leg

Flying into a headwind on base leg, you can afford to delay the turn to final.

A headwind on base leg will decrease your speed over the ground, and so you can:

- **delay descent** until later than usual;

- **delay the turn onto final** until almost in line with the runway; and
- **stop the turn short** of runway heading to anticipate the expected drift.

If you turn too early then you may not reach final, and a positive turn will have to be made into wind to become established. **If you turn too late** and fly through final, fly the runway heading and the wind will most probably carry you back onto the extended centreline. Once in line with the runway, lay off drift to track directly down final.

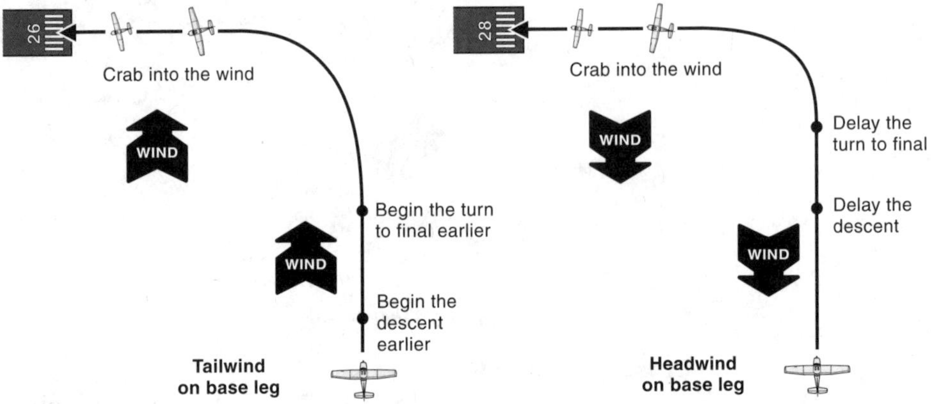

■ *Figure 13f-6* ***Allow for wind effect when turning final***

Tracking Down Final

Positively control tracking down final.

Because of the 'crab' angle needed to maintain the extended centreline, the runway will appear to one side of the nose, but will still look symmetrical. On final for a crosswind landing, you should have a view directly down the runway centreline. If the aeroplane drifts downwind, then make a very definite turn into wind and regain final without delay (do not just aim the nose of the aeroplane at the runway!). Keep the aeroplane in balance.

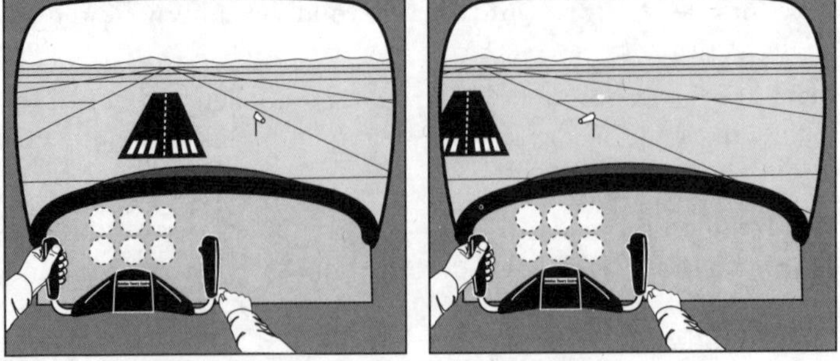

■ *Figure 13f-7* ***An into-wind approach; and a crosswind approach***

Wind strength often decreases near the ground, so continual adjustments to heading will have to be made to maintain your track down final. This is especially the case in strong and gusty conditions.

■ *Figure 13f-8* ***Get tracking under control early on final approach***

Once tracking is under control, then achieving a stabilised descent path and a workmanlike landing becomes a simpler task. It is particularly true in the crosswind case that a good landing requires a good approach.

Align the Wheels

Following a crosswind approach, align the wheels with the runway prior to touchdown.

While an aeroplane is airborne, the fact that its longitudinal axis is not aligned with the runway is not significant. It would be uncomfortable to touch down in this situation, however, since the wheels are not aligned with the path of the aeroplane down the runway in a crosswind. A strong sideways force on the undercarriage could do structural damage or, in an extreme case, tip the aeroplane over. On touchdown, the wheels should be aligned with the runway direction.

The trick in a crosswind landing is to:

- **align the axis of the aeroplane** (i.e. the wheels) with the runway direction prior to touchdown; and to
- **avoid any sideways drift** across the runway before the wheels touch down.

To do this requires the coordinated use of the controls (ailerons, rudder, elevator and power). As your skills develop with practice, you will gain great satisfaction from consistently performing good crosswind landings.

There are three accepted crosswind landing techniques:

(a) The crab method.

(b) The wing-down method.

(c) The combination method (incorporating the best features of each of the above) – a crab approach and a wing-down landing.

Your flying instructor will teach you his or her preferred method. A description of each method begins on page 251.

General Considerations

Strong crosswinds are often accompanied by gusts and turbulence, and consideration should be given to using only partial or zero flap and a slightly higher approach speed than normal to give you better controllability.

The **flare** in a crosswind landing is normal, but the hold-off should not be prolonged (otherwise sideways drift could develop). The aeroplane should be placed on the ground, wheels aligned with the runway, while the flight controls are effective and with the aeroplane tracking along the runway centreline.

Remember to flare, but do not prolong the hold-off.

Once on the ground, directional control is more easily achieved if the nosewheel is lowered onto the ground at an early stage in the landing run. Forward pressure on the control column may be required. You must retain firm control throughout the whole manoeuvre until the aeroplane is stopped or at least has slowed to taxiing speed.

During the landing run:

- **keep straight with rudder** (the crosswind will cause an into-wind weathercocking tendency);
- **lower the nosewheel** to the ground to assist in directional control;
- **keep the wings level** with progressive into-wind aileron as the airspeed decreases (the crosswind will tend to lift the into-wind wing). Full into-wind control column may be required by the end of the landing run.

On the ground, keep on the centreline with rudder and keep wings level with aileron.

Airmanship

Be firm and positive in your handling of the aeroplane. Be decisive!

Airmanship is being positive and alert to the effects of a crosswind.

Remember that your crosswind circuit may conflict with the standard circuit, so keep a good lookout.

If at any stage you feel distinctly unhappy about the approach and landing, go around and start again.

Method (a) – The Crab Method

In the crab method, drift should be laid off all the way down final and through the flare. This will keep the aeroplane tracking down the centreline, but the wheels will not be aligned with the landing direction.

Just prior to touchdown, yaw the aeroplane straight with smooth and firm rudder pressure to align its longitudinal axis (and the wheels) with the centreline of the runway. Keep the wings level with ailerons.

The hold-off period should not be prolonged and the main wheels of the aeroplane should be lowered onto the runway before any sideways drift has a chance to develop. Do not allow the nosewheel to touch first as this could cause a bounce as well as overstress the structure; however, the nosewheel should be lowered to the ground early in the landing run to aid in directional control.

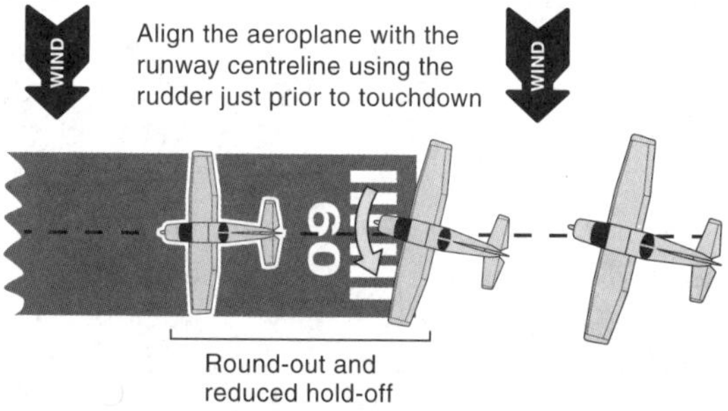

■ *Figure 13f-9* ***In crab method, align the aeroplane just prior to touchdown***

Judgement and Timing

Judgement and timing are important when using the crab method. Failing to remove the crab angle prior to landing will result in the wheels touching down sideways; removing it too early will allow a sideways drift to develop and, as well as landing downwind of the centreline, the wheels will still touch down with a sideways component. In both cases the landing will feel heavy and the undercarriage will be unnecessarily stressed. A reasonable touchdown can only be achieved with fine judgement in removing drift and contacting the ground.

If any sideways drift looks like developing before touchdown, it can be counteracted by:

- **a small amount of wing-down** into wind; and
- **keeping straight with rudder.**

This is really a lead-in to the next method of crosswind landing, the wing-down or forward slip method.

Airwork 13f, Part (ii), Method (a)
Crab Method of Crosswind Landing

Aim *To carry out a crosswind approach and landing by crabbing into wind until just prior to wheel contact on touchdown.*

1. *On Final Approach*

- Track down extended centreline by heading aircraft into wind.
- Control airspeed with elevator, flightpath with power and keep in balance with rudder. The wings should be level except when adjusting crab angle.

2. *During the Flare*

- Reduce power and raise nose normally.
- Maintain track above centreline by crabbing into wind.

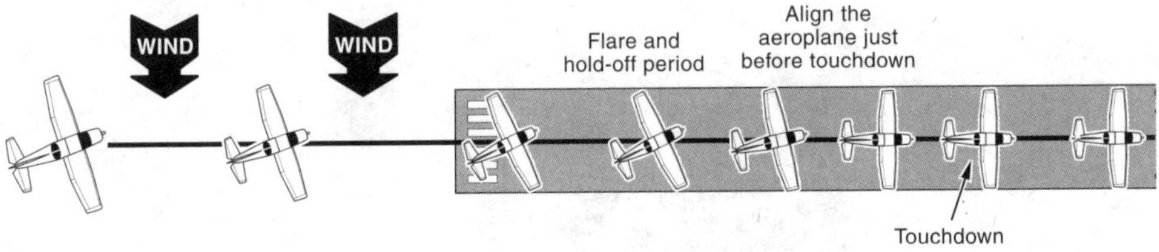

3. *Just Prior to Touchdown*

- Align the aeroplane with the centreline with smooth, firm rudder pressure.
- Hold wings level with aileron.

4. *The Landing Run*

- Keeping straight with rudder, lower the nosewheel onto the ground.
- Keep wings level with progressive into-wind aileron.
- Hold nosewheel on the ground to obtain positive steering.

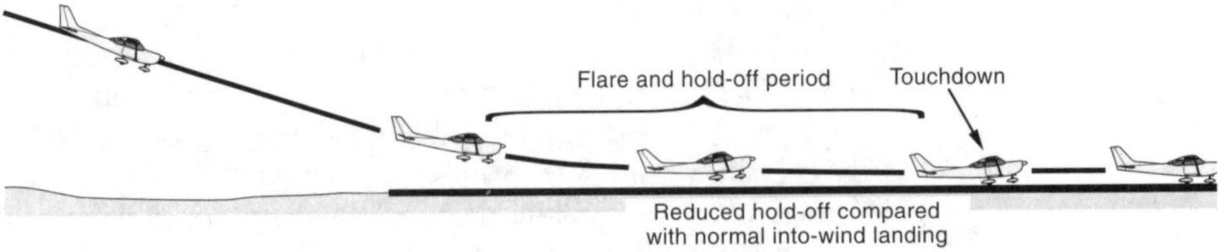

Method (b) – The Wing-Down Method

This method can be employed in the latter stages of the approach. In some places it is taught to be used all the way down final – in others, just for the last few feet. At this stage of your training we will discuss this method as applying to the last 300 ft or so.

The aeroplane is made to track down the extended centreline, not by crabbing, but by 'slipping'. Because the aeroplane tracks 'forward' towards the runway in a 'slip', this manoeuvre is called a **forward-slip.**

To initiate a forward-slip:
- **lower the into-wind wing** a few degrees; and
- **apply opposite rudder pressure** to stop the aeroplane turning and to align its longitudinal axis with the runway centreline.

The aeroplane is out-of-balance and so the balance ball will not be centred. The stronger the crosswind, the more wing-down and opposite rudder required.

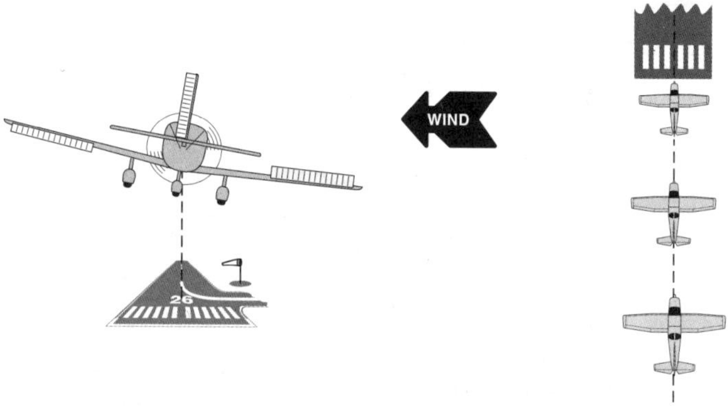

■ *Figure 13f-10* **The wing-down or forward-slip crosswind technique**

Drift Control

Control drift with wing-down, and heading with rudder.

If the aeroplane starts to drift **downwind** across the runway, you have applied insufficient wing-down, so:
- **lower the wing** a few degrees further; and
- **keep straight with rudder.**

If the aeroplane starts to slip **into wind** across the runway, you have applied too much wing-down, so:
- **raise the wing** a few degrees; and
- **keep straight with rudder.**

Stay aligned by varying the amount of wing-down and rudder pressure.

In gusty conditions especially, you will be continually varying the degree of wing-down and opposite rudder to remain aligned with the runway centreline.

The Touchdown

Touch down on the into-wind main wheel.

The wing-down and opposite rudder is held on through the flare and touchdown, which will occur on the into-wind main wheel. Throughout the manoeuvre the aeroplane will be tracking straight down the runway with its longitudinal axis aligned with the centreline. No sideways drift across the runway should be allowed to develop.

■ Figure 13f-11 **The view from the cockpit in a left crosswind**

When the wing-down main wheel touches first, there may be a tendency for the aeroplane to yaw into wind, but the aeroplane can easily be kept straight with rudder. The other main wheel will touch down naturally, after which you should lower the nosewheel onto the ground to allow more positive directional control.

In the landing run:

In the ground roll, keep straight with rudder and wings level with aileron.

- **keep straight with rudder,** holding the nosewheel on the ground; and
- **keep wings level** with into-wind aileron – full control wheel into wind perhaps being required as the aeroplane slows down.

Advantages of the Wing-Down Method

Less judgement and timing is required in the actual touchdown using this method, since the aeroplane is aligned with the runway centreline throughout the flare and hold-off. There is no crab angle to remove and no sideways drift. It is of less importance if the aeroplane touches down a little earlier or a little later than expected, whereas with the crab method good judgement in aligning the aeroplane just before touchdown is required.

Airwork 13f, Part (ii), Method (b)
Wing-Down Crosswind Landing

Aim *To land the aeroplane in a crosswind following a wing-down approach.*

1. On Final Approach, Aligned with Runway Centreline

- Lower the into-wind wing and use rudder to remain aligned with runway centreline.
- Control airspeed with elevators, flightpath with power and the track with wing-down (and opposite) rudder.

2. During the Flare

- Reduce power and raise nose normally.
- Maintain track along the centreline with wing down and opposite rudder.

3. The Touchdown

- The touchdown will be on the into-wind wheel because of that wing being down.
- The other main wheel will follow naturally.

4. The Landing Run

- Keep straight with rudder.
- Lower the nosewheel to the ground.
- Wings level with into-wind aileron.

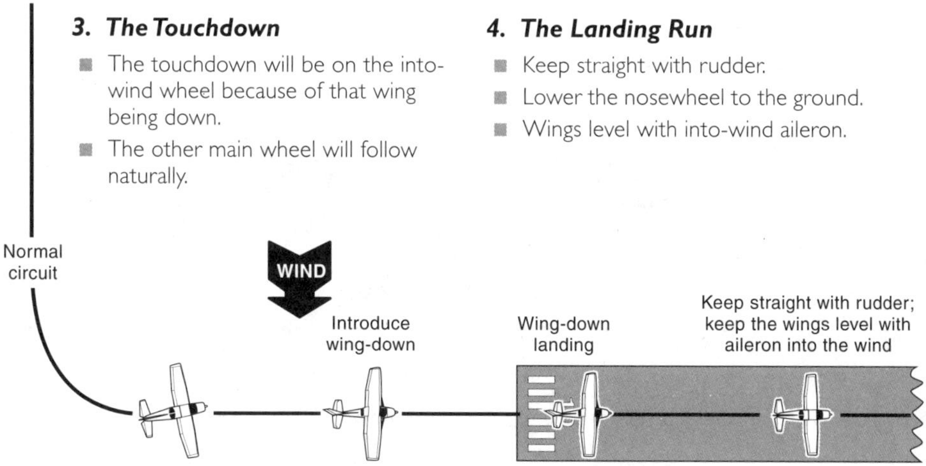
Normal circuit
WIND
Introduce wing-down
Wing-down landing
Keep straight with rudder; keep the wings level with aileron into the wind

Method (c) – The Combination Method

Crab Approach Followed by a Wing-Down Landing

A distinct disadvantage of the wing-down technique being used all the way down final is that the controls are crossed and the aeroplane is out of balance (i.e. the ball is not centred). This is both inefficient and uncomfortable.

Crab into wind on approach.

A more comfortable approach can be flown if drift is laid-off to maintain the extended runway centreline by 'crabbing' and the aeroplane is flown in balance (ball centred, pilot and passengers comfortable).

Before touchdown, yaw the nose straight with rudder and prevent drift with wing-down

An easier crosswind landing can be made if, prior to touchdown, the wing-down method is employed by lowering the into-wind wing, simultaneously applying opposite rudder to align the aeroplane. This aligns the wheels with the track along the runway – the amount of 'wing-down' and opposite rudder required being determined by the strength of the crosswind.

At just what point you transfer from the crab to the wing-down depends on your experience and the wind conditions. Initially, it may be better to introduce the wing-down at about 100 ft above ground level but, as you become more experienced, this can be delayed until in the flare below 20 ft. In **strong and gusty crosswinds,** it is better to introduce the wing-down earlier than in steady conditions.

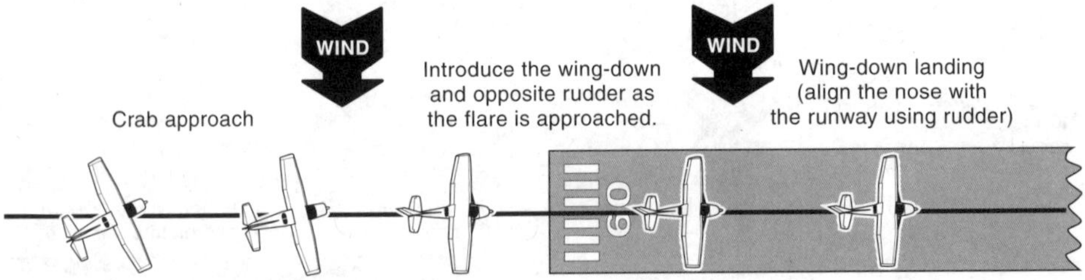
WIND
Crab approach
Introduce the wing-down and opposite rudder as the flare is approached.
WIND
Wing-down landing (align the nose with the runway using rudder)
09

■ *Figure 13f-12* ***The combination method of crosswind landing***

Airwork 13f, Part (ii), Method (c)
The Combined Crab Approach and Wing-Down Crosswind Landing

Aim *To land the aeroplane in a crosswind using a crab approach followed by a wing-down landing.*

1. On Final Approach

- Adjust the heading to track (crab) down final along the extended runway centreline.
- Keep the wings level, and balance with rudder pressure.

2. At or Approaching Flare Height

(about 20 ft above the runway, or hangar height)

- Use smooth rudder pressure to align aeroplane with runway centreline – and stay aligned.
- Lower the into-wind wing to prevent sideways drift.

3. During the Flare

- Reduce power and raise the nose normally.
- Maintain centreline with wing-down and opposite rudder.

4. The Touchdown

- Touch down on the into-wind main wheel and allow the other main wheel to follow.
- Maintain directional control with rudder.

5. The Landing Run

- Keep straight with rudder.
- Lower nosewheel to runway.
- Wings level with into-wind aileron (full control wheel movement may be required).

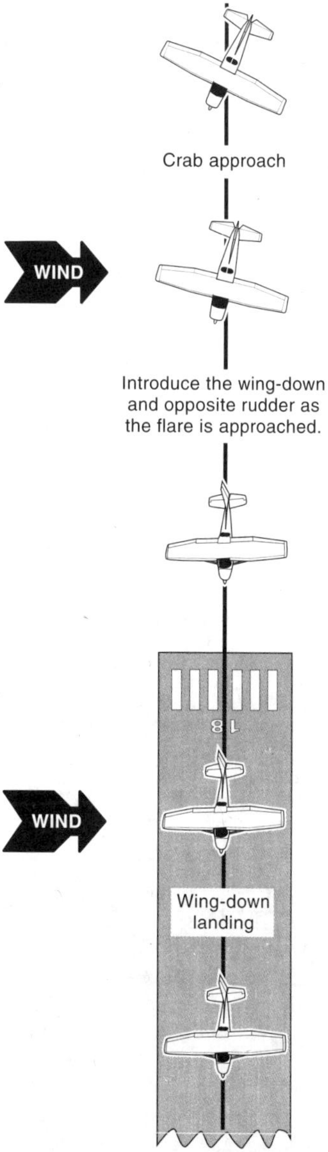
Crab approach
WIND
Introduce the wing-down and opposite rudder as the flare is approached.
18
WIND
Wing-down landing

Exercise 13g
Short-Field Operations

Aim

To operate safely and efficiently out of and into a short field.

Considerations

What is a Short Field?

A short field is one at which the **runway length available** and/or the **obstacle-clearance gradients** are only just sufficient to satisfy take-off and landing requirements.

Performance Charts

The take-off and landing performance charts for your aeroplane should be consulted to ensure that a short field in a confined area is indeed adequate for the planned operations under the existing conditions. An inspection on foot of the proposed take-off and landing surface and the surrounding area may be necessary. During the inspection remember that the take-off is not complete until all obstacles are cleared in the climb-out, so not only the take-off surface, but also the surrounding area, need to be considered.

Refer to the appropriate performance charts for your aeroplane.

CONDITIONS:
Flaps 10°
Full Throttle Prior to Brake Release
Paved, Level, Dry Runway
Zero Wind

TAKEOFF DISTANCE

SHORT FIELD

SAMPLE ONLY
not to be used
in conjunction
with flight operations
or flight planning

NOTES:
1. Short field technique as specified in Section 4.
2. Prior to takeoff from fields above 3000 feet elevation, the mixture should be leaned to give maximum RPM in a full throttle, static runup.
3. Decrease distances 10% for each 9 knots headwind. For operation with tailwinds up to 10 knots, increase distances by 10% for each 2 knots.
4. For operation on a dry, grass runway, increase distances by 15% of the "ground roll" figure.

WEIGHT LBS	TAKEOFF SPEED KIAS		PRESS ALT FT	0°C		10°C		20°C		30°C		40°C	
	LIFT OFF	AT 50 FT		GRND ROLL	TOTAL TO CLEAR 50 FT OBS	GRND ROLL	TOTAL TO CLEAR 50 FT OBS	GRND ROLL	TOTAL TO CLEAR 50 FT OBS	GRND ROLL	TOTAL TO CLEAR 50 FT OBS	GRND ROLL	TOTAL TO CLEAR 50 FT OBS
1670	50	54	S.L.	640	1190	695	1290	755	1390	810	1495	875	1605
			1000	705	1310	765	1420	825	1530	890	1645	960	1770
			2000	775	1445	840	1565	910	1690	980	1820	1055	1960

■ *Figure 13g-1* **Consult the performance charts**

Flying the Manoeuvre

The Short-Field Take-Off

There are generally two considerations in the short-field take-off:

1. Use of only a short ground run.
2. Avoidance of obstacles in the take-off and climb-out flightpath.

A short-field take-off is a normal take-off, except that you should pay special attention to the following points to achieve the shortest ground run and steepest climb-out:

- Take off as much into wind as possible.
- Use the best flap setting for take-off.
- Ensure that the take-off run is commenced from as close to the end of the field as possible.
- Apply power with toe-brakes on, holding the control column back to avoid damage to the propeller, releasing the brakes as full power is reached (although, if loose stones could damage the propeller, a rolling start is preferred).
- Lift off at the minimum recommended flying speed with elevator.
- Assume the nose attitude for the best-angle climb to avoid obstacles (a higher pitch attitude than in a normal climb).
- At a safe height, when clear of obstacles, enter a normal climb.

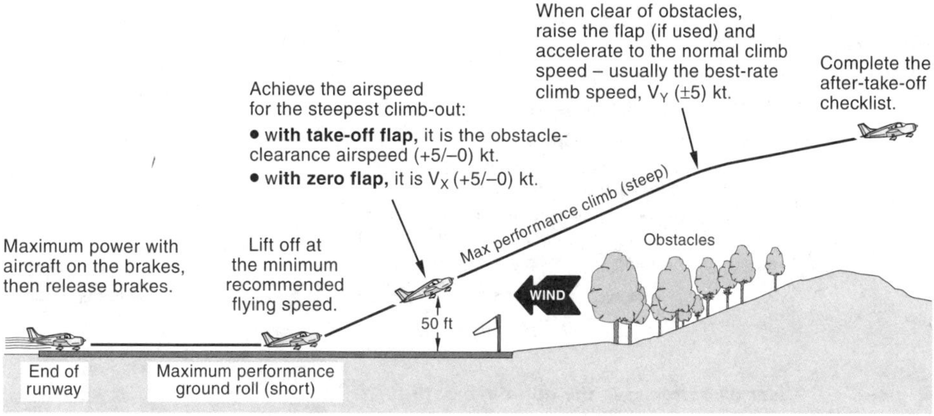

■ *Figure 13g-2* ***The short-field take-off***

The Short-Field Landing

The short-field landing is useful when the chosen landing area:

- is of marginal length (obviously); or
- has a surface of which the pilot is unsure.

Land as much into wind as possible, since this will allow a steeper approach and a shorter landing run. Position the aeroplane as for a normal approach – the preferred technique being a power-assisted approach at a low speed, with an aiming point as close to the threshold as practicable. The aeroplane should touch down without much float as soon as the throttle is closed.

Fly as slow an approach speed as is safe. Full flap is preferred if wind conditions are suitable (i.e. no significant gustiness), since this allows a lower approach speed and there will be less float prior to touchdown due to the extra drag. A shorter landing distance will result. The recommended approach speed for a short-field landing may be less than for the normal approach (check your Pilot's Operating Handbook); however, it should never be less than 1.3 times the actual stall speed to give you a 30% safety buffer over the stall when on approach.

Use power to control the flightpath and elevator to maintain airspeed. If you are on 'the back side of the power curve' (also known as 'the back side of the drag curve'), then frequent and positive adjustments to power and attitude will be required to maintain the desired flightpath and airspeed.

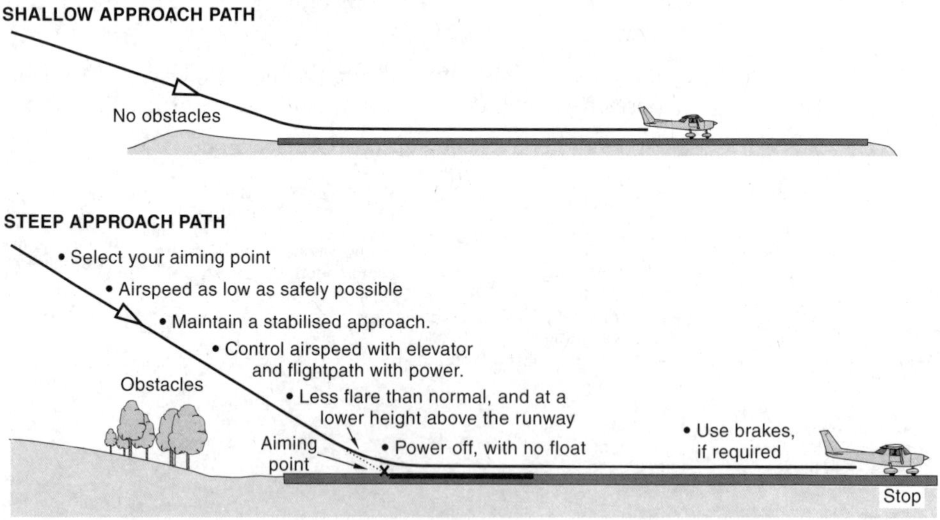
SHALLOW APPROACH PATH
No obstacles
STEEP APPROACH PATH
• Select your aiming point
• Airspeed as low as safely possible
• Maintain a stabilised approach.
• Control airspeed with elevator and flightpath with power.
Obstacles
• Less flare than normal, and at a lower height above the runway
Aiming point
• Power off, with no float
• Use brakes, if required
Stop

■ *Figure 13g-3* ***Clear all obstacles in the approach path***

Fly the approach so as to clear all obstacles. Obstacles in the approach path may require that an aiming point further into the short field be chosen. Having cleared the obstacles, do not reduce power unduly, otherwise a high sink rate and a heavy touchdown may result (since at a low speed the aeroplane has less-effective controls and a reduced flaring capability). Given a choice, you should select an approach path that does not have obstacles.

If there are no obstacles in the approach path, then a slightly undershooting approach may be considered, with power being used to ensure that you clear the nearside fence safely.

Aim to cross the airfield boundary at the selected speed and at the minimum height consistent with adequate obstacle clearance and with power on. Do not prolong the hold-off and touchdown; then use brakes as required.

Since the nose will be higher than in a normal landing due to the lower speed and higher power, not as great a flare will be required and the round-out should be commenced closer to the ground than normal. Some power should be left on at the commencement of flare if the speed is low; touchdown will follow immediately the throttle is closed.

If a high sink rate develops add power to prevent a heavy landing. Power may be required all the way to the ground – if so, close the throttle as soon as the wheels touch.

If an especially short landing run is required, brakes may be used once all the wheels are firmly on the ground. Early in the landing run, the wings will still be producing some lift and so all of the weight will not be on the wheels. Excessive braking at this time may cause skidding.

Exercise 13h
Soft-Field Operations

Aim

To operate safely and efficiently from a 'soft' field.

Considerations

What is a Soft Field?

A soft field could be an area which has a soft surface such as sand or snow, a wet grassy surface or a rough surface. A soft field may be quite long and with no obstacle-clearance problems in the climb-out or approach path. It may also be short, which means the short-field considerations of obstacle-clearance also becomes important. For this exercise, we assume a long take-off surface and no obstacle-clearance problems.

Soft surfaces degrade acceleration.

Soft surfaces create extra frictional drag and stress on the wheels and therefore degrade the acceleration in the take-off run. The wheels may have a dangerous tendency to 'dig-in'. Only use a soft field if you are totally satisfied that a safe take-off and/or landing can be made.

Flying the Manoeuvre

The Soft-Field Take-Off

The main concern in a soft-field take-off is to shift the weight from the wheels to the wings as soon as possible and achieve a short ground run. Consequently optimum flap and maximum power should be used.

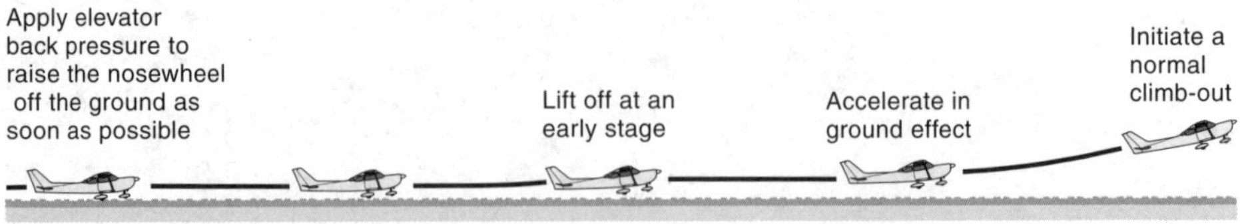
Apply elevator back pressure to raise the nosewheel off the ground as soon as possible
Lift off at an early stage
Accelerate in ground effect
Initiate a normal climb-out

■ *Figure 13h-1* ***The soft-field take-off***

During the take-off run, keep the weight off the nosewheel with the control column held well back. Lift the aeroplane off the ground as soon as possible (at a lower speed than in a normal take-off) and accelerate to climb speed close to the ground. The aeroplane can fly in ground effect at a lower speed than when it is well away from the ground. For this reason, do not climb more than about 10 ft above the ground until a safe flying speed is attained, at which time a normal climb-out can proceed.

The Soft-Field Landing

Since the tendency on a soft field is for the nosewheel (and, to a lesser extent, the main wheels) to dig in, the aim should be to:

- **land as slowly as possible;** and
- **hold the nose up as long as possible** during the landing roll.

Use full flap if conditions permit. Full flap reduces the stalling speed and so touchdown can be made at a very low speed. If field length is not a problem, a normal approach can be flown, with a slightly modified round-out. Some power can be left on in the flare as the nose is raised higher than normal in a prolonged hold-off. The higher the nose attitude and the lower the speed on touchdown, the better.

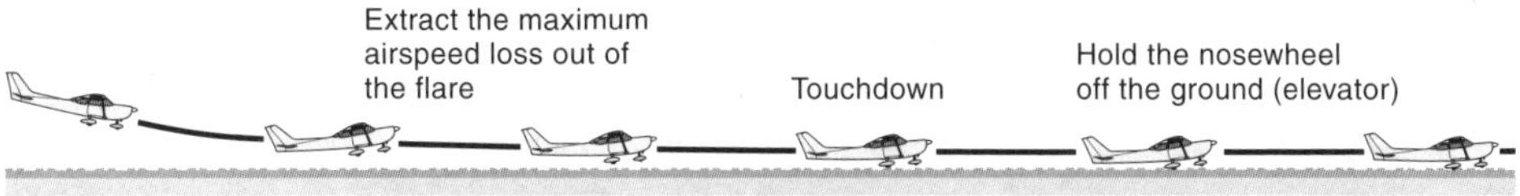
Extract the maximum airspeed loss out of the flare
Touchdown
Hold the nosewheel off the ground (elevator)

■ *Figure 13h-2* ***The soft-field landing***

Exercise 14
First Solo

Aim

To fly solo and be the pilot-in-command of an aeroplane for the first time.

Flying the Manoeuvre

First solo is a great experience! When your instructor steps out of the aeroplane and leaves you to your first solo flight you are being paid a big compliment. You may feel a little apprehensive, but remember that he or she is trained to judge the right moment to send you solo. Your instructor will have a better appreciation of your flying ability than anybody (including you).

Fly your first solo circuit in the same manner as you flew those circuits before the instructor stepped out. The usual standards apply to your take-off, circuit and landing. Maintain a good look out, fly a neat circuit, establish a stabilised approach and carry out your normal landing. Be prepared for better performance of the aeroplane without the weight of your instructor on board. If at any stage you feel uncomfortable, go around.

If an emergency, such as engine failure, occurs – and this is an extremely unlikely event – carry out the appropriate emergency procedure that you have been well trained in. Your flying instructor, when sending you solo, not only considers you competent to fly a circuit with a normal take-off and landing, but also considers you competent to handle an emergency.

One take-off, circuit and landing will admit you to the family of pilots!

Consolidation Flying

Further refinement and consolidation of the basic skills that you now possess will follow, with solo periods being interspersed with dual periods. The dual flights allow your flying instructor to refine your skills and develop them further. In the solo periods you will develop the skills of a captain, making your own decisions and acting on them.

Your initial solo flights will be in the circuit area, practising take-offs and landings, but, quite soon, you will be proceeding solo to the local training area to practise other manoeuvres.

Exercise 15a
The Steep Level Turn

Aim

To perform a steep level turn, maintaining constant height and airspeed.

Considerations

A steep turn is a turn in which the bank angle exceeds 45°. It is a high-performance manoeuvre which requires good coordination and positive control.

Increased Lift

A steep level turn requires increased lift, and this requires back pressure on the control column.

In straight and level flight, the lift produced by the wings balances the weight of the aeroplane. In turns, the lift force is tilted and consequently the lift generated by the wings must be increased to provide not only a vertical component to balance the weight but also a horizontal component (known as the *centripetal force*) to pull the aeroplane into the turn. In a 60° banked turn, for example, the lift produced must be double the weight if height is to be maintained.

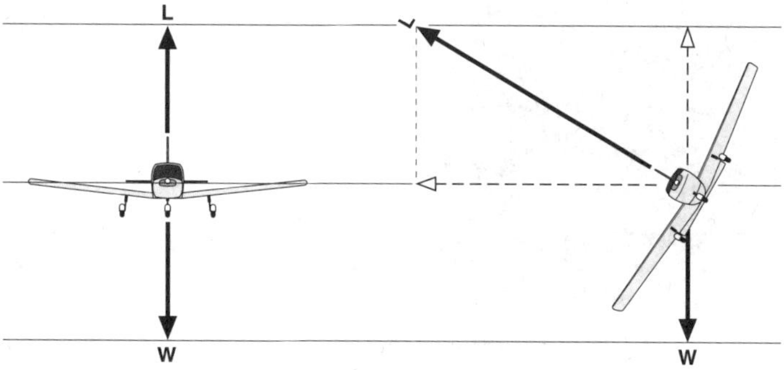

■ *Figure 15a-1* ***A steep level turn requires increased lift***

Increased lift in a turn is generated by an increased angle of attack.

The increased lift in a turn is generated by back pressure on the control column which increases the angle of attack. The back pressure required to maintain height is quite significant in a steep turn.

Increased Load Factor

When you feel an increased g-loading during a turn you are simply experiencing an increased load factor (which is the ratio *lift/weight*). The normal load factor is one (1) when the aeroplane is either stationary on the ground or in steady, straight and level flight. You experience this as '1g', i.e. your normal weight. In a 60° banked turn the load factor is 2 and you will feel *twice* your normal weight because the lift generated by the wings is now double the aeroplane's weight. The human body soon becomes accustomed to these g-forces.

Load factor and stalling speed increase significantly in a steep turn.

The steeper the turn, the greater the angle of attack required to generate sufficient lift, and consequently the stalling angle of attack will be reached at a higher airspeed than when the wings are level. In a 60° banked turn, for example, the stalling speed is some 40% greater (e.g. an aeroplane which stalls at 50 kt straight and level will stall at 70 kt when pulling 2g).

The greater the load factor, the higher the stalling speed. Feeling a g-force is a signal that the aeroplane structure is under additional stress and that stalling speed has increased. At any hint of stalling in a steep turn, some of the back pressure on the control column should be released. This will reduce the angle of attack and move the wings away from the stalling angle. Reducing the bank angle or adding power (if there is any in reserve) will also assist in avoiding a stall in this situation.

The greater the load factor, the higher the stalling speed.

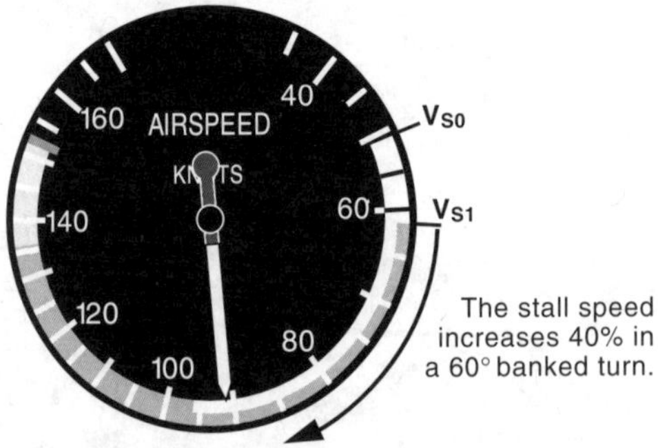

■ *Figure 15a-2* ***Be alert to the stall speed increase in a steep turn***

Increased Drag

The greater angle of attack used to generate the increased lift required in a steep turn also creates additional induced drag. This must be balanced by increased thrust if the aeroplane is to maintain airspeed. Whereas it was acceptable to lose a few knots in medium turns, it is very important to maintain airspeed in steep turns because of the higher stalling speed.

Drag increases significantly in steep turns, so additional thrust is required to maintain speed.

As well as coordinating the use of aileron, rudder and elevator (as in medium turns), power now becomes an added ingredient as the **maximum achievable bank angle** in a steady steep turn is determined by the amount of power available.

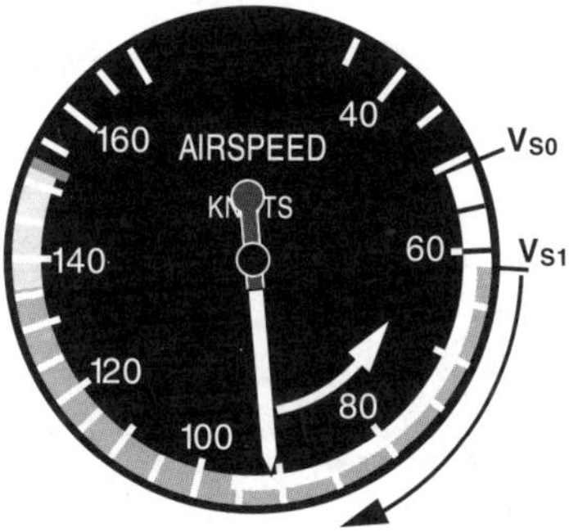

■ *Figure 15a-3* ***Use power to maintain airspeed in a steep turn***

Flying the Manoeuvre

The g-forces in a 45° steep turn are nowhere near as great as in a 60° banked turn. For this reason, you may find it easier to practise steep turns at a 45° bank angle initially, progressing to 60° bank angle turns later on in your training.

Prior to practising steep turns, your training organisation may require you to carry out the pre-aerobatic HASELL check (as described in Exercise 10a).

Rolling into a Steep Level Turn

Be on speed, on altitude, and in trim before rolling into a steep turn.

Trim the aeroplane for straight and level flight at the desired airspeed and height. Look out for other aeroplanes and select a reference point on the horizon for the roll-out.

Roll into the turn just as you would into a normal medium turn except that as the bank angle increases through 30°:

- **smoothly add power;**
- **progressively increase the back pressure** on the control column;
- **adjust the bank angle and back pressure** to place the nose in the correct position relative to the horizon; and
- **balance with rudder.**

Do not apply too much back pressure entering the turn or the aeroplane will climb – just gradually increase it as you steepen the bank. The back pressure required in a steep turn will probably be much greater than you had anticipated. Do not trim as the turn is only a transient manoeuvre.

Maintaining a Steep Level Turn

Add power to maintain airspeed.

The secret of flying an accurate steep level turn is to hold the nose in the correct position relative to the horizon (even if it takes a lot of back pressure), ensuring the airspeed is maintained by adding sufficient power.

Keep a very good lookout during the steep turn to monitor the nose position and the approach of your roll-out reference point, as well as to look for other aircraft, especially in the direction of your turn.

An occasional glance at the instruments will confirm that the turn is proceeding satisfactorily, but do not sacrifice your outside reference by concentrating on the instruments. In just a second or two you can quickly check:

- **height** on the altimeter and vertical speed indicator;
- **airspeed** on the airspeed indicator;
- **bank angle** on the attitude indicator;
- **balance** on the balance indicator (ball in the centre).

Adjusting the bank angle and nose position is a continuing requirement throughout the steep turn and keeps the pilot quite busy. That is why it is such a good training manoeuvre! The sooner the corrections are made, the smaller they can be and the better the steep turn.

IF HEIGHT IS BEING GAINED in the steep turn, it means that the vertical component of the lift force is too great, and so either:

- steepen the bank angle; and/or
- relax some of the back pressure.

IF HEIGHT IS BEING LOST then the vertical component of the lift force is insufficient. To regain height:

- reduce the bank angle slightly;
- raise the nose with back pressure; and
- once back on height, reapply the desired bank angle and back pressure.

IF THE NOSE DROPS BELOW THE HORIZON during a steep turn, trying to raise the nose with back pressure will only tighten the turn rather than raise the nose. Should the height loss rapidly increase, roll out to straight and level, climb back to your desired height and start again.

Stall Buffet

If the aeroplane turns through more than 360°, you may in fact strike your own slipstream and feel some turbulence. This is not the stall buffet, but the sign of a well-executed steep turn. If, however, the stall buffet is felt, then **release some of the back pressure** to reduce the angle of attack before the stall actually occurs. To avoid losing height, you will have to decrease the bank angle slightly as back pressure is released.

When practising steep turns aim to achieve an accuracy of ±200 ft and ±10 kt initially and then, as your training progresses, accept no variations at all.

■ *Figure 15a-4* ***Typical nose attitudes while flying the manoeuvre***

Rolling Out of a Steep Turn

This is the same as rolling out of a medium turn, except that:

- greater anticipation is required to roll out on your reference point;
- there is a great deal more back pressure to be released, otherwise height will be gained; and
- after the airspeed has been regained, power must be reduced to cruise power.

Remember to keep the aeroplane in balance with rudder.

Concentration is required in the roll-out, especially to avoid gaining height since you may be a little reluctant to relax all of the back pressure. Rolling out of a 45° banked turn, relaxing back pressure is usually sufficient. Rolling out of a 60° banked turn the release of back pressure is so great that it may feel as though you have to push the control column forward.

Do not forget to reduce the power as you roll out, otherwise airspeed will rapidly increase.

After some practice at steep turns to the left and right, your flying instructor may suggest that you roll from a steep turn one way immediately into a steep turn the other way.

Airmanship

Airmanship is keeping a good lookout, and flying the aeroplane positively.

Practise steep turns in an appropriate area and keep a very good look out for other aircraft.

Note various landmarks that will assist in orientation during and after the turn. It is easy for an inexperienced pilot to become disoriented in steep turns which involve large changes of heading.

Handle the power smoothly and monitor the gauges to ensure engine limitations are not exceeded.

Exert smooth, but firm, control over the aeroplane.

Airwork 15a
Steep Level Turns

Aim *To perform a steep level turn, maintaining constant height and airspeed.*

1. *Entry*

- Complete the HASELL check.
- Look out.
- Select a reference point on the horizon.
- Roll on bank with aileron.
- Balance with rudder.
- Apply sufficient back-pressure on control column to maintain height.
- Add power progressively to maintain airspeed.

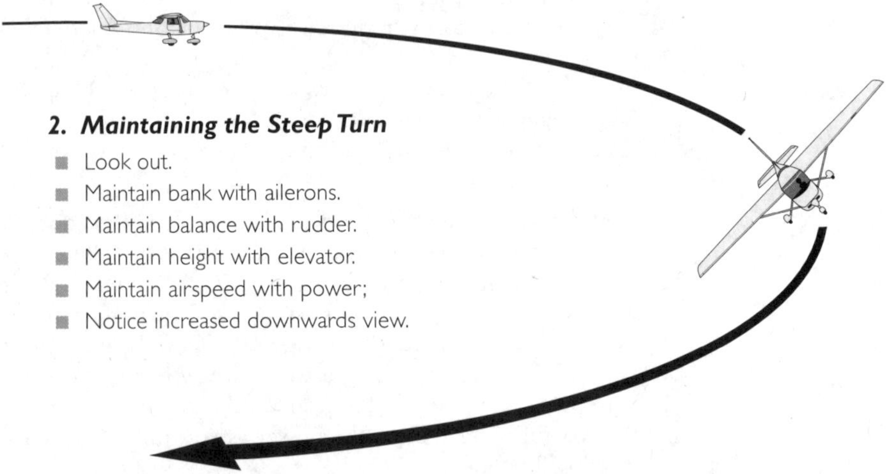

2. *Maintaining the Steep Turn*

- Look out.
- Maintain bank with ailerons.
- Maintain balance with rudder.
- Maintain height with elevator.
- Maintain airspeed with power;
- Notice increased downwards view.

If height is gained:

- Reduce back pressure and consider steepening the bank angle temporarily, but do not over-bank.

If height is lost:

- Reduce bank angle.
- Raise nose with increased back pressure; and then reapply bank.

3. *Roll Out*

- Look out.
- Locate roll-out reference point (anticipate by 30°).
- Roll off bank with ailerons.
- Balance with rudder.
- Release elevator back pressure to maintain height.
- Progressively reduce power to maintain the required cruise airspeed.

Further Points

Maximum Performance Turns

Maximum bank angle possible in a steady steep turn is limited by power.

A maximum performance steep level turn at a particular airspeed is flown like a normal steep turn except that power is progressively applied as the bank angle is increased, until maximum power is reached.

The ability to maintain height and airspeed in this manoeuvre depends on the amount of power available. For most training aeroplanes, the performance limit is reached at about 65° of bank.

Turning performance is measured in terms of:
- **the rate of turn** (the greater, the better); and
- **the radius of turn** (the smaller, the better).

At a **constant airspeed,** turning performance increases with bank angle.

At a **constant bank angle,** turning performance is better at low airspeeds. Therefore, the best turning performance can be achieved at a relatively low airspeed and a high bank angle (providing the aeroplane is not stalled or the airframe overstressed).

Overstressing

Do not overstress the airframe in a steep turn.

The lift which can be generated by the wings with full rearward movement of the control column is far greater at high airspeeds than at low airspeeds and results in greater load factors occurring. For example, pulling the control column fully back at 150 kt will increase the g-loading considerably more than at 50 kt. At **high airspeeds,** therefore, there is a danger of overstressing the airframe by exceeding the maximum allowable load factor (+3.8g for most training aeroplanes).

Manoeuvring Speed (V_A)

Large elevator deflection at high airspeed can cause the wings to generate so much lift that the aeroplane's **limit-load-factor** is exceeded without the wings reaching their stalling angle of attack. At low airspeeds the aeroplane will stall before the limit-load-factor is reached, i.e. the airframe is 'protected' aerodynamically.

Maximum turning performance is achieved at the manoeuvring speed (V_A).

The airspeed at which maximum elevator deflection causes the stall to occur right at the limit-load-factor is called the manoeuvring speed (V_A). The **best aerodynamic turning performance** can be achieved at this speed provided sufficient power is available.

For most training aeroplanes the engine performance is the limiting factor in maximum-performance steep turns.

V_A for maximum weight is specified in the Flight Manual. At airspeeds *less* than manoeuvring speed (V_A), full elevator deflection will not overstress the airframe; above V_A it will. At lesser weights, when stalling speed is lower, the actual V_A will be a few knots less than that published.

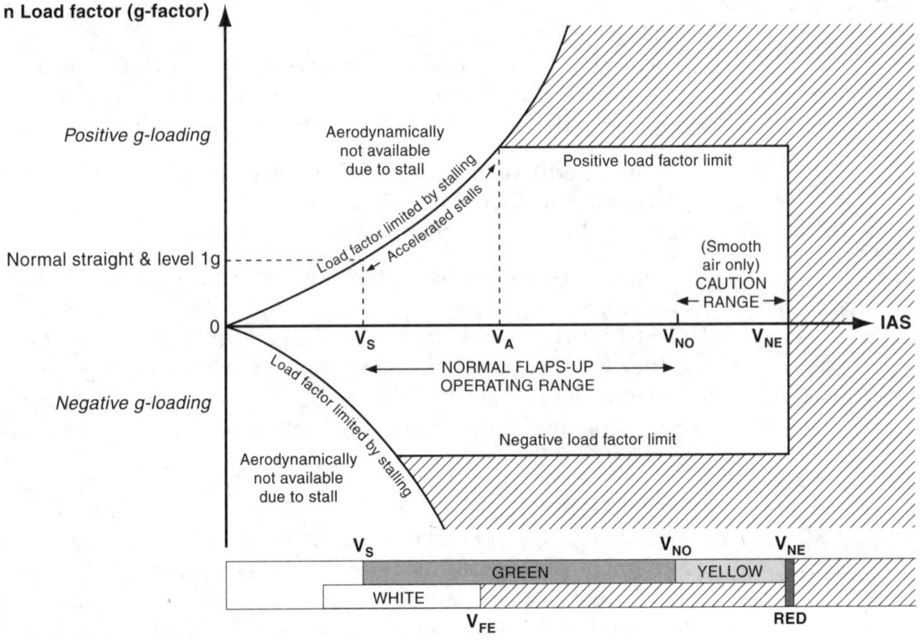

■ *Figure 15a-5* ***Airspeed (V) versus allowable load factor (n)***

Exercise 15b
Recovery from Unusual Attitudes

Aim

To recognise and recover from an unusual aeroplane attitude that may develop into a potentially hazardous situation.

Considerations

While a steep turn should be a straightforward manoeuvre, it is possible that early in your steep turn training some unusual attitudes may develop. It would be appropriate for you to reread Exercises 10 and 11 at this stage.

What is an Unusual Attitude?

The two fundamental unusual attitudes are:

- **nose-high** with a decreasing airspeed; or
- **nose-low** with an increasing airspeed.

Unusual attitudes generally result from some form of mishandling by the pilot. For example, the relatively low power available in most training aeroplanes will not allow a steady climb to be maintained in a steep turn. A **nose-high/low-speed** unusual attitude can result if the nose is raised in an attempt to achieve a steep climbing turn.

Flying the Manoeuvre

Nose High and Decreasing Airspeed

Nose high and decreasing airspeed – beware of a stall or spin.

If the nose is well above the horizon and the speed is low and/or decreasing, a stall is a possibility.

To recover from a **nose-high/low-airspeed** unusual attitude following a stall:

- **ease the control column centrally forward;**
- **apply sufficient rudder** to prevent further yaw;
- **apply maximum power;** and
- **when the airspeed increases** as the wings become unstalled, **level the wings** with coordinated use of rudder and ailerons, **ease out of the descent** and resume the desired flightpath.

If a full spin develops from a mishandled steep turn, probably as a result of the nose being raised too high and the speed allowed to drop too low, then recover using the recommended **spin recovery.**

The spin-recovery technique is:
- **throttle closed,** flaps up and ailerons neutral;
- **verify the spin direction** on the turn coordinator;
- **apply full opposite rudder;**
- **pause;**
- **move the control column centrally forward** (to unstall the wings) until the rotation stops;
- **centralise the rudder** once the rotation has stopped;
- **level the wings** and gently **ease out of the ensuing dive;** and
- **as the nose rises** through the horizon, add power and climb away.

Nose Low and Increasing Airspeed

Nose low and increasing airspeed – beware of an overspeed or spiral dive.

If the nose is low, especially if power is applied, exceeding the **maximum allowable airspeed** (V_{NE} – shown on the ASI as a red line) is a danger as this could overstress the aeroplane. A steep bank angle and a low nose attitude may develop into a spiral dive.

To recover from a **nose-low/high-airspeed** unusual attitude:
- **reduce power** (close the throttle);
- **roll the wings level** with aileron and rudder;
- **ease out of the ensuing dive;** and
- **as the nose passes through the horizon,** reapply power and climb away.

A **nose-low/increasing-speed** attitude, if not corrected, can develop into a **spiral dive,** which can be recognised by:
- **a high g-loading;**
- **a rapidly increasing airspeed** (that distinguishes it from a spin); and
- **a rapid loss of height,** probably with the rate of descent increasing.

The recovery from the spiral dive is the same as that for a *nose-low/high-speed* situation, but it is especially important to avoid excessive elevator deflection when easing out of the dive, otherwise the limit load factor for the aeroplanes could be exceeded, overstressing the airframe. It is permissible to use the ailerons as firmly as needed to roll the wings level.

Airwork 15b
Recovery from Unusual Attitudes

Aim *To recognise and recover from an unusual aeroplane attitude which has developed.*

1. Nose High/Low Airspeed

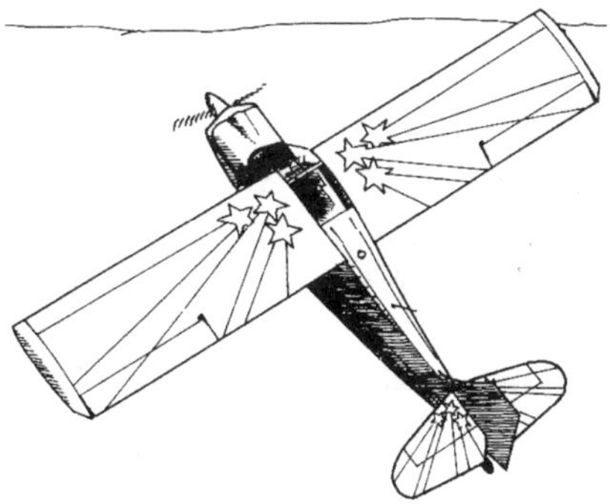

Recognised primarily from ASI.

Recovery:

- Simultaneously ease control column forward and roll wings level.
- Add power.
- If close to stall, do not use aileron until certain the wings are unstalled.

2. Nose Low/High Airspeed

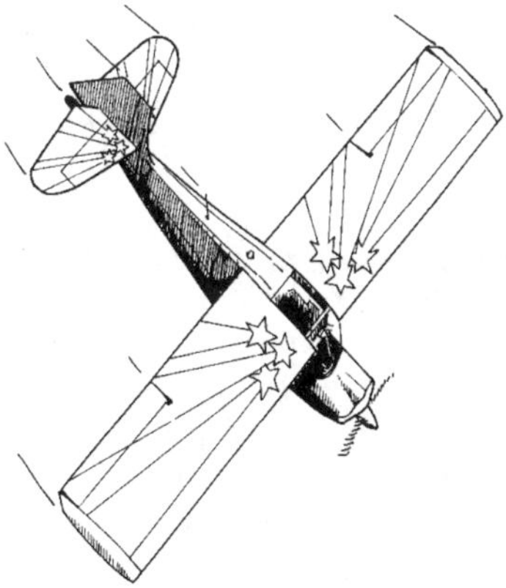

Recognised primarily from airspeed and vertical speed indicators.

Recovery:

- Reduce power.
- Roll wings level with aileron and balance with rudder.
- Ease out of dive.
- Add power as nose passes through the horizon.

Exercise 15c
The Steep Descending Turn

Aim

To perform a steep turn while descending.

Considerations

A steep descending turn can be made in:
- **a glide;** or
- **a powered descent.**

Fly Faster

It is usual to increase the flying speed as a steep descending turn is commenced to retain an adequate safety margin above the stalling speed (which increases during a turn). Typical speed increases are:
- **10 kt for a 45°** steep descending turn; and
- **20 kt for a 60°** steep descending turn.

Fly faster in a steep descending turn because of the increased stalling speed.

In a steep gliding turn, the rate of descent will increase markedly. It can be controlled by reducing the bank angle or by adding power.

Flying the Manoeuvre

A steep descending turn is flown like a steep level turn except that the **increased airspeed** is maintained with the elevator.

The nose will tend to drop in a descending turn and so, even though the nose position is lower to achieve a higher airspeed, some back pressure on the control column will be needed to stop it dropping too far.

If airspeed becomes excessive:
- **ease off the bank angle** with ailerons;
- **raise the nose** with elevator; and
- **re-establish** the desired steep turn.

The lack of slipstream in a glide will mean that more rudder is required when rolling in one direction than when rolling in the other.

Simply exerting increased back pressure on the control column in a steep descending turn may *tighten* the turn and increase the g-loading beyond acceptable limits. A spiral dive may also result if attitude and airspeed are not monitored.

Keep a good lookout, especially below. The steep descending turn described here is without reference to any ground object – the aim is to hold a steady bank angle, which means you will descend through a 'cylinder' of air. In nil-wind conditions, you will remain over the same patch of ground, but in a wind you will be carried along with it.

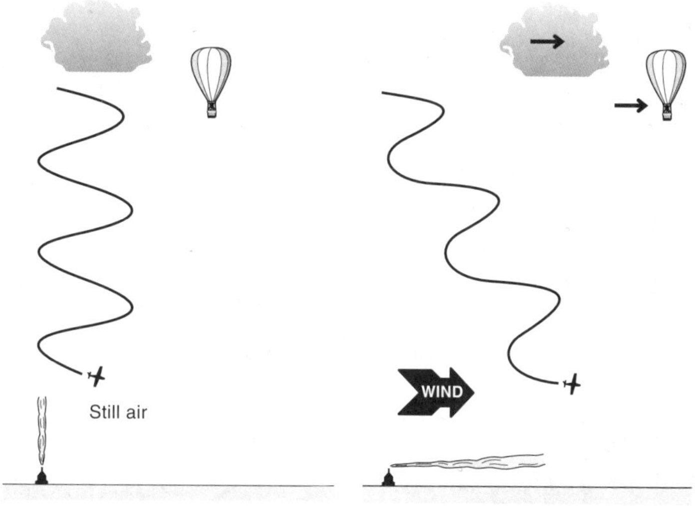

■ Figure 15c-1 ***In a steep descending turn the aeroplane will be carried along by the wind***

Airmanship

Airmanship is remaining aware of your altitude and ground clearance.

Be aware of your proximity to the ground since the rate of descent will be quite high in a gliding steep turn.

Allow the airspeed to increase and maintain a safe margin above the stall, but do not let a spiral dive develop.

Keep a very good lookout, especially below.

Airwork 15c
Steep Descending Turns

Aim *To perform a steep turn while descending.*

1. *Entry to the Turn*

- Complete HASELL check.
- Look out.
- Select horizon reference point.
- Roll on bank with aileron.
- Balance with rudder.
- Hold nose in slightly lower attitude to maintain increased airspeed (necessary due to higher stalling speed).

2. *Maintaining the Steep Descending Turn*

- Look out.
- Maintain bank angle with aileron.
- Balance with rudder.
- Maintain desired airspeed with back pressure.

If airspeed increases:

- Reduce bank angle.
- Raise nose with elevator.
- Reapply bank angle.

3. *Roll Out*

- Look out.
- Roll off bank with ailerons.
- Balance with rudder.
- Select desired pitch attitude with elevator.

Maintain airspeed with elevator. If desired, control rate of descent with power.

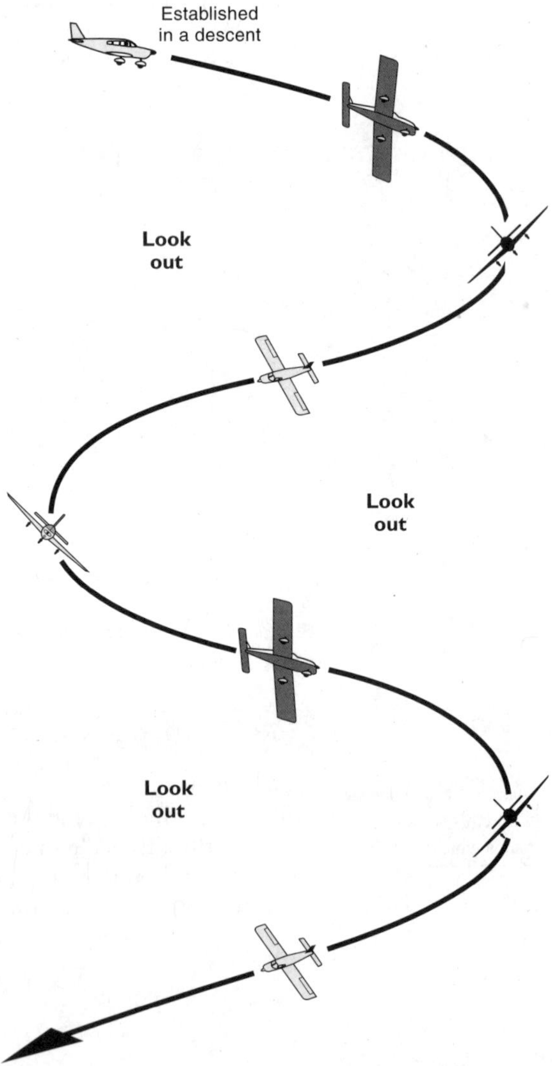

Exercise 16 Ex. 18b JAR-FCL Navigation at Minimum Level and in Reduced Visibility

Aim

1. To fly the aeroplane safely at a low level.
2. To observe the misleading visual effects caused by a strong wind at low levels.

Considerations

Why Fly at a Low Level?

Low-level flying is at 500 ft agl or below.

A low level is generally considered to be 500 ft above ground level or lower. Low-level flying may be necessary:

- **in poor weather conditions** such as low cloud and/or poor visibility;
- **to inspect a field** in preparation for a forced landing with power available;
- **in the VFR Entry/Exit Lanes** that provide access to certain aerodromes beneath airspace reserved for Instrument Flight Rules (IFR) operations.

Pilot Responsibilities

Remain aware of your pilot responsibilities when low flying.

Do not fly within 500 ft of any person, building, animal, etc., except when taking off or landing. There are other restrictions regarding flight over built-up areas (1,500 ft) and large open-air gatherings (1,000 metres), which are covered in the Aviation Law section of Vol. 2 of *The Air Pilot's Manual.*

Low cloud or some other unforeseen situation may force you below the minimum legal levels. As a visual pilot, you are not qualified to enter cloud and this should be avoided at all costs. If low cloud is encountered, it is better to fly slowly beneath it closer to the ground and turn back as soon as possible, rather than to enter it. This is because, in cloud, all visual contact with the ground and the horizon will be lost and the consequences for an untrained pilot are usually fatal!

Be aware that **radio communication,** which depends on line-of-sight transmission, may be poor at low levels.

Around the country there are areas that have been set aside for local training. Other aircraft may be operating in these areas at the same time as you, so keep a good lookout for them (and for obstructions such as TV masts and transmission wires). Do not forget that balloons, helicopters, sailplanes, hang-gliders and microlight aircraft may also be operating at low levels.

Obstacle Clearance

A close study of charts of the area is advisable prior to flight – special attention being given to the height of the ground above sea level, the nature of the terrain and the position of obstacles.

Watch out for radio towers and elevated cables when low flying, especially in valleys.

Flying at a low level you have a limited field of vision and surface features move rapidly through it. You need to **anticipate any ground features** and recognise them quickly. Obstacles such as overhead cables, radio masts, chimneys and rising ground deserve particular attention. Note these prior to commencing low-level flight.

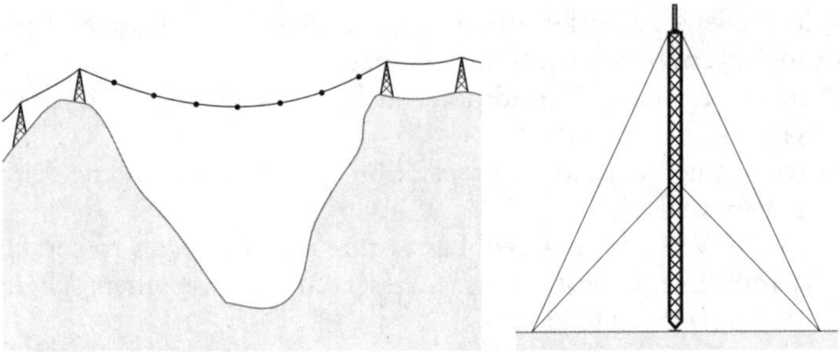

■ *Figure 16-1* ***Elevated cables and the guy wires supporting transmission towers can be almost invisible***

Aeronautical charts may not show elevations below 500 ft above mean sea level (amsl) and obstacles below 300 ft above ground level (agl). Consequently, an obstacle that is 798 ft amsl may not be shown on your chart, so always keep a sharp lookout, especially in poor visibility.

If you fly 500 ft higher than the highest spot height shown on the chart for the area, your obstacle clearance may in fact be only 200 ft. Flying at 300 ft you may have no obstacle clearance at all, especially if altimeter errors have crept in. Charts specify terrain and obstacles in terms of height above mean sea level. If you are using a chart to determine vertical clearance from obstacles, then QNH should be set in the subscale so that the altimeter reads height amsl.

Some common sense rules for obstacle clearance are:

- **anticipate rising ground** and climb early to remain at the desired height above it;
- **ensure that the aeroplane** can actually out-climb the rising ground, especially if a wind is blowing down its slopes;
- **avoid areas of rising ground** under a lowering cloud base;
- **always be prepared to turn back.**

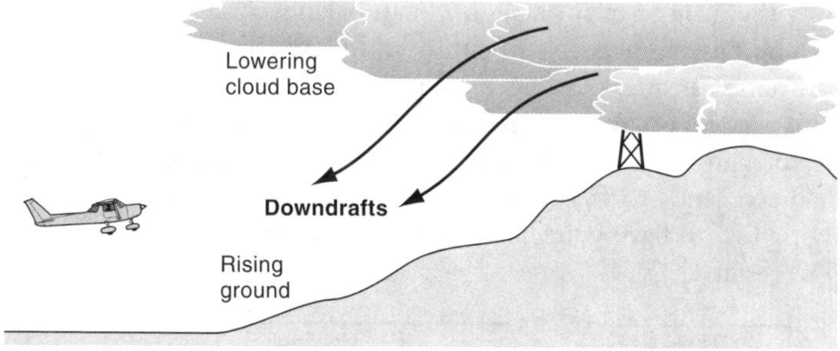

Figure 16-2 ***Avoid a lowering cloud base and rising ground***

Ground Features

Features with vertical characteristics are good landmarks for low-level navigation. Hills, peaks, high monuments, factory chimneys and radio or television masts fall into this category.

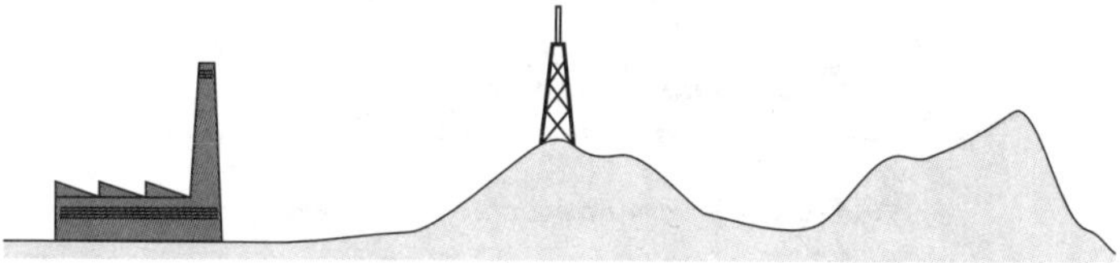

Figure 16-3 ***Choose landmarks suitable for low-level flight***

Misleading Visual Effects

Be careful of the visual illusions caused by wind when low flying.

When flying at high levels, you are less aware of your passage over the ground, which may seem to be in slow motion. In low-level flight, however, both speed and drift are very obvious.

The aeroplane flies in the air mass – its indicated airspeed has much more significance than its groundspeed, and balanced flight is achieved when the ball is centred (even if it appears to be slipping or skidding over the ground because of a crosswind).

A TAILWIND causes a false impression of high speed. An aeroplane flying with an airspeed of 70 kt in a 25 kt tailwind will have a groundspeed of 95 kt. The nearness of the ground will give an impression of speed much greater than 70 kt, but you must resist any temptation to slow down. Reducing the groundspeed to what feels like 70 kt would require an airspeed of 45 kt, which may be below the stalling speed. Check the airspeed on the ASI regularly.

IN A HEADWIND the reverse is the case. The groundspeed is lower than the airspeed, giving an impression of low (rather than high) speed. Since there is no temptation to slow down, this situation is not as dangerous as the former one.

SIDEWAYS DRIFT over the ground due to a crosswind causes false impressions of balance. In strong crosswinds, especially if the airspeed is low, the aeroplane will experience a large drift angle over the ground even though it is in balance.

Keep your hand on the throttle when flying low.

The false impression of slip or skid, especially when turning, can tempt an inexperienced pilot to use rudder to counteract it. This would place the aeroplane out of balance and degrade its performance. Confirm balance with the balance ball. Since airspeed tends to fall in a turn, it is also good airmanship when flying low to have your hand on the throttle to adjust the airspeed if necessary.

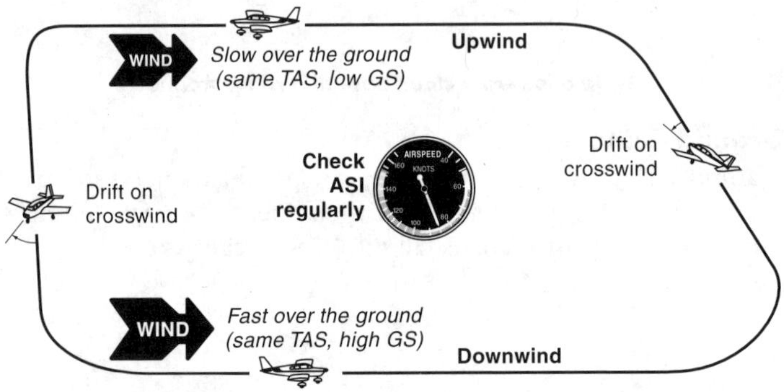

■ *Figure 16-4* ***Wind effect is very noticeable in low-level flight***

Obstacles

Remain **downwind** of obstacles, especially when turning, to avoid the wind carrying the aeroplane into them.

Turbulence and Windshear

Expect increased turbulence and windshear at low levels.

The air is often more turbulent near the ground than at higher levels for various reasons – the main ones being:

- **surface friction** slowing down strong winds;
- **changes in wind speed** and/or direction (windshear); and
- **uneven heating** of the earth's surface creating convection currents.

The possibility of turbulence at low level is another reason why it is good airmanship to keep your hand on the throttle most of the time to enable an immediate response to airspeed variations if they occur.

NOTE See Chapter 15 in Vol. 3 of *The Air Pilot's Manual* for more on low-level navigation. See Chapter 17 for low-level routes.

Aircraft Configuration

Consider the precautionary configuration for low flying.

In good visibility and over open country, the normal cruise configuration of 'clean' wings may be suitable for low-level flying. In poor visibility or in confined areas where good manoeuvrability is required, however, the **precautionary configuration** with an early stage of flap lowered may be preferable.

Using the precautionary configuration allows:

- **better vision** because of the lower nose attitude with flap extended;
- **a lower cruise speed** because of the reduced stalling speed;
- **better manoeuvrability** and smaller-radius turns because of the lower airspeed;
- **better response** to elevator and rudder, due to the extra power required causing a greater slipstream effect.

A disadvantage of having flap extended for long periods, however, is the increased fuel consumption and the reduced range capability.

Flying the Manoeuvre

Preparation

Be well prepared before descending to a low level.

As it is important that the pilot maintains a very good lookout when flying at a low level, a **low-flying check** of items in the cockpit should be completed prior to descending. The FREHA check, outlined previously, may be adequate:

FREHA IN-FLIGHT CHECK	
F	***Fuel*** *Fuel on and sufficient.* *Fuel tank usage monitored.* *Mixture rich.* *Fuel pump on (if fitted) and fuel pressure checked.*
R	***Radio*** *Radio frequency correctly selected, volume and squelch satisfactory.* *Make any necessary radio calls (reception will decrease at low levels).*
E	***Engine*** *Engine oil temperature and pressure; mixture set correctly; carburettor heat if required; check of other systems (ammeter for electrical system; suction gauge for air-driven gyroscopes if installed).*
H	***Heading*** *Heading indicator aligned with magnetic compass, and your position on the map checked.*
A	***Altitude*** *Altitude checked and subscale setting correct (normally Regional QNH, possibly QFE if joining a bad-weather circuit).*

Additional check items prior to low-level flight should include:
- **the security of the aeroplane** (doors and harnesses) and take steps to make the aeroplane more visible (landing lights, rotating beacon and strobe lights on if appropriate);
- **check the surface wind direction;**
- **assume the desired configuration** ('clean' or an early stage of flap in the precautionary configuration);
- **trim.**

A good lookout is essential! View the ground even before you commence the descent to a low level to ensure that an adequate height above obstacles can be maintained and also look out for other aircraft. **Beware of rising ground,** especially if a wind is blowing down its slopes.

Vital points when flying low are:
- **monitor the airspeed** (resisting any temptation to slow down in a tailwind);
- **keep in balance;**
- **stay well clear of obstacles** and turn downwind of them.

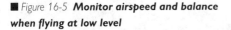

■ *Figure 16-5* ***Monitor airspeed and balance when flying at low level***

Allow for Aeroplane Inertia

The aeroplane will take time to respond to any control movements due to inertia (resistance to change). Commence climbs and turns early to avoid obstacles. Avoid harsh manoeuvres (such as steep turns or high-g pull-ups) which may lead to an accelerated (or high-speed) stall.

Trim

Keep in trim when low flying.

An aeroplane that is correctly trimmed is easier to fly and more likely to maintain height. Since your attention is directed out of the cockpit for most of the time in low-level flying, a well-trimmed aeroplane is essential. A very slight nose-up trim will help ensure that an unintentional descent does not occur.

Airmanship

Maintain a high visual awareness. Keep a good lookout for other aircraft and also for birds. Avoid congested areas and maintain a suitable altitude (at least 500 agl). Also, avoid annoying people or farm animals. Select a suitable area with good ground references.

Beware of false impressions caused by the wind effect, best counteracted by reference to the airspeed indicator and the balance ball. Be aware of false horizons.

Divide your time appropriately between:

- **aeroplane control;**
- **maintaining and adjusting** the path over the ground, keeping coordinated with rudder pressure; and
- **maintaining a visual scan** so that you can see and avoid other aircraft or obstacles, if necessary.

Apply the necessary wind drift corrections in straight flight by adjusting heading, and in constant ground radius turns by adjusting bank angle (but not to exceed 45°). Entering a manoeuvre with the wind behind you will mean that the first turn will be the steepest.

Turbulence may be greater at low levels, so ensure that you are strapped in securely.

Hold the chosen speed to within 10 kt and altitude to within 100 feet. Avoid bank angles in excess of 45°.

Airwork 16
Low-Level Flying

Aims *(a) To fly the aeroplane safely at a low level.*
(b) To observe the misleading visual effects caused by a strong wind at low levels.

1. Prior to Descending to Low Level

- Complete FREHA check (refer to full version on page 232):
  - **F** – Fuel system checks.
  - **R** – Radio correctly set.
  - **E** – Engine and systems for normal operation.
  - **H** – Heading indicator aligned correctly and position on map checked.
  - **A** – Altitude and altimeter subscale checked (QNH or perhaps QFE set).
- Additional considerations:
  - Security of the aeroplane (doors and harnesses, etc.) and its visibility (landing lights, beacons, strobes ON).
  - Note surface wind direction.
  - Aeroplane configuration (clean or early stage of flap).
  - Trim.
  - Decide on suitable IAS for the operation.
- Awareness of low flying regulations.

***Look out** for obstacles and other aircraft – including balloons, microlights, gliders, parachutists, airships, towers, masts, hang-gliders, large birds and flocks of birds.*

Airwork 16

2. Descent to Low Level

- Commence descent, hand on throttle, keeping a good lookout.
- Fly no lower than 500 ft agl (or as advised by your flying instructor).
- Estimate height visually, with back-up from the altimeter and known height amsl of the ground.

3. Establish Cruise Flight at the Desired Level

- Set desired airspeed and height.
- Trim.
- Consider increasing power in the medium turns to maintain airspeed.

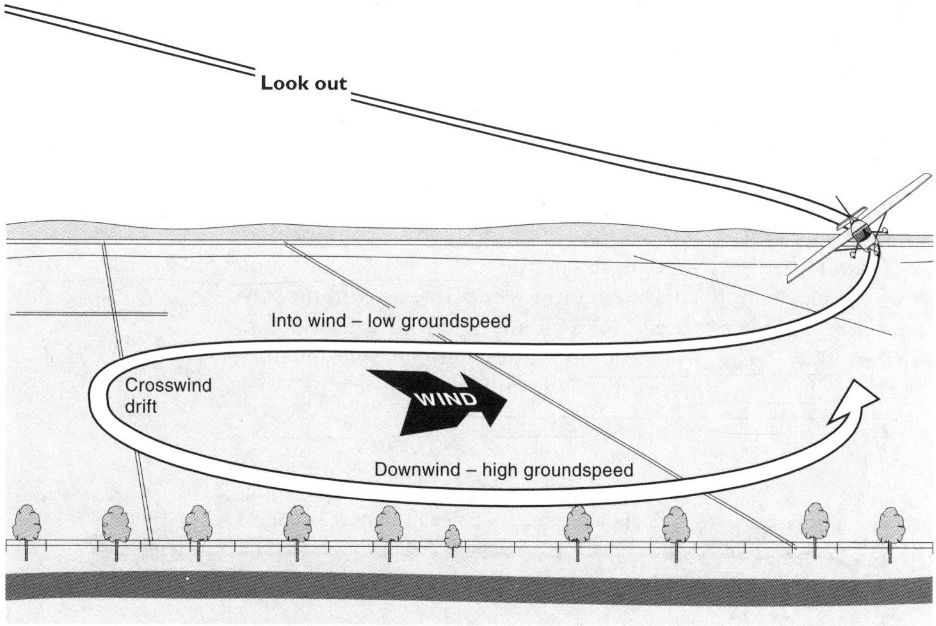

4. Observe the Various Effects of Wind – Look Out

These are more noticeable as you near the ground:

- For the same IAS, there is a low groundspeed into wind – check the airspeed indicator.
- At same IAS, there is a high groundspeed downwind, so do not remove power without checking ASI first.
- Noticeable drift on crosswind legs – check that the balance ball is centred.
- Significant downwind drift in turns (check ball for balance) and do not fly close to obstacles.

Further Points

Low Flying in Bad Weather

Poor visibility, a descending cloud base or rising ground may require some unplanned low flying. If you are 'caught-out' in really marginal conditions, maintain as much separation from the ground as possible, but avoid entering cloud – an estimated 100 ft beneath it is adequate.

Use any aircraft systems that can assist you in coping with bad weather, such as carburettor heat (if required), pitot heaters, window demisters, etc. Make your aeroplane more visible by switching the rotating beacon and strobe on.

If the legal requirements of minimum visibility and distance from cloud cannot be satisfied, then consideration should be given to either:

- **diverting** to an area where better weather exists;
- **landing** at a nearby aerodrome, or requesting radar guidance if navigation is a problem; or
- making a **precautionary landing** in a field (this procedure is discussed in Exercise 17).

The Bad-Weather Circuit

A circuit in bad weather (i.e. poor visibility and/or a low cloud base) should be flown so that visual contact with the field is not lost. This may require a tight circuit flown at low level in the *precautionary* configuration. Aim for a circuit height of at least 500 ft above ground level if possible, but do not enter cloud! Maintain a clearance of at least 300 ft vertically from obstacles.

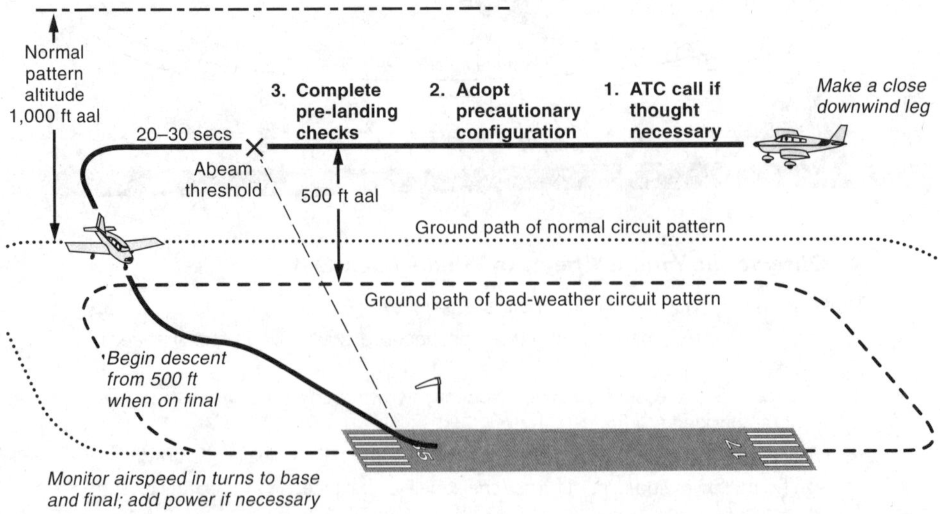

■ *Figure 16-6* ***The bad-weather circuit***

Exercise 17a ⁘ Ex. 16 JAR-FCL
The Forced Landing Without Power

Aim

To carry out a safe approach and landing following engine failure.

Considerations

Why Would an Engine Fail?

A forced landing due to a mechanical malfunction or a structural problem is a rare event with modern aeroplanes. However, occasionally it happens, so be prepared.

Always check the fuel prior to flying.

Fuel starvation is often the cause of an engine stopping in flight. Fuel gauges can be inaccurate and fuel agents have on rare occasions loaded incorrect or contaminated fuel. A visual inspection of the fuel tanks and of the fuel itself during your pre-flight inspection should prevent insufficient or incorrect fuel causing a forced landing.

Always check your fuel selection and use the mixture and carburettor heat controls correctly.

Forgetting to switch from a near-empty fuel tank in flight to an alternative tank, incorrect use of the mixture control and failure to use carburettor heat can all lead to an engine stoppage through fuel starvation.

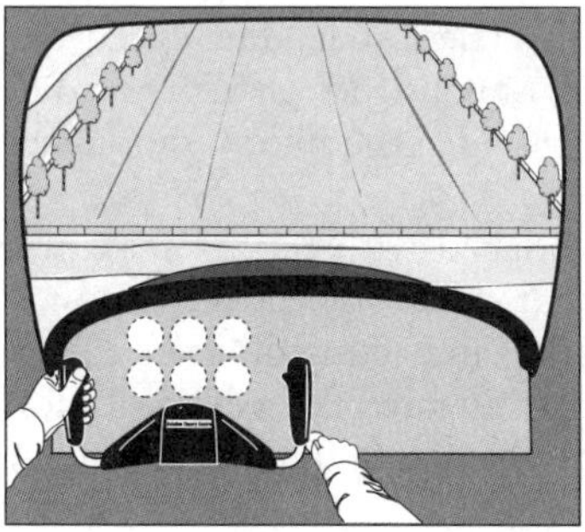

■ *Figure 17a-1* ***Safe forced landings can be made in small fields***

Performance data published in Flight Manuals is obtained from test results achieved by experienced test pilots flying new aeroplanes under ideal conditions. Similar results will be difficult to achieve for an average pilot in a well-used aeroplane. The published fuel consumption and range figures assume **correct leaning** of the mixture. If this is not done by the pilot when cruising at 75% maximum continuous power or less, the manufacturer's range figures will not be attained.

As the captain of an aeroplane, you must show good airmanship and always be aware of the real fuel situation. Never allow fuel starvation to force you into an unwanted landing.

Other possible causes of engine stoppage include faults in the magneto system, in ancillary equipment (e.g. a carburettor malfunction or a broken fuel line), mechanical failure (possibly due to insufficient oil) or an engine fire. Bad luck sometimes plays a role – for instance, a bird-strike damaging the propeller.

Ratification of an engine stoppage by the pilot is generally limited to checking that the engine controls are providing the correct amount of fuel and air to the engine (i.e. fuel selector, mixture control, throttle and carburettor heat), or experimentation with the ignition system (e.g. eliminating a faulty magneto system by selecting the opposite magneto).

Always be prepared to cope with engine failure.

This is not to say that you will have to cope with an engine stoppage each and every time you go flying – it is not unusual for a pilot to go through a whole career without a real engine failure, although simulated engine failures will have been practised many times. A well-trained pilot is well prepared for an engine failure at any time in flight or on the ground. A disciplined approach to checklists and the sequence of events during training is important, as the recall of procedures can be extremely difficult when faced with a real emergency.

Forced Landings without Power

Forced landings without power can be made quite safely.

All pilots must be able to cope with an emergency landing without the use of engine power, possibly on an unprepared surface. This can be done quite successfully. The low landing speed of a modern training aircraft and its robust construction allow it to be landed safely in quite small fields, provided the pilot positions the aeroplane accurately.

No new flying aspects are introduced with this exercise; it is simply a matter of putting together what you already know – making sound decisions fairly quickly and acting on them.

An aeroplane that glides at 700 ft/min rate of descent will allow the pilot only 3 minutes from a height of 2,000 ft agl. Always be aware that:

- **flying the aeroplane** is your number one priority – maintain a satisfactory airspeed and keep it in trim;
- **planning and executing the approach** comes next, with an attempt (if you think it advisable) to restart the engine.

Partial power from an engine that has not completely failed may give you extra time and the possibility of gaining some extra distance, but do not rely on it. The engine may fail completely at a most inopportune moment, so plan your approach and landing as if no power is available.

Engine Failure at Altitude

Height is time.

Height means time to a pilot, and the amount of time that you have available determines what options you have. If the engine fails, convert any excess speed into height by a gentle climb or into useful distance by maintaining height until the airspeed decays to gliding speed, and then **establish a glide** with the aeroplane in trim.

When the aeroplane is comfortably under control, perform some simple emergency actions and attempt an engine restart – provided that you think restarting the engine is a good idea. It is possible that a restart is not advisable, say following an engine fire or mechanical damage. This is a command decision that only the pilot-in-command can make.

Engine Restart

An immediate engine restart may be possible.

An experienced pilot may decide very quickly to attempt an immediate restart and will perform the required actions while allowing the aeroplane to slow down to gliding speed.

A less-experienced pilot may be advised to concentrate just on flying the aeroplane – first establishing it in the glide and trimming it *before* performing any restart actions. Your flying instructor will advise you on this point.

Rectify the problem if possible.

If the propeller is still turning, rectification of the fuel or ignition problem (if that is the cause) will see the engine fire up again without any need to use the starter. Some obvious items to be considered in an attempted restart of the engine are:

- **A fuel problem:**
  - change fuel tanks;
  - fuel pump on (if fitted);
  - mixture RICH;
  - primer locked.
- **An ignition problem:**
  - check magneto switches individually (BOTH – LEFT – RIGHT). If the engine operates on one magneto as a result of a fault in the other magneto system, then leave it there, otherwise return to BOTH.
- **An icing problem:**
  - carburettor heat FULL HOT.

NOTE Following a **mechanical failure** or **fire,** the engine should be stopped immediately. If the failure is partial, resulting in reduced or intermittent running, then use the engine at your discretion. There is a likelihood that it may fail at a critical stage, so it may be best not to rely on it and simply assume a total failure. Following a failure due to **faulty operation** by the pilot, restart the engine in the glide.

Part (i)
Forced Landing Without Power

Flying the Manoeuvre

Forced Landing Scenario

Many scenarios are possible and your actions will depend on the situation at the time, the height above ground at which the failure occurs, the surface wind and the availability of suitable landing fields (possibly even an airfield).

We will consider a very general situation which is capable of modification to suit your precise set of conditions.

If the engine fails at a reasonable height (say 3,000 ft or more above ground level), a basic pattern that may be followed is:

- **convert excess speed** to height or to useful distance;
- **set up a safe glide;**
- **attempt a restart;**
- **select a suitable field** and plan an approach to it;
- **make a distress** (Mayday) radio call;
- **attempt to resolve the emergency** (while maintaining a safe glide);
- **carry out a safe approach and landing** (in the case of training, a go-around rather than a landing will usually be performed).

Always Know the Ground Wind

While flying along, it is good airmanship (common sense) to keep an eye on the surface wind. A forced landing into wind is generally safer because of the lower groundspeed on touchdown and the shorter landing run.

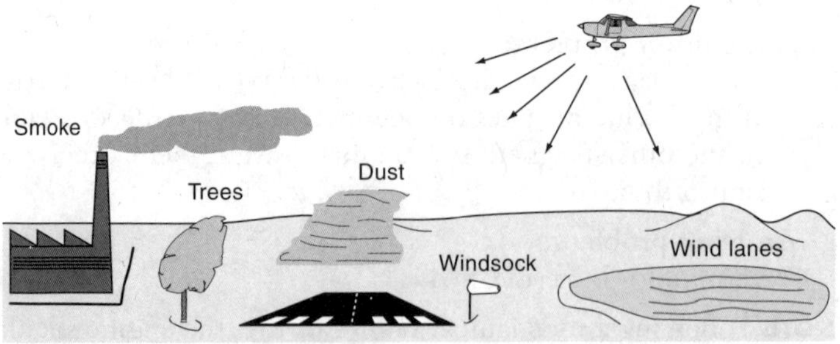

■ *Figure 17a-2* ***Always be aware of the surface wind direction***

Good indicators of surface wind include:

- **smoke;**
- **a windsock;**
- **cloud shadows** on the ground (especially if the clouds are low);

- **the drift angle** of the aeroplane over the ground;
- **wind lanes** on water.

Estimate the Gliding Range

Fly at the recommended gliding speed to achieve the best gliding range.

A typical training aircraft has a *best lift/drag ratio* of approximately 9:1, which means that, when flown at the correct gliding speed, 9,000 ft (or 1.5nm) can be gained horizontally for each 1,000 ft lost in height.

Losing 1,000 ft vertically in 9,000 ft horizontally is an angle of depression (down from the horizontal) of about 7° (easy to work out using the 1-in-60 rule, from your navigation studies).

To estimate gliding range in still air conservatively, lower your arm about 10° from the horizontal. You should be pointing at a position on the ground to which a glide in still air is possible. Of course, the closer the chosen field is, the more certain you are of reaching it comfortably.

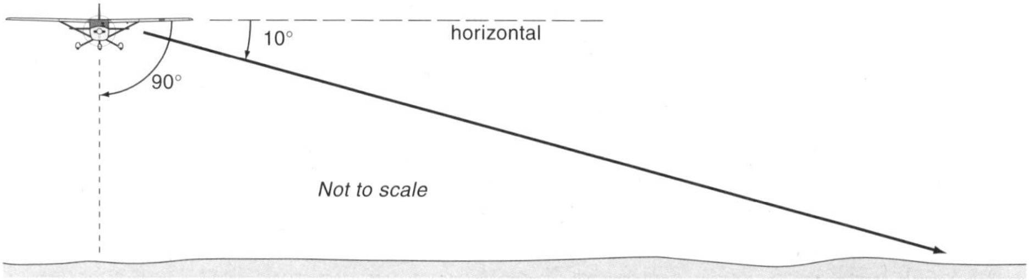

■ *Figure 17a-3* ***An approximate estimate of gliding range in nil wind***

A **headwind** will reduce the gliding range; a **tailwind** will increase it. A windmilling or stopped propeller will also decrease it. In your training so far, you have become familiar with the glidepath achievable with the engine idling and the propeller turning over.

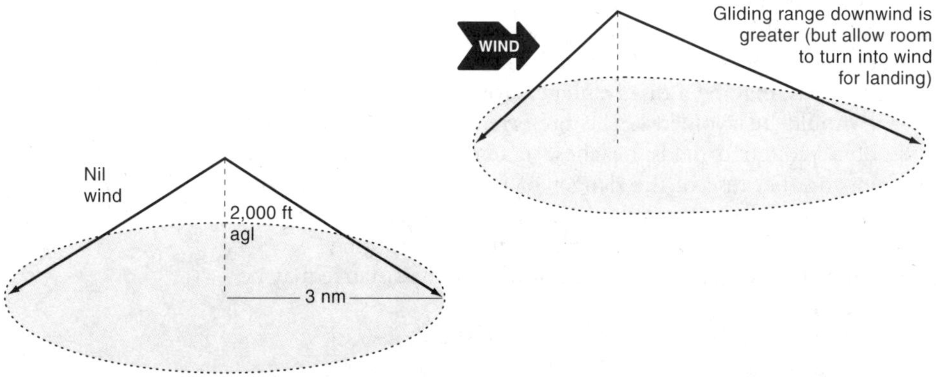

■ *Figure 17a-4* ***Wind affects gliding range over the ground***

If the engine has failed, the propeller (either stopped or windmilling) will cause a significant increase in drag. The nose of the aeroplane will have to be lowered to maintain airspeed and the rate of descent will increase. The increased drag will mean a steeper glidepath and a reduced gliding range.

Select a Suitable Field

Following an engine failure, convert excess speed above gliding speed to height or useful distance, then adopt the gliding attitude and speed and trim the aeroplane. Change fuel tanks.

Choose a forced landing field well within your gliding range.

An experienced pilot might attempt a restart at this stage but, at all times, it is most important to fly the aeroplane first.

When settled into the glide, select a suitable field for a forced landing. It is safest to select a field well within your gliding range and to fly a pattern around it, rather than to try a long straight glide to a distant field. This makes correct judgement of the glide easier and gives you more flexibility and room to correct if your original estimates are not perfect.

The easiest place to look for a field is out of the left window. But do not fail to look out to the right, just in case a perfectly suitable field is available there. Manoeuvre the aircraft if necessary, and look beneath it. Ideally, select a field downwind of your present position, since that is where the gliding range of the aeroplane will be greatest.

Make all turns towards the field and do not turn your back on it – it is possible to lose sight of the field and waste time re-identifying it.

Make all turns towards the field.

The forced landing field should:

- **be well within gliding range;**
- **be large** and preferably surrounded by other suitable fields;
- **have no obstacles** on the approach and overshoot areas;
- **be level or slightly uphill;**
- **have a suitable surface** (ideally an aerodrome, but pasture or stubble may be satisfactory; wetness, often indicated by dark green areas, may be a disadvantage; crops and beaches in general should be avoided – the preferred order being pasture, stubble, ploughed fields, beaches, standard crops. Avoid roads if possible, because of the danger of vehicles, power lines and roadside posts or signs, although, especially after heavy rain, a quiet, straight country road might be the best option).
- **be close to civilisation** (communication and assistance may be valuable).

Apply the mnemonic wosssss:

'WOSSSSS' FORCED LANDING CHECK	
W	***Wind***
O	***Obstacles*** *(on surface: trees, rocks, etc.)*
S	***Size and Shape of field*** *(in relation to wind)*
S	***Surface and Slope***
S	***'Shoots'*** *(undershoot and overshoot areas)*
S	***Sun*** *(position relative to final approach planned)*
S	***S(c)ivilisation*** *(proximity for assistance after landing)*

Planning the Approach

Use key points in planning the approach.

The basic plan that you formulate depends mainly on your height above the ground. Various patterns and **key points** around a field can assist you in flying a suitable glide descent.

Each flying training organisation and each flying instructor will have a preferred technique, but the aim is the same in every case – consistently good positioning for a glide approach and landing. We discuss various planning techniques. Your flying instructor will give you sound advice on which to use.

Method (a):
The 1,000 ft agl Close Base Leg Technique

The basic aim using this technique is to arrive at 1,000 ft agl on a close base leg, from which a comfortable glide well into the field can be made. If the engine is stopped, the drag from the propeller will steepen the glidepath compared to the glide angle when the engine is idling (as in the practice manoeuvre), so allow for this possibility.

A close base leg gives flexibility.

A wide base leg allows little room for error, but a close base leg gives flexibility in the case of over- or under-shooting the field, allowing adjustments to be made quite easily. According to your position when the engine fails, choose either a left or right 1,000 ft base area, with a long base leg and a short final. Left turns provide a better view of the field for the pilot. Noting a ground reference point near the 1,000 ft position will assist in re-identifying the turning-base point if you are distracted.

Stay close to the field and make all turns towards it.

A suitable distance for the downwind leg is approximately ⅓ nm from the selected landing path. In flying a square pattern around the selected field, approximately 1,000 ft per leg will be lost, and this must be considered in your planning.

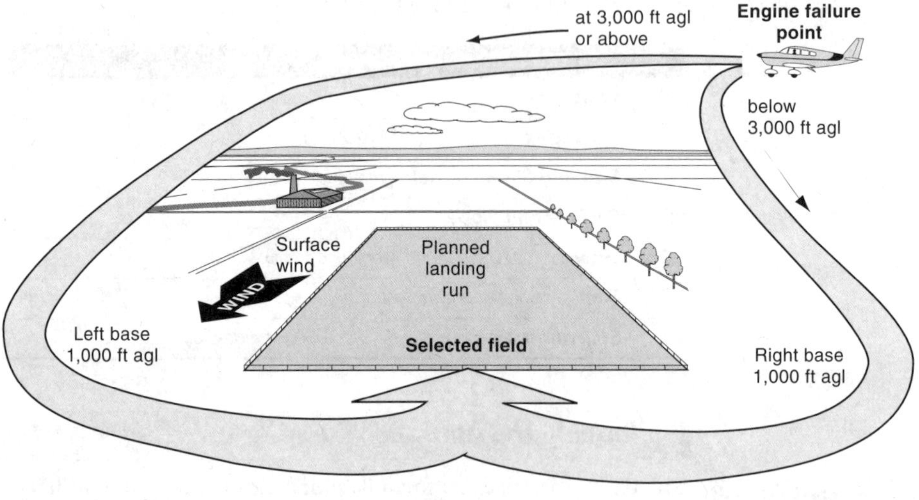

■ *Figure 17a-5* ***A very basic circuit plan for a forced landing***

Method (b): The High Key and Low Key Technique

The advantage of using the *high key* and the *low key* is that they are closely related to the selected landing strip and therefore are easily re-identified:

- **The low key** – 1,500 ft agl about ⅓ nm abeam the landing threshold (a similar position to where the aeroplane would be using Method (a)).
- **The high key** – 2,500 ft agl in line with and about ¾ to 1 nm upwind of the far end of the selected landing strip.

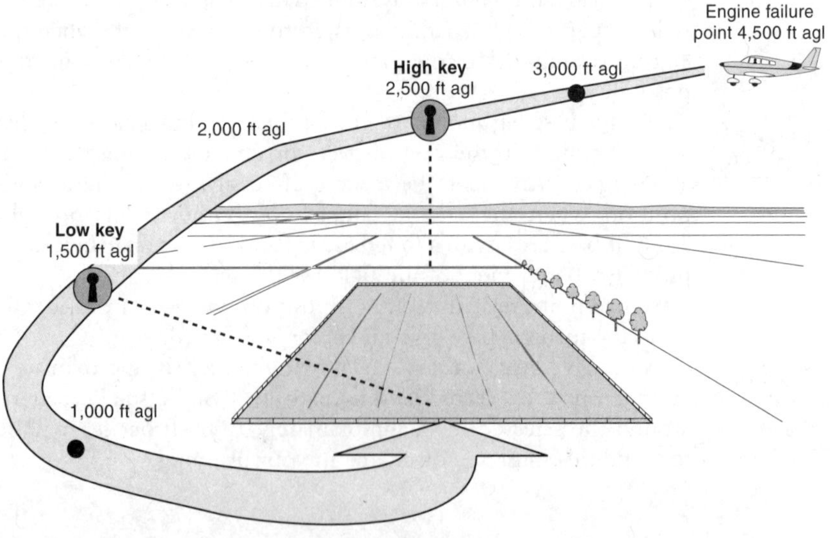

■ *Figure 17a-6* ***The high key and the low key***

The first aim in the descent is to glide to the high key, keeping the field in sight. The purpose of the high key is simply to assist your judgement in reaching the low key, which is of course the more important key point. After some practice glide descents, you may find that you can glide direct to the low key without any definite consideration of the high key.

Engine failure at a low height (say 2,000 ft agl) will also mean flight direct to the low key.

Plan your descent for a long base and a short final.

Monitor descent to the key points and plan on a long base and a short final. If too high, widen out; if too low, cut in.

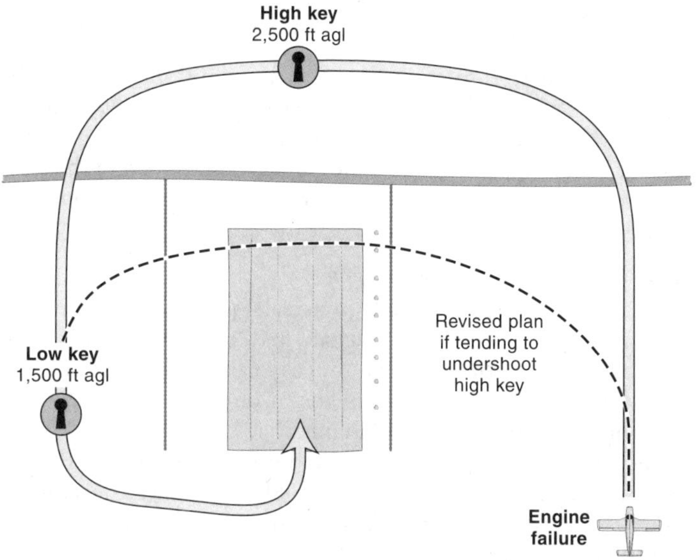

■ *Figure 17a-7* ***Monitor the descent to the key points***

Estimates of familiar heights (such as 1,000 ft agl circuit height) will generally be reasonably accurate. You should develop the same skill with other heights.

Assess the wind during the descent.

Assess the wind during the descent to assist in choosing a suitable base point. A reasonably long base leg allows:

- **more time** to judge wind strength (using the drift angle on base);
- **better judgement of height** (since it is easier to judge height out to one side of the aeroplane than straight ahead);
- **flexibility** in adjusting the descent path:
  - cutting in if too low;
  - widening out, lengthening the base leg or extending flap if too high.

A short final allows for a glidepath steeper than expected.

Rectifying the Problem

When established in the glide, there may be time to look for the cause of the engine failure and to remedy it. The Pilot's Operating Handbook will contain a list of the appropriate items to check. It will include:

Attempt to rectify the engine problem.

- fuel;
- mixture;
- carburettor heat;
- throttle linkage;
- fuel pump on (if fitted);
- primer (locked);
- magneto switches.

If the propeller is rotating, then fuel and ignition ON should be enough to restart the engine, otherwise the starter may be required. While attempting to rectify the problem, the continuing descent towards the key points should be monitored and the suitability of the field confirmed. If you decide that your chosen field is unsuitable, then select another as early as possible.

Do not neglect to control the flightpath.

Radio Calls and Passenger Briefing

Make a **Mayday distress call** (in a real forced landing, but not when practising). VHF radio signals may not be effective from very low levels, so the sooner a Mayday call is made in the glide the better. The Mayday call should be made on 121.5 MHz as this frequency secures best ATC assistance.

Advise others of your forced landing.

Keep radio conversations brief and do not be distracted from your main duty, which is to fly the aeroplane. Squawk transponder code 7700, as this helps ATC radar to identify an aeroplane experiencing an emergency.

Advise your passengers of your intentions. Request them to remain calm, to remove sharp objects from their pockets, to remove glasses and dentures and ensure that their seatbelts are fastened securely. Use of soft clothing or pillows will protect them if a sudden deceleration or impact is expected. Harnesses should remain fastened until the aeroplane stops. Be firm and tolerate no interference. Request silence.

Do not be distracted from your main duty, which is to fly the aeroplane.

Approaching the Low Key Point – 1,500 ft agl

As normal circuit height is approached, all of your attention needs to be focused on positioning for the approach and landing. Further attempts to re-start would only distract you from this. **Secure the aeroplane,** placing it in a safer condition for a landing on an unprepared field by carrying out the required **security check** (also known as the *crash* or *impact check*):

Secure the aircraft for touchdown on a rough surface.

- **fuel** OFF;
- **ignition** OFF;

- **radio** OFF;
- **master switch** OFF (unless flaps are electrically operated);
- **cabin heater** OFF;
- **brakes** OFF;
- **harnesses** very secure;
- **doors** unlatched (if appropriate to your aeroplane type);
- **all loose items secured** and the position of safety items noted (e.g. fire extinguisher, first-aid kit).

Where to Turn onto Base Leg

Extend downwind according to the wind.

From the low key abeam the touchdown point, extend downwind according to the wind. The stronger the wind, the shorter the extension of the downwind leg, bearing in mind that it is preferable to be a little high on final approach than to be too low. If the surface wind is:

- **greater than 20 kt,** commence base turn at the **low key** point abeam the aiming point for landing, i.e. at about 1,500 ft agl;
- **between 10 and 20 kt,** commence base turn when the aiming point for landing appears about one-half chord length behind the trailing edge (for a low-wing aeroplane), which will occur at about 1,300 ft agl;
- **less than 10 kt,** commence base turn when the aiming point for landing appears about one chord length behind the trailing edge (for a low-wing aeroplane), which will occur at about 1,100 ft agl.

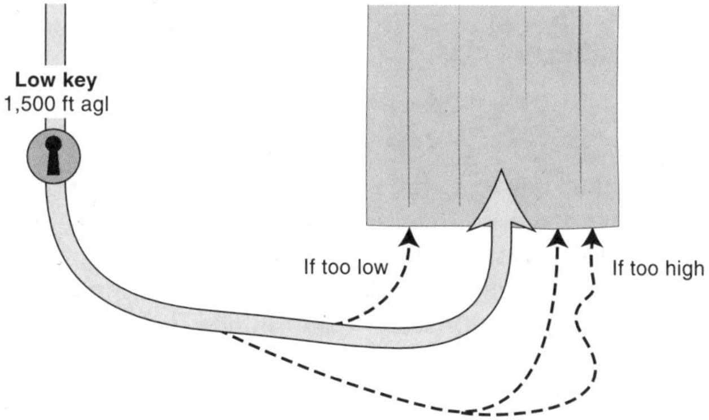

■ *Figure 17a-8* ***Manoeuvre for a long base and a short final***

When To Use Flaps

A typical technique is to lower:

- **the first stage of flap** at the low key on downwind leg;
- **the second stage** when turning base leg;
- **full flap** on final and when assured of 'getting in'.

If the aeroplane appears to be **high on base leg,** then:
- **lengthen the base leg;** or
- **widen the base leg;** or
- **extend some flap;** or
- **sideslip** (if permitted – refer to the Pilot's Operating Handbook); or
- **carry out some S-turns** (but try and avoid this).

If the aeroplane appears to be **low on base leg,** then you can:
- **shorten the base leg;**
- **cut in** towards the field for a shorter final; or
- **delay the use of flap.**

A long base leg and a short final give you the greatest flexibility.

Monitor Airspeed and Bank Angle

It is most important that you maintain the correct gliding speed, especially when turning. A gliding turn near the ground should *not* be steep because:
- **stalling speed increases** with increasing bank angle and wing loading; and
- **rate of descent in a glide increases** with bank angle.

Monitor airspeed and bank angle closely in the gliding turn to final.

Be very conscious of your airspeed during the turn onto final and limit the angle of bank to 15–20° (30° maximum). Do not stall or even allow the aeroplane to approach the stall!

Turn onto final so that the aiming point is well into your chosen field, say ½ to ⅓ into the field, to ensure that you make it. It is better to land too far in than to undershoot the field and hit a fence or some other obstacle. It is best of course, to land comfortably over the field boundary and have sufficient distance to stop well before the far boundary without any drama.

Final Approach

Once certain that you can glide well into the field, continue extending flap in stages to steepen your approach and bring the aiming point closer to you.

Keep the aiming point comfortably past the near boundary so that, even if an undershoot occurs, a safe landing in the field can still be made. It is safer to hit an obstacle at the far end at slow speed than to hit the fence before landing. It is safest, of course, to judge your aiming point so that neither occurs and so that you land comfortably into the field. Ensure that the master switch is OFF once electrically operated flaps have been placed in the landing position.

If you are **too high** on final approach:
- **extend flap;**
- **make shallow S-turns** (but avoid this if possible);
- **dive-off excess height** (but avoid this also if possible).

If you are **too low** on final approach, delay extending flap. Do not fall into the trap of trying to stretch the glide by raising the nose. Airspeed will fall and the flightpath will in fact be steeper. In an extreme case you may have to land in a nearer field.

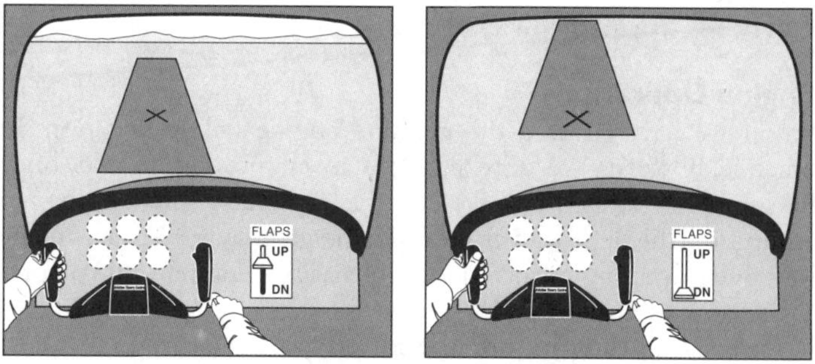

■ *Figure 17a-9* ***Use of more flap brings the aiming point closer***

The Landing

A forced landing with **full flap** is generally safest because:

- **the touchdown speed is low** (due to the lower stalling speed);
- **the landing run is shorter;** and
- **the stress on the airframe** will be less if the field is rough.

Hold the nosewheel off during the landing.

Touch down on the main wheels, holding the (less-robust) nosewheel off to avoid unnecessary stress. Brakes can be used as desired to shorten the ground run.

Unseen obstacles and ditches could be a problem. If collision with an obstacle is imminent (say the far fence), apply rudder, braking on one side only to initiate a controlled ground loop if possible.

Aeroplane at Rest

Secure the aeroplane and evacuate.

A forced landing is not complete until the aeroplane is stopped, the passengers evacuated, the aeroplane made secure and assistance obtained. So as soon as the aeroplane stops:

- **set the brakes** to PARK;
- **secure** the aeroplane (check all switches OFF, fuel OFF, control locks IN);
- **evacuate;**
- **chock** the aeroplane;
- **remove any items** thought necessary;
- **protect the aeroplane,** e.g. keep animals away;
- **seek assistance** and telephone the chief flying instructor and the appropriate authorities. If possible, leave someone in charge of the aeroplane.

Do not attempt to take off!

Part (ii)
Simulated Forced Landing

Flying the Manoeuvre

Engine Operation

Ensure correct engine operation.

So far we have covered the genuine engine-failure situation. In practice, however, we only simulate an engine-failure and, once having demonstrated that we could have made a safe landing, go around off the approach from a safe height (say 500 ft agl in the low flying training area). To ensure that the engine will respond at the time of go-around:

- **ensure that the mixture** is RICH and move the carburettor heat control to HOT to avoid carburettor icing (prior to reducing power in the simulated engine-failure). If a fuel pump is fitted, switch it ON;
- **clear the engine** and keep it warm by increasing rpm for a few seconds every 500 or 1,000 ft on descent;
- **when applying power** for the go-around, check mixture RICH and carburettor heat full COLD (most engine manufacturers recommend applying power first, then moving carburettor heat to COLD).

Simulate the trouble check, Mayday call and security check that you would carry out in a real forced landing, i.e. call them out at the appropriate time in your glide descent, but do not action them. For example, call "fuel OFF, magneto switches OFF", and so on, but do not move the switches.

Keep a good lookout. Other aircraft may be practising glide approaches to the same field in the training area, possibly from the other direction in calm wind conditions. Ensure that the climb-out area following the go-around is clear of obstacles. Check this well before you descend to a point where the go-around could become marginal.

Practising forced landings requires steady concentration. It is practising for an emergency and has its own peculiar risks. You are calling out items associated with a real forced landing, yet operating the aeroplane so that it will function normally when you carry out a go-around from a safe height. Be quite clear that, while practicing, you should not do anything that would endanger the aeroplane (e.g. actually stop the engine).

Practising forced landings *without* the use of engine power (i.e. with the engine idling) is good training in developing the skills of command. One of these skills is to manage your resources effectively and efficiently in an emergency situation.

Airmanship

Airmanship is flying well and making sound decisions.

When practising forced landings without the use of engine power:

- **Look out,** especially in the latter stages of the glide approach – other aircraft may be practising forced landings into the same or a nearby field.
- **Clear the engine** by increasing rpm at least every 1,000 ft on descent.
- **Do not descend below** the authorised **break-off height.**
- **Know your checks thoroughly** and execute them in the correct sequence.
- **Do not turn your back on the field** – keep it in sight at all times.
- **Do not make unnecessary changes** in your field selection.
- **Make command decisions** in a calm but firm manner.

An Actual Forced Landing

When carrying out an *actual* forced landing without the use of engine power, most of the points above related to practising also apply in the real forced landing situation:

- **Do not rely on a partially failed engine.**
- **Ensure the trouble check,** Mayday call and security check are actioned and not just called out, as in practice. To be effective, the Mayday call must be made at a reasonable height. It may be made earlier in the sequence, according to circumstances at the time. For instance, if the engine fails at a low height, the Mayday call could be made as the last item of step 1 in the following Airwork diagram. If the engine fails at height, then the Mayday call can be made at position 5 as shown.
- **Be certain to know** (and to action) door position either OPEN or CLOSED as specified in the Pilot's Operating Handbook for a forced landing.
- **Ensure the safety** of your aeroplane and passengers after landing, stopping and securing the aeroplane.
- **Notify the authorities** as soon as possible following the landing.

Airwork 17a
Practising the Forced Landing

5. *Simulate Distress Call*

- Mayday
  Mayday
  Mayday
- (Name of station addressed)
- (Your callsign and type)
- (Nature of emergency)
- (Your intention)
- (Present position, altitude and heading)
- (Pilot qualification)

Squawk transponder code 7700, (Mode C, if fitted)

4. *Simulate Trouble Check*

as in Pilot's Operating Handbook:

....

....

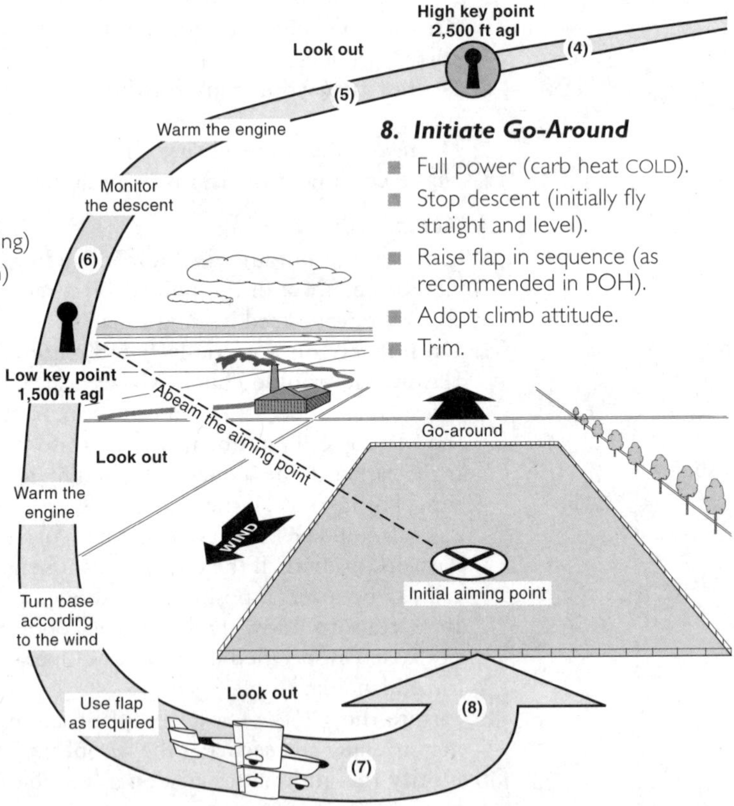

8. *Initiate Go-Around*

- Full power (carb heat COLD).
- Stop descent (initially fly straight and level).
- Raise flap in sequence (as recommended in POH).
- Adopt climb attitude.
- Trim.

6. *Simulate Security Check*

as in Pilot's Operating Handbook:

....

....

- But complete the normal pre-landing checks:

....

....

7. *Adjust Base and Final*

Use flap as required to reduce aiming point.

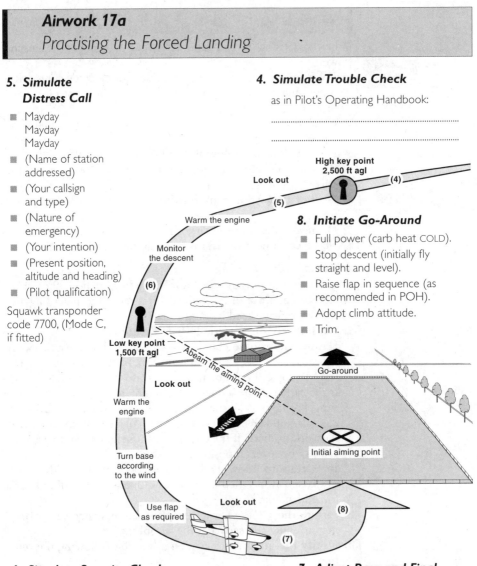

Airwork 17a

3. Plan the Approach

- Select key positions.
- Keep turns towards the field.

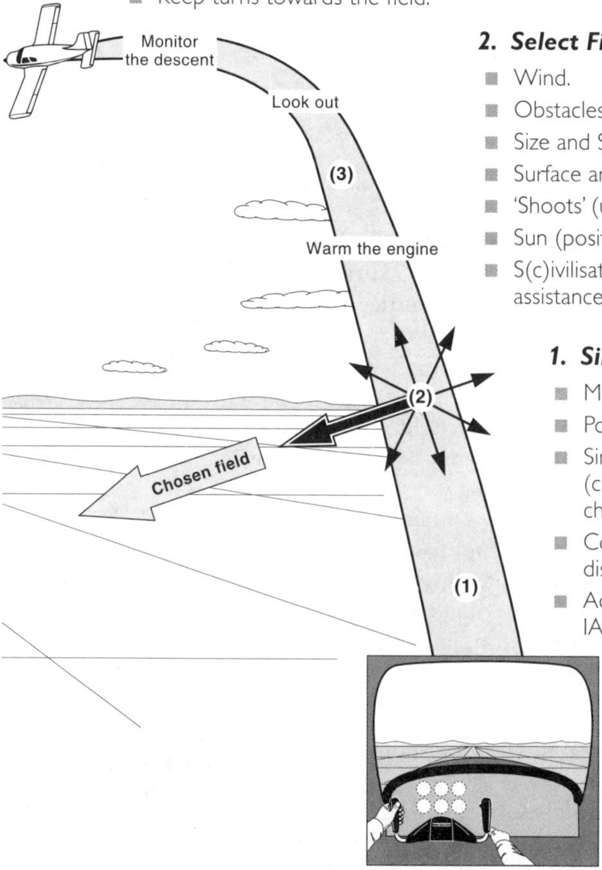

2. Select Field: (W O S S S S S)

- Wind.
- Obstacles (on surface).
- Size and Shape (in relation to wind).
- Surface and Slope.
- 'Shoots' (under-/over-shoot areas).
- Sun (position relative to final).
- S(c)ivilisation (proximity for assistance).

1. Simulated Engine Failure

- Mixture rich.
- Power OFF (carb heat HOT).
- Simulate emergency check (change fuel tanks, magneto check, carburettor ice check).
- Convert excess speed to distance or height.
- Adopt gliding attitude. IAS .... kt and trim.

Prior to Practising Forced Landings

START HERE

Check:

- Correct local flying training area.
- At a suitable height above the ground.
- Look out for other aircraft.
- Maintain awareness of low flying regulations.

Exercise 17b ⁘ Ex. 17 JAR-FCL
The Precautionary Search and Landing

Aim

To carry out a safe powered approach and landing at an unfamiliar field.

Considerations

Why Land on an Unfamiliar or Unprepared Field?

A pilot may be faced with the decision to land away from an aerodrome for a number of reasons. These include suspected engine or airframe problems; a sudden deterioration in weather, with low cloud and decreasing visibility making further flight unsafe; or as a result of deficient flight planning or navigation. Being totally lost, having insufficient fuel or insufficient daylight remaining are good enough reasons to consider making a precautionary landing in a field.

Impending incapacitation of the pilot, say due to food poisoning, is best coped with on the ground. Land sooner rather than later, but ensure that the field chosen for landing is suitable.

If you are about to land at an unfamiliar field, then you should consider a **precautionary inspection** before landing, especially if there is no other activity at the field.

Decision to Land

Make an early decision to land.

If any doubt exists as to the advisability of continuing the flight, make the decision to land while there is still time to do so with the aeroplane under full control and before conditions deteriorate to a dangerous level. It is better to land before you run out of either fuel, daylight or visibility, even if the landing is in a field rather than at an aerodrome.

Estimate what time you do have available. Slowing the aeroplane down and possibly lowering some flap may help enormously. Slow flight gives you more time to observe the ground and to plan, as well as making the aeroplane more manoeuvrable. Turning performance is better at slow speeds and forward vision from the cockpit is improved. Slow flight may reduce the problems facing you and may even eliminate them.

Flying the Manoeuvre

Search for a Suitable Landing Area

Once the decision to land has been taken, immediately search for a suitable landing area. Ideally, choose an active aerodrome; otherwise select the most suitable landing field as outlined in *Select a Suitable Field* on page 296. Consider advising Air Traffic Control of your intentions by radio on the normal frequency and, if not satisfactory, on the emergency frequency 121.5 MHz.

Items to consider when selecting a field include:

- **its alignment** with respect to the surface wind;
- **size** (large is better than smaller);
- **no obstacles** in the approach or go-around areas;
- **level or slightly uphill** (a downslope is not good);
- **a firm surface** with no obstructions;
- **near civilisation.**

If no suitable field is obvious, then searching downwind will allow you to have a higher groundspeed and so cover more area.

Aircraft Configuration

Consider adopting the precautionary configuration.

If low cloud, poor visibility or a restricted manoeuvring area is involved, then adopt the precautionary (or bad weather) configuration. Use the optimum stage of flap, which may be just the first stage. Extending some flap allows:

- **slower speeds** (due to reduced stalling speed);
- **a smaller turn radius** and a higher rate of turn (due to the reduced speed);
- **better visibility** from the cockpit (due to lower nose position); and
- **improved elevator and rudder response** due to higher power and greater slipstream effect over the tail (possibly).

Staying in the one configuration allows you to fly the whole sequence (descents, straight and level, and climbs) at a constant airspeed, thereby removing one variable. Fly the attitude for the desired speed, and control descent, level flight and climb-out with the use of power.

Field Inspection

Inspect the selected landing area.

Several inspection runs should be made in the precautionary configuration and a circuit pattern and circuit height established. With no restrictions, a normal circuit pattern should be suitable.

In bad weather, a low and tight circuit (e.g. 500 ft agl) may be advisable. The heights at which the circuits are flown and the number of inspection runs carried out depend on the situation. Command decisions must be made by the pilot.

The low flying check should be completed before descent to a low level. It is good airmanship to keep your workload to a minimum in low-level flight. Flying low to inspect a surface means accurate flying and a good lookout. Keep the aeroplane in trim or, if anything, trim slightly nose-up so that the aeroplane will have no tendency to descend while your attention is directed outside.

Airmanship

Fly the aeroplane into a position for a normal engine-assisted approach. Consider making a short-field landing to minimise stress on the aeroplane during the touchdown and landing run if the field is rough. Complete the appropriate pre-landing checks. If time is not a consideration, be prepared to go around if not totally satisfied with the approach.

Be aware of the usual illusions of low flying resulting from the wind effect. Keep your turns accurate and balanced in spite of the deceptive appearance of the ground if there is a strong wind. Add power to maintain airspeed in the turn if necessary and monitor the airspeed indicator.

Even though three preliminary circuits are shown in *Airwork 17b* on page 312, adapt the procedure according to your requirements. Learn to make command decisions quickly and efficiently.

Learn to make command decisions quickly and efficiently.

Adapt your plan to suit the conditions (e.g. low cloud, imminent darkness, low fuel). Possibly a 500 ft agl, close-in circuit with only one inspection run might be called for, with no delay in making a landing.

When practising the precautionary search and landing:

- **Ensure** that you are in the correct local flying area and keep a good lookout for other aircraft.
- **Consider any regulations** or local rules (such as no descents below 500 ft agl, do not frighten animals, etc.), and obey them.
- **Align the heading indicator** with the landing direction (either on 360 or 180) to help with orientation.

Your flying instructor will give you plenty of practice at this procedure in many different situations. Adapt to each situation as you see fit.

Further Points

Three Inspection Circuits

If there are no time, fuel or weather restrictions, and three inspection circuits are considered necessary, a suitable plan might be:

CIRCUIT 1. At 1,000 ft agl to establish circuit and note landmarks and magnetic headings. Some flying instructors may consider this preliminary circuit superfluous. Complete low flying checks before descent.

CIRCUIT 2. To select and make a preliminary evaluation of the actual landing path. Descend on final and make a 500 ft agl run (or 300 ft agl run – refer to your flying instructor) slightly right of the landing path to give you a good view of the approach path and the landing surface out of your left cockpit window. Search for large obstacles and obstructions, ditches, animals, wires, fences, etc. Return to circuit height as you near the end of the field.

CIRCUIT 3. Descend on final and make a run to the right of and along the landing path at a lower, but still safe, level (say 100 ft or 50 ft agl) for a closer inspection of the landing surface itself. Return to circuit height.

CIRCUIT 4. A normal circuit followed by a short-field landing. Make each inspection run alongside the selected landing path at a constant height and not as a slow descent that necessitates a frantic climb at the far boundary to avoid obstacles.

Airwork 17b
The Precautionary Search and Landing

Aim *To carry out a safe approach and landing at an unfamiliar field with engine power available.*

For the purpose of this exercise, the scenario is a cloud base of 600 ft agl, poor visibility and 20 minutes' flight time available before night sets in.

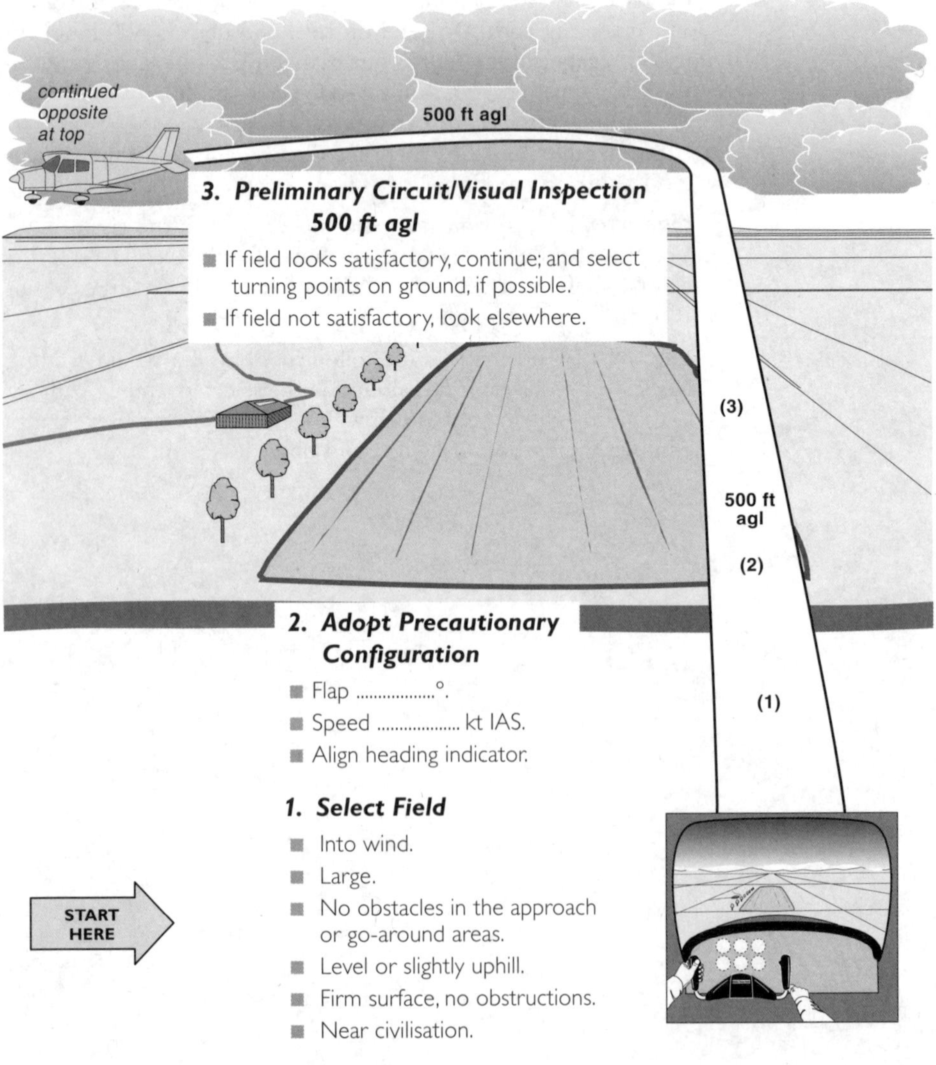

continued opposite at top
500 ft agl
3. Preliminary Circuit/Visual Inspection 500 ft agl
■ If field looks satisfactory, continue; and select turning points on ground, if possible.
■ If field not satisfactory, look elsewhere.
(3)
500 ft agl
(2)
2. Adopt Precautionary Configuration
■ Flap ....°.
■ Speed .... kt IAS.
■ Align heading indicator.
(1)
1. Select Field
■ Into wind.
■ Large.
■ No obstacles in the approach or go-around areas.
■ Level or slightly uphill.
■ Firm surface, no obstructions.
■ Near civilisation.
START HERE

Airwork 17b

Run 1. 200 ft agl,
To right of landing path

Look for:

- Large obstacles.
- Obstructions.
- Ditches.
- Transmission wires.

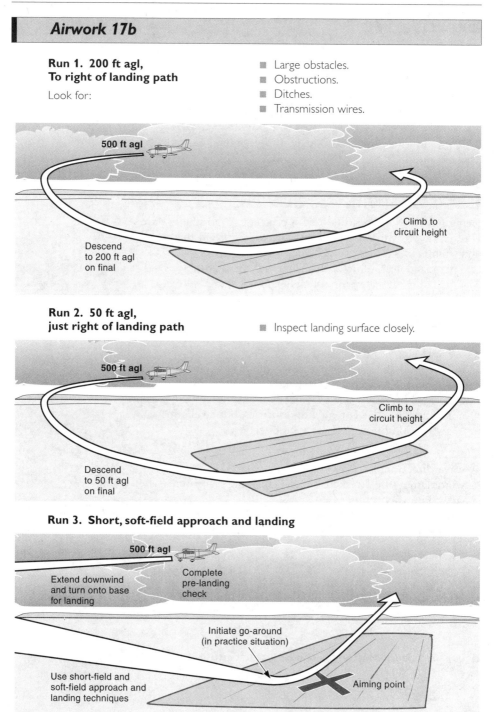

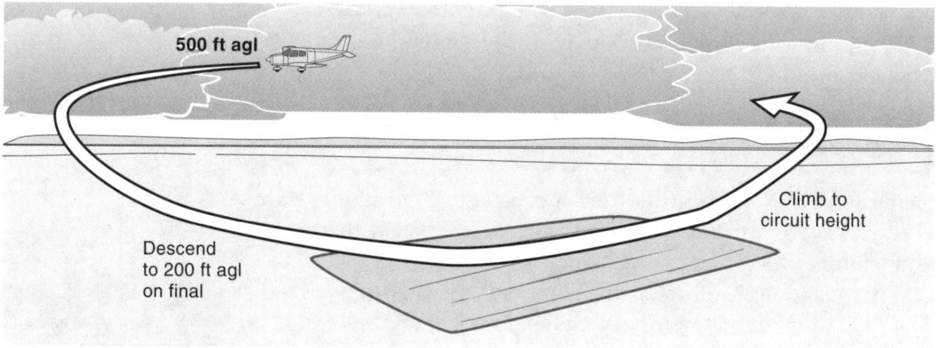
500 ft agl
Climb to
circuit height
Descend
to 200 ft agl
on final

Run 2. 50 ft agl,
just right of landing path

- Inspect landing surface closely.

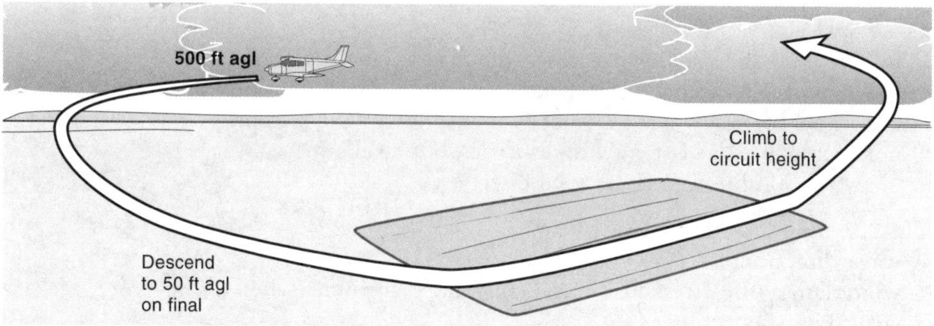
500 ft agl
Climb to
circuit height
Descend
to 50 ft agl
on final

Run 3. Short, soft-field approach and landing

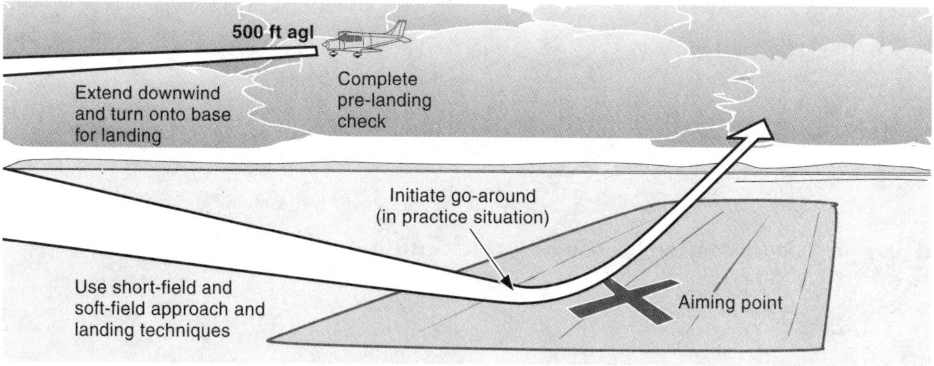
500 ft agl
Complete
pre-landing
check
Extend downwind
and turn onto base
for landing
Initiate go-around
(in practice situation)
Use short-field and
soft-field approach and
landing techniques
Aiming point

Exercise 17c
Ditching in Water

Aim

To alight on water as successfully as possible, if ditching is the best available option.

Considerations

Being forced to ditch in the ocean is a remote possibility; however, it is worthwhile having a suitable procedure in the back of your mind.

Try to land near a ship or in a shipping lane if possible. Make a Mayday radio call before too much height is lost to ensure the best chance of reception by ground stations.

Make emergency radio calls before ditching.

Landing Direction

If the water is smooth, or smooth with a very long swell, then land into wind.

If there is a large swell or rough sea, then land along the swell, even if you have to accept a crosswind. This avoids the danger of nosing into a big wave. **Waves** generally move downwind except near a shoreline or in fast-moving estuaries, but **swells** may not bear any relationship to surface wind direction.

Clues to wind direction include:

- **wave direction;**
- **wind lanes** (the streaked effect being more apparent when viewed downwind);
- **gust ripples** on the water surface;
- **aeroplane drift.**

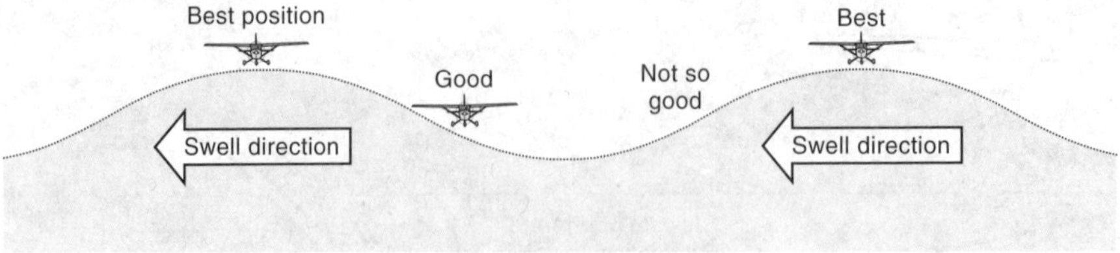

■ *Figure 17c-1* ***Touch down on top of a swell, or just after it***

Flying the Manoeuvre

Use a powered approach, if possible, for ditching.

If your engine is running, use a powered approach for ditching. From altitude, water generally appears to be calmer than it is. Fly low and study the water surface before ditching.

Generally ditch with an early stage of flap set, using a low speed, a high nose attitude (tail-down) and a low rate of descent controlled by power (if available). Power gives you a lot more control over the touchdown point, so avoid running out of fuel prior to ditching.

Touch down with as low a flying speed as possible, but do not stall in.

Alert the Passengers

Warn the passengers. Buckle up and don life-jackets, if available, but do not inflate them until in the water, as they may restrict the evacuation. Remove headsets and anything else that may get in the way during the evacuation.

Be prepared for a double impact – the first when the tail strikes the water, the second (and greater) when the nose hits the water. The aircraft may also slew to one side.

Evacuation (if possible) should be carried out as calmly as possible, life-jackets being inflated outside the cabin. The pilot-in-command should supervise.

Exercise 18
Pilot Navigation

Aim

To fly cross-country, navigating with visual reference to the ground.

JAR-FCL1 requires radio navigation to be studied (Ex. 18c). This is not required for the UK national syllabus. JAR-FCL students should read this introductory chapter to navigation, and then go to Vol. 3 of *The Air Pilot's Manual*, where all aspects of navigation, including radio navigation, are covered in depth.

Considerations

When you have completed most, or all, of your basic flying training, the next challenge awaiting you is to deal with cross-country navigation. Flying to another aerodrome, perhaps quite distant, requires the additional knowledge and skills encompassed in flight planning and navigation. In this exercise, we have summarised the knowledge which is covered in detail in Volume 3 of this series, *Air Navigation*. Volume 3 prepares you for the CAA PPL exam in this subject.

Flight Management

Control the progress of your flight from the planning stage to closing the flight plan.

As the pilot-in-command of a cross-country flight you have certain duties to perform, both on the ground and in flight. The main flight management tasks are:

- **to fly the aeroplane;** and
- **to navigate it to the destination,** which involves:
  - flight planning; and
  - en route navigation.

You have limited resources in the cockpit which need to be managed efficiently. For example, it is difficult to measure tracks and distances on a chart in flight while trying to fly in rough air. Better management would have seen the chart work done on the ground prior to flight. The better the flight planning, the easier the en route navigation!

Personal Navigation Equipment

The two most important instruments in visual navigation are the **magnetic compass** and the **clock,** so always carry a serviceable watch. Provided that the aeroplane's position has been fixed within the previous twenty minutes or so, and its speed is known (at least approximately), its position during flight can be deduced from the direction it has travelled and the time taken from the fix.

A flight case, satchel or 'nav bag' that fits comfortably within reach in the cockpit should be used to hold your navigation equipment. A typical flight case should contain:

- **relevant charts** covering at least 50 nm either side of your planned track;
- **a navigation computer;**
- **a scale rule** and **protractor** (or a plotter);
- **pens,** pencils and spare flight log forms;
- appropriate **flight information** publications, e.g. *Pooley's Flight Guide;*
- **sunglasses.**

The Flight Log

The flight log is designed to keep the necessary navigation data and calculations orderly. There are various presentations and the one illustrated below is typical.

Pilot H. Lawson				**Aircraft** G-BATC				**Date** 1-2-97				**ETD** 1430 UTC			
From/To	**Safety ALT**	**ALT** / **Temp**	**RAS**	**TAS**	**W/V**	**TR °T**	**Drift**	**HDG °T**	**Var**	**HDG °M**	**GS**	**Dist**	**Time**	**ETA**	**HDG °C**

■ Figure 18-1 **Layout of a typical flight log form**

Flight Planning

Weather and Operational Considerations

Obtain a thorough pre-flight briefing.

Before you start to plan any flight, you should check the likely weather to be found on the planned route, including a forecast of winds and temperatures. Although you are not obliged to obtain a met forecast for flights of less than 50 nm from your departure aerodrome, good airmanship dictates that you take advantage of the facilities available and get a **weather briefing** for your planned areas and aerodromes of operation.

Weather information is available:

- **in aerodrome briefing offices** (where, at certain aerodromes, print-outs and facsimiles of Area Forecasts and Aerodrome Forecasts are available – as advised in UK AIP GEN 3-5);
- **by telephone** from the AIRMET automated text information service, using the AIRMET program shown in AIP GEN 3-5; or

- **by facsimile** from the dial-up MET-Fax service, which supplies a variety of graphic area forecasts and AIRMET regional forecasts, along with actual weather reports and aerodrome forecasts.

NOTE For flights outside the area of coverage of UK Area Forecasts, a Special Forecast may be obtained from a weather office, but two hours' notice is required (four hours' if the route distance exceeds 500 nm). Refer to the *Weather Forecasts and Reports* chapter in Vol. 2 of this series.

Make an informed go/no-go decision.

Establish from the forecasts that the planned flight can be completed in visual conditions. Note the Altimeter Setting Regions (ASRs) you will pass through en route. You must check for any **operational factors** affecting your route, referring to:

- **NOTAMs** for urgent and short notice items;
- **AICs** (Aeronautical Information Circulars), the **AIP** (UK Aeronautical Information Publication) and **AIP Supplements** for 'permanent' items of long standing.

Compiling a Flight Log

Select a suitable route.

Select the route over which you want to fly. Terrain, cultural features and aeronautical information are shown on the CAA 1:500,000 aeronautical chart series, as well as the 1:250,000 series. (1:250,000 charts have airspace information only up to 3,000 ft amsl, however.) Note the nature of the terrain and of the airspace along the chosen route and to either side of it:

- **terrain** – check the height of any obstacles within (say) 10 nm of track;
- **airspace** – check the route for:
  - controlled airspace, including CTRs and overlying TCAs and CTAs;
  - Prohibited Areas, Restricted Areas or Danger Areas;
  - Aerodrome Traffic Zones (ATZs) and Military Aerodrome Traffic Zones (MATZs);
  - Radar Advisory Service Areas;
  - other aerodromes.

It may be best to avoid particularly high or rugged terrain and areas of dense air traffic.

Choose turning points and checkpoints that will be easily identified in flight, and cannot be confused with other nearby ground features. Mark the route on your chosen aeronautical chart and enter the checkpoints on the navigation flight log.

Look for suitable en route alternate aerodromes.

Note any suitable **alternate aerodromes** on or adjacent to the route, in case of an unscheduled landing becoming necessary. Also note the en route radio frequencies and any other relevant information.

Safety Altitudes and Cruising Altitudes

Select a safe cruising altitude.

For each leg of the flight, calculate a **safety altitude** that is 1,000 ft higher than any obstacle within a specified distance either side of track (15, 10 or 5 nm, as recommended by your training organisation), and enter it on the flight log. A more general safety altitude can be obtained quickly from the maximum elevation figures (MEFs) shown for each latitude/longitude quadrangle on the UK 1:500,000 charts.

A reasonable minimum altitude is very handy if, for instance, cloud forces you to fly lower than planned. Also check the meteorological information to confirm that the forecast cloud base is above this safety altitude.

Select a suitable **cruising altitude** for each leg and enter it in the flight log.

Considerations should include:
- **terrain;**
- **overlying airspace restrictions;** and
- **the cloud base.**

Tracks and Distances

For each leg of the flight, mentally estimate the track in degrees true and the distance in nautical miles before measuring it accurately (ensuring that you are using the correct scale). Mentally estimating track and distance prior to actual measurement will avoid gross errors. Insert these measured figures on the flight log.

From/To	Safety ALT	ALT / Temp	RAS	TAS	W/V	TR °T	Drift	HDG °T	Var	HDG °M	GS	Dist	Time	ETA	HDG °C
Elstree															
						069						60			
Ipswich															
						286						40			
Cambridge															
						208						38			
Elstree															
											Total	**138**			

■ *Figure 18-2* **The flight log at this stage**

Distance Markers or Time Markers

To assist you in flight, it is suggested that each leg be subdivided and small marks placed at intervals on the track lines drawn on the chart. The usual means of subdividing (your flying instructor will recommend a method) is to use one of the following:
- **distance markers** each 10 nm; or
- **distance markers** at ¼, ½, and ¾ points; or

- **time markers** each 10 minutes; or
- **time markers** at the ¼, ½ and ¾ points.

NOTE The time markers will, of course, have to wait until you have calculated groundspeeds and time intervals. Once in flight, these may vary from the flight-planned values, unlike the distance markers.

Track Guides

To allow easier in-flight estimation of any deviation from the desired track, it is useful to draw in 5° and 10° guides either side of track emanating from each turning point. This avoids having to use a protractor or plotter in flight.

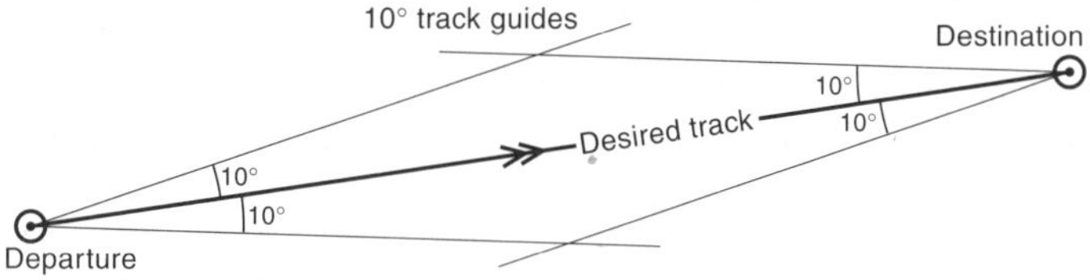

■ *Figure 18-3* **Track guides and distance markers**

Groundspeeds and Time Intervals

Insert the forecast winds for each leg, the selected cruising altitude and the TAS onto the flight log.

Remember that for a given indicated airspeed, the true airspeed will be greater at higher altitudes and temperatures because of the decreased air density. Converting IAS to TAS is easily done on the calculator side of the computer.

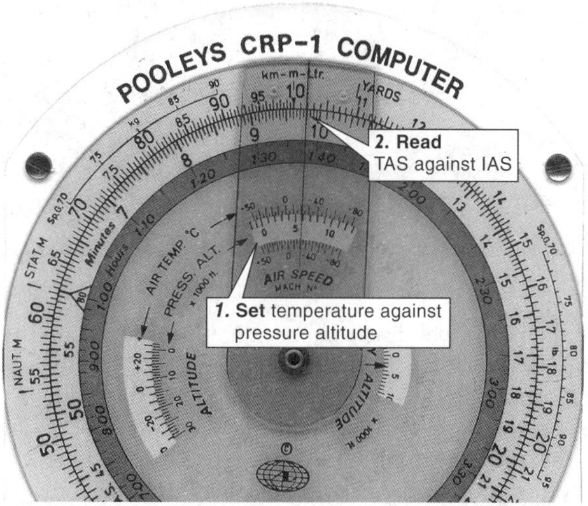

■ *Figure 18-4* **If necessary convert IAS to TAS (using pressure altitude and temperature)**

On the wind side of the computer, use the forecast wind to set up the **triangle of velocities** and calculate drift, heading and groundspeed.

NOTE It is most important when using the wind side of the computer that you work either completely in degrees true or completely in degrees magnetic. Do not mix them! Either method is satisfactory, but it is most common for PPL holders in the UK to work in degrees true. Using the navigation computer is covered in detail in Volume 3 of this series.

Having obtained the values for groundspeed (GS) and heading HDG(T), insert them on the flight log. Magnetic variation, found on the chart, is then used to convert the true heading into magnetic heading – required when using the magnetic compass and the heading indicator during the flight.

Having measured the distance of each leg and calculated the expected groundspeed, determine the estimated time interval and insert it on the flight log.

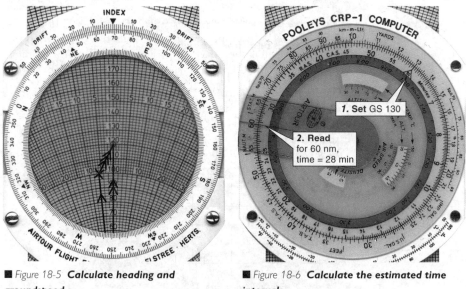

■ *Figure 18-5* ***Calculate heading and groundspeed***

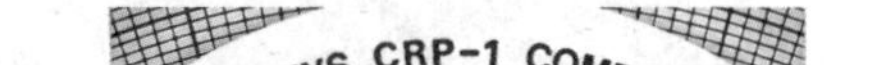

■ *Figure 18-6* ***Calculate the estimated time intervals***

Add all of the individual time intervals together and obtain the **total time interval** for the whole flight.

It is good airmanship at this point to compare this with the total distance for the flight and verify that it is a reasonable result, considering the average groundspeed expected to be achieved. Also, confirm that you will arrive with adequate daylight remaining.

From/To	Safety ALT	ALT / Temp	RAS	TAS	W/V	TR °T	Drift	HDG °T	Var	HDG °M	GS	Dist	Time	ETA	HDG °C
Elstree															
	1920	2400 / +10	98	102	270/30	069	–6	063	4W	067	130	60	28		
Ipswich															
	1768	2400 / +10	98	102	270/30	286	–5	281	4W	285	73	40	33		
Cambridge															
	1920	2400 / +10	98	102	270/30	208	+15	223	4W	227	84	38	27		
Elstree															
											Total	**138**	**88**		

■ Figure 18-7 ***The flight log at this stage***

Fuel Calculations

The fuel consumption for various power settings is published in the Flight Manual and Pilot's Operating Handbook. These figures assume **correct leaning** of the fuel/air mixture at higher levels (usually above 5,000 ft) when cruising at less than 75% maximum continuous power. Leaning the mixture correctly can decrease fuel consumption by up to 20%.

At least 45 minutes' reserve fuel is recommended.

From the estimated time interval for the whole flight and the published fuel consumption rate, calculate the expected **flight fuel.** Reserve fuel should also be carried to allow for in-flight contingencies, including diversions, fuel consumption poorer than that published, unexpected headwinds en route, etc. At least 45 minutes' reserve fuel is recommended.

Insert the fuel calculations onto the flight log.

CONSUMPTION RATE *7 USG/hr*

Stage	min	US gal
Route	88	10.3
Reserve	45	5.3
Fuel required	133	15.6 = 16
Margin	180	21.0
Total carried	313	37.0

■ Figure 18-8 ***Fuel calculations***

Weight and Balance

The aeroplane must be loaded within its weight and balance limits.

At this stage in your flight planning, knowing the fuel required and the passenger and baggage load, it is appropriate to consider weight and balance. For a flight to be legal, the aeroplane must not exceed any weight limitation and must be loaded so that the centre of gravity lies within the approved range throughout the flight. Complete a load sheet (if necessary) to verify that the requirements are met.

SAMPLE LOADING PROBLEM	SAMPLE AIRPLANE WEIGHT (LBS.)	SAMPLE AIRPLANE ARM (IN.)	SAMPLE AIRPLANE MOMENT (LB.-IN. /1000)	YOUR AIRPLANE WEIGHT (LBS.)	YOUR AIRPLANE ARM (IN.)	YOUR AIRPLANE MOMENT (LB.-IN. /1000)
*1. Licensed Empty Weight (Typical)	1262	83.4	105.25	1267		105.05
2. Oil (8 qts.) 1 qt. = 1.875 lbs.	15	32.0	.48	15	32.0	.48
3. Fuel (in excess of unuseable) Standard Tanks (37 gal.)	222	90.9	20.18	222	90.9	20.18
Long Range Tanks (51 gal.)		94.81		—	94.81	—
4. Pilot and Co-Pilot	340	90.6	30.80	340	90.6	30.80
5. Rear Seat Passengers	340	126.0	42.84	—	126.0	—
*6. Baggage (in baggage compartment) Max. allowable 120 lbs.	21	151.0	3.17	45	151.0	6.80
7. Cargo Area Max. allowable 340 lbs.		116.4		20	116.4	2.32
8. Total Airplane Weight (loaded)	2200	92.17	202.72	1909		165.63

NOTE: Change in moment from upright to fold-down position of rear seat is negligible.

*Maximum allowable is 120 pounds if C.G. is within Center of Gravity Envelope. Refer to Cargo Loading and Weight and Balance Section for cargo loading instructions.

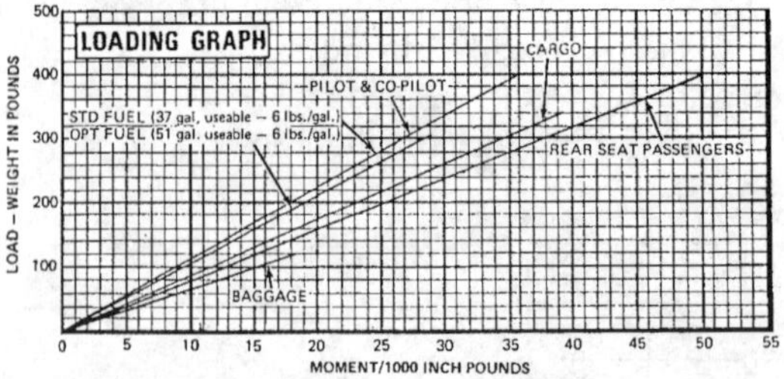

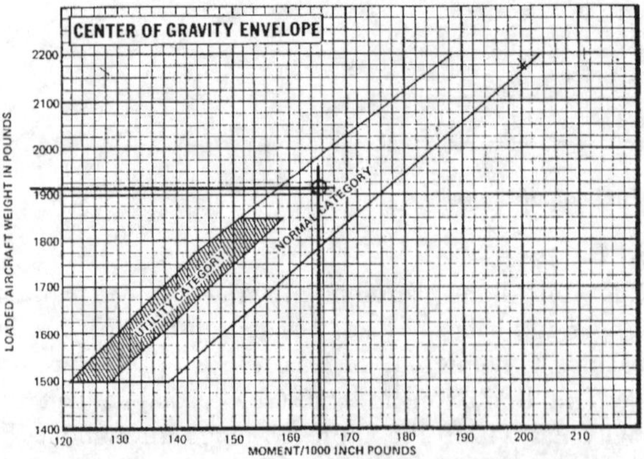

■ *Figure 18-9* ***A typical load sheet***

Take-Off and Landing Performance

Check that runways are adequate.

Having considered weight and balance, you will know the expected take-off weight and landing weight of the aeroplane. If any doubt exists regarding the suitability of the departure, destination and alternate aerodromes, then reference should be made to the take-off and landing **performance charts** in the Flight Manual. The official source of **aerodrome data** is the AD section of the Aeronautical Information Publication (AIP). Meteorological data affecting the performance (i.e. wind and temperature) can be obtained from the forecast.

UNITED KINGDOM
SUPPLEMENT

GULFSTREAM AMERICAN
MODEL AA-5A CHEETAH

TAKEOFF DISTANCE (AA-5A United Kingdom)

Sample only
Not to be used
for operational
purposes

ASSOCIATED CONDITIONS:
POWER – MAXIMUM
FLAPS – UP
RUNWAY – HARD SURFACE (LEVEL & DRY)
FUEL MIXTURE – FULL THROTTLE CLIMB, MIXTURE LEANED ABOVE 5000 FT TO SMOOTH ENGINE OPERATION.

NOTES:
1. DECREASE DISTANCE 4% FOR EACH 5 KNOTS HEADWIND. FOR OPERATION WITH TAILWINDS UP TO 10 KNOTS, INCREASE DISTANCE BY 10% FOR EACH 2.5 KNOTS.
2. IF TAKEOFF POWER IS SET WITHOUT BRAKES APPLIED, THEN DISTANCES APPLY FROM POINT WHERE FULL POWER IS ATTAINED.
3. FOR TAKEOFF FROM A DRY, GRASS RUNWAY, INCREASE GROUND RUN AND TOTAL DISTANCE TO CLEAR A 50 FT OBSTACLE BY 12.5% OF THE HARD SURFACE RUNWAY TOTAL TO CLEAR 50 FT OBSTACLE.

WEIGHT KGS	TAKEOFF SPEED KIAS (MPH) LIFT OFF	CLEAR 50 FT	PRESS. ALT FT	0°C (32°F) METRES GND RUN	50 FT	10°C (40°F) METRES GND RUN	5(…) F(…)
998	56 (64)	63 (73)	SL	230	419	255	46
			2000	273	495	304	54
			4000	326	587	362	65
			6000	391	698	434	77
			8000	469	832	520	92
907	53 (61)	60 (69)	SL	183	336	203	37
			2000	218	397	241	44
			4000	260	471	288	52
			6000	311	560	345	62
			8000	373	668	414	74
816	50 (58)	57 (66)	SL	142	263	158	29
			2000	169	312	187	34
			4000	202	369	221	40
			6000	241	439	268	48
			8000	290	523	321	58

GULFSTREAM AMERICAN
MODEL AA-5A CHEETAH

UNITED KINGDOM
SUPPLEMENT

LANDING DISTANCE (AA-5A United Kingdom)

SAMPLE ONLY
Not to be used in conjunction
with Flight Operations or
Flight Planning

ASSOCIATED CONDITIONS:
POWER – OFF
FLAPS – DOWN
RUNWAY – HARD SURFACE (LEVEL & DRY)
BRAKING – MAXIMUM

NOTES:
1. DECREASE DISTANCE 4% FOR EACH 5 KNOTS HEADWIND.
2. FOR OPERATIONS WITH TAILWINDS UP TO 10 KNOTS, INCREASE DISTANCE BY 9% FOR EACH 2.5 KNOTS.
3. WHEN LANDING ON A DRY GRASS RUNWAY, INCREASE GROUND RUN AND TOTAL DISTANCE OVER 50 FT. OBSTACLE BY 20% OF THE HARD SURFACE RUNWAY TOTAL DISTANCE OVER A 50 FT OBSTACLE.

WEIGHT KGS	SPEED AT 50 FT		PRESS ALT FT.	0°C (32°F) METRES		10°C (40°F) METRES		20°C (68°F) METRES		30°C (86°F) METRES		40°C (104°F) METRES	
	KIAS	MPH		GND RUN	CLEAR 50 FT	GND RUN	CLEAR 50 FT	GND RUN	CLEAR 50 FT	GND RUN	CLEAR 50 FT	GND RUN	CLEAR 50 FT
998	68	78	SL	123	410	127	422	130	434	133	445	137	458
			2000	130	434	134	447	138	460	141	473	145	487
			4000	138	461	142	476	146	490	150	504	155	519
			6000	147	492	151	507	156	523	161	539	165	555
			8000	157	526	162	543	167	560	172	578	177	595
907	65	75	SL	115	362	118	392	121	402	124	413	127	424
			2000	121	403	125	414	128	426	131	438	135	449
			4000	128	427	132	440	135	452	139	465	143	478
			6000	136	454	140	468	144	482	148	496	152	511
			8000	145	484	149	500	154	515	158	531	163	547
816	61	71	SL	107	353	110	362	112	371	115	380	118	390
			2000	112	371	115	381	118	392	121	402	121	412
			4000	118	393	122	404	125	415	128	426	131	438
			6000	125	416	129	429	132	441	136	454	140	467
			8000	133	443	137	457	141	471	145	485	149	499

■ *Figure 18-10* ***Consider if performance charts need to be consulted***

Flight Notification

Prior to flight you should contact the relevant Air Traffic Services (ATS) unit and either:

- **book out**; or
- **file a flight plan.**

A flight plan may be filed with ATC for any flight and is advisable when planning to fly more than 10 nm from the coast or over sparsely populated or mountainous areas, especially if the aeroplane is not equipped with a radio. A flight plan must be filed for certain flights, e.g. in Class D controlled airspace. The AIP and AICs detail the requirements. Notification can be in the form of a full flight plan, or an abbreviated flight plan containing the limited information needed to obtain a clearance for a portion of a flight. The abbreviated flight plan can be filed on the radio or by telephone prior to take-off.

For most visual flights, however, it is sufficient to **book out** with the ATS unit. This may be done by radio prior to taxiing, by telephone, or in person if necessary. Booking out details should include the aircraft registration, the destination, flight time, endurance and the number of persons on board.

Aeroplane Documentation and Flight Preparation

Check that the Certificate of Airworthiness is valid and that the maintenance document confirms that the aeroplane is airworthy.

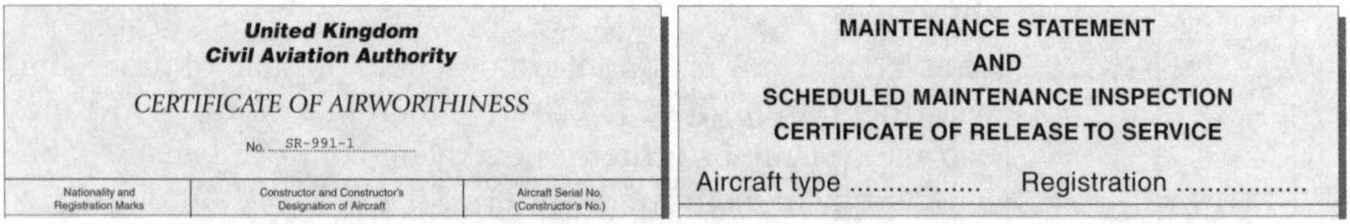
United Kingdom
Civil Aviation Authority

CERTIFICATE OF AIRWORTHINESS

No. SR-991-1

Nationality and Registration Marks	Constructor and Constructor's Designation of Aircraft	Aircraft Serial No. (Constructor's No.)

MAINTENANCE STATEMENT
AND
SCHEDULED MAINTENANCE INSPECTION
CERTIFICATE OF RELEASE TO SERVICE

Aircraft type .... Registration ....

■ *Figure 18-11* ***Check the CofA and the maintenance document***

Ensure that there is **adequate fuel on board** and complete your normal pre-flight duties, i.e. the external (walk-around) inspection and internal inspection. Never rush this aspect of the flight. It is more important that the pre-flight preparation is thorough and, even if you are running behind schedule because of flight planning taking longer than expected (a common reason), do not rush your normal pre-flight duties.

Prepare the aeroplane in an orderly manner. Do not rush!

Settle into the cockpit and place your navigation equipment and charts where they are readily accessible. Ensure that the charts are folded so that at least 20 nm either side of track is visible. Ensure that no metallic or magnetic objects are placed near the magnetic compass. Check on the comfort of your passengers (at this stage, your flying instructor).

These final checks are worthwhile since, once the engine starts, the noise level will be higher, communication will be slightly more difficult and you will be busier with the normal workload of manipulating the aeroplane.

The Flight

Start-Up and Taxi

Following normal procedures, start the engine, switch on the radio, book out with the ATS unit (if this has not already been done) and taxi to the take-off position. If in any doubt about the exact time, confirm it with an ATS unit and ensure that your clock is set correctly. Complete all of the normal pre-flight checks.

Ensure that your navigation equipment is accessible, but will not restrict the controls in any way.

Take Off and Set Heading

When aligned on the runway, but not accelerating, check that the magnetic compass is reading correctly and that the heading indicator is aligned with it.

Following take-off, the easiest method of **setting heading** is from directly overhead the airfield, at which time you would mentally note your 'set heading' time (or actual time of departure).

NOTE For various reasons, it is not always possible to set heading over the top (for example, at aerodromes with a low-level Entry/Exit Lane or if there is overlying controlled airspace) and you must fly to intercept the planned track some short distance en route. Once on track, you should estimate what the actual time of departure from overhead would have been.

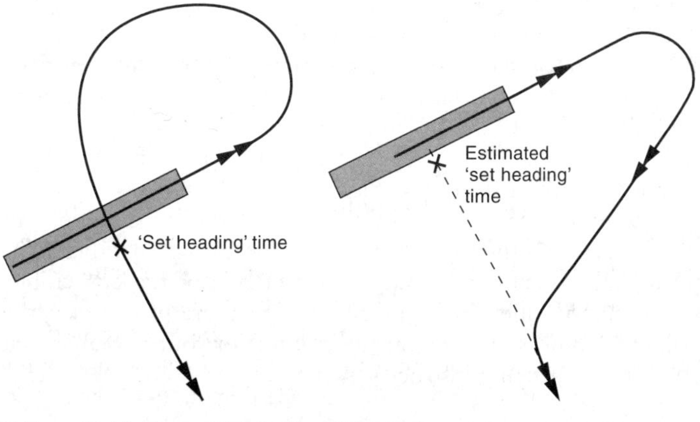

■ *Figure 18-12* ***Two methods of setting heading***

To use the magnetic compass precisely, you should refer to the compass deviation card in the cockpit so that the magnetic heading can be modified if necessary to the slightly more accurate compass heading. (Deviation is usually less than 3° and so is not operationally significant.)

Once well clear of the circuit area, enter the 'set heading' time of the flight log and estimate the arrival time at the destination and at selected points en route. Regional QNH (obtainable by radio from an ATS unit) should be set in the altimeter subscale so that height **above mean sea level** is indicated, i.e. altitude. Look well ahead to ensure that visual flight and the required separation from cloud can be maintained and, if not, consider a diversion.

When established outbound from the aerodrome:

- **Arrange the chart** so that your planned track runs up the page, making it easier for you to read from map to ground.
- **Confirm** that the heading indicator is aligned correctly with the magnetic compass.
- **Positively check** a definite ground feature or group of features within the first 10 nm to ensure that you are indeed on track and that no gross error has been made – misreading the compass or misaligning the heading indicator is always a possibility.

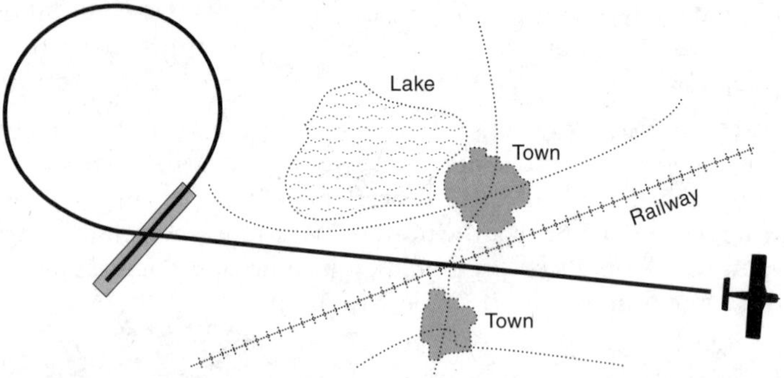

■ *Figure 18-13* ***Check that tracking is correct soon after setting heading***

En Route Navigation

It is important to maintain steady headings for known times when flying cross-country.

There is no need to refer to the chart all the time, but be sure to keep it handy (and usually on your lap). It is best to select ground features that will appear at intervals of 10 minutes or so (which at a groundspeed of 120 kt puts them about 20 nm apart) to verify that you are on or near track. Selecting checkpoints this far apart allows time for your other duties, which include flying the aeroplane, making radio calls and carrying out periodic checks of the aeroplane systems (see FREHA check, page 232).

Know from the chart which features to expect ahead.

At the appropriate time, look ahead for the next checkpoint which should be coming into view – in other words, look at the chart, note the features that should shortly come into view and then look outside with the expectation of seeing them. **Read from map to ground** – then use features to either side of track and well ahead to confirm your position.

Groundspeed Checks

Make regular checks of the groundspeed and revise your ETAs.

The actual groundspeed is easily calculated from *distance/time,* using the time and distance between two fixes or crossing two position lines. For example, if you cover 5 nm in 3 minutes, then the groundspeed is 100 kt (3 minutes = $\frac{1}{20}$ of an hour, therefore GS = 20 × 5 = 100 kt). These calculations can be done mentally or on the computer. Mentally is better if you can manage it.

Once you know the GS, you can revise your ETA for the next check-point (and others further on). Again, this can be done mentally or by computer. For example, if it is 40 nm to the next checkpoint, then at 100 kt this should take $\frac{40}{100}$ ($\frac{4}{10}$) of 1 hour = 4 × 6 minutes = 24 minutes. If the time now is 1343 UTC, ETA at the checkpoint is 1407 UTC.

Checking the actual time at the ¼, ½ or ¾ points along the way makes the mental calculation of the next ETA very easy. Also, it is good airmanship to log the times at fixes (or mark them on the map), so that you have some record of what positions the aeroplane passed over and when.

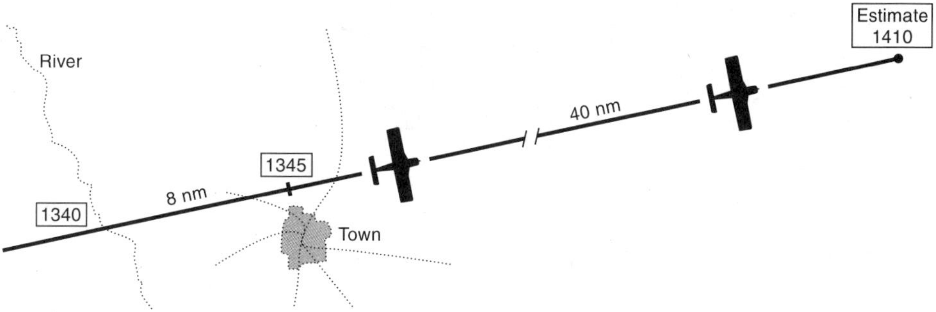

■ *Figure 18-14* ***Calculate groundspeed and revise ETAs***

Off-Track Corrections

Adjust heading as necessary.

It is usual to find that the actual track made good over the ground differs from the desired track plotted on the map, possibly because the wind is different to that forecast.

Whatever the cause, it is quite a simple calculation to revise the heading to reintercept track. There are various means of doing this and your flying instructor will recommend a method. It can be done by computer or it can be done mentally (which leaves your hands free for other duties and avoids having your 'head in the cockpit' for too long). It is good airmanship to log the heading changes and the time at which they were made.

In each of the three methods in the next figure, the same result (turn 12° to the right) is obtained. Having regained track, turn 4° left to maintain it.

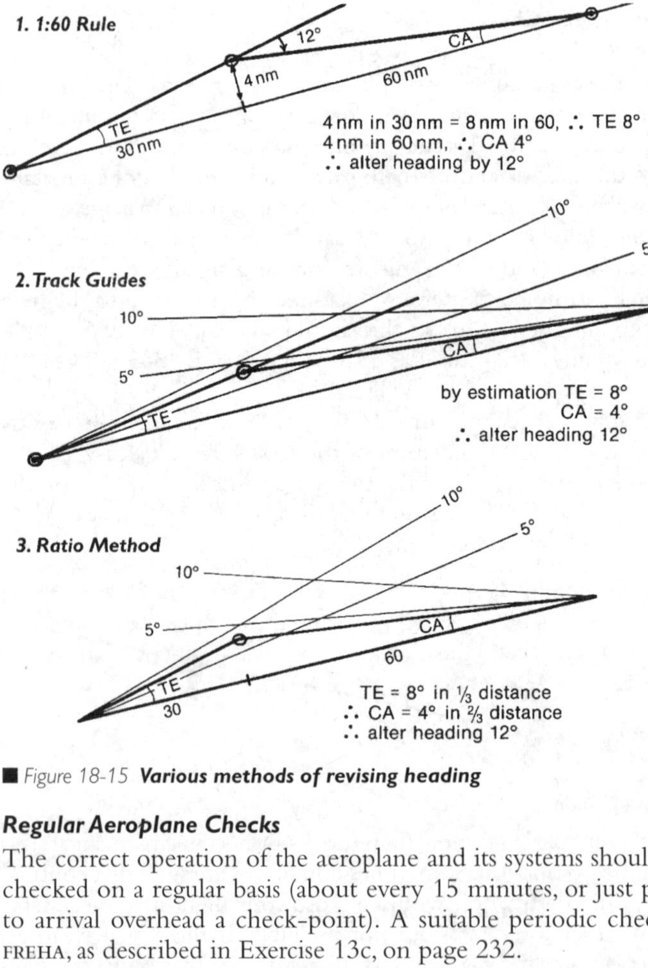

■ Figure 18-15 **Various methods of revising heading**

Regular Aeroplane Checks

Periodically check the aeroplane systems.

The correct operation of the aeroplane and its systems should be checked on a regular basis (about every 15 minutes, or just prior to arrival overhead a check-point). A suitable periodic check is FREHA, as described in Exercise 13c, on page 232.

Turning Points

Just prior to reaching a turning point, check that the HI is indeed aligned with the magnetic compass (part of the FREHA check). Take up the new heading over the turning point, log the time and calculate the ETA for the next checkpoint. Then, within 10 nm of passing the turning point, confirm from ground features that you are on the desired track and that no gross error has been made.

Use of the Radio

The radio is a very useful aid. En route and outside controlled airspace, you will normally select the FIR frequency (shown on the charts) to enable immediate contact with the Air Traffic Service unit if desired. If passing close to Aerodrome Traffic Zones, Military Air Traffic Zones, regulated airspace, etc., make sure you contact the appropriate R/T frequency prior to penetrating the airspace.

Do not be afraid to request the Radar Advisory Service if it is available in your area.

A typical **position report** will contain your:

- **aircraft identification (callsign);**
- **position;**
- **time;**
- **level;**
- **next position and ETA.**

Arrival at the Destination

If appropriate, make contact with the ATS unit at the aerodrome some 10 minutes prior to your ETA. This will allow time for you to obtain the aerodrome information (e.g. the wind, runway in use, and the QFE or QNH) so that you can plan your arrival.

Normal procedures are either to join on downwind leg at circuit height or to overfly at 2,000 ft above aerodrome level and let down to circuit height on the 'dead side' of the traffic pattern. The latter method is preferred at non-radio fields.

Having landed and taxied in, secure the aeroplane and book in. Refuelling may be a consideration, as well as payment of any landing fees.

Further Points

Diversions

A successful cross-country flight does not necessarily mean arriving at the destination. Sometimes conditions are such that continuing to the destination would expose your flight to unnecessary risk. Weather forecasters are not infallible. If the actual weather conditions ahead deteriorate to such a degree that onward visual flight would be unsafe (or less safe than you like it to be), then to divert is good airmanship.

Never be afraid to divert if you think it is the appropriate thing to do.

There will always be pressures to press on from, for example, passengers wanting to get home, a sense of failure if you do not make it to the planned destination, the inconvenience of having to stay overnight away from home unexpectedly, etc.

When faced with an operational decision of whether to divert or not, forget all of these secondary problems! They are irrelevant. Your decision should be based on **flight safety** grounds alone.

Having decided to divert, perhaps in difficult conditions such as turbulence, there is a **basic diversion procedure** that you should follow:

- Make your decision to divert earlier rather than later.
- If possible, plan to divert from a prominent ground feature ahead, so that the diversion is commenced from a known point (e.g. a town).
- Mark the diversion track on the chart (freehand if necessary) and estimate track and distance – estimate the track in degrees true with reference to the latitude-longitude grid and estimate the distance.
- At the prominent feature, take up the estimated diversion heading, which you have calculated from the estimated track, allowing for magnetic variation and wind drift. Your heading is extremely important at this stage – even more important than distance (within reason).
- Log the time at the diversion point and your new heading.
- Refer to the chart and look for a positive ground feature soon after altering heading to ensure that no gross error has been made.
- When time permits, measure the track and distance accurately (ideally this would be done prior to the actual diversion).
- Estimate the GS and ETA at the diversion aerodrome or next turning point.
- Inform the nearest Air Traffic Service unit by radio of your actions.

Inform an ATS unit of your revised intentions.

- Continue with normal navigation until you reach the diversion aerodrome (i.e. adjust heading and ETAs as required, contact the ATS unit at the diversion field when about 10 nm away, obtain QNH or QFE, landing direction and other information).
- Join the circuit normally, land, and book in (and consider if the original destination aerodrome should be advised), and then advise your home base of the situation.

Low-Level Navigation

If a diversion is due to a lowering cloud base you may find yourself involved in low-level navigation. Low-level flying was covered in Exercise 16, but navigation aspects worth noting are:

- If possible, perform any required checks before descent to a low level.
- Consider using the *precautionary* configuration (which allows slower flight, a better forward view, better manoeuvrability, but poorer fuel consumption).
- Your field of vision at low level is small and the speed that ground features pass through it is greater.
- Check features need to be close to track to fall within this field of vision and must be prominent in profile (i.e. when seen from the side).
- You must anticipate reaching the ground features, because they may not be in your field of vision for long.
- Keep your eyes *out of the cockpit* as much as possible.

Uncertain of Position

Being *temporarily uncertain of your position* is not the same as being lost. A DR (dead reckoning) position can be calculated which, hopefully, can shortly be backed up with a positive fix over or abeam a ground feature.

If, at any time, you are uncertain of your position:

1. Log your heading (compass and heading indicator) and the time.
2. If the HI is incorrectly set, then you have the information needed to make a reasonable estimate of your actual position. Reset the HI and calculate a HDG and time interval to regain the desired track.
3. If the HI is aligned correctly with the compass, then the non-appearance of a landmark, while it will perhaps cause you some concern, need not indicate that you are grossly off track. You may not have seen the landmark for some perfectly legitimate reason (bright sunlight, poor visibility, a change in features not reflected on the chart, cloud, etc.).
4. If you think it is appropriate, make an **urgency call** (Pan-Pan Pan-Pan Pan-Pan, etc.) on the frequency in use or on the emergency frequency 121.5 MHz, and squawk the appropriate conspicuity code on your transponder.
5. If still unable to fix your position, follow the procedures on the next page.

Procedure when Lost

Becoming lost is usually the result of some human error. Careful pre-flight planning followed by in-flight attention to the simple navigation tasks will ensure that you never become lost. You may become *temporarily uncertain of your exact position,* but this is not being *lost* because you can calculate an approximate DR position.

If you ever become lost, **formulate a plan of action** and do not just fly around aimlessly. Make use of the Radar Advisory Service, if available (refer to point 4 above).

When lost:

1. It is important that you initially maintain the HDG (if terrain, visibility and what you know of the proximity of controlled airspace permit) and carry out a sequence of positive actions.
2. If a vital checkpoint is not in view at your ETA, then continue to fly for 10% of the time since your last positive fix.
3. Start from the chart position of your last known fix, check the headings flown since that last fix, and ensure that:
   - the magnetic compass is not being affected by outside influences such as a camera, portable radio, or other metal objects placed near it;
   - the gyroscopic heading indicator (HI) is aligned with the magnetic compass correctly;
   - magnetic variation and drift have been correctly applied to obtain your HDGs flown;
   - an estimate of the track direction on the chart against that shown on the flight plan is correct.
4. When lost, read from ground to chart, i.e. look for significant ground features or combinations of features and try to determine their position on the chart.
5. Establish a **most probable area** in which you think you are. This can be done in several ways – your flying instructor will recommend a method. Two suggested methods of establishing a most probable area follow.

Establishing A Most Probable Area

Use one of these two methods to establish the most probable area that you are in.

METHOD 1. Estimate the distance flown since the last fix and apply this distance, plus or minus 10%, to an arc 30 degrees either side of what you estimate the probable track made good (TMG) to be.

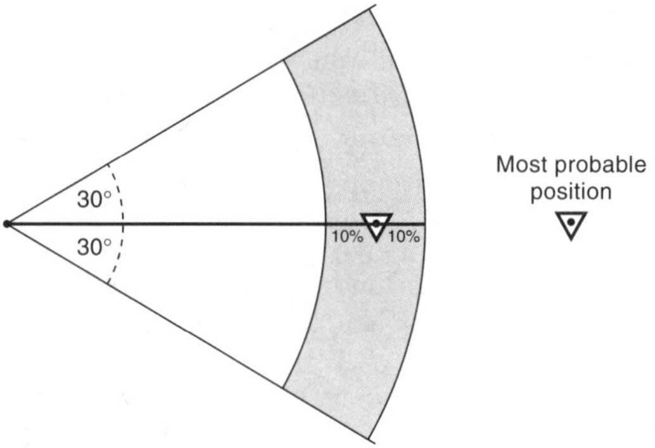

■ *Figure 18-16* ***Estimating the most probable area that you are in***

METHOD 2. Estimate your most probable position and around it draw a circle of radius equal to 10% of the distance flown since the last fix.

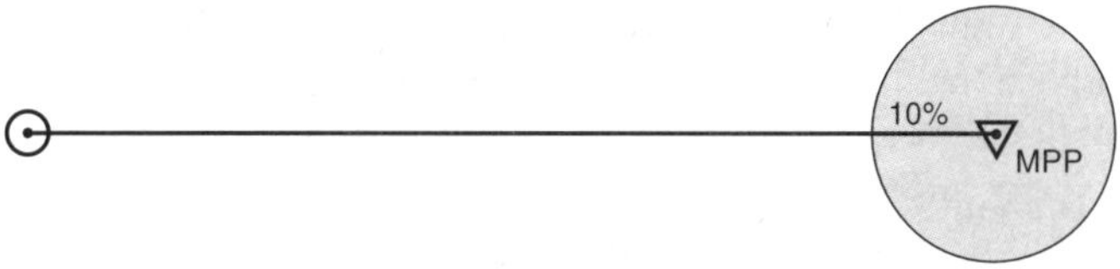

■ *Figure 18-17* ***Another means of estimating the most probable position***

Establish a safety altitude to ensure adequate clearance of all obstacles in what you consider the general area to be – being especially careful in conditions of poor visibility or low cloud.

Check large features within this area of the chart with what can be seen on the ground. Try and relate features seen on the ground with those shown on the chart, i.e. read from ground to chart. Confirm the identification of any feature by closely observing secondary details around the feature.

At all times continue to fly the aircraft safely, maintaining an awareness of time, especially with respect to ***last light*** *and your* ***fuel state.***

When you do positively establish a fix, recheck your HI and recommence normal navigation activity. Calculate the HDG, GS and ETI for the next check feature and set course for it.

If you are still unable to fix your position, you should consider taking one of the following actions:

1. Increase your most probable area by 10%, 15% or 20% of the distance flown since the last fix.
2. Climb to a higher altitude to increase your range of vision.

3. Turn towards a prominent 'line feature' known to be in the area, e.g. a coastline, large river, railway line or road, and then follow along it to the next town, where you should be able to obtain a fix.
4. Steer a reciprocal heading and attempt to return to your last fix.

Important Points

- If you want to cover as much ground as possible with the fuel available, you should fly the aeroplane for **best range.**
- Keep a **navigation log** going.
- Remain positively aware of time. Keep your eye on the fuel and on the amount of time remaining until last light. If last light is approaching, remember that it will be darker at ground level than at altitude and, if you are flying in the tropics, that it will become dark very quickly following sunset.
- If you decide to carry out a precautionary search and landing, allow sufficient time and fuel to do this, because two or three inspections might have to be made before finding a suitable landing area.

Why Did You Become Lost?

If at any stage you became lost, try to determine the reason systematically (either in flight or post flight) so that you can learn from the experience.

Common reasons for becoming lost include:
- **incorrectly calculated HDGs, GSs, and ETIs** (hence the need to make mental estimates of approximate answers to these items);
- **an incorrectly synchronised heading indicator** (HI), i.e. the gyroscopic HI not aligned correctly with the magnetic compass – the HI should be checked every 10 or 15 minutes against the compass;
- **a faulty compass reading** (due to transistor radios, cameras and other metal objects placed near the compass);
- **incorrectly applied variation** (*variation west, magnetic best,* etc.);
- **incorrectly applied drift** (compared to track, heading should be into wind);
- **an actual wind velocity** significantly different to that forecast, and not allowed for in flight by the pilot;
- **a deterioration in weather,** a reduced visibility, or an increased cockpit workload;
- **an incorrect fix,** i.e. misidentification of a check feature;

- **a poorly planned diversion** from the original desired track;
- **not paying attention** to carrying out normal navigation tasks en route.

With regular checks of the HI alignment with the compass, reasonably accurate flying of heading, and with position fixes every 10 or 15 minutes, none of the above errors should put you far off-track. It is only when you are slack and lets things go a bit too far that you become lost.

Exercise 19
Instrument Flying

Introduction to Attitude Instrument Flying

As an instrument pilot, you must learn to trust what you see on the instruments.

We normally use our **vision** to orientate ourselves with our surroundings, supported by other bodily senses that can sense gravity, such as *feel* and *balance*. Even with the eyes closed, however, we can usually manage to sit, stand and walk on steady ground without losing control. This becomes much more difficult standing on the bed of an accelerating or turning truck, or even in an accelerating elevator.

■ *Figure 19-1* **Flying on instruments**

In an aeroplane, which can accelerate in three dimensions, the task becomes almost impossible without using your eyes.

The eyes must gather information from the external ground features, including the horizon, or, in poor visibility, gather **substitute information** from the instruments.

A pilot's eyes are very important, and the starting point in your instrument training will be learning to use your eyes to derive information from the instruments.

Fundamental Skills.

The three fundamental skills in instrument flying are:

- **instrument cross-check** (also known as *scanning* the instruments);
- **instrument interpretation** (understanding their message); and
- **aeroplane control** (directing the aeroplane along the desired flightpath at the desired airspeed using attitude flying).

Cockpit

Instrument flying is much easier if you are comfortable in the cockpit and know your aeroplane well. Adjust the seat position prior to flight to ensure that you can reach all of the controls easily, and so that you have the correct **eye position.**

Attitude Flying

Power plus attitude equals performance.

Attitude flying is the name given to the technique of using a selected power and a selected attitude to achieve the desired performance of the aeroplane in terms of flightpath and airspeed.

For a given aeroplane weight and configuration, a particular attitude combined with a particular power setting will always result in a similar flightpath through the air, be it a straight and level flightpath, a climb, a descent or a turn. Any change of power and/or attitude will result in a change of flightpath and/or airspeed.

Aeroplane attitude has two aspects – pitch and bank, i.e. nose position against the horizon, and bank angle. **Pitch attitude** is the angle between the longitudinal axis of the aircraft and the horizontal. **Bank angle** (or bank attitude) is the angle between the lateral axis of the aeroplane and the horizontal.

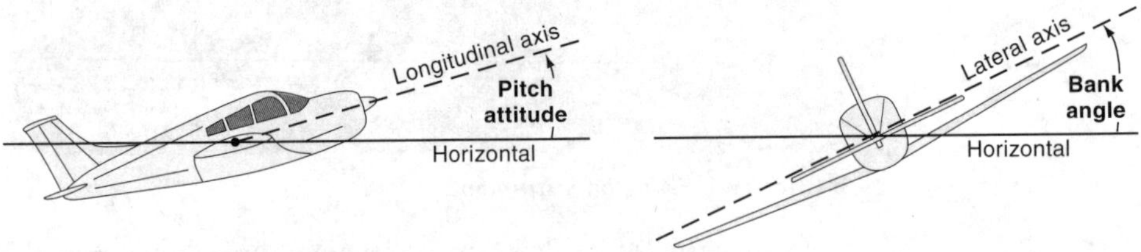

■ *Figure 19-2* ***Pitch attitude (left) and bank angle (right)***

Pitch Attitude

*Pitch attitude is **not** angle of attack.*

The pitch attitude is the geometric relationship between the longitudinal axis of the aeroplane and horizontal. Pitch attitude refers to the aeroplane's inclination to the horizontal, and not to where the aeroplane is actually going.

The angle of attack, however, is the angle between the wing chord and the relative airflow. The angle of attack, therefore, is closely related to flightpath.

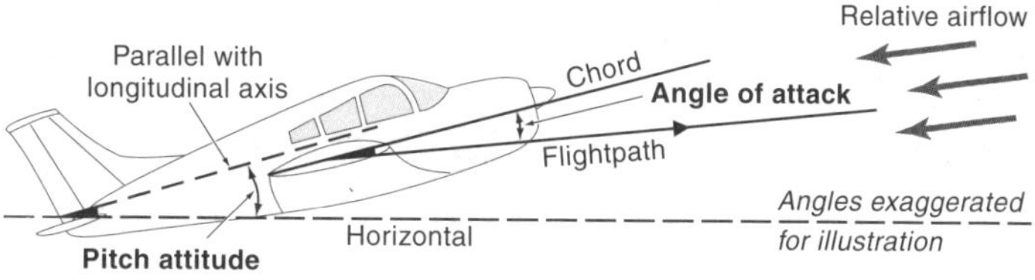

■ *Figure 19-3* ***Pitch attitude and angle of attack are not the same***

Pitch attitude and angle of attack are different, but they are related in the sense that if the pitch attitude is raised, then the angle of attack is increased. Conversely, if the pitch attitude is lowered, the angle of attack is decreased.

Attitude Flying on Instruments

Attitude flying on instruments is an extension of visual flying, with your attention gradually shifting from external visual cues to the instrument indications in the cockpit, until you are able to fly accurately on instruments alone.

You select pitch attitude using the elevator. In visual conditions, you select the desired pitch attitude by referring the nose position to the external natural horizon. In instrument flight, **pitch attitude** is selected with reference to the attitude indicator, using the position of the centre dot of the wing bars relative to the horizon bar. The centre dot represents the nose of the aeroplane.

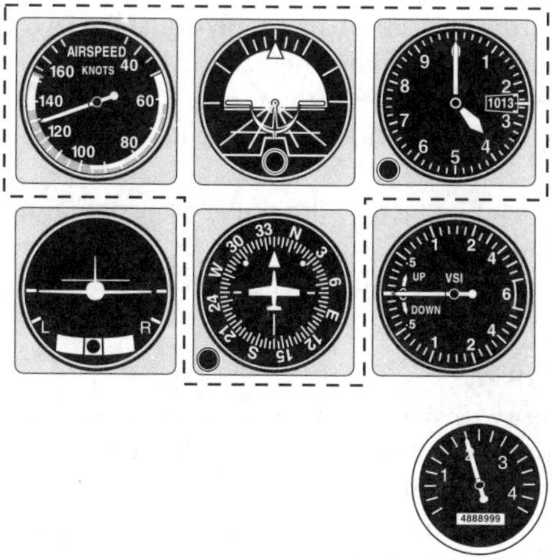

■ *Figure 19-4* ***The full panel***

You select bank angle using the ailerons. In visual conditions, you refer to the angle made by the external natural horizon in the windscreen. On instruments, you select **bank angle** on the attitude indicator, either by estimating the angle between the wing bars of the miniature aeroplane and the horizon bar, or from the position of the bank pointer on a graduated scale at the top of the attitude indicator.

■ Figure 19-5 **Low pitch attitude, and wings level**

■ Figure 19-6 **High pitch attitude, and right bank**

Check the attitude indicator every few seconds.

Most of your attention during flight, both visual and on instruments, is concerned with achieving and holding a suitable attitude. A very important skill to develop when flying on instruments, therefore, is to check the attitude indicator every few seconds. There are other tasks, of course, to be performed, and there are other instruments to look at as well, but the eyes should always return fairly quickly to the AI.

To achieve the desired **performance** (in terms of flightpath and airspeed), you must not only place the aeroplane in a suitable **attitude** with the flight controls, you must also apply suitable **power** with the throttle. Just because the aeroplane has a high pitch attitude does *not* mean that it will climb – it requires climb power as well as climb attitude to do this. With less power, it may not climb at all.

Attitude flying is the name given to the skill – controlling the aeroplane's flightpath and airspeed with changes in attitude and power. The techniques used in attitude flying are the same visually or on instruments.

Scanning the Instruments

Scanning the instruments with your eyes, interpreting their indications, and applying this information is a vital skill to develop if you are to become a good instrument pilot.

Power is selected with the throttle, and can be checked on the power indicator. Pitch attitude and bank angle are selected using the control column, with frequent reference to the attitude indicator. With both correct power and attitude set, the aeroplane will perform as expected. The attitude indicator and the power indicator, because they are used when controlling the aeroplane, are known as the **control instruments.**

The actual performance of the aeroplane, once its power and attitude have been set, can be cross-checked on what are known as the **performance instruments** – the altimeter for altitude, the airspeed indicator for airspeed, the heading indicator for heading, and so on.

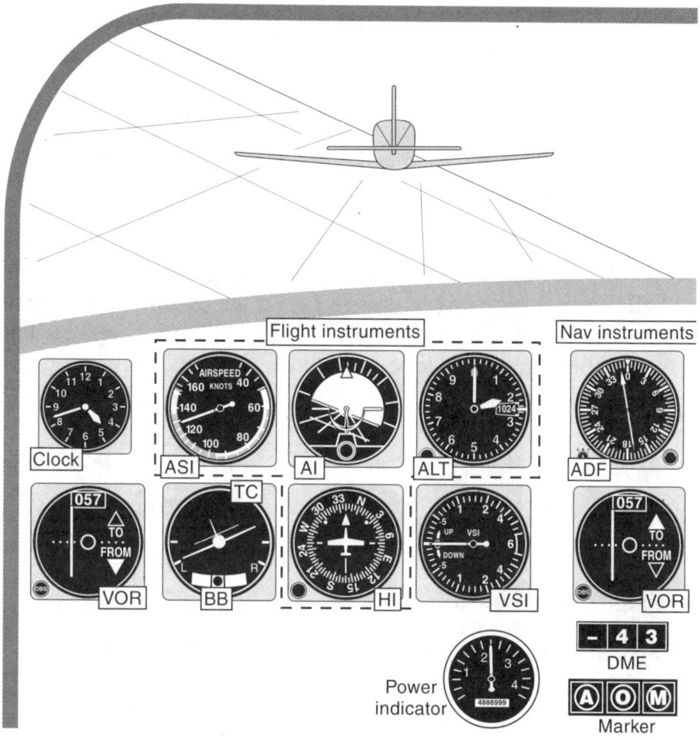

■ *Figure 19-7* ***Layout of a typical instrument panel***

Your main scan is across six basic instruments:
• ASI • AI • ALT
• TC • HI • VSI

Scanning is an art that will develop naturally during your training especially when you know what to look for. The main scan to develop initially is that of the six basic flight instruments, concentrating on the AI and radiating out to the others as required. Having scanned the instruments, interpreted the message that they contain, built up a picture of where the aeroplane is and where it is going, you can control it in a meaningful way.

Controlling the Aeroplane

During instrument flight, the aeroplane is flown using the normal controls according to the picture displayed on the instrument panel. From this picture, you will, with practice, know what control movements (elevator, aileron, rudder and throttle) are required to either maintain the picture as it is, or change it.

When manoeuvring the aeroplane, a suitable **control sequence** to follow (the same as in visual flight) is:

1. **Visualise** the desired new flightpath and airspeed.
2. **Select the attitude and the power required** to achieve the desired performance by moving the controls, and then checking when the aeroplane has achieved the estimated attitude on the AI.
3. **Hold the attitude** on the AI, allowing the aeroplane to settle down into its new performance, and allowing the pressure instruments that experience some lag to catch up.
4. **Make small adjustments** to attitude and power until the actual performance equals the desired performance.
5. **Trim** (which is essential, if you are to achieve accurate and comfortable instrument flight). Heavy loads can be trimmed off earlier in the sequence to assist in control, if desired, but remember that the function of trim is to relieve control on the pilot, and not to change aircraft attitude.

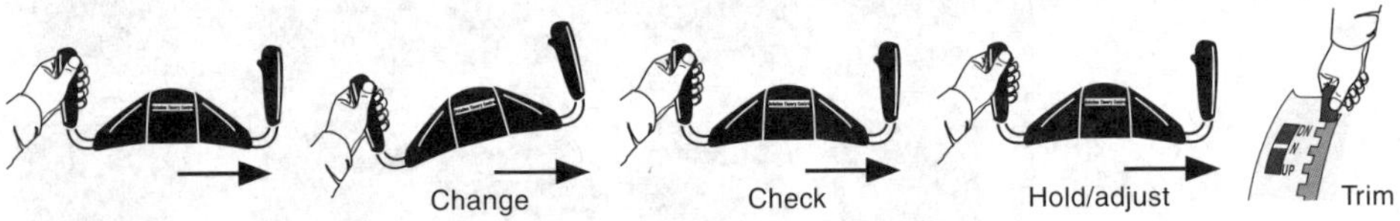

■ *Figure 19-8* ***Control sequence***

Some helpful hints follow:

- **Derive the required information** from the relevant instrument, e.g. heading from the heading indicator, altitude from the altimeter.
- **Respond to deviations** from the desired flightpath and/or airspeed. Use the AI as a control instrument, with power as required. For instance, if you are 50 ft low on altitude, then raise the pitch attitude on the AI slightly and climb back up to height. Do *not* accept steady deviations – it is just as easy to fly at 3,000 ft as it is to fly at 2,950 ft. A lot of instrument flying is in the mind and, in a sense, instrument flying is a test of character as well as of flying ability. Be as accurate as you can!
- **Do not over-control.** Avoid large, fast or jerky control movements, which will probably result in continuous corrections, over-corrections and then re-corrections. This can occur if attitude is changed without reference to the AI, or it might be caused by the aeroplane being out-of-trim, or possibly by a pilot who is fatigued or tense.

- **Do not be distracted** from a scan of the flight instruments for more than a few seconds at a time, even though other duties must be attended to, such as checklists, radio calls and navigation tasks.
- **Be relaxed.** Easier said than done at the beginning, but it will come with experience.

Sensory Illusions

Sensory illusions can lead you astray.

Most people live in a 1g situation most of the time, with their feet on the ground (1g means the force of gravity). However, some variations to 1g do occur in everyday life – for instance, when driving a car. Accelerating a car, hard braking, or turning on a flat bend will all produce g-forces on the body different to the 1g of gravity alone. Passengers with their eyes closed could perhaps detect this by bodily feel or with their sense of balance.

A right turn on a flat road, for instance, could be detected by the feeling of being thrown to the left – but it might be more difficult to detect if the curve was perfectly banked for the particular speed. A straight road sloping to the left (and causing the passenger to lean to the left) might give the passenger the false impression that the car is turning right, even though it is in fact not turning at all. The position-sensing systems of the body, using nerves all over the body to transmit messages of feel and pressure to the brain, can be fooled in this and other ways.

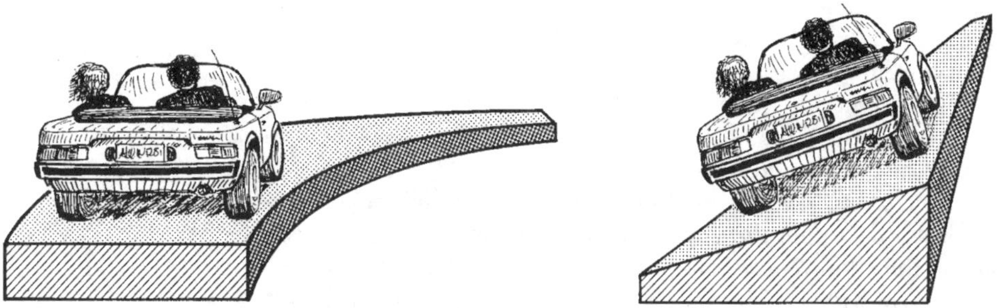

■ Figure 19-9 ***Turning right – or simply leaning?***

The organs within the inner ear, used for balance and to detect accelerations, can also be deceived. For instance, if you are sitting in a car travelling around a suitably banked curve, the sensing system in your ears falsely interprets the g-force holding you firmly and comfortably in the seat as a vertical force, as if you were moving straight ahead rather than in a banked turn.

The inner ear organs have other limitations, one being that a constant velocity is not detected, nor is a very gradual change in velocity. If you are sitting in a train, for instance, and there is another train moving slowly relative to you on an adjacent track, it is sometimes difficult to determine which train is moving, or if indeed both are moving.

False impressions of motion can also be caused by unusual g-forces – for instance, by rapid head motion, or by lowering the head. If you happen to drop your pencil while instrument flying, don't just lower your eyes and lean down to look for it in one motion – take it very carefully step by step to avoid any feelings of vertigo.

Because an aeroplane moves in three dimensions, it is possible to accelerate and decelerate in three dimensions, and this can lead to more complicated illusions. Pulling up into a steep climb, for instance, holds a pilot tightly in his seat, which is exactly the same feeling as in a steep turn. With your eyes closed, it is sometimes difficult to say which manoeuvre it is.

Another example is decelerating while in a turn to the left, which may give a false impression of a turn to the right. Be aware that your sense of balance and bodily feel can lead you astray in an aeroplane, especially with rapidly changing g-forces in manoeuvres such as this. The one sense that can resolve most of these illusions is **sight.** If the car passenger could see out, or if the pilot had reference to the natural horizon and landmarks, then the confusion would be easily dispelled.

The senses of balance and bodily feel can be misleading; trust your eyes and what the instruments tell you.

Unfortunately, in instrument flight you do *not* have reference to ground features, but you can still use your sense of sight to **scan the instruments,** and obtain substitute information. Therefore, an important instruction to the budding instrument pilot is: believe your eyes and what the instruments tell you.

An instrument pilot must learn to believe the instruments.

While sight is the most important sense, and must be protected at all costs, also make sure that you avoid anything that will affect your balance or position-sensing systems.

Avoid alcohol, drugs (including smoking in the cockpit) and medication. Do not fly when ill or suffering from an upper respiratory infection (e.g. a cold). Do not fly when tired or fatigued. Do not fly with a cabin altitude higher than 10,000 ft amsl without using oxygen. Avoid sudden head movements and avoid lowering your head or turning around in the cockpit.

Despite all these *don'ts,* there is one very important *do – do trust what your eyes tell you from the instruments.*

Developing a Scan Pattern

The performance of an aeroplane is, as always, determined by the power set and the attitude selected.

In **visual flying conditions,** the external natural horizon is used as a reference when selecting pitch attitude and bank angle. The power indicator in the cockpit is only referred to occasionally, for instance when setting a particular power for cruise or for climb.

In **instrument conditions,** when the natural horizon cannot be seen, pitch attitude and bank angle information is still available to the pilot in the cockpit from the **attitude indicator.** Relatively large pitch attitude changes against the natural horizon are reproduced in miniature on the attitude indicator.

In straight and level flight, for instance, the wings of the miniature aeroplane should appear against the horizon line, while in a climb they should appear one or two bar widths above it.

In a turn, the wing bars of the miniature aeroplane will bank along with the real aeroplane, while the horizon line remains horizontal. The centre dot of the miniature aeroplane represents the aeroplane's nose position relative to the horizon.

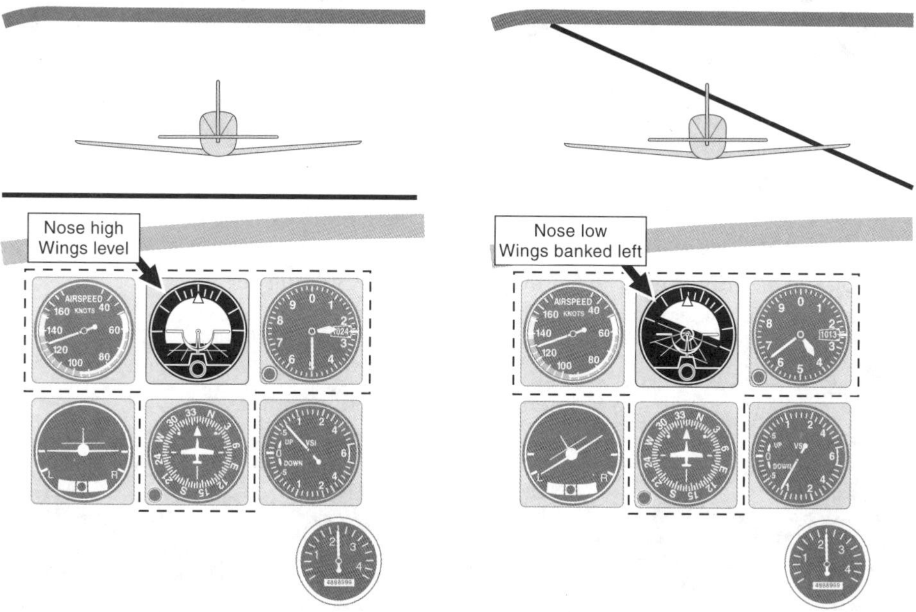

■ *Figure 19-10* ***The AI is the master instrument for pitch attitude and bank angle***

Simple Scans

BALANCE (COORDINATION). The AI, while it shows pitch attitude and bank angle directly, does not indicate balance (coordination) or yaw. Balance or coordination information can be obtained simply by moving the eyes from the attitude indicator diagonally down to the left to check that the **balance ball** in the turn coordinator is indeed being centred with rudder pressure. The eyes should then return to the AI.

HEADING. Directional information can be obtained from the **heading indicator (HI)** or from the magnetic compass. From the AI, the eyes can be moved straight down to the HI to absorb heading information, before returning to the AI.

Each eye movement to obtain particular information is very simple, starting at the attitude indicator and radiating out to the relevant instrument, before returning again to the AI.

■ *Figure 19-11* ***A simple scan for balance (coordination)***

■ *Figure 19-12* ***A simple scan for heading***

AIRSPEED. Airspeed information is also very important, and this is easily checked by moving the eyes left from the AI to the **airspeed indicator (ASI)**, before returning them to the AI.

ALTITUDE. The **altimeter** is the only means of determining the precise height of the aeroplane, in visual as well as in instrument conditions.

To obtain height information, the eyes can move from the AI towards the right where the altimeter is located, before moving back to the AI.

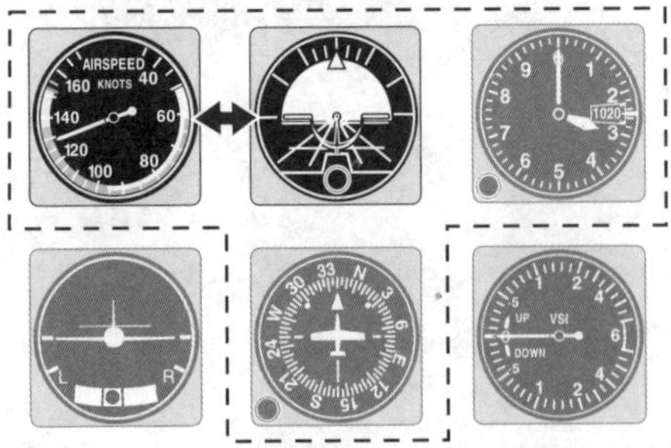

■ *Figure 19-13* ***A simple scan for airspeed***

■ *Figure 19-14* ***A simple scan for altitude***

VERTICAL SPEED. The rate of change of height, as either a rate of climb or a rate of descent in feet per minute, can be monitored on the **vertical speed indicator (VSI)** by moving the eyes from the AI diagonally down to the right to the VSI, before returning them to the AI.

The VSI, since it is often used in conjunction with the altimeter, is located directly beneath it on most instrument panels.

TURNING. A turn is entered using the AI to establish bank angle and the ball to confirm balance (coordination). Additional information on the turning rate is available from the **turn coordinator** once the bank angle is established.

The normal rate of turn in instrument flying is 3° per second, known as **rate 1** or **standard rate,** and this is clearly marked on the turn coordinator (or turn-and-slip indicator).

■ *Figure 19-15* ***A simple scan for vertical speed information***

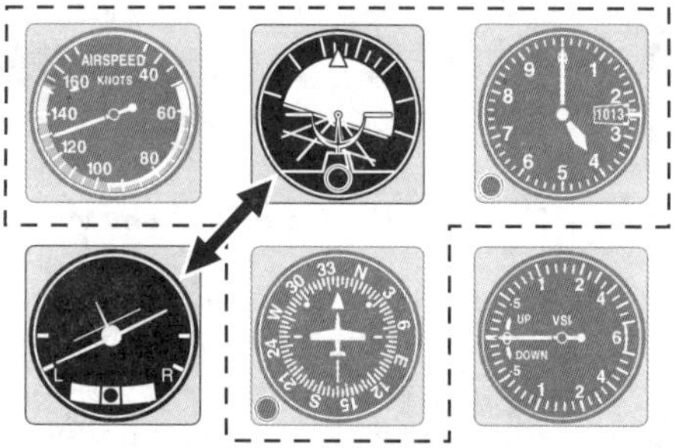

■ *Figure 19-16* ***A simple scan for turn rate***

With these **six basic flight instruments,** plus the **power indicator,** it is possible to fly the aeroplane very accurately and comfortably without any external visual reference, provided the instruments are scanned efficiently, and the pilot controls the aeroplane adequately in response to the information that he derives from them.

Control and Performance

Control the aeroplane to achieve the desired performance. The attitude selected on the **attitude indicator** and the power set on the **power indicator** determine the performance of the aeroplane; hence these two instruments are known as the **control instruments.**

The attitude indicator is located centrally on the instrument panel directly in front of the pilot, so that any changes in attitude can be readily seen. Because continual reference to the power indicator is not required, it is situated slightly away from the main group of flight instruments, easy to scan occasionally, but not in the main field of view.

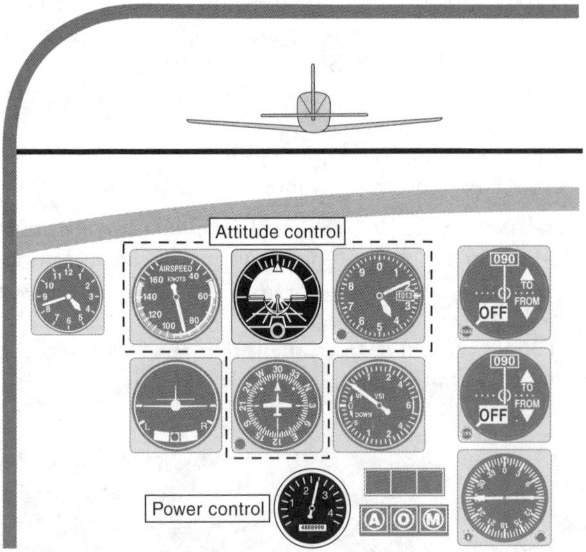

■ *Figure 19-17* ***Use the control instruments to select attitude and power***

The other flight instruments are **performance instruments** that display how the aeroplane is performing (as a result of the power and attitude selected) in terms of:

- **altitude** – on the altimeter and VSI;
- **heading** – on the HI and turn coordinator; and
- **airspeed** – on the ASI.

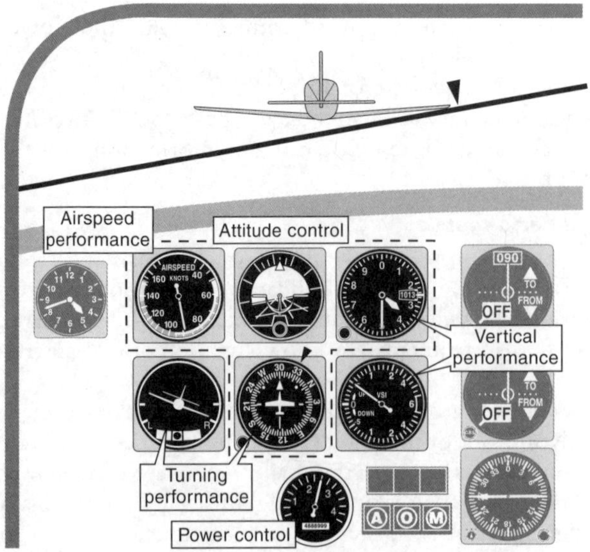

■ *Figure 19-18* ***The performance instruments***

Changes in **pitch attitude** are shown directly on the AI, and are reflected on the altimeter, VSI and ASI. Changes in **bank angle** are shown directly on the AI, and are reflected on the turn coordinator and the heading indicator. The quality of flight is shown by the balance ball.

■ *Figure 19-19* **The pitch instruments**

■ *Figure 19-20* **The bank instruments**

The Selective Radial Scan

Of the six main flight instruments, the **attitude indicator** is the master instrument. It gives you a direct and immediate picture of pitch attitude and bank angle. It will be the one most frequently referred to (at least once every few seconds in most stages of flight).

The eyes can be directed selectively towards the other instruments to derive relevant information from them as required, before returning to the AI. This eye movement radiating out and back to selected instruments is commonly known as the **selective radial scan.**

For instance, when climbing with full power selected, the estimated climb pitch attitude is held on the attitude indicator, with subsequent reference to the airspeed indicator to confirm that the selected pitch attitude is indeed correct. If the ASI indicates an airspeed that is too low, then lower the pitch attitude on the AI (say by a half bar width or by one bar width), allow a few seconds for the airspeed to settle, and then check the ASI again.

Correct pitch attitude in the climb is checked on the airspeed indicator.

The key instrument in confirming that the correct attitude has been selected on the AI during the climb is the airspeed indicator. Because it determines what pitch attitude changes should be made on the AI during the climb, the airspeed indicator is the primary performance guide for pitch attitude in the climb. It is supported by the AI and the VSI.

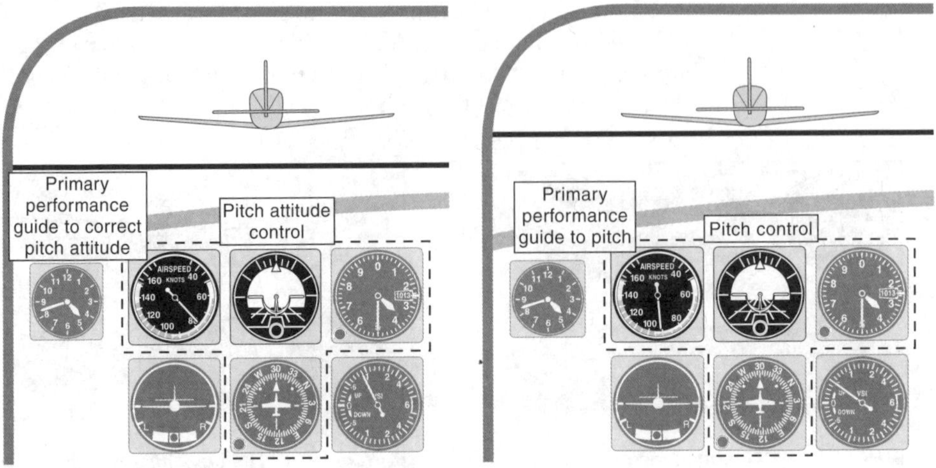

■ *Figure 19-21* ***ASI is the primary instrument in the climb to confirm correct pitch attitude***

Correct pitch attitude when cruising is checked on the altimeter.

Approaching the desired cruise level, however, more attention should be paid to the altimeter to ensure that, as pitch attitude is lowered on the AI, the aeroplane levels off at the desired height. When cruising, any minor deviations from height detected on the altimeter can be corrected with small changes in pitch attitude. Because the altimeter is now the instrument that determines if pitch attitude changes on the AI are required to maintain level flight, the altimeter is the primary performance guide for pitch attitude in the cruise. It is supported by the AI and the VSI.

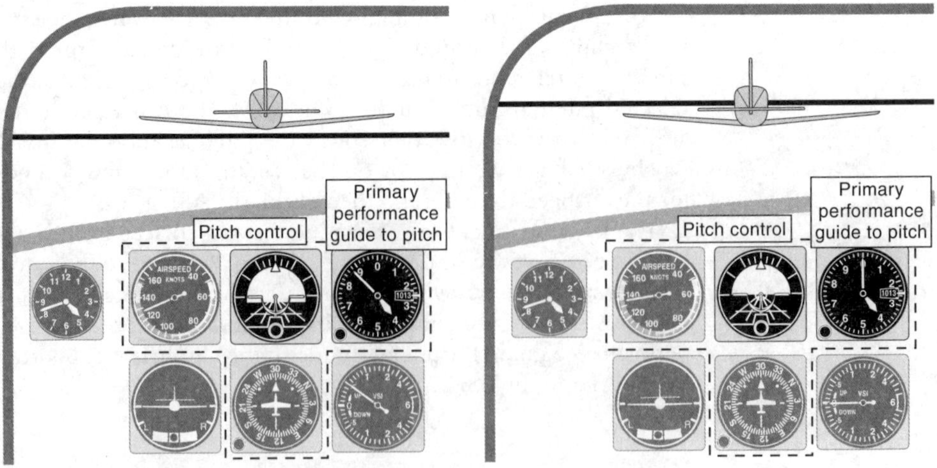

■ *Figure 19-22* ***The altimeter is the primary instrument in the cruise to confirm correct pitch attitude***

If climb power is still set after the aeroplane has been levelled off at cruise height, then the aeroplane will accelerate, shown by an increasing airspeed on the ASI. At the desired speed, the power should be reduced to a suitable value.

Correct power when cruising is checked on the airspeed indicator.

While it is usual simply to set cruise power and then accept the resulting airspeed, it is possible to achieve a precise airspeed by adjusting the power. Because the ASI indications will then determine what power changes should be made during level flight, the airspeed indicator is the primary performance guide to power requirements in the cruise.

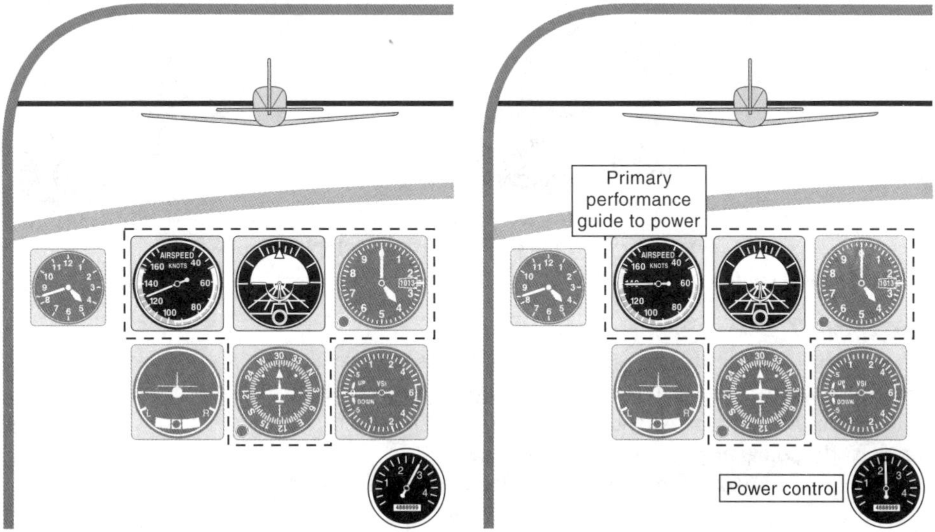

■ *Figure 19-23* ***The ASI is the primary instrument in the cruise to confirm correct power***

Check wings level on the heading indicator.

Heading is maintained with reference to the heading indicator (HI), any deviations being corrected with gentle balanced (coordinated) turns. Because the indications on the HI will determine what minor corrections to bank angle should be made on the attitude indicator during straight flight, the heading indicator is the primary performance guide to zero bank angle in maintaining a constant heading for straight flight. It is supported by the turn coordinator and the AI.

Keep the balance ball centred.

The ball should be centred to keep the aeroplane in balance, avoiding any slip or skid, i.e. to provide coordinated straight flight.

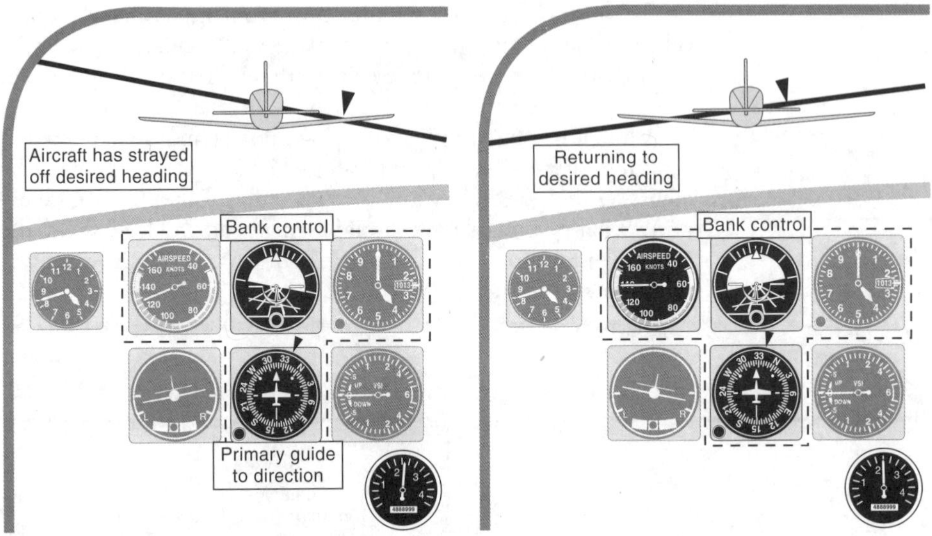

■ *Figure 19-24* ***The heading indicator is the primary instrument in straight flight to confirm wings level***

The Basic-T Scan

A basic scan suitable for straight and level flight (where altitude, direction and airspeed need to be monitored) is centred on the AI, and radiates out and back, following the basic-T pattern on the panel, to the relevant performance instrument:

- **the HI to confirm heading** (and correct with shallow turns on the AI);
- **the altimeter to confirm altitude** (and correct with pitch changes on the AI);
- **the ASI to confirm airspeed** (and, if desired, correct with power changes).

■ *Figure 19-25* ***The basic-T scan in cruise flight***

If cruise power is set and left alone, with the resulting airspeed being accepted (often the case in a normal cruise), then scanning the ASI need not be as frequent, and the scan can concentrate on the AI, HI, and altimeter.

Also, once established and well trimmed on the cruise, the aeroplane will tend to maintain height because of its longitudinal stability, making it less essential to scan the altimeter continually compared to when the aeroplane is out of trim. The aeroplane may not be as stable laterally as it is longitudinally, however, and so the heading indicator should be scanned quite frequently to ensure that heading is maintained.

Non IMC-rated pilots are already well-practised at scanning the altimeter regularly, since it is the only means of accurately maintaining height, but they may not be used to scanning the HI quite so frequently as is necessary in instrument conditions. This skill must be developed.

What About the Other Flight Instruments?

In smooth air, the VSI will show a trend away from cruise height often before it is apparent on the altimeter, and can be used to indicate that a minor pitch attitude correction is required if height is to be maintained. The VSI provides supporting pitch information to that provided by the altimeter, although it is of less value in turbulence which causes the VSI needle to fluctuate.

If the wings are held level on the AI, and heading is being maintained on the HI, then it is almost certain that the aeroplane is in balance (coordinated), with ball centred. Normally, the balance ball does not have to be scanned as frequently as some of the other instruments, but it should be referred to occasionally, especially if heading is changing while the wings are level, or if the 'seat of your pants' tells you that the aeroplane is skidding or slipping.

The turn coordinator will show a wings-level indication during straight flight, and provides supporting information regarding bank to that provided by the heading indicator. In a rate 1 turn, it is the primary performance guide to confirm that the bank angle is correct.

Choice of Scan Pattern

Use a logical scan for each manoeuvre.

Starting with your eyes focused on the AI, scan the performance instruments that provide the information required. Relevant information can be obtained from different instruments, depending on the manoeuvre.

Primary pitch information (to confirm whether or not the pitch attitude selected on the AI is correct) is obtained from the altimeter during cruise flight, but from the ASI during climbs and descents. There is no need to memorise particular scan patterns, since they will develop naturally as your training progresses.

Keep the eyes moving, and continually return to the attitude indicator.

Do not allow the radial scan to break down. Avoid fixation on any one instrument because the resulting breakdown in the radial scan will cause delayed recognition of deviations from the desired flightpath and/or airspeed. Fixation on the HI, for instance, can lead to heading being maintained perfectly, but in the meantime altitude and airspeed may change – tendencies which would have been detected (and corrected for) if the altimeter,VSI and ASI had been correctly scanned. Keep the eyes moving, and continually return to the AI.

Occasionally, the eyes will have to be directed away from the main flight instruments for a short period, for instance when checking the power indicator during or following a power change, or when periodically checking the oil temperature and pressure gauges, fuel gauges, the ammeter, or the suction (vacuum) gauge, or when realigning the heading indicator with the magnetic compass. Do not neglect the radial scan for more than a few seconds at a time, even though other necessary tasks have to be performed.

Avoid omitting any relevant instrument. For instance, after rolling out of a turn, check the HI to ensure that the desired heading is being achieved and maintained. The wings might be level and the aeroplane flying straight, but you may be on the wrong heading.

Use all available resources. For instance, with correct power set and the correct attitude selected on the AI, it is possible to maintain height, at least approximately, using only the AI and the power indicator but, if precision is required, then the altimeter must be included in the scan as the primary reference for altitude.

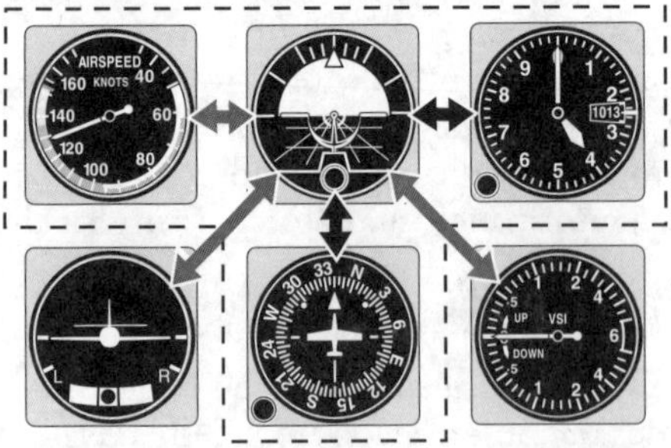

■ *Figure 19-26* ***A suitable scan during straight and level flight***

Furthermore, do not forget that supporting instruments can provide additional information to back-up primary instruments.

For instance, altitude is indicated directly on the altimeter, but any tendency to depart from that height may first be indicated on the VSI (especially in smooth air), which makes it a very valuable supporting instrument to the altimeter.

Other Scans

It is necessary on some occasions to have a fast scan, such as on final for an instrument approach. On other occasions, however, the scan can be more relaxed, for instance when cruising with the autopilot engaged. It may then be suitable just to have a fairly relaxed **circular scan.**

■ *Figure 19-27* ***A circular scan***

If you are performing other tasks while flying a constant heading, such as map reading, then a very simple scan to make sure things do not get out of hand is a **vertical scan** from the AI down to the heading indicator and back again.

If at any time, you suspect an **instrument failure,** then a very efficient means of establishing what instrument or system has failed is to commence an **inverted-V scan,** centred on the AI and radiating to the turn coordinator and the VSI.

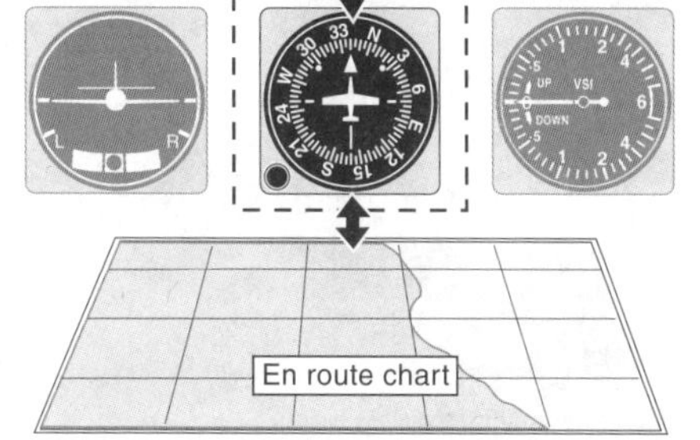

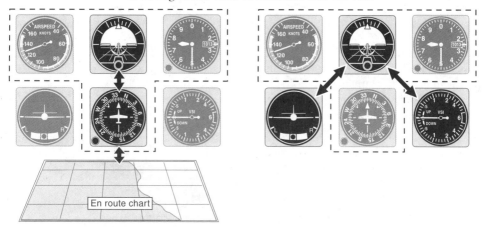

Figure 19-28 ***The vertical scan***

Figure 19-29 ***The inverted-V scan***

Each of these instruments normally has a different power source – the vacuum system for the AI, the electrical system for the turn coordinator, and the static system for the VSI – so a false indication on one should not be reflected on the others. Confirmation of attitude and flightpath can then be achieved using the other instruments.

With practice, you will develop scans to suit every situation.

Performance Table

To help you adjust to a new aeroplane type, we have included a type performance table. You can fill in this table as you become familiar with the power settings and attitudes required to achieve the desired performance in the various phases of flight.

Attitude can be shown on the AI by inserting a horizon line. The table allows for aircraft with retractable landing gear – if yours has a fixed undercarriage, then just pencil the wheels in on the chart, and only fill in the power settings and attitudes that you need. Knowing the numbers simplifies the game.

Airmanship

Never proceed into instrument conditions without a flight instructor unless you are properly qualified (with a valid instrument rating) in a suitably equipped aeroplane, and within the limitations of your ability and licence rating privileges.

Always calculate a lowest safe altitude *before* entering instrument conditions.

Keep in practice! Use smooth and coordinated control movements.

Airmanship is never proceeding into instrument conditions unless you and the aircraft are properly equipped to handle them.

Airwork

The basic manoeuvres will be practised initially while you have visual reference to the outside world, and then solely by reference to the cockpit instruments.

This introduction to instrument flying may best be handled in the following four separate parts:

- **Part (i)** Straight and Level
- **Part (ii)** Climb, Cruise and Descent
- **Part (iii)** Turning
- **Part (iv)** Recovery from Unusual Flight Attitudes

PERFORMANCE TABLE

	Configuration *Flaps* *Gear*	**Power** *MP* *rpm*	**Attitude**	**Performance** *Airspeed* *VSI*	**V-speeds**
Take-off	 ....° *down*		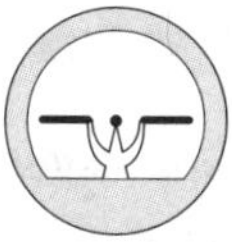		
	 ....° *up*		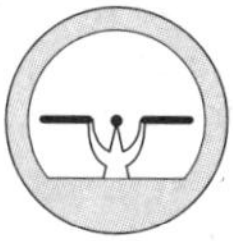		
Climb	 ....° *up*		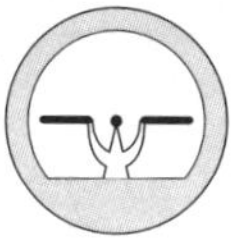		V_{S1} = ... *(stall speed, clean)* V_X = ... *(best angle)* V_Y = ... *(best rate)*
Cruise			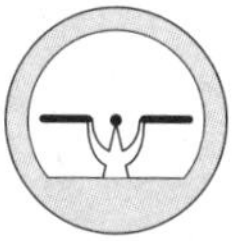		V_A = ... *(manoeuvring speed)* V_{NO} = ... *(normal maximum)* V_{NE} = ... *(never exceed)*
Cruise descent *(500 ft/min)*			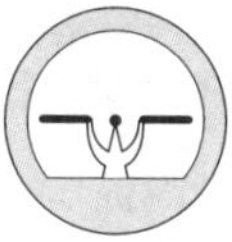		
Slow-speed cruise **1.** *Clean*			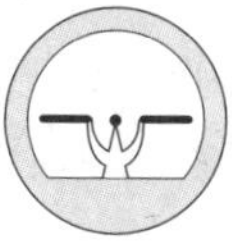		
2. *Flaps extended*	 ....° *up*		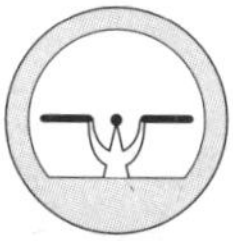		V_{FE} = ... *(flaps extended)*
3. *Flaps and landing gear extended*	 ....° *down*		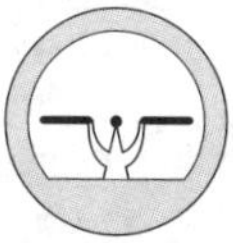		V_{LO} = ... *(landing gear operation)* V_{SO} = ... *(landing flaps and landing gear extended)*

Airwork 19, Part (i)
Flying Straight and Level on Instruments

Aim *To maintain a steady cruise, straight and level, with reference to the flight instruments only.*

1. To Establish Straight and Level Flight

- Select power for level flight.
- Set pitch attitude for level flight by positioning the miniature aeroplane against the horizon line of the attitude indicator.
- Hold the attitude and allow aeroplane to stabilise.
- Monitor: AI-ALT-AI-HI-AI-ASI-AI-VSI-AI-TC-AI-ALT, etc.
- Trim the aeroplane carefully so that it will fly 'hands-off'.

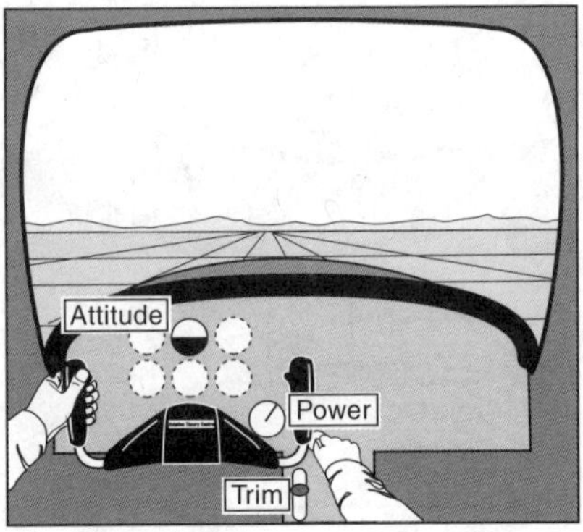

2. Raising the Nose at Constant Power

- Place the miniature aeroplane a little above the horizon line on the AI (say one-half or one bar width) and hold.
- The ASI will show a gradual decrease and finally settle on a lower indicated airspeed (IAS).
- The altimeter, after some lag, will start showing an increase in height.
- The VSI, after some initial fluctuations, will settle on a steady rate of climb.

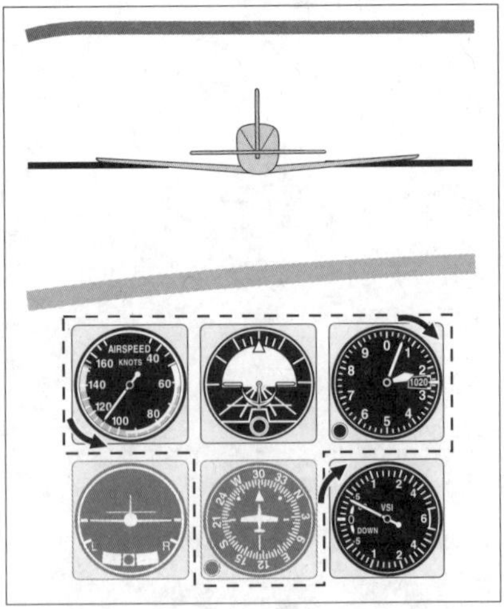

Airwork 19, Part (i)

3. Lowering the Nose at Constant Power

- Place the miniature aeroplane a little below the horizon line on the AI and hold this attitude.
- The ASI will show a gradual increase and finally stabilise at a higher IAS. Note that a relatively large airspeed change will occur after a small change in attitude.
- The altimeter, after some lag, will start showing a gradual decrease in height.
- The VSI will eventually stabilise on a steady rate of descent.

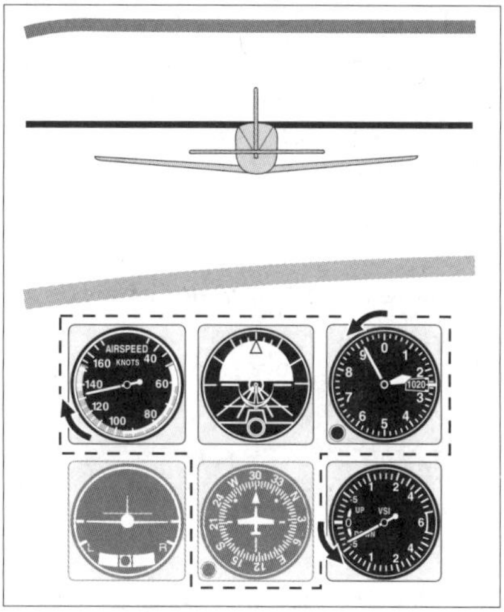

4. Maintaining Straight and Level at Constant Power

Suggested accuracy: • airspeed ±10 kt • heading ±10° • altitude ±100 ft

Correct variations in:

- **Altitude** by making very small changes in the position of the miniature aeroplane relative to the horizon line on AI. Within ±100 ft is acceptable.*
- **Heading** by using small bank angles and checking that the aeroplane is balanced. Within ±10° is acceptable.*
- **Airspeed** by adjustments in power, followed by as a consequence, a small change in attitude. Within ±10 kt is acceptable.*

Keep in trim.

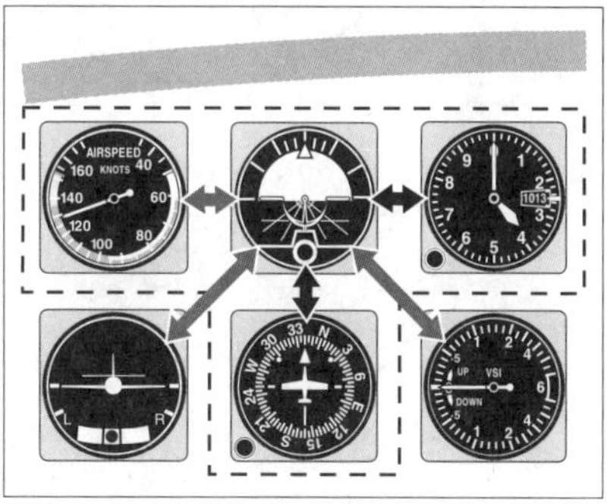

■ ***Monitoring straight and level flight***

*Aim to have airspeed, altitude and heading precisely on the desired numbers. If they are not, take corrective action immediately.

Airwork 19, Part (i)

5. *Changing Airspeed, Straight and Level*

(a) To increase airspeed at a constant height:

- Add power with the throttle (balance with rudder and forward pressure on the control column).
- Gradually lower the pitch attitude to avoid climbing, and allow the airspeed to increase to the desired value.
- Adjust power to maintain desired airspeed, and hold the pitch attitude.
- Trim.

(b) To decrease airspeed at a constant height:

- Reduce power with the throttle (balance with rudder and hold nose up with elevator back pressure).
- Gradually raise the pitch attitude to avoid descending and allow airspeed to reduce to desired value.
- As the desired airspeed is approached, adjust power to maintain it, and hold the pitch attitude.
- Trim.

Normal cruise Fast cruise Slow cruise

■ ***Different pitch attitudes for different speeds***

Airwork 19, Part (ii)
Climbing, Cruising and Descending on Instruments

Aim *To climb, cruise and descend, and to change from one to another, with reference only to the flight instruments.*

1. Climb, Cruise and Descent at a Constant Airspeed

Climb, cruise and descent speeds are usually different. However, by using a constant airspeed in these initial manoeuvres, we simplify the task by removing one of the variables.

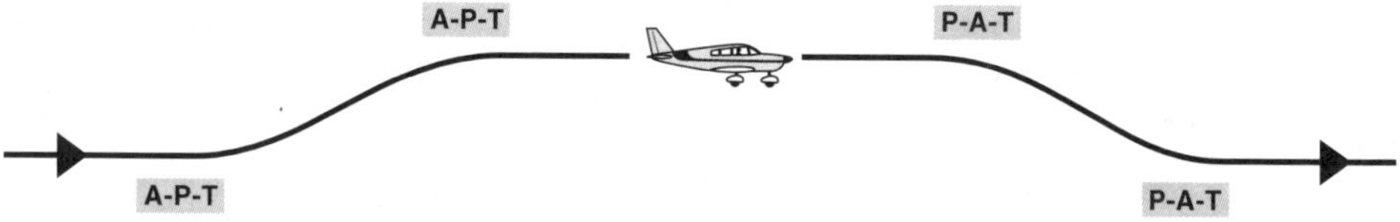

(a) From straight and level, enter a climb at a constant airspeed:

- Settle into straight and level flight (a cruise) and note airspeed.
- Smoothly open throttle to full power (balance with rudder).
- Simultaneously raise nose slightly to maintain airspeed, and hold attitude.
- Note the VSI shows a rate of climb and altimeter a gain in height.
- Trim.

(b) From a climb, level off and maintain a constant airspeed:

- Lower the nose to maintain a constant airspeed.
- Reduce the power to normal cruise as set before (balance with rudder).
- Note the VSI shows zero and the altimeter a constant height.
- Trim.

(c) From straight and level, commence a descent:

- Reduce power by (300 rpm or so), balance with rudder.
- Lower the nose to maintain a constant airspeed.
- Note the VSI shows a rate of descent and the altimeter shows a decrease in height.
- Trim.

(d) From a descent, enter a climb:

- Smoothly open the throttle to full power (balance with rudder) and simultaneously allow nose to rise to the climb attitude.
- Hold the attitude to maintain desired airspeed.
- Note the VSI shows a rate of climb and the altimeter a change in height.
- Trim.

Suggested accuracy: • airspeed ±10 kt • heading ±10°

Airwork 19, Part (ii)

2. *Initiating a Climb at Normal Climb Speed*

Generally the normal climb speed is less than cruise speed. As in normal visual flight, a climb is initiated in the sequence A-P-T: Attitude–Power–Trim.

Procedure:

- Settle in straight and level flight and note the airspeed.
- Raise the nose to the pitch attitude for climb.
- Increase power to the climb figure (balance with rudder).
- Hold the new attitude as airspeed decreases to the desired climbing speed. The VSI will show a rate of climb and the altimeter an increase in height.
- Make minor pitch attitude adjustments to achieve and maintain the correct climb airspeed.
- Trim.

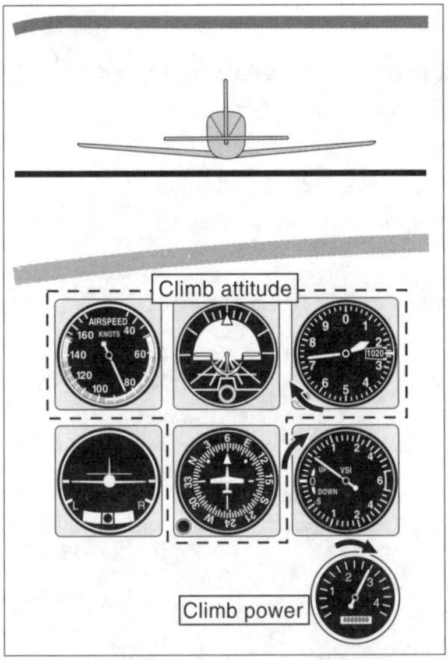

Suggested accuracy:
• airspeed ±10 kt • heading ±10°

NOTE If desired, you can trim earlier in the sequence, while holding the new attitude as airspeed decreases, to off-load some control-column pressure. However, a final trim adjustment will need to be made. Do not use trim to change the attitude; pitch attitude must only be changed with elevator. The trim is used solely to relieve sustained control pressures.

A steady climb is maintained with reference to all flight instruments, with the ASI confirming that you are indeed holding the correct attitude for climbing, as set on the AI.

Airwork 19, Part (ii)

3. Levelling Off from a Climb

As in visual flight, levelling off from a climb follows the sequence A-P-T: Attitude–Power–Trim. Since cruise speed is normally greater than climb speed, acceleration is allowed to occur before the power is reduced from climb to cruise power.

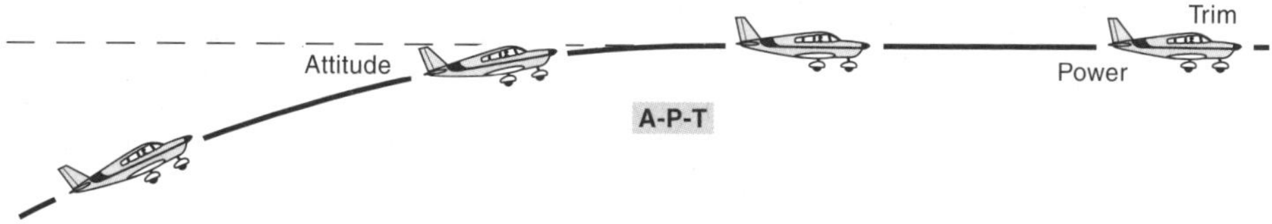
Trim
Attitude
Power
A-P-T

To level off at the desired height:

- Smoothly lower the nose to the cruise position slightly before the desired height is reached – a suitable amount of 'lead' being approximately 10% of the rate of climb. (For example, at 500 ft/min rate of climb, begin lowering the nose 50 ft prior to reaching the desired height).
- Allow the airspeed to increase towards the cruise figure.
- Reduce power to cruise rpm as the cruise speed is reached.
- Make minor adjustments to maintain height, heading and airspeed.
- Trim.

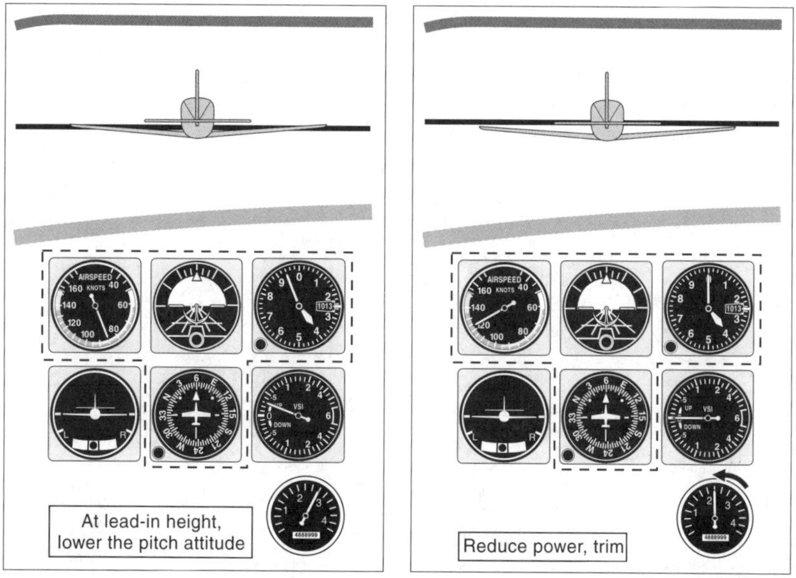
At lead-in height, lower the pitch attitude
Reduce power, trim

Suggested accuracy: • airspeed ±10 kt • heading ±10° • altitude ±100 ft

NOTE Steady, straight and level flight is maintained by reference to all flight instruments, with the altimeter confirming that you are holding the correct attitude for straight and level, as set on the attitude indicator.

Airwork 19, Part (ii)

4. Initiating a Descent on Instruments

As in normal visual flight, a descent is initiated in the order P-A-T: Power–Attitude–Trim. Descent speed is usually less than cruise speed – decelerate to descent speed at the cruise height before lowering the nose to descend.

The standard rate of descent in instrument flying is 500 ft/min. This may be achieved by a reduction of 300 rpm or so from the cruise power-setting. However, you may remove more power and descend at a greater rate, if desired. Also, a glide descent may be made, with the throttle fully closed.

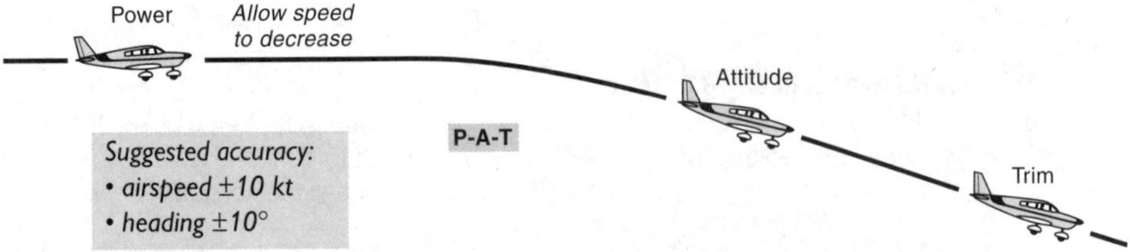
Power
Allow speed to decrease
Attitude
P-A-T
Trim

Suggested accuracy:
- *airspeed ±10 kt*
- *heading ±10°*

Procedure:

- Reduce power (balance with rudder and exert back pressure on the control column as necessary to maintain height).
- Allow the airspeed to decrease towards descent speed.
- At descent speed, lower the nose to the estimated descent attitude.
- Hold the new attitude to allow descent speed to stabilise (VSI will show rate of descent and altimeter a decrease in height).
- Make minor adjustments to achieve the desired descent speed and rate of descent (control airspeed with attitude and rate of descent with power).
- Trim.

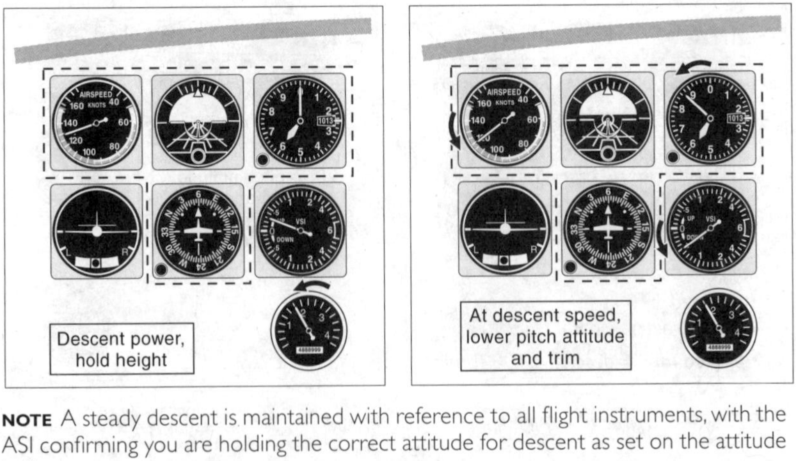
Descent power, hold height
At descent speed, lower pitch attitude and trim

NOTE A steady descent is maintained with reference to all flight instruments, with the ASI confirming you are holding the correct attitude for descent as set on the attitude indicator.

Airwork 19, Part (ii)

5. Controlling the Rate of Descent at a Constant Airspeed

To achieve any desired rate of descent while maintaining a constant airspeed, both the power and attitude must be adjusted. Rate of descent is indicated to the pilot by the:

- vertical speed indicator (primarily); or the
- altimeter and clock.

(a) To increase the rate of descent:

- Reduce power.
- Lower the pitch attitude to maintain airspeed.
- Trim.

(b) To decrease the rate of descent:

- Increase power.
- Raise the pitch attitude to maintain airspeed.
- Trim.

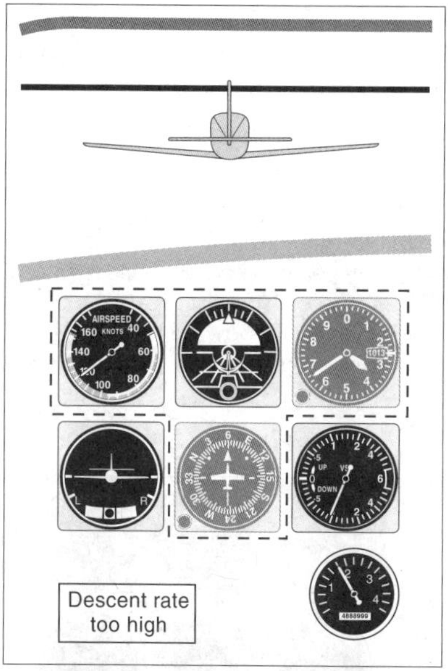
Descent rate
too high

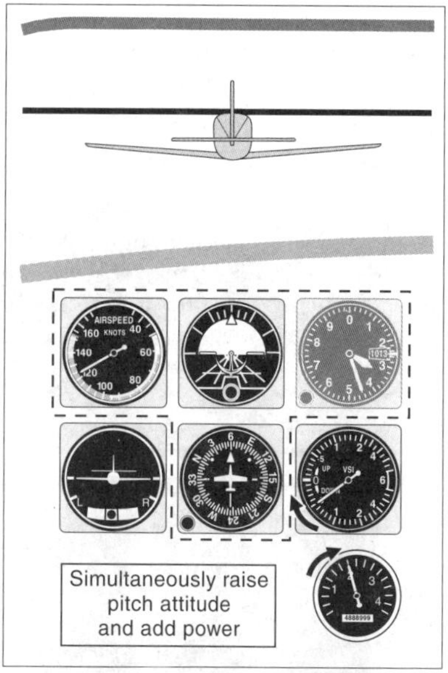
Simultaneously raise
pitch attitude
and add power

Suggested accuracy:
- *airspeed ±10 kt*
- *heading ±10°*
- *desired rate of descent ±100 ft/min*

Airwork 19, Part (ii)

6. Levelling Off from a Descent

As in normal visual flight, levelling off from a descent follows the sequence P-A-T: Power–Attitude–Trim.

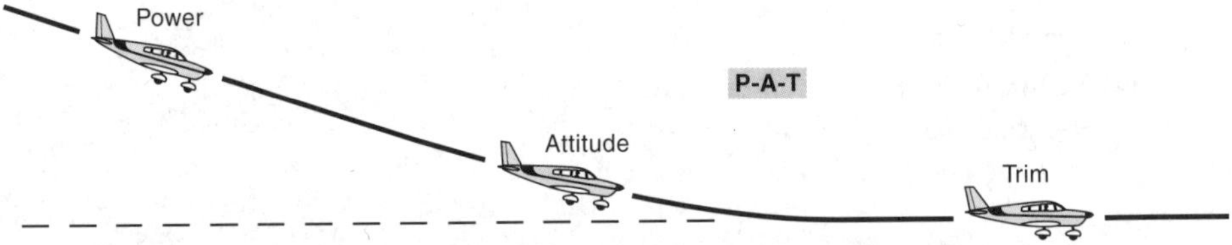
Power
P-A-T
Attitude
Trim

Suggested accuracy: • altitude ±100 ft • airspeed ±10 kt • heading ±10°

To level off at a specific height, increase the power and gradually raise the nose towards the cruise position just before that height is reached – the amount of 'lead' being approximately 10% of the rate of descent. For example, at 500 ft/min rate of descent, start increasing power and raising the nose 50 ft prior to reaching the desired height.

- Increase power to cruise rpm (and balance with rudder pressure).
- Raise the pitch attitude to the cruise position.
- Make minor adjustments to maintain height.
- Trim.

Steady straight and level flight is maintained with reference to all flight instruments – with the altimeter confirming that you are holding the correct attitude for straight and level as set on the attitude indicator.

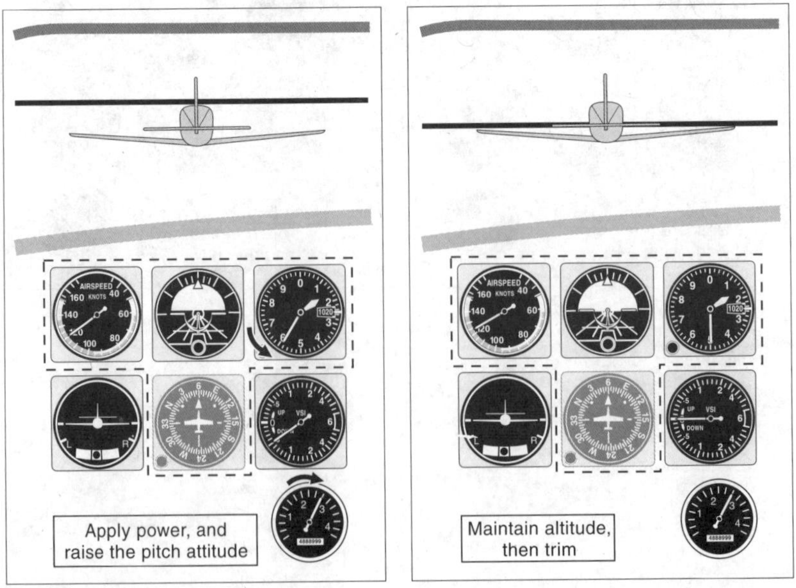
Apply power, and raise the pitch attitude
Maintain altitude, then trim

Airwork 19, Part (ii)

7. Climbing Away from a Descent

The procedure is the same as levelling off from a descent, except that climb power and climb attitude are selected instead.

Be prepared for strong nose-up and yawing tendencies as climb power is applied. Even though the climb attitude is higher than the descent attitude, it may initially require forward pressure to stop the nose rising too far. Rudder will of course be required to balance the increase in slipstream effect.

Trim off any steady pressure remaining on the control column.

Procedure:

- Apply climb power, balance with rudder.
- Set the desired pitch attitude for the climb.
- Trim.

Suggested accuracy:
- *airspeed ±10 kt*
- *heading ±10°*

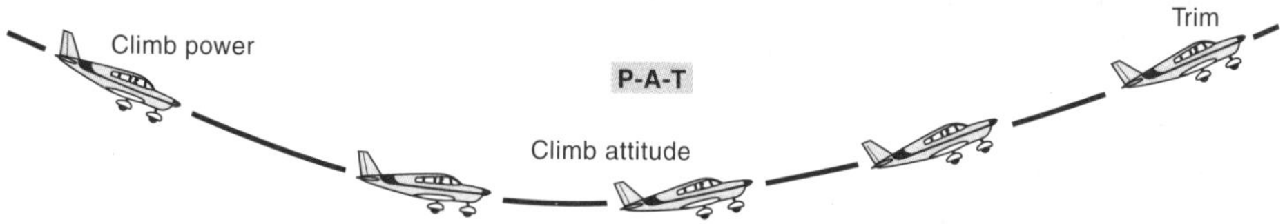

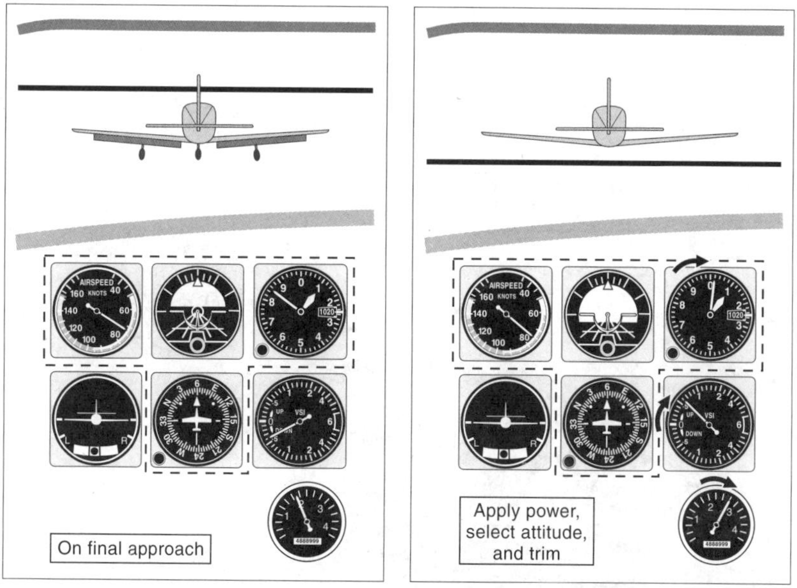

NOTE If making a go-around from an approach, you should apply maximum power (keeping ball centred with rudder), hold a higher pitch attitude to establish a climb, and then raise the flaps in stages. If your aeroplane has a retractable undercarriage, you would retract it once you have a positive rate of climb.

Airwork 19, Part (iii)
Turning Using the Flight Instruments

Aim *To turn the aeroplane solely by reference to the flight instruments.*

1. A Rate 1 Level Turn

The required bank angle for a rate 1 turn will equal $\frac{1}{10}$ the airspeed plus half of that. At 80 kt, the bank angle required will be (8 + 4) = 12°.

- Trim for straight and level flight.

To enter and maintain the turn:

- Roll into the turn using ailerons, balancing with rudder pressure.
- Hold a constant bank angle and keep the balance ball centred.
- Hold the correct pitch attitude to maintain height using elevator.
- Do not use trim in a turn, since turning is normally only a transient manoeuvre (although you may trim for a sustained turn).

The rate of turn is indicated to the pilot by:

- The turn coordinator (rate 1 = 3° per sec, or 360° in 2 min); or
- The heading indicator and clock.

To stop the turn on a desired heading:

- Anticipate and begin recovery from the turn about 5° prior to reaching the desired heading.
- Roll the wings level, and balance with rudder.
- Lower the pitch attitude to that required for straight and level flight.
- Trimming will not be necessary, if trim was not adjusted during turn.

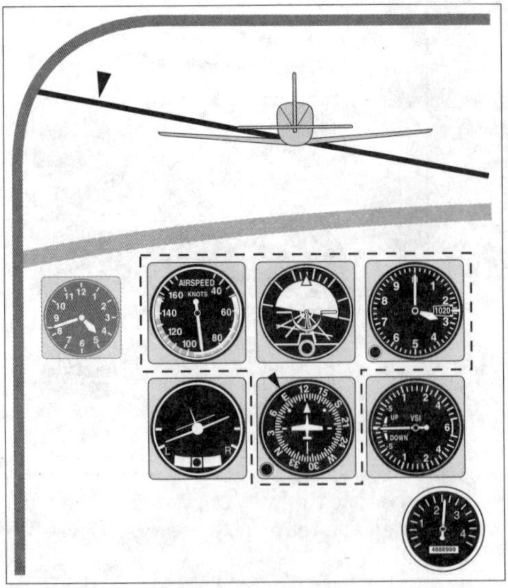

Suggested accuracy:
- *height ±100 ft*
- *bank angle ±5°*
- *heading ±10°*

■ ***A rate 1 level turn to the left***

Airwork 19, Part (iii)

NOTE A rate 1 turn may also be achieved by using the clock and the heading indicator. By holding the calculated bank angle you should achieve a turn rate of 3°/sec, which will give a 45° heading change in 15 seconds, a 90° heading change in 30 seconds, a 180° heading change in one minute and 360° heading change in two minutes (hence the 2 MIN that is marked on many turn coordinators).

2. A 30° Banked Level Turn

At the speeds achieved by most training aircraft, a 30° banked turn is greater than rate 1. A steeper bank angle requires greater back pressure to maintain height, so the airspeed will decrease a little further – by about 5 or 10 kt. The pitch attitude will be slightly higher than for straight and level flight.

The rate of turn can be estimated from the turn coordinator, or by using the clock and the heading indicator (bearing in mind that the turn coordinator may be limited by stops at about rate 2 (twice rate 1, or 360°/min) – so that steeper bank angles will not be accompanied by an increased rate-of-turn indication).

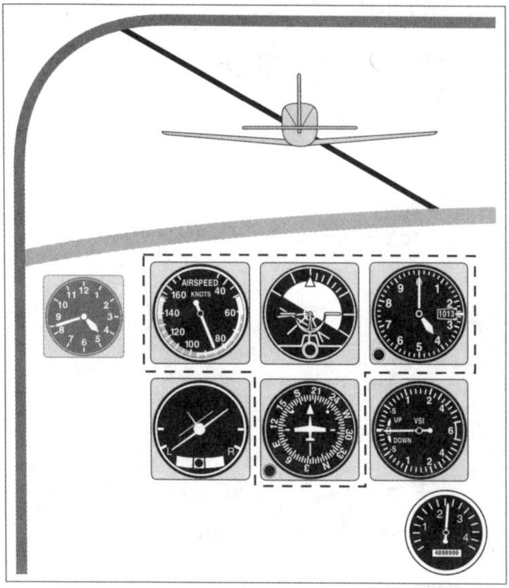

■ ***A 30° banked level turn***

Suggested accuracy:
- *height ±100 ft*
- *bank angle ±5°*
- *heading ±10°*

Airwork 19, Part (iii)

3. The Climbing Turn

The climbing turn will normally be entered from a straight climb. To ensure adequate climb performance, do not exceed a 20° bank angle in a typical training aeroplane. The pitch attitude will have to be lowered slightly to maintain a constant airspeed in a climbing turn. (In climbing and descending turns, speed is maintained with elevator, whereas in level turns it is height which is maintained.)

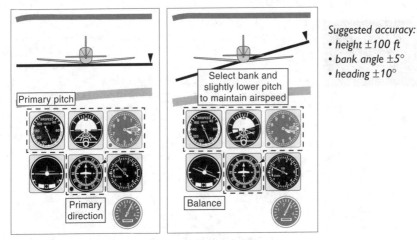

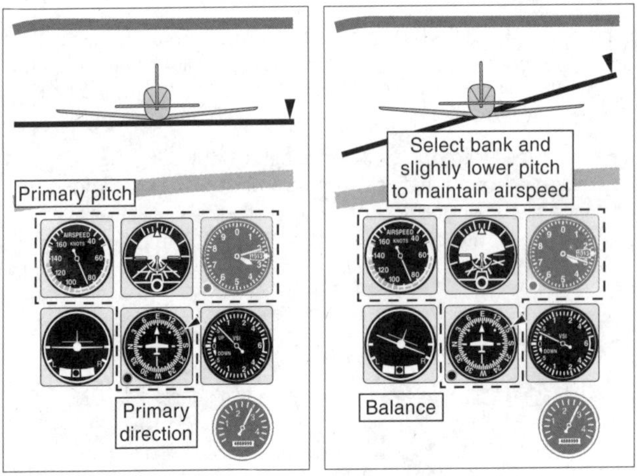

Suggested accuracy:
- *height ±100 ft*
- *bank angle ±5°*
- *heading ±10°*

■ ***Entering and maintaining a climbing turn to the right***

4. Descending Turns

The descending turn will normally be entered from a straight descent. A lower pitch attitude will be required in the turn to maintain airspeed. The rate of descent will increase – it can be controlled with power, if you wish.

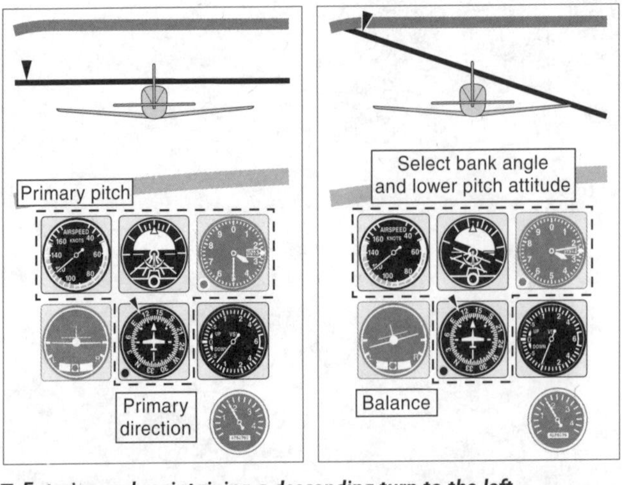

Suggested accuracy:
- *height ±100 ft*
- *bank angle ±5°*
- *heading ±10°*

■ ***Entering and maintaining a descending turn to the left***

Airwork 19, Part (iv)
Recovery from Unusual Attitudes

Aim *To recognise a potentially hazardous flight attitude from instrument indications and recover before a hazardous attitude develops.*

An unusual attitude is considered to be a potentially hazardous attitude where either:

- the aeroplane's nose is unusually high with the airspeed decreasing; or
- the aeroplane's nose is unusually low with the airspeed increasing.

The aeroplane may also be banked.

The easiest recovery from an unusual attitude is not to get into one! In extreme attitudes, the attitude indicator (a gyroscopic instrument) may tumble, depriving you of your most important instrument. Most of its information can be derived, however, from other sources:

- Approximate pitch attitude can be determined from the airspeed indicator (increasing or decreasing airspeed) and the altimeter and vertical speed indicator (descent or climb). A decreasing airspeed indication and a decreasing rate of climb would indicate an unusually high nose-up attitude; conversely a rapidly increasing airspeed and rate of descent would indicate a nose-low attitude.
- Turning can be detected on the turn coordinator. The heading indicator (a gyroscopic instrument) may have tumbled and the magnetic compass will probably not be giving a steady reading if there is any significant turn occurring. The turn coordinator is gyroscopic but will not topple.

1. Nose High and Steep Bank – Beware of Stall

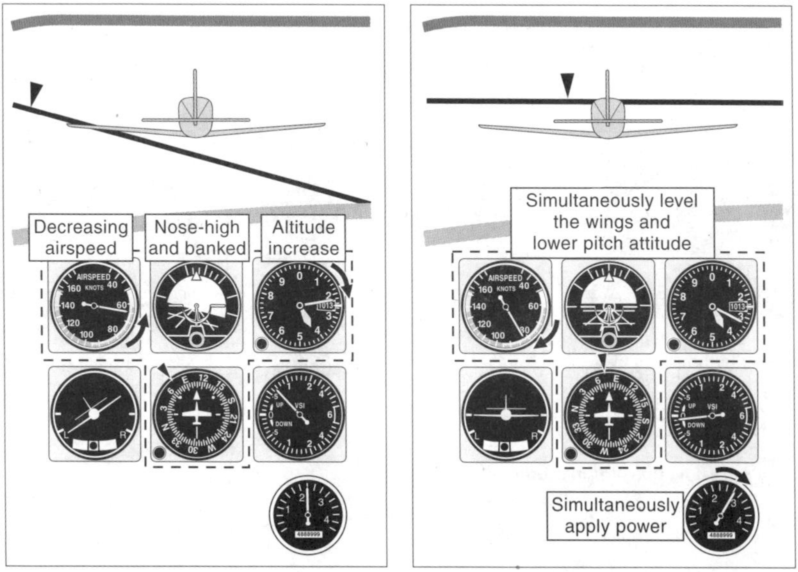
Decreasing airspeed
Nose-high and banked
Altitude increase
Simultaneously level the wings and lower pitch attitude
Simultaneously apply power

■ ***A nose-high unusual attitude***

Airwork 19, Part (iv)

Recovery Procedure:

(a) If close to the stall:

- Simultaneously lower the nose to the level pitch attitude (referring to the AI); and
- Apply full power (balance with rudder).
- As speed increases, level the wings (refer to the AI).

(b) If not close to the stall:

- Select straight and level flight (refer to the AI):
  - add power as necessary;
  - roll wings level with aileron (ailerons can be used as the wings are not stalled);
  - balance with rudder;
  - lower the nose to the level pitch attitude.
- Adjust power as necessary.

2. *Nose Low and High Airspeed*

Beware of an overspeed or a spiral dive.

Recovery Procedure:

- Reduce the power (throttle closed).
- Roll the wings level with aileron and rudder.
- Ease out of the ensuing dive into straight and level attitude (AI).
- Reapply power.
- Regain height, if necessary.

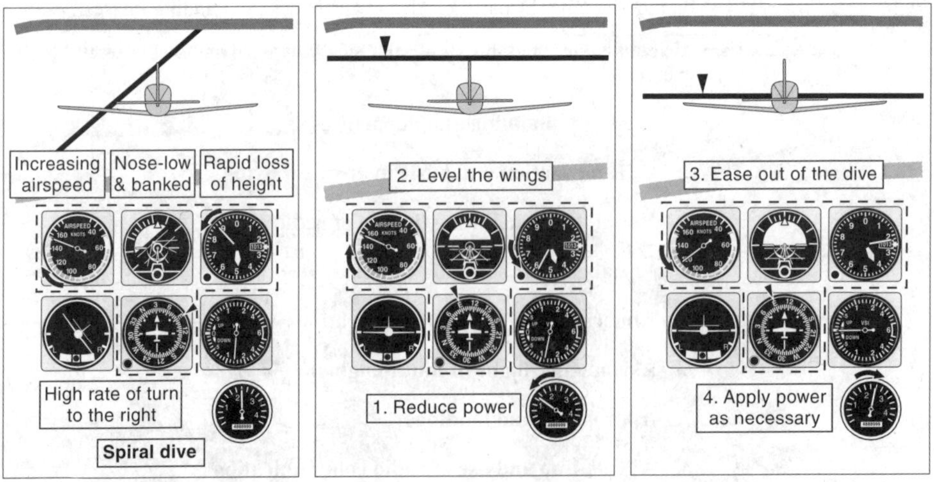

■ ***A nose-low unusual attitude and recovery***

The PPL(A) Skill Test

The following is reproduced from CAP 53, *The Private Pilot's Licence and Associated Ratings,* courtesy of the CAA and the Joint Aviation Authorities (JAA) Flight Crew Licensing. It is an outline of what you can expect to be asked to demonstrate for your PPL(A) Skill Test in a single-engine piston aircraft.

The oral examination and Aircraft Class Rating qualification is also covered at the time you take your flight test. Details of this test are included in Vol. 4 of *The Air Pilot's Manual.*

PPL(A) SKILL TEST

This syllabus lists all the items which should be covered during training and which will be examined during the Skill Test. It applies to the test for single-engine and multi-engine piston aircraft and is similar for SLMG (self-launching motor gliders). Microlight aircraft will, for the time being, remain with the existing syllabus for the UK National Licence.

The Skill Test will cover the following items and the candidate will be required to demonstrate satisfactory standards of knowledge and handling in each section.

The flight may be conducted in two parts with the agreement of the examiner, that is the Enroute Section (Navigation) may be conducted on a separate flight test. However, if this option is taken up the applicant will be reassessed on the Planning, Departure, Arrival and Precision Landing Phases.

The applicant is required to demonstrate proficiency in the following exercises:

1. **Pre-flight planning and departures**
2. **VFR navigation and basic instrument flying**
3. **Visual flying including the use of radio aids**
4. **Visual general handling exercises**
5. **Abnormal and emergency operations**
6. **Asymmetric flight (if multi-engine)**
7. **Approaches and landings**
8. **ATC liaison and use of radio communication**
9. **Post-flight procedures**
10. **Aircraft systems and operation of the aircraft used for the flight test.**

Below is an example of a completed Report Form for the PPL(A) Skill Test – note that the applicant was successful!

Serial No: 014502

CIVIL AVIATION AUTHORITY

APPLICATION AND REPORT FORM FOR THE PPL(A) SKILL TEST

SERIES No: 1 ATTEMPT No: 1

SURNAME: HUCKLE CAA REF. No: 319411L

FORENAMES: JOANNA SIGNATURE: (Applicant)

IT IS AN OFFENCE TO MAKE, WITH INTENT TO DECEIVE, ANY FALSE REPRESENTATIONS FOR THE PURPOSE OF PROCURING THE GRANT, ISSUE, RENEWAL OR VARIATION OF ANY CERTIFICATE, LICENCE, APPROVAL, PERMISSION OR OTHER DOCUMENT. PERSONS SO DOING RENDER THEMSELVES LIABLE, ON SUMMARY CONVICTION TO A FINE NOT EXCEEDING THE STATUTORY MAXIMUM (CURRENTLY £5000) OR IN NORTHERN IRELAND £2000 AND ON CONVICTION ON INDICTMENT TO AN UNLIMITED FINE OR IMPRISONMENT FOR A TERM NOT EXCEEDING 2 YEARS OR BOTH.

Date of Test: 1-1-99 Base: CRANFIELD.

Aircraft Type & Regn.	Block Times			Examiners name & Licence No.
	Dep.	Arr.	Duration	202574D
PA-38 9BGGM	1000	1220	2:20	P.D. GODWIN

Route: STRADISHALL-DESBRO'-DIVERT HENLOW

TEST SECTIONS:	1	2	3	4	5	6
SECTIONS TO BE TAKEN:	✓	✓	✓	✓	✓	✓
RESULT:	PASS	PASS	PASS	PASS	PASS	PASS
a	✓	✓	✓	✓	✓	N/A
b	✓	✓	✓	✓	✓	N/A
c	✓	✓	✓	✓	✓	N/A
d	✓	✓	✓	✓	✓	N/A
e	✓	✓	✓	✓		PASS
f	✓	✓	✓	✓		N/A
g	✓	✓	✓	✓		PASS
h	✓	✓		✓		
Re-test:						
Test sections incomplete due:						
Items not completed:						

EXAMPLE

Retraining Requirement: A/c: Sim:

Remarks:

Signed: Peter Godwin (Flight Examiner) Date: 1-1-99

Received: (Applicant)

FTO	BONUS AV'
Date flying training completed	23-12-98

White – Applicants Copy, Pink – FCLD Copy
Yellow – Examiners Copy, Blue – CFEs Copy

1

FORM FCL 684
200898

The reverse side describes each manoeuvre from each section, item by item.

Civil Aviation Authority Regulation 6
Regulation 6(5) of the Civil Aviation Authority Regulations, 1991 as follows: Any person who has failed any test or examination which he is required to pass before he is granted or may exercise the privileges of a personnel licence may within 14 days of being notified of his failure request that the Authority determine whether the test or examination was properly conducted. In order to succeed you will have to satisfy the Authority that the examination or test was not properly conducted. Mere dissatisfaction of the result is not enough.

SECTION 1. PRE FLIGHT OPERATIONS AND DEPARTURE	
a	Pre flight documentation and weather brief
b	Mass and balance and performance calculation
c	Aeroplane inspection and servicing
d	Engine starting and after starting procedures
e	Taxying and aerodrome procedures, pre take off procedures
f	Take off and after take off checks
g	Aerodrome departure procedures
h	ATC liaison and compliance, R/T procedures, Airmanship

SECTION 2. AIRWORK +	
a	ATC liaison and compliance, R/T procedure, Airmanship
b	Straight and level flight with speed changes
c	Climbing: i. Best rate of climb ii. Climbing turns iii Levelling off
d	Medium turns (30° bank)
e	Steep turns (360° left and right - 45° bank) including recognition and recovery from a spiral dive.
f	Flight at critically low airspeed with and without flaps. Best angle of climb
g	Stalling: i. Clean stall and recovery with power ii. Approach to stall descending turn with bank angle 20°, approach configuration. iii. Approach to stall in landing configuration.
h	Descending: i. With and without power ii. Descending turns (steep gliding turns) iii. Levelling off

SECTION 3. EN-ROUTE PROCEDURES +	
a	Flight plan, dead reckoning and map reading
b	Maintenance of altitude, heading and speed
c	Orientation, timing and revision of ETAs, log keeping
d	Diversion to alternate aerodrome, planning & implementation
e	Use of radio navigation aids, position fix and tracking
f	Basic instrument flying (180° turn in simulated IMC)
g	Flight management (checks, fuel, systems and carburettor icing etc.) ATC liaison and compliance, R/T procedures, Airmanship.

SECTION 4. APPROACH AND LANDING PHOCEDURES	
a	Aerodrome arrival procedures
b	* Precision landing (short field landing), cross wind (if suitable conditions available)
c	* Flapless landing
d	Approach and landing with idle power (Single engine only)
e	Touch and go
f	Go around from low height
g	ATC liaison and compliance, R/T procedures, Airmanship
h	Actions after flight including documentation

SECTION 5. ABNORMAL AND EMERGENCY OPERATIONS * +	
This section may be combined with Sections 1 through 4.	
a	Simulated engine failure after take off (Single engine only)
b	* Simulated forced landing. (Single engine only)
c	Simulated precautionary landing (Single engine only)
d	*Simulated emergencies

SECTION 6. SIMULATED ASYMMETRIC FLIGHT (if applicable)* AND RELEVANT CLASS/TYPE RATING ITEMS	
This section may be combined with sections 1 through 5.	
a	Simulated engine failure during take off (at a safe altitude unless carried out in a FNPT II or a flight simulator)
b	Asymmetric approach and go around
c	Asymmetric approach and full stop landing
d	Engine shutdown and restart (if applicable)
e	ATC liaison and compliance, R/T procedures, Airmanship
f	As determined by the Flight Examiner - any relevant items of the class/type rating skill test to include, if applicable: i. Aeroplane systems including handling of auto pilot ii. Operation of pressurisation system iii Use of de-icing and anti icing system
g	Oral questions

+ Additionally, Items a, b and h of Section 4 shall be assessed within any re-test or split test.

*** Some of these items may be combined at the discretion of the Flight Examiner**

Reproduced with kind permission of the Civil Aviation Authority

Index

D

E

F

U

V

W

Y